Frommer's®

Nashville & Memphis

9th Edition

by Linda Romine

Wiley Publishing, Inc.

ABOUT THE AUTHOR

Linda Romine has been a professional writer for nearly 2 decades. With a background in music, she has worked on the editorial staffs of various newspapers and magazines as a reporter, music critic, travel editor, and restaurant reviewer.

Published by:

WILEY PUBLISHING, INC.

111 River St.
Hoboken, NJ 07030-5774

ISBN 978-0-470-59152-9

Editor: Matthew Brown with Ian Skinnari
Production Editor: Jana M. Stefanciosa
Cartographer: Guy Ruggiero
Photo Editor: Richard Fox
Production by Wiley Indianapolis Composition Services
Front cover photo: Neon sign outside of The Stage on Broadway in Nashville ©Brian Jannsen / Alamy Images
Back cover photo: Graffiti on the wall of Graceland, Memphis ©Chris Floyd / Reportage / Getty Images

For information on our other products and services or to obtain technical support, please contact our Customer Care Department within the U.S. at 877/762-2974, outside the U.S. at 317/572-3993 or fax 317/572-4002.

Wiley also publishes its books in a variety of electronic formats. Some content that appears in print may not be available in electronic formats.

Manufactured in the United States of America

5 4 3 2 1

CONTENTS

LIST OF MAPS vii

1 THE BEST OF NASHVILLE 1

1 Frommer's Most Unforgettable Travel Experiences 2
2 The Best Splurge Hotels. 2
3 The Best "Green" Hotel. 2
4 The Most Unforgettable Dining Experiences 3
5 The Best Things to Do for Free (Or Almost) 3
6 The Best Art Deco Architecture. 3
7 The Best (Year-round) Christmas Lights .4

2 NASHVILLE IN DEPTH 5

1 The Nashville Sound 5
Eclectic Playlist for Nashville/ Tennessee Travel .7
2 Looking Back at Nashville 8
Dateline 8
African-American History in Nashville 11
3 The Lay of the Land 12
4 Nashville in Film, TV & Music 13
5 Eating & Drinking in Nashville 14

3 PLANNING YOUR TRIP TO NASHVILLE & MEMPHIS 15

1 When to Go. 16
Nashville Calendar of Events 16
Memphis Calendar of Events. 20
2 Entry Requirements 22
3 Getting There & Getting Around 23
4 Money & Costs. 30
What Things Cost in Nashville & Memphis 31
5 Health 31
6 Safety. 32
7 Specialized Travel Resources 32
8 Sustainable Tourism. 33
General Resources for Green Travel 34
9 Special-Interest Trips & Escorted General-Interest Tours. 35
10 Staying Connected. 36

4 SUGGESTED NASHVILLE ITINERARIES 37

Neighborhoods in Brief.............37
1 The Best of Nashville in 1 Day.....39
2 The Best of Nashville in 2 Days....42
3 The Best of Nashville in 3 Days....43

5 GETTING TO KNOW MUSIC CITY 45

1 Nashville Orientation..............45

6 WHERE TO STAY IN NASHVILLE 49

1 The Best Hotel Bets...............50
2 Downtown Area, Music Row & the West End.....................50
Family-Friendly Hotels.............56
3 Music Valley & the Airport Area....59

7 WHERE TO DINE IN NASHVILLE 65

1 The Best Dining Bets..............65
2 Restaurants by Cuisine............66
3 Downtown, the Gulch & 12th Avenue South...............68
Family-Friendly Restaurants........72
4 Germantown & Jefferson Street...74
5 Music Row, the West End & Areas Southwest..................75
6 Music Valley & East Nashville......82
7 Barbecue & Hot Chicken..........85
8 Cafes, Delis, Bakeries & Pastry Shops.......................86
Best Tennessee-Based Eateries......87

8 EXPLORING NASHVILLE 88

1 On the Music Trail.................88
Notable Songs & Albums Recorded in Music City.............94
2 More Attractions..................96
3 Especially for Kids............... 104
4 Strolling Around Nashville....... 105
Walking Tour: Downtown Nashville........................ 105
5 Organized Tours.................. 109
Nashville Name Game........... 110
6 Outdoor Activities............... 111
7 Spectator Sports................ 112

9 SHOPPING IN NASHVILLE 113

1 The Nashville Shopping Scene... 113
2 Nashville Shopping A to Z....... 113

10 NASHVILLE AFTER DARK 124

1 The Country Music Scene....... 125
Know Before You Go............. 128
2 Rock, Blues, Jazz & More......... 130
3 The Bar & Pub Scene............ 133
More Nightlife.................... 135
4 The Performing Arts............. 135

11 SIDE TRIPS FROM NASHVILLE 138

1 Franklin, Columbia & Scenic U.S. 31 138
2 Distilleries, Horses & a Battlefield 141

12 THE BEST OF MEMPHIS 144

1 Frommer's Most Unforgettable Travel Experiences 144
2 The Best Splurge Hotels 145
3 The Best Moderately Priced Hotels 145
4 The Most Unforgettable Dining Experiences 145
5 The Best Things to Do for Free (Or Almost) 146

13 MEMPHIS IN DEPTH 147

1 Memphis Today 147
2 Looking Back at Memphis 147
Dateline 148
3 The Lay of the Land 152
4 Memphis in Books & Film 153
5 Eating & Drinking in Memphis 153

14 SUGGESTED MEMPHIS ITINERARIES 155

Neighborhoods in Brief *155*
1 The Best of Memphis in 1 Day 156
2 The Best of Memphis in 2 Days 157
3 The Best of Memphis in 3 Days 160

15 GETTING TO KNOW THE HOME OF THE BLUES 162

1 Orientation 162

16 WHERE TO STAY IN MEMPHIS 166

1 Best Hotel Bets 167
2 Downtown 168
The Peabody Ducks 169
3 Midtown 174
4 East Memphis 175
Family-Friendly Hotels 176
Starting the Chain: The Story of the Holiday Inn 178
5 The Airport & Graceland Areas 179

17 WHERE TO DINE IN MEMPHIS 182

1 Best Dining Bets 182
2 Restaurants by Cuisine 183
3 Downtown 185
Family-Friendly Restaurants 188
4 Midtown 192
5 East Memphis 196
6 South Memphis & Graceland Area 201
7 Barbecue 202
8 Delis, Cafes & Bakeries 203

18 EXPLORING MEMPHIS 204

1 Graceland, Beale Street & More. 204

Elvis Trivia 209

Elvis Beyond the Gates of Graceland 211

2 Nonmusical Memphis Attractions. 212

3 African-American Heritage in Memphis. 218

4 Especially for Kids 219

5 Strolling Around Memphis 220

Walking Tour: Downtown Memphis. 220

6 Organized Tours. 223

7 Outdoor Activities. 224

8 Spectator Sports 225

9 Side Trips From Memphis 225

Southern Foodways Alliance: It's Gravy 229

The Blind Side: A Memphis Movie 230

19 SHOPPING IN MEMPHIS 232

1 The Shopping Scene. 232

2 Shopping A to Z 232

20 MEMPHIS AFTER DARK 244

1 Beale Street & Downtown. 244

2 The Rest of the Club & Music Scene 248

3 Bars, Pubs & Lounges. 249

4 The Performing Arts. 252

Gambling on the Mississippi 254

21 FAST FACTS 255

1 Fast Facts: Nashville 255

2 Fast Facts: Memphis. 259

3 Airline, Hotel & Car-Rental Websites. 261

INDEX 255

General 263

Accommodations: Nashville and Environs 272

Accommodations: Memphis and Environs 273

Restaurants: Nashville and Environs 273

Restaurants: Memphis and Environs 274

LIST OF MAPS

Nashville & Memphis 17
Suggested Nashville Itineraries . . . 40
Nashville Orientation 47
Nashville Accommodations: Downtown Area, Music Row & the West End 52
Nashville Accommodations: Music Valley & the Airport Area 61
Nashville Dining: Downtown Area, Music Row & the West End 70
Nashville Dining: Music Valley & East Nashville 83
Nashville Attractions: Downtown Area & Music Row 90
Nashville Attractions: Music Valley 92
Walking Tour: Downtown Nashville 107
Nashville Shopping 114
Nashville After Dark 126
Side Trips from Nashville 139
Suggested Memphis Itineraries . . 158
Memphis Orientation 163
Memphis Accommodations: Downtown & Midtown 170
East Memphis Accommodations 177
Memphis Dining: Downtown & Midtown 186
East Memphis Dining 197
Memphis Attractions: Downtown & Midtown 206
Walking Tour: Downtown Memphis 221
Side Trips from Memphis 227
Memphis Shopping: Downtown & Midtown 234
East Memphis Shopping 237
Memphis After Dark 246

HOW TO CONTACT US

In researching this book, we discovered many wonderful places—hotels, restaurants, shops, and more. We're sure you'll find others. Please tell us about them, so we can share the information with your fellow travelers in upcoming editions. If you were disappointed with a recommendation, we'd love to know that, too. Please write to:

Frommer's Nashville & Memphis, 9th Edition
Wiley Publishing, Inc. • 111 River St. • Hoboken, NJ 07030-5774

AN ADDITIONAL NOTE

Please be advised that travel information is subject to change at any time—and this is especially true of prices. We therefore suggest that you write or call ahead for confirmation when making your travel plans. The authors, editors, and publisher cannot be held responsible for the experiences of readers while traveling. Your safety is important to us, however, so we encourage you to stay alert and be aware of your surroundings. Keep a close eye on cameras, purses, and wallets, all favorite targets of thieves and pickpockets.

FROMMER'S STAR RATINGS, ICONS & ABBREVIATIONS

Every hotel, restaurant, and attraction listing in this guide has been ranked for quality, value, service, amenities, and special features using a **star-rating system.** In country, state, and regional guides, we also rate towns and regions to help you narrow down your choices and budget your time accordingly. Hotels and restaurants are rated on a scale of zero (recommended) to three stars (exceptional). Attractions, shopping, nightlife, towns, and regions are rated according to the following scale: zero stars (recommended), one star (highly recommended), two stars (very highly recommended), and three stars (must-see).

In addition to the star-rating system, we also use **seven feature icons** that point you to the great deals, in-the-know advice, and unique experiences that separate travelers from tourists. Throughout the book, look for:

Finds	Special finds—those places only insiders know about
Fun Facts	Fun facts—details that make travelers more informed and their trips more fun
Kids	Best bets for kids and advice for the whole family
Moments	Special moments—those experiences that memories are made of
Overrated	Places or experiences not worth your time or money
Tips	Insider tips—great ways to save time and money
Value	Great values—where to get the best deals

The following **abbreviations** are used for credit cards:

AE American Express **DISC** Discover **V** Visa
DC Diners Club **MC** MasterCard

TRAVEL RESOURCES AT FROMMERS.COM

Frommer's travel resources don't end with this guide. Frommer's website, **www.frommers.com,** has travel information on more than 4,000 destinations. We update features regularly, giving you access to the most current trip-planning information and the best airfare, lodging, and car-rental bargains. You can also listen to podcasts, connect with other Frommers.com members through our active-reader forums, share your travel photos, read blogs from guidebook editors and fellow travelers, and much more.

1

The Best of Nashville

Nashville may be the capital of Tennessee, but it's better known as Music City, the country music mecca. Yet it is so much more. Combining small-town warmth with an unexpected urban sophistication, Nashville is an increasingly popular tourist destination that boasts world-class museums and major-league sports teams; an eclectic dining and after-hours scene; and an eye-catching skyline ringed by a beautiful countryside of rolling hills, rivers and lakes, and wide-open green spaces.

Ultimately, though, Nashville is the heart and soul of country music, that uniquely American blend of humble gospel, blues, and mountain music that has evolved into a $2-billion-a-year industry. At its epicenter, Nashville is still the city where unknown musicians can become overnight sensations, where the major record deals are cut and music-publishing fortunes are made, and where the *Grand Ole Opry* still takes center stage.

Symbolic of Nashville's vitality is downtown, an exciting place that is finally breathing new life. Once-tired and -abandoned warehouses now bustle in the entertainment area known as the District. This historic neighborhood teems with tourist-oriented nightclubs and restaurants, including B. B. King's Blues Club & Grill, the ubiquitous Hard Rock Cafe that's become a staple of most large cities, and the one-and-only Wildhorse Saloon (the most famous boot-scootin' dance hall in the land). Luckily, the District isn't yet all glitz and tour-bus nightclubs. Along lower Broadway, there are still half a dozen or more dive bars where the air reeks of stale beer and cigarettes and live music plays day and night. In these bars, aspiring country bands lay down their riffs and sing their hearts out in hopes of becoming tomorrow's superstars. With so many clubs, restaurants, shops, and historic landmarks, the District is one of the South's most vibrant nightlife areas.

Folks looking for tamer entertainment head out to the Music Valley area, home to the *Grand Ole Opry,* the radio show that started the whole country music ball rolling back in 1925. Clustered in this land the locals sometimes refer to as "Nashvegas" are other music-related attractions, including the epic Opryland Resort; the nostalgic *General Jackson* showboat; several modest souvenir shops posing as museums; and theaters featuring family entertainment, with the majority showcasing performers from the *Grand Ole Opry.* Dozens of other clubs and theaters around the city also feature live music of various genres.

Country isn't the only music you'll hear in this city. Mainstream rock stars are also being lured by the city's intangible vibe. (Jack White and Kid Rock are just a few of the high-profile musicians to have moved here recently.) They come here for inspiration, to record new material, or for crossover collaborations with local music pros. No matter the genre, the city seems to attract more musicians each year, which means there's enough live music here in Nashville to keep your toes tappin' even long after you hit the highway home.

1 FROMMER'S MOST UNFORGETTABLE TRAVEL EXPERIENCES

- **Catching a Show at the Ryman Auditorium:** Known as the "Mother Church of Country Music," the Ryman Auditorium, 116 Fifth Ave. N. (© **615/254-1445;** www.ryman.com), was the home of the *Grand Ole Opry* for more than 30 years. Now restored, it once again has country music coming from its historic stage. And, yes, the old church pews are still there and just as uncomfortable as they always were. See p. 95.
- **Attending the *Grand Ole Opry:*** This live radio broadcast is an American institution and is as entertaining today as it was when it went on the air nearly 80 years ago. Luckily, the current Grand Ole Opry House, 2804 Opryland Dr. (© **800/SEE-OPRY** [733-6779]; www.opry.com), is quite a bit more comfortable than the old Ryman Auditorium, where the *Opry* used to be held. See p. 129.
- **Checking Out Up-and-Comers at the Bluebird Cafe:** With its excellent acoustics and two shows a night, the Bluebird Cafe, 4104 Hillsboro Rd. (© **615/383-1461;** www.bluebirdcafe.com), is Nashville's most famous venue for country songwriters. Only the best make it here, and many of the people who play the Bluebird wind up getting "discovered." See p. 130.

2 THE BEST SPLURGE HOTELS

- **The Hermitage Hotel,** 231 Sixth Ave. N. (© **888/888-9414** or 615/244-3121; www.thehermitagehotel.com): Built in 1910 in the Beaux Arts style, the Hermitage boasts the most elegant lobby in the city. The marble columns, gilded plasterwork, and stained-glass ceiling recapture the luxuries of a bygone era. This is a classic grand hotel, conveniently located in the heart of downtown Nashville. See p. 50.
- **Loews Vanderbilt Hotel,** 2100 West End Ave. (© **800/23-LOEWS** [235-6397] or 615/320-1700; www.loewsvanderbilt.com): If you want to be near the trendy West End area of town, treat yourself to a stay at this sophisticated luxury hotel. European tapestries and original works of art adorn the travertine-floored lobby. Service is gracious and attentive. See p. 51.

3 THE BEST "GREEN" HOTEL

- The **Hutton Hotel,** 1808 West End Ave. (© **615/340-9333;** www.huttonhotel.com), sets a new standard of excellence for sustainability, from the decor of reclaimed wood and bamboo furnishings, to its use of biodegradable cleaning products and energy-saving lighting, plumbing, and elevators. Even the hotel's two luxury courtesy vehicles are hybrid SUVs. See p. 54.

4 THE MOST UNFORGETTABLE DINING EXPERIENCES

- **Slurping a Chocolate Shake at the Elliston Place Soda Shop,** 2111 Elliston Place (✆ **615/327-1090**): Sure, every city has its retro diner these days, but the Elliston Place Soda Shop is the real thing. It's been in business since 1939 and makes the best chocolate shakes in Nashville. See p. 80.
- **Sopping up Red-Eye Gravy with Homemade Biscuits at the Loveless Cafe,** 8400 Tenn. 100 (✆ **615/646-9700;** www.lovelesscafe.com): This perennially popular country cookin' outpost serves the best traditional Southern breakfasts in the entire area. But be prepared to wait for a table. See p. 78.
- **Lingering Over Coffee and Biscotti after an Exquisite Lunch at Marché Artisan Foods,** 1000 Main St. (✆ **615/262-1111;** www.marcheartisanfoods.com): This sunny East Nashville eatery is probably my favorite place for gourmet food in a casual setting. Chef/owner Margot McCormack oversees a menu featuring artisanal breads, luscious salads, and creamy quiches. Imported olive oils, pestos, and pastas are artfully displayed around wooden farmhouse tables. See p. 84.

5 THE BEST THINGS TO DO FOR FREE (OR ALMOST)

- **Pretending You're at the Parthenon in Greece:** Nashville's lovely Centennial Park, in the West End, offers everything you could want in a city park—playgrounds, picnic areas, gorgeous shade trees—and, believe it or not, a replica of Greece's famed Parthenon. Admire the amazing architectural detail for free, or go tour the art galleries inside, for a nominal fee. See p. 97.
- **Getting That Old-Time Religion at Cowboy Church,** Texas Troubadour Theatre, 2416 Music Valley Dr. (✆ **615/859-1001**): If you're looking for a down-home dose of gospel-music ministry, make it to the Cowboy Church on time. The old-timey, nondenominational services kick off Sundays at 10am sharp. Come as you are, or don your best Stetson and bolo tie. Either way, you'll fit right in with the eclectic, all-ages congregation of locals and tourists alike, who pack the pews every week for a patriotic praise-and-worship service. See p. 129.

6 THE BEST ART DECO ARCHITECTURE

- The **Frist Center for the Visual Arts,** 919 Broadway (✆ **615/244-3340;** www.fristcenter.org): Located in a building that dates back to 1934, this was originally Nashville's main post office. The Art Deco building is a city landmark and on the National Register of Historic Places. See p. 99.

7 THE BEST (YEAR-ROUND) CHRISTMAS LIGHTS

- Aside from Opryland's dazzling holiday display of electrical excess, the Christmas lights with the most colorful history can be seen, year-round, in **Historic RCA Studio B,** on Music Row (✆ **800/852-6437** or 615/416-2001; www.countrymusichalloffame.com). The modest building where Elvis Presley recorded more than 250 of his songs still has the red, blue, and green lights that were used during the sessions from one of Elvis's Christmas albums. The story goes that The King had trouble showing the holiday spirit while recording in July, so his crew put up an artificial Christmas tree and lights. See p. 93.

2

Nashville in Depth

Though Nashville's fortunes aren't exclusively those of the country music industry, the city is inextricably linked to its music. These days, country music is enjoying greater popularity than ever before (it's now a $2-billion-a-year industry), bringing newfound importance to this city. On any given night of the week downtown, you can hear live music in clubs and bars—and not all of the music is country music. There are blues bars, jazz clubs, alternative-rock clubs, even Irish pubs showcasing Celtic music.

Nashville also has its share of shopping malls, theme restaurants, stadiums, and arenas, but it is music that drives this city. Nashville delights not only fans of country music but just about anyone who enjoys a night on the town. With all the new developments taking place, it is obvious that Nashville is ascendant, rising both as a city of the New South and as Music City.

1 THE NASHVILLE SOUND

Country music is everywhere in Nashville. You can hardly walk down a street here without hearing the strains of a country melody. In bars, in restaurants, in hotel lobbies, in the airport, and on the street corners, country musicians sing out in hopes that they, too, might be discovered and become the next big name. Nashville's reputation as Music City attracts thousands of hopeful musicians and songwriters every year, and though very few of them make it to the big time, they provide the music fan with myriad opportunities to hear the occasional great, undiscovered performer. Keep your ears tuned to the music that's the pulse of Nashville and one day you just might be able to say, "I heard her when she was a no-name playing at a dive bar in Nashville, years ago."

As early as 1871, a Nashville musical group, the Fisk University Jubilee Singers, had traveled to Europe to sing African-American spirituals. By 1902, the city had its first music publisher, the Benson Company; and today, Nashville is still an important center for gospel music. Despite the fact that this musical tradition has long been overshadowed by country music, there are still numerous gospel-music festivals throughout the year in Nashville.

The history of Nashville in the 20th century is, for the most part and for most people, the history of country music. Though traditional fiddle music, often played at dances, had been a part of the Tennessee scene from the arrival of the very first settlers, it was not until the early 20th century that people outside the hills and mountains began to pay attention to this "hillbilly" music.

In 1925, radio station WSM-AM went on the air and began broadcasting a show called The *WSM Barn Dance,* which featured live performances of country music. Two years later, it renamed the show the *Grand Ole Opry,* a program that has been on the air ever since, and is the longest-running radio show in the country. The

Big Business

Nashville's economy is diversified. Scores of well-known corporations and associations have their headquarters and/or other major facilities in the area. These include BellSouth, Bridgestone/Firestone, Broadcast Music Inc. (BMI), Caterpillar Financial, Dell, Gibson Guitar Corp./Baldwin Pianos, Lifeway Christian Resources, National Federation of Independent Business, Nissan Motor Manufacturing USA, O'Charley's Inc., and Tractor Supply Co.

same year that the *Grand Ole Opry* began, Victor Records sent a recording engineer to Tennessee to record the traditional country music of the South. These recordings helped expose this music to a much wider audience than it had ever had, and interest in country music began to grow throughout the South and across the nation.

In 1942, Nashville's first country music publishing house opened, followed by the first recording studio in 1945. By the 1960s, there were more than 100 music publishers in Nashville and dozens of recording studios. The 1950s and early 1960s saw a rapid rise in the popularity of country music, and all the major record companies eventually opened offices here. Leading the industry at this time were brothers Owen and Harold Bradley, who opened the city's first recording studio not affiliated with the *Grand Ole Opry.* CBS and RCA soon followed suit. Many of the industry's biggest and most familiar names first recorded in Nashville at this time, including Patsy Cline, Hank Williams, Brenda Lee, Dottie West, Floyd Cramer, Porter Wagoner, Dolly Parton, Loretta Lynn, George Jones, Tammy Wynette, Elvis Presley, the Everly Brothers, Perry Como, and Connie Francis.

During this period, country music evolved from its "hillbilly music" origins. With growing competition from rock 'n' roll, record producers developed a cleaner, more urban sound for country music. Production values went up and the music took on a new sound, the "Nashville sound." You can tour the old recording studio where many of those hits were recorded—Historic RCA Studio B.

In 1972, the country music–oriented Opryland USA theme park (now supplanted by a shopping mall) opened on the east side of Nashville. In 1974, the *Grand Ole Opry* moved from the Ryman Auditorium, its home of more than 30 years, to the new Grand Ole Opry House just outside the gates of Opryland.

In more recent years, country music has once again adapted to maintain its listenership. Rock and pop influences have crept into the music, opening a rift between traditionalists (who favor the old Nashville sound) and fans of the new country music, which for the most part is faster and louder than the music of old. However, in Nashville, every type of country music, from Cajun to contemporary, bluegrass to cowboy, honky-tonk to Western swing, is heard with regularity. Turn on your car radio anywhere in America and run quickly through the AM and FM dials: You'll likely pick up a handful of country music stations playing music that got its start in Nashville.

Eclectic Playlist for Nashville/Tennessee Travel

"The Brand New Tennessee Waltz" **Joan Baez**
"East Nashville Easter" **Yonder Mountain String Band**
"Killing Time in Nashville" **The Lost Cartographers**
"Nashville" **Indigo Girls**
"Nashville" **Liz Phair**
"Nashville Blues" **The Louvin Brothers**
"Nashville Casualty & Life" **Kinky Friedman**
"Nashville Cats" **The Kingston Trio**
"Nashville Moon" **Charlie Daniels Band**
"Nashville Parent" **Lambchop**
"Nashville Pickin'" **Doc Watson**
"The Nashville Scene" **Hank Williams, Jr.**
"Nashville Shores" **Jemima Pearl**
"Nashville Skyline" **Dishwalla**
"Nashville Skyline Rag" **Bob Dylan**
"Nashville Tears" **John Anderson**
"Nashville Toupee" **Southern Culture on the Skids**
"Nashville West" **The Byrds**
"Nashville Woman's Blues" **Bessie Smith**
"Pete the Best Coon Dog in Tennessee" **Jimmy Martin**
"South Nashville Blues" **Steve Earle**
"Tennessee" **Arrested Development**
"Tennessee" **BadMonkey**
"Tennessee" **Carl Perkins**
"Tennessee" **NRBQ**
"Tennessee" **The Shakes**
"Tennessee" **Shawn Colvin**
"Tennessee Blues" **Clarence "Gatemouth" Brown**
"Tennessee Courage" **Vern Gosdin**
"The Tennessee Jump" **Chet Atkins**
"Tennessee Line" **Daughtry**
"Tennessee Pusher" **Old Crow Medicine Show**
"Tennessee Toddy" **Marty Robbins**
"Tennessee Twister" **Bob James and the Bob Cats**
"Tennessee Waltz" **Les Paul and Mary Ford**
"Tennessee Waltz" **Norah Jones**
"Tennessee Waltz" **Otis Redding**
"Tennessee Waltz/Tennessee Mazurka" **The Chieftains**
"Tennessee Whiskey" **David Allan Coe**
"Tennessee Woman" **Charlie Musselwhite**

2 LOOKING BACK AT NASHVILLE

Long before the first Europeans set foot in middle Tennessee, Native Americans populated this region of rolling hills, dense forests, and plentiful grasslands. Large herds of deer and buffalo made the region an excellent hunting ground. However, by the late 18th century, when the first settlers arrived, continuing warfare over access to the area's rich hunting grounds had forced the various battling tribes to move away. Though there were no native villages in the immediate area, this did not eliminate conflicts between Native Americans and settlers.

FRONTIER DAYS The first Europeans to arrive in middle Tennessee were French fur trappers and traders: Charles Charleville, who established a trading post at a salt lick, and Timothy Demonbreun, who made his home in a cave on a bluff above the Cumberland River. By the middle part of the century, the area that is now Nashville came to be known as French Lick because of the salt lick.

Throughout the middle part of the century, the only other whites to explore the area were so-called long hunters. These hunters got their name from the extended hunting trips, often months long, that they would make over the Appalachian Mountains. They would bring back stacks of buckskins, which at the time sold for $1. Thus, a dollar came to be called a "buck." Among the most famous of the long hunters was Daniel Boone, who may have passed through French Lick in the 1760s.

The Indian Treaty of Lochaber in 1770 and the Transylvania Purchase in 1775 opened up much of the land west of the Appalachians to settlers. Several settlements had already sprung up on Cherokee land in the Appalachians, and these settlements had formed the Watauga Association, a sort of self-government. However, it was not until the late 1770s that the first settlers began to arrive in middle Tennessee. In 1778, James Robertson, a member of the Watauga Association, brought a scouting party to the area in his search for a place to found a new settlement.

The bluffs above the Cumberland River appealed to Robertson, and the following year he returned with a party of settlers. This first group, composed of men only, had traveled through Kentucky and arrived at French Lick on Christmas Eve 1779. The women and children, under the leadership of John Donelson, followed by flatboat, traveling 1,000 miles by river to

DATELINE

- **9000 B.C.** Paleo-Indians inhabit area that is now Nashville.
- **A.D. 1000–1400** Mississippian-period Indians develop advanced society characterized by mound-building and farming.
- **1710** French fur trader Charles Charleville establishes a trading post in the area.
- **1765** A group of long hunters camp at Mansker's Lick, north of present-day Nashville.
- **1772** Watauga Association becomes first form of government west of the Appalachians.
- **1775** Transylvania Purchase stimulates settlement in middle Tennessee.
- **1778** James Robertson scouts the area and decides to found a settlement.
- **1779** Robertson's first party of settlers arrives on Christmas Eve.
- **1780** Second of Robertson's parties of settlers, led by Col. John Donelson, arrives by boat in April; in May, settlement of Nashborough founded.
- **1781** Battle of the Bluffs fought with Cherokee Indians.

reach the new settlement and arriving in April 1780. This new settlement of nearly 300 people was named Fort Nashborough, after North Carolinian General Francis Nash. As soon as both parties were assembled at Fort Nashborough, the settlers drew up a charter of government called the Cumberland Compact. This was the first form of government in middle Tennessee.

Fort Nashborough was founded while the Revolutionary War was raging, and these first settlers very soon found themselves battling Cherokee, Choctaw, and Chickasaw Indians—whose attacks were incited by the British. The worst confrontation was the Battle of the Bluffs, which took place in April 1781, when settlers were attacked by a band of Cherokees.

By 1784, the situation had grown quieter, and, in that year, the settlement changed its name from Nashborough to Nashville. Twelve years later, in 1796, Tennessee became the 16th state in the Union. Nashville at that time was still a tiny settlement in a vast wilderness, but in less than 20 years, the nation would know of Nashville through the heroic exploits of one of its citizens.

In 1814, at the close of the War of 1812, Andrew Jackson, a Nashville lawyer, led a contingent of Tennessee militiamen in the Battle of New Orleans. The British were soundly defeated and Jackson became a hero. A political career soon followed, and in 1829, Jackson was elected the seventh president of the United States.

In the early part of the 19th century, the state government bounced back and forth between eastern and middle Tennessee, and was twice seated in Knoxville, once in Murfreesboro, and had once before been located in Nashville before finally staying put on the Cumberland. By 1845, work had begun on constructing a capitol building, which would not be completed until 1859.

THE CIVIL WAR & RECONSTRUCTION By 1860, when the first rumblings of secession began to be heard across the South, Nashville was a very prosperous city, made wealthy by its importance as a river port. Tennessee reluctantly sided with the Confederacy and became the last state to secede from the Union. This decision sealed Nashville's fate. The city's significance as a shipping port was not lost on either the Union or the Confederate army, both of which coveted the city as a means of controlling important river and railroad transportation routes. In February 1862, the Union army occupied Nashville, razing many homes in the process. Thus, Nashville became the first state capital to fall to the Union troops.

- **1784** The small settlement's name changed from Nashborough to Nashville.
- **1796** Tennessee becomes the 16th state.
- **1814** Andrew Jackson, a Nashville resident, leads the Tennessee militia in the Battle of New Orleans and gains national stature.
- **1840** Belle Meade plantation home built.
- **1843** State capital moved from Murfreesboro to Nashville.
- **1850** Nashville is site of convention held by nine Southern states that jointly assert the right to secede.
- **1862** Nashville becomes first state capital in the South to fall to Union troops.
- **1864** Battle of Nashville, last major battle initiated by the Confederate army.
- **1866** Fisk University, one of the nation's first African-American universities, founded.
- **1873** Vanderbilt University founded.
- **1897** The Parthenon built as part of the Nashville Centennial Exposition.
- **1920** Nashville becomes center of nation's attention as Tennessee becomes 36th state to give women the

continues

Epic Athena

In 1897, Nashville built a replica of the ancient Greek Parthenon in Centennial Park. Why? With more than a dozen colleges and universities, and a growing reputation as a center of learning and higher education, Nashville earned a reputation as the "Athens of the South." Inside the Nashville Parthenon is a statue of Athena. At 41-feet tall, she's the largest piece of indoor sculpture in the Western World.

Throughout the Civil War, the Confederates repeatedly attempted to reclaim Nashville, but to no avail. In December 1864, the Confederate army made its last stab at retaking Nashville, but during the Battle of Nashville they were roundly rebuffed.

Though the Civil War left Nashville severely damaged and in dire economic straits, the city quickly rebounded. Within a few years, the city had reclaimed its important shipping and trading position and also developed a solid manufacturing base. The post–Civil War years of the late 19th century brought a newfound prosperity to Nashville. These healthy economic times left the city with a legacy of grand classical-style buildings, which can still be seen around the downtown area.

Fisk University, one of the nation's first African-American universities, was founded in 1866. Vanderbilt University was founded in 1873, and in 1876, Meharry Medical College, the country's foremost African-American medical school, was founded. With this proliferation of schools of higher learning, Nashville came to be known as the "Athens of the South."

THE 20TH CENTURY At the turn of the century, Nashville was firmly established as one of the South's most important cities. This newfound significance had culminated 3 years earlier with the ambitious Tennessee Centennial Exposition of 1897, which left as its legacy to the city Nashville's single most endearing structure—a full-size reconstruction of the Parthenon. Though Nashville's Parthenon was meant to last only the duration of the exposition, it proved so popular that the city left it in place. Over the years, the building deteriorated until it was no longer safe to visit. At that point, the city was considering demolishing this last vestige of

vote, thus ratifying the 19th amendment to the U.S. Constitution.

- **1925** WSM-AM radio station broadcasts first *Grand Ole Opry* program.
- **1943** *Grand Ole Opry* moves to Ryman Auditorium, in downtown Nashville.
- **1944** Nashville's first recording studio begins operation at WSM-AM radio.
- **1950s** Numerous national record companies open offices and recording studios in Nashville.
- **Late 1950s to early 1960s** Record company competition and pressure from rock 'n' roll change the sound of country music, giving it a higher production value that comes to be known as the "Nashville sound."
- **1972** Opryland USA theme park opens in Nashville.
- **1974** *Grand Ole Opry* moves to a new theater at the Opryland USA theme park.
- **1993** Ryman Auditorium closes for a renovation that will make the *Grand Ole Opry*'s most famous home an active theater once again.

African-American History in Nashville

- Nashvillian **William Edmonson** was the first black artist to be honored with a one-man exhibit at New York's Museum of Modern Art, in 1937. (Today, visitors to Nashville can see his work in a permanent exhibit at Cheekwood Botanical Garden.)
- From the 1940s to the 1960s, **Jefferson Street** was known as the jazz, blues, and R&B district of Nashville. Legendary performers, ranging from Duke Ellington and Ella Fitzgerald to Ray Charles, Little Richard, and Ike and Tina Turner, played in nightclubs (now long gone) such as the Del Morocco and New Era.
- Civil Rights pioneer and lawmaker **John Lewis** was a seminary student in Nashville in February 1960. He helped organize sit-ins at segregated lunch counters across the city.
- **Wilma Rudolph,** a track star with Tennessee State's Tigerbelles, won three gold medals at the 1960 Summer Olympic Games in Rome. Known as the "fastest woman in the world," she was the first American woman to win three gold medals in one Olympics.
- Former Nashville resident **Oprah Winfrey** was a Tennessee State University sophomore when she became the first female and the first African-American in Nashville to anchor a local newscast.
- The nation's oldest African American architectural firm, **McKissack & McKissack,** was founded in Nashville.

the Centennial Exposition, but public outcry brought about the reconstruction, with more permanent materials, of the Parthenon.

About the same time the Parthenon was built, trains began using the new Union Station, a Roman-Gothic train station. The station's grand waiting hall was roofed by a stained-glass ceiling, and, with its

- **1994** With the opening of the Wildhorse Saloon and the Hard Rock Cafe, and the reopening of the Ryman Auditorium, Nashville becomes one of the liveliest cities in the South.
- **1996** Nashville Arena opens in downtown Nashville.
- **1997** Bicentennial Capitol Mall State Park opens north of state capitol building.
- **1999** NFL Tennessee Titans move into new Coliseum, and NHL Nashville Predators move into Gaylord Entertainment Center (now Sommet Center) downtown.
- **2000** Titans take a trip to the Super Bowl as AFC champs. Opry Mills, a 1.2-million-square-foot entertainment and shopping complex, rises from the ashes of the demolished Opryland amusement park.
- **2001** Two new world-class venues open downtown: the Frist Center for the Visual Arts and the Country Music Hall of Fame. The CMA Fest (formerly known as Fan Fair) moved from its long-time home at the Tennessee State Fairgrounds to downtown Nashville.

continues

And the Rest is History

In 1925, the *WSM Barn Dance* was a popular Saturday-night radio program that followed a broadcast of classical music from New York City. Preparing for the *Barn Dance* program one night, announcer George Hay joked, "For the last hour, we have been listening to music taken largely from grand opera and the classics. We now present our own 'Grand Ole Opry.'" And that's how the *Grand Ole Opry* got its name.

gilded plasterwork and bas-reliefs, was a symbol of the waning glory days of railroading in America. Today, Union Station has been restored and is one of Nashville's two historic hotels.

In 1920, Tennessee played a prominent role in the passing of the 19th Amendment to the U.S. Constitution, which gave women the right to vote in national elections. As the 36th state to ratify the 19th Amendment, the Tennessee vote became the most crucial battle in the fight for women's suffrage. Surprisingly, both the pro-suffrage and the anti-suffrage organizations were headquartered in the Beaux Arts–style Hermitage Hotel. In 1994, this hotel was completely renovated; now known as the Hermitage, it is the city's premier historic hotel.

The 20th century also brought the emergence of country music as a popular musical style. The first recordings of country music came from Tennessee, and though it took a quarter of a century for "hillbilly" music to catch on, by 1945 Nashville found itself at the center of the country music industry. The city embraced this new industry and has not looked back since.

3 THE LAY OF THE LAND

Nashville has a striking skyline, with its mix of new high-rises and historic buildings. Incidentally, the skyscraper with the pointy-looking "ears" belongs to AT&T, but locals call it like they see it (the Batman Building). Although downtown

- **2005** Centennial Park, a 132-acre green oasis and home to the Parthenon in Nashville's West End, becomes one of the first parks in the U.S. to get wireless Internet access.
- **2006** Nashville celebrates its bicentennial. The Schermerhorn Symphony Center, modeled after the ornate concert halls of Old Europe, opens downtown.
- **2009** Nashville's Gulch neighborhood is the first neighborhood in the South to receive "LEED for Neighborhood Development" (LEED ND) certification.

Nashville was built around the Cumberland River, the city's sprawl extends for miles in all directions. Outlying areas include beautiful farmland, scenic parks and lakes, and rolling foothills that hint of the Appalachians in the eastern part of the state.

4 NASHVILLE IN FILM, TV & MUSIC

Even before such modern-day television reality shows as *Nashville Star,* Music City's place in pop-culture history was forever sealed with the long-running musical-comedy program *Hee Haw.* Hosted by country entertainers Buck Owens and Roy Clark, the corny weekly variety show was filmed in Nashville and featured all the greats of the 1960s and '70s. If that was before your time, you can still check out DVDs of the popular program.

Television retains a huge presence here, as The Nashville Network (TNN), Country Music Television (CMT), and Great American Country (GAC) continue to showcase the area's Southern charms. In addition, Nashville entertainer Bobby Jones hosts his self-titled gospel music show on BET (Black Entertainment Television). It has become the longest-running show at that network.

In addition to its myriad country artists, Nashville is also a burgeoning enclave for big-name talents in other musical genres, including pop, rock, bluegrass, jazz, and especially contemporary Christian music. Such artists as Bon Jovi, Matchbox Twenty, and the White Stripes have come here to write and record music. Well-known musicians, including Michael McDonald, Donna Summer, Peter Frampton, Sheryl Crow, and Jack White, have homes in Nashville.

With rags-to-riches stories around every corner, Nashville has been the inspiration behind some memorable movies. Over the past 4 decades, there have been several cinematic standouts, beginning with *Nashville* (1975). The late director Robert Altman's comic parody looks at the lives of assorted characters who converge in Music City during the early 1970s. *In Coal Miner's Daughter* (1980), Sissy Spacek earned an Academy Award for her portrayal of Loretta Lynn, a poor Kentucky girl who became one of country music's first female legends. One of my personal favorites, this film is especially appealing in the way it accurately portrays Nashville's heyday in the 1940s and 1950s, when such country pioneers as Hank Williams and others were in their prime.

Another unforgettable biopic is *Sweet Dreams* (1985). Jessica Lange plays music star Patsy Cline, a friend to Loretta Lynn. The film follows the singer's tumultuous marriage and short-lived career. Cline was killed in a plane crash at the height of her fame.

Another, lesser-known country-music coming-of-age story that has held up pretty well over the years is *The Thing Called Love* (1993). Directed by Peter Bogdanovich and starring Samantha Mathis (and a then-unknown Sandra Bullock), it's perhaps best remembered as the

Kids' Play

The Nashville Children's Theatre, renowned for the high quality of its productions, is the oldest children's theater in the U.S.

last movie made by the promising young actor River Phoenix, who died shortly thereafter.

Sibling Joaquin Phoenix struck box-office gold more than a decade later with another big-budget blockbuster, *Walk the Line.* In that Oscar-winning musical biography, Phoenix channels the "Man in Black," Johnny Cash, who was born in Arkansas, launched his career at Sun Records, in Memphis, and became one of Nashville's most outspoken entertainers. Nashville native Reese Witherspoon portrays his wife, June Carter Cash, for which she won an Oscar.

If you're looking for the real deal instead of actor portrayals and period pieces, I recommend *Down from the Mountain* (2000), an acclaimed documentary that showcases musicians featured in the soundtrack to the Coen Brothers' *O Brother, Where Art Thou?,* starring George Clooney. Performances and interviews by Ralph Stanley, Emmylou Harris, and many others are featured.

Last, and perhaps least expected among the movies filmed in Nashville, is *The Green Mile* (1999), starring Tom Hanks. Novelist Stephen King's gripping story focuses on death-row guards at a penitentiary in the 1930s.

5 EATING & DRINKING IN NASHVILLE

Although still known and loved for its Southern traditions, including sweet iced tea and plate-lunch specials known as the "meat-and-three" (an entree with sides), Nashville has stretched its culinary wings in recent years. With noted up-and-coming chefs, nationally-recognized restaurants, and an array of bistros, cafes, and ethnic eateries throughout the metro area, the dining scene is more sophisticated and diverse than you might expect.

Chain restaurants are everywhere these days, but Nashville has plenty of great, locally owned, independent eateries. With consistent food and service, they have been able to build loyal clientele while attracting tourists, as well. For food lovers, Nashville is a tempting mix that could have you starting your day with biscuits and sausage gravy, sampling sushi at lunch, and feasting on German sauerbraten at supper.

Drinking in Nashville can be equally adventurous. The city boasts an eclectic blend of beer dives, microbreweries, trendy cocktail spots, and gourmet restaurants with extensive wine lists. The hard stuff is also a point of pride. After all, this is Jack Daniel's and George Dickel country. Those two nearby historic whiskey distilleries draw their fair share of tourists, and their products are prominently featured on many restaurant and bar menus throughout the region and beyond.

3

Planning Your Trip to Nashville & Memphis

Nashville and Memphis have many things in common. But boiled down to basics, both are large, modern cities that retain the flavor and hospitality of the American South—and both are bona fide, world-renowned tourist destinations for fans of American music, including the blues, folk, rock, soul and, of course, country and bluegrass. So it makes sense that if you're traveling a significant distance to get here, you might as well do both destinations in a single trip.

Nashville and Memphis are within a half-day's drive of each other, making it feasible to stay a few nights in one city before heading down the highway to the other. You'll have to drive, or book an escorted tour that covers both locales. A good place to start planning is the **Tennessee Department of Tourism Development,** P.O. Box 23170, Nashville, TN 37202 (✆ **800/836-6200** or 615/741-2158). For more information and suggested itineraries, visit their website at www.tnvacations.com. However, it's not necessary to do both cities. Both are equally accessible to travelers throughout the U.S. and around the world.

Before heading to Music City, you can get more information by contacting the **Nashville Convention & Visitors Bureau,** 150 Fourth Ave. N. (✆ **800/657-6910** or 615/259-4700).

You can also find information about Nashville at the following websites.

- Nashville Convention & Visitors Bureau: **www.visitmusiccity.com**
- *Nashville Scene,* Nashville's main arts and entertainment weekly: **www.nashvillescene.com**
- *The Tennessean,* Nashville's morning daily newspaper: **www.tennessean.com**

For information on Memphis, contact the Memphis Convention & Visitors Bureau, 47 Union Ave., Memphis, TN 38103 (✆ **800/8-MEMPHIS** [863-6744] or 901/543-5300). You can also get information online at www.memphistravel.com and the following websites.

- The *Memphis Flyer,* is Memphis's main arts and entertainment weekly: **www.memphisflyer.com.**
- *The Commercial Appeal,* is Memphis's morning daily newspaper: **www.commercialappeal.com.**

For additional help in planning your trip and for more on-the-ground resources, please turn to "Fast Facts: Nashville & Memphis," on p. 255.

1 WHEN TO GO

Summer is the peak tourist season in Nashville and Memphis. Unless you're specifically visiting Nashville for the Country Music Fan Fair in June, or going to Graceland for Elvis Week in August, you might want to avoid traveling during these times, when hotels sell out and prices go through the roof.

Summer is also when both cities experience their worst weather. During July and August, and often in September, temperatures can hover around 100°F, with humidity at close to 100%. (Can you say "muggy"?) Spring and fall, however, last for several months and both are quite pleasant. Days are often warm and nights cool, though during these two seasons the weather changes, so bring a variety of clothes. Heavy rains can hit any time of year, and if you spend more than 3 or 4 days in town, you can almost bet on seeing some rain. Winters can be cold, with daytime temperatures staying below freezing, and snow is not unknown.

CALENDAR OF EVENTS

For an exhaustive list of events beyond those listed here, check http://events.frommers.com, where you'll find a searchable, up-to-the-minute roster of what's happening in cities all over the world.

NASHVILLE CALENDAR OF EVENTS

"Awesome April"

The **GMA (Gospel Music Association) Dove Awards,** the **CMT Music Awards,** and the **Tin Pan South** songwriters' festival all take place in this action-packed month, when Nashville weather is at its prettiest. Also on tap are the Music City Walk of Fame Induction Ceremony, the Nashville Film Festival, and the Country Music Marathon. For more detailed information on each of these events, and for tour packages and tickets, contact the Nashville Convention and Visitors Bureau (✆ **800/657-6910;** www.visitmusiccity.com). All month.

May

Tennessee Renaissance Festival, in Triune (20 miles south of downtown Nashville). Maidens, knights, gypsies,

Average Temperature & Rainfall in Nashville

	Jan	Feb	Mar	Apr	May	June	July	Aug	Sept	Oct	Nov	Dec
Temp. (°F)	38	41	50	60	68	76	80	79	72	61	49	41
Temp. (°C)	3	5	10	15	20	24	26	26	22	16	9	5
Rainfall (in.)	4.3	4.2	5	4	4.6	3.8	3.8	3.3	3.4	2.7	3.9	4.6

Average Temperature & Rainfall in Memphis

	Jan	Feb	Mar	Apr	May	June	July	Aug	Sept	Oct	Nov	Dec
Temp. (°F)	40	45	53	63	71	79	83	81	74	63	52	44
Temp. (°C)	4	7	11	17	21	26	28	27	23	17	11	6
Rainfall (in.)	4.7	4.5	5.2	5.6	4.9	3.9	3.9	3.4	3.2	2.9	4.8	5.3

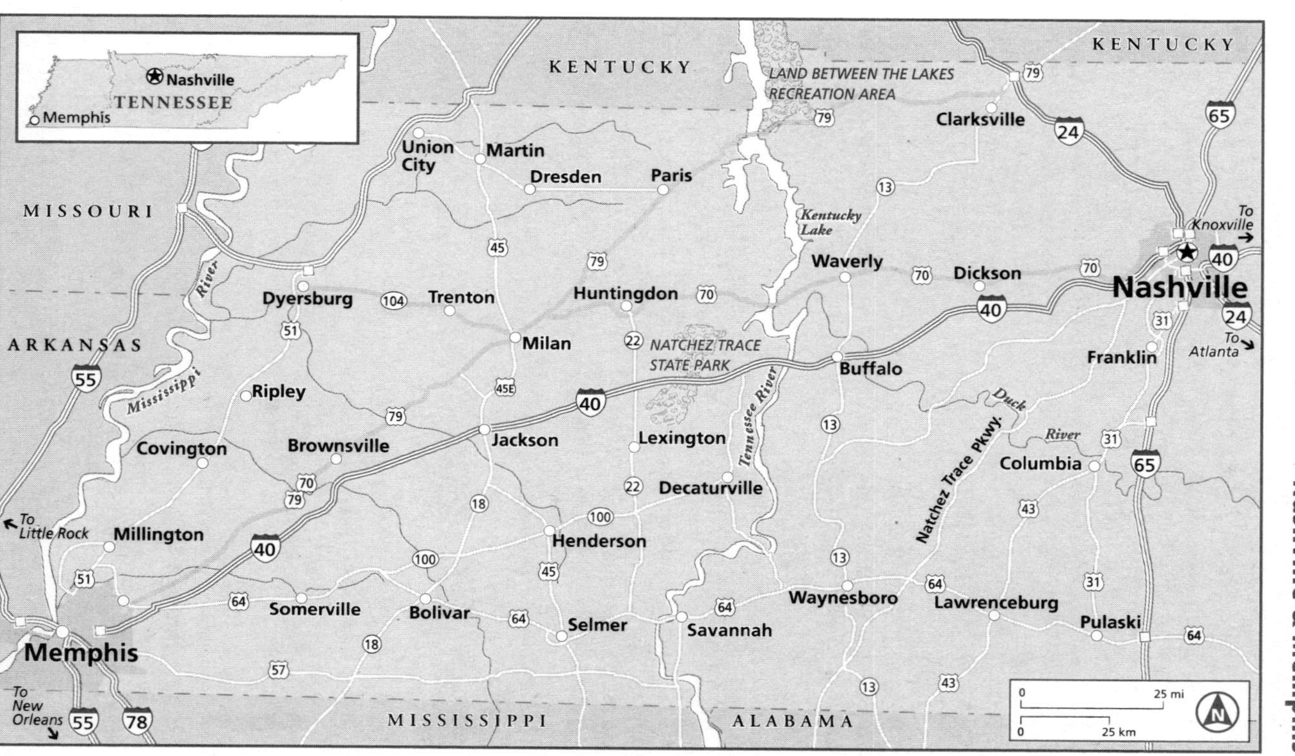

Nashville
TENNESSEE
Memphis
KENTUCKY
KENTUCKY
MISSOURI
ARKANSAS
MISSISSIPPI
ALABAMA
LAND BETWEEN THE LAKES RECREATION AREA
Kentucky Lake
NATCHEZ TRACE STATE PARK
Natchez Trace Pkwy.
Tennessee River
Duck River
Mississippi River
To Knoxville
To Atlanta
To Little Rock
To New Orleans
Clarksville
Union City
Martin
Dresden
Paris
Waverly
Dickson
Nashville
Dyersburg
Trenton
Huntingdon
Milan
Buffalo
Franklin
Ripley
Jackson
Lexington
Covington
Brownsville
Decaturville
Columbia
Millington
Henderson
Somerville
Bolivar
Selmer
Savannah
Waynesboro
Lawrenceburg
Pulaski
Memphis
0 25 mi
0 25 km

jugglers, jousters, games, and food—think whole turkey legs that you can eat like a barbarian—are some of the diversions you'll find at this medieval fair held on the grounds of the **Castle Gwynn** (✆ **615/395-9950;** www.tnrenfest.com). Weekends in May, including Memorial Day.

Tennessee Craft Fair, Centennial Park. With the largest display of Tennessee crafts, this fair opens the summer season. Food, demonstrations, and children's craft activities (✆ **615/385-1904;** www.tennesseecrafts.org). Early May.

Iroquois Steeplechase, Percy Warner Park. This horse race has been a Nashville ritual for more than 50 years. A benefit for Vanderbilt Children's Hospital, the event is accompanied by tailgate picnics (✆ **615/322-4814** or 615/343-4231; www.iroquoissteeplechase.org). Second Saturday in May.

Tennessee Jazz & Blues Society's Jazz on the Lawn, various locations. Every Sunday evening May through October, the society performs on lawns of historic homes such as Cheekwood Botanical Garden, the Hermitage, and Belle Meade Plantation (✆ **615/301-5121;** www.jazzblues.org). Sundays May through October.

June

Bluegrass Nights at the Ryman, Ryman Auditorium. Thursday nights at the historic Ryman Auditorium play host to top-name bluegrass acts such as Alison Krauss and Ricky Skaggs (✆ **615/889-3060;** www.ryman.com). Thursdays June through July.

CMA (Country Music Association) Music Festival (formerly Fan Fair), Various downtown locations. This is a chance for country artists and their fans to meet and greet each other in a week-long music celebration. Glitzy stage shows and picture/autograph sessions with country music stars are all part of the action. A Texas barbecue and tickets for sightseeing are included in the price of a ticket, along with a bluegrass concert and the Grand Masters Fiddling Championship. This is the biggest country music event of the year in Nashville, so book your tickets far in advance. Contact the CMA Office (✆ **615/244-2840;** www.cmaworld.com) for ticket information. Four days in mid-June.

American Artisan Festival, Centennial Park. Artisans from 35 states present a wide range of crafts, from blown glass to leather and quilts. Children's art booth and music, too (✆ **615/298-4691**). Mid-June.

July

Music City July 4th: Let Freedom Sing!, Riverfront Park. This family-oriented, alcohol-free event attracts 100,000 people for entertainment, food, and fireworks. Top-name entertainers, such as Taylor Swift and Wynonna Judd, have headlined the patriotic, televised extravaganza (✆ **800/657-6910;** www.musiccityjuly4th.com). July 4.

Impressions

Take of London fog 30 parts; malaria 10 parts; gas leaks 20 parts; dewdrops gathered in a brickyard at sunrise 25 parts; odor of honeysuckle 15 parts. Mix. The mixture will give you an approximate conception of a Nashville drizzle.

—O. Henry, "A Municipal Report," in *Strictly Business,* 1910

August

Tennessee Walking-Horse National Celebration, Celebration Grounds, Shelbyville (40 miles southeast of downtown Nashville). The World Grand Championship of the much-loved Tennessee walking horse, plus trade fairs and dog shows (✆ **931/684-5915;** www.twhnc.com). Late August.

September

Music City Jazz, Blues & Heritage Festival, Riverfront Park. The festival coincides with the John Merritt Classic football game (and battle of the marching bands) at Tennessee State University (✆ **800/791-8368** or 615/506-5114; www.nb14u.com/MCJHF.htm). Labor Day weekend.

Tennessee State Fair, Tennessee State Fairgrounds. Sprawling livestock and agriculture fair, with 4-H Club and Future Farmers of America members well represented—and a midway, of course (✆ **615/862-8980;** www.tennesseestatefair.org). Early to mid-September.

Belle Meade Plantation Fall Fest, Belle Meade Plantation. Antiques, crafts, children's festival, garage treasures sale, and food from local restaurants (✆ **800/270-3991** or 615/356-0501; www.bellemeadeplantation.com). Mid-September.

African Street Festival, Tennessee State University, main campus. Featured entertainment includes gospel, R&B, jazz, reggae music, and children's storytelling (✆ **615/251-0007;** www.aacanashville.org). Mid-September.

TACA Fall Craft Fair, Centennial Park. This upscale fine-crafts market features artisans from throughout Tennessee (✆ **615/385-1904;** www.tennesseecrafts.org). Late September.

October

Southern Festival of Books, War Memorial Plaza. Sponsored by the National Endowment for the Humanities, the region's largest, free literary festival is a feast for book lovers. More than 200 authors gather for a variety of special events over 3 days (✆ **615/770-0006;** www.humanitiestennessee.org/festival). Second full weekend in October.

Oktoberfest, Historic Germantown, at the corner of Eighth Avenue North and Monroe Street. Tours of Germantown, polka dancing, accordion players, and lots of authentic German food (✆ **615/256-2729;** www.nashvilleoktoberfest.com). Early to mid-October.

Annual Fall Festival & Tennessee State Pow Wow, place to be determined. Native Americans from the United States and Canada gather for this powwow, sponsored by the Native American Indian Association (✆ **615/232-9179;** www.naiatn.org/powwow). Mid-October.

Birthday of the *Grand Ole Opry*, Grand Ole Opry House. Three-day party with performances, autographs, and picture sessions with *Opry* stars. In recent years, the all-star lineup has run the gamut from Ralph Stanley to Alan Jackson (✆ **615/889-3060;** www.gaylordopryland.com). Mid-October.

November

Longhorn World Championship Rodeo, Tennessee Miller Coliseum, outside Murfreesboro. Professional cowboys and cowgirls participate in this rodeo to win championship points (✆ **800/357-6336** or 615/876-1016; www.longhornrodeo.com). Third weekend in November.

Christmas at Belmont, Belmont Mansion, Belmont University Campus. The opulent antebellum mansion is decked out in Victorian Christmas finery, and the gift shop is a great place to shop for Christmassy Victorian reproductions

(✆ **615/460-5459;** belmontmansion.com). Late November to late December.

A Country Christmas, Opryland Resort. More than two million Christmas lights are used to decorate the grounds of the hotel. Musical revues change every few years, with headliners ranging from Pam Tillis and Louise Mandrell to "Charlie Brown" and the Radio City Music Hall Rockettes (✆ **888/777-OPRY** [6779] or 615/889-1000; www.gaylordhotels.com). November 1 to December 25.

MEMPHIS CALENDAR OF EVENTS

January

Elvis Presley's Birthday Tribute, Graceland. International gathering of Presley fans to celebrate the birthday of "The King" (✆ **800/238-2000;** www.elvis.com). Around January 8.

Martin Luther King, Jr.'s, Birthday, citywide. Events to memorialize Dr. King take place on the nationally observed holiday (✆ **901/521-9699;** www.civilrightsmuseum.org). Mid-January.

February

Beale Street Zydeco Music Festival, along Beale Street. More than 20 acts perform during this 2-day event (✆ **901/529-0999**). Mid-February.

Regions Morgan Keegan Tennis Championship, Racquet Club of Memphis. World-class players compete in this famous tour event (✆ **901/765-4400;** www.memphistennis.com). Mid- to late February.

April

Dr. Martin Luther King, Jr., Memorial March, downtown. This somber event remembers the assassination of the civil rights leader (✆ **901/525-2458**). April 4.

Memphis International Film Festival, Midtown. Filmmakers and cinema lovers converge in Memphis (✆ **901/273-0014;** www.onlocationmemphis.org). Second week in April.

Africa in April Cultural Awareness Festival, downtown. A several-day festival centering on African music, dance, theater, exhibits, arts, and crafts (✆ **901/947-2133;** www.africainapril.org). Third week in April.

May

Memphis in May International Festival, citywide. A month-long celebration of a different country each year with musical, cultural, and artistic festivities; business, sports, and educational programs; and food unique to the country. More than a million people come to nearly 100 sanctioned events scheduled throughout the city. The most important happenings are the Memphis in May Beale Street Music Festival (first weekend in May), the World Championship Barbecue Cooking Contest (mid-May), and the Sunset Symphony (last weekend of May). Call ✆ **901/525-4611;** or visit www.memphisinmay.org. Entire month of May.

FedEx Cup St. Jude Classic, Tournament Players Club at Southwind. A benefit for St. Jude Children's Research Hospital, this is a PGA event (✆ **901/748-0534;** www.stjudeclassic.com). Late May to early June.

June

Carnival Memphis, citywide. Almost half a million people join in the exclusive activities of exhibits, music, crafts, and events (✆ **901/278-0243;** www.carnivalmemphis.org). Early June.

Germantown Charity Horse Show, Germantown Horse Show Arena. Four-day competition for prizes (✆ **901/754-0009;** www.gchs.org). Second week in June.

July

Star-Spangled Celebration, Shelby Farms. Fourth of July entertainment and fireworks (✆ **901/726-0469;** www.shelbyfarmspark.org). July 4.

Blues on the Bluff, downtown. Volunteer- and member-supported radio station WEVL-FM presents two concerts on the grounds of the National Ornamental Metal Museum, overlooking the Mississippi River (✆ **901/528-0560;** www.wevl.org). Late July and early August.

August

Elvis Tribute Week, Graceland and citywide. Festival commemorating the influences of Elvis (✆ **800/238-2000;** www.elvis.com). Second week in August.

September

Beale Street Labor Day Music Festival, Beale Street. Memphis musicians are featured Labor Day (and night) in restaurants and clubs throughout the Beale Street district (✆ **901/526-0110**). Labor Day weekend.

Memphis Music & Heritage Festival, Center for Southern Folklore. A celebration of the diversity of the South (✆ **901/525-3655;** www.southernfolklore.com). Early September.

Cooper-Young Festival, Midtown. Neighborhood festival featuring food, arts, crafts, and family activities (✆ **901/276-7222;** www.cooperyoungfestival.com). Mid-September.

Mid-South Fair, Mid-South Fairgrounds. Ten days of fun-filled rides, food, games, shows, a midway, and a rodeo (✆ **901/274-8800;** www.midsouthfair.org). Last week of September.

Southern Heritage Classic, Midtown. Classic college football rivalry at the Liberty Bowl Memorial Stadium (✆ **901/398-6655;** www.southernheritageclassic.com). A Saturday in September.

October

River Arts Festival, South Main Historic District. Painters, jewelers, sculptors, woodworkers and other artists and musicians converge on the South Main Historic District in downtown Memphis for this high-quality, juried festival (✆ **901/826-3629;** riverartsfestmemphis.org). Late October.

November

Freedom Awards, downtown. Human rights activists are honored by the National Civil Rights Museum (✆ **901/521-9699;** www.civilrightsmuseum.org) with public lectures and other ceremonies. Past recipients include Oprah Winfrey, Bono, Colin Powell, and Bill Clinton. Late October or early November.

Mid-South Arts and Crafts Show, Memphis Cook Convention Center. Artists and craftspeople from more than 20 states sell their handiwork (✆ **423/430-3461**). Third week in November.

International Blues Competition. Blues musicians from around the country meet for performances at various venues, with the W. C. Handy Awards and post-show jam. For more information, call the Blues Foundation at ✆ **901/527-BLUE** (2583); or log on to www.blues.org. Throughout November.

December

Merry Christmas Memphis Parade, downtown. Christmas parade with floats and bands (✆ **901/575-0540**). Early December.

AutoZone Liberty Bowl Football Classic, Liberty Bowl Memorial Stadium. Intercollegiate game that's nationally televised (✆ **901/274-4600;** www.libertybowl.org). Late December.

Bury Your Blues Blowout on Beale, Beale Street. New Year's Eve celebration both inside the clubs and outside on Beale Street (✆ **901/526-0110**). December 31.

2 ENTRY REQUIREMENTS

PASSPORTS

Virtually every air traveler entering the U.S. is required to show a passport. All persons, including U.S. citizens, traveling by air between the United States and Canada, Mexico, Central and South America, the Caribbean, and Bermuda are required to present a valid passport. U.S. and Canadian citizens entering the U.S. at land and sea ports of entry from within the Western Hemisphere will need to present government-issued proof of citizenship, such as a birth certificate, along with a government issued photo ID, such as a driver's license. A passport is not required for U.S. or Canadian citizens entering by land or sea, but it is highly encouraged to carry one.

VISAS

For information on obtaining a Visa, please visit "Fast Facts: Nashville & Memphis," on p. 255.

The U.S. Department of State has a **Visa Waiver Program (VWP)** allowing citizens of the following countries to enter the United States without a visa for stays of up to 90 days: Andorra, Australia, Austria, Belgium, Brunei, Denmark, Finland, France, Germany, Iceland, Ireland, Italy, Japan, Liechtenstein, Luxembourg, Monaco, the Netherlands, New Zealand, Norway, Portugal, San Marino, Singapore, Slovenia, Spain, Sweden, Switzerland, and the United Kingdom. Citizens of Czech Republic, Estonia, Hungary, Latvia, Lithuania, Malta, Republic of Korea, and Slovakia are soon to be admitted to the VWP. (*Note:* This list was accurate at press time; for the most up-to-date list of countries in the VWP, consult http://travel.state.gov/visa.) Even though a visa isn't necessary, in an effort to help U.S. officials check travelers against terror watch lists before they arrive at U.S. borders, visitors from VWP countries must register online through the Electronic System for Travel Authorization (ESTA) before boarding a plane or a boat to the U.S. Travelers will complete an electronic application providing basic personal and travel eligibility information. The Department of Homeland Security recommends filling out the form at least 3 days before traveling. Authorizations will be valid for up to 2 years or until the traveler's passport expires, whichever comes first. Currently, there is no fee for the online application. ***Note:*** Any passport issued on or after October 26, 2006, by a VWP country must be an **e-Passport** in order for VWP travelers to be eligible to enter the U.S. without a visa. Citizens of these nations also need to present a round-trip air or cruise ticket upon arrival. E-Passports contain computer chips capable of storing biometric information, such as the required digital photograph of the holder. If your passport doesn't have this feature, you can still travel without a visa if it is a valid passport issued before October 26, 2005, and includes a machine-readable zone, or between October 26, 2005, and October 25, 2006, and includes a digital photograph. For more information, go to **http://travel.state.gov/visa**. Canadian citizens may enter the United

States without visas; they will need to show passports (if traveling by air) and proof of residence, however.

Citizens of all other countries must have (1) a valid passport that expires at least 6 months later than the scheduled end of their visit to the U.S., and (2) a tourist visa.

CUSTOMS

What You Can Bring Into the U.S.

Every visitor more than 21 years of age may bring in, free of duty, the following: (1) 34 ounces of wine or hard liquor; (2) 200 cigarettes, 100 cigars (but not from Cuba), or 3 pounds of smoking tobacco; and (3) $100 worth of gifts. These exemptions are offered to travelers who spend at least 72 hours in the United States and who have not claimed them within the preceding 6 months. It is forbidden to bring into the country almost any meat products (including canned, fresh, and dried meat products such as bullion, soup mixes, and such). Generally, condiments including vinegars, oils, spices, coffee, tea, and some cheeses and baked goods are permitted. Avoid rice products, as rice can often harbor insects. Bringing fruits and vegetables is not advised, though not prohibited. Customs will allow produce depending on where you got it and where you're going after you arrive in the U.S. International visitors may carry in or out up to $10,000 in U.S. or foreign currency with no formalities; larger sums must be declared to U.S. Customs on entering or leaving, which includes filing form CM 4790. For details regarding U.S. Customs and Border Protection, consult your nearest U.S. embassy or consulate, or **U.S. Customs** (www.customs.gov).

What You Can Take Home from the U.S.

For information on what you're allowed to bring home, contact one of the following agencies:

Canadian Citizens: Canada Border Services Agency (✆ **800/461-9999** in Canada, or 204/983-3500; www.cbsa-asfc.gc.ca).

U.K. Citizens: HM Revenue & Customs (✆ **0845/010-9000,** or 020/8929-0152 from outside the U.K.; www.hmce.gov.uk).

Australian Citizens: Australian Customs and Border Protection Service (✆ **1300/363-263;** www.customs.gov.au).

New Zealand Citizens: New Zealand Customs Service, The Customhouse, 17–21 Whitmore St., Box 2218, Wellington (✆ **04/473-6099** or 0800/428-786; www.customs.govt.nz).

MEDICAL REQUIREMENTS

Unless you're arriving from an area known to be suffering from an epidemic (particularly cholera or yellow fever), inoculations or vaccinations are not required for entry into the United States.

3 GETTING THERE & GETTING AROUND

GETTING TO NASHVILLE & MEMPHIS

By Plane

Nashville (airport code: BNA) is served by the following major airlines: **American Airlines** (✆ 800/433-7300); **Continental** (✆ 800/525-0280); **Delta** (✆ 800/221-1212); **Northwest-KLM** (✆ 800/225-2525); **Southwest** (✆ 800/435-9792); **United Airlines** (✆ 800/241-6522); and **US Airways** (✆ 800/428-4322).

Southwest is the city's largest carrier, with some 87 daily flights out of the city. Most Southwest flights will depart and arrive from the airport's Concourse C. Southwest Airlines also offers air/hotel packages. For details, visit **Southwest Airlines Vacations** online at **www.swavacations.com**, or call ✆ **800/423-5683.**

Memphis is served by the following airlines: **American Airlines** (✆ 800/433-7300); **Delta** (✆ 800/221-1212); **KLM** (✆ 800/374-7747); **Northwest** (✆ 800/225-2525); **Southwest** (✆ 800/435-9792); **United Airlines** (✆ 800/241-6522); and **US Airways** (✆ 800/428-4322).

Northwest has a hub in Memphis and is the city's largest carrier. It's also your best bet for package deals. For details, visit **Northwest Airlines** online, at **www.nwavacations.com**, or call ✆ **800/225-2525.**

Some large airlines offer transatlantic or transpacific passengers special discount tickets under the name **Visit USA,** which allows mostly one-way travel from one U.S. destination to another at very low prices. Unavailable in the U.S., these discount tickets must be purchased abroad in conjunction with your international fare. This system is the easiest, fastest, cheapest way to see the country.

Getting Into Nashville from the Airport

Nashville International Airport (✆ **615/275-1600**) is located about 8 miles east of downtown Nashville and is just south of I-40. It takes about 15 minutes to reach downtown Nashville from the airport. See below for information on car-rental facilities at the airport. Many hotels near the airport offer a complimentary shuttle service, while others slightly farther away have their own fee shuttles; check with your hotel when you make your reservation.

The **Super Shuttle International** (✆ **800/258-3826** or 615/361-6034) offers transportation from the airport to Nashville and surrounding areas. Departures leave the airport every 15 minutes, and they leave downtown and West End hotels for the airport every 30 minutes. The **Gray Line Airport Express** (✆ **615/275-1180**) operates shuttles between the airport and downtown and West End hotels. These shuttles operate from the airport every 15 to 20 minutes daily between 6:30am and 11pm; in addition to the hotels listed below, a few other hotels are on call. The downtown shuttle stops at the following hotels: Hilton, Union Station, Courtyard by Marriott (Fourth and Church), Holiday Inn Express, Renaissance Nashville Hotel, Nashville Sheraton, The Hermitage, and Doubletree Hotel Nashville. The West End shuttle stops at the following hotels: Loews Vanderbilt Plaza Hotel, Embassy Suites–West End, Holiday Inn Select, Courtyard by Marriott, Marriott-Vanderbilt, Guest House Inn, Hampton Inn–Vanderbilt, Hampton Inn and Suites–Elliston Place, and Days Inn–Vanderbilt. Rates are $11 one-way and $17 round-trip.

Metropolitan Transit Authority **buses** connect the airport and downtown Nashville. Buses run 7 days a week. One-way fares are $2. All-day, unlimited-ride passes are $4.80. Buses from the airport leave at the ground-level curbside. Buses to the airport leave from the new Music City Central downtown transit station, at 400 Charlotte Ave. It's located between Fourth Avenue North and Fifth Avenue North. For current schedule information, call ✆ **615/862-5950** Monday to Friday 6:30am to 6pm and Saturday 8am to 1pm.

Taxi service is another option. There is a $25 flat fare in the triangle between the airport, downtown, and Gaylord Opryland Resort and Convention Center. Between any two points, the fare is $25 for up to four people. Outside this geographical triangle, the meter starts at $7. Taxis are available on the ground level of the airport terminal. For information, call the Transportation Licensing Commission (TLC) at ✆ **615/862-6777.**

Getting Into Memphis from the Airport

The **Memphis International Airport** (✆ **901/922-8000**) is located approximately 11 miles south of downtown Memphis, off I-240. From the airport to East Memphis, it's about 9 miles. The route into either downtown or East Memphis is on I-240 all the way. Generally, allow about 20 minutes for the trip between the airport and downtown, and 15 minutes between the airport and East Memphis—up to an hour more during rush hour. See below for information on car-rental facilities at the airport.

Although there is no direct bus service from the airport to downtown Memphis, it is possible (though impractical), with a change of bus en route, to get downtown on **Memphis Area Transit Authority** buses (✆ **901/274-6282**). These buses, however, do not run very often and are not very convenient for visitors. The buses run every 1 to 2 hours until about 5:30pm Monday through Saturday, and until 5:15pm on Sunday, and the fare is $1.25. From the lower level at the airport, take no. 32, the East Parkway/Hollywood bus, and transfer to no. 10, the Lamar bus (which runs about every hour Mon–Fri, fewer times on Sat), or the no. 56, the Union/Kimball bus (running about every half-hour Mon–Fri), which will take you downtown. If you want to take the bus, the best bet is to call MATA or ask a bus driver for the latest schedule information.

A taxi from the airport to downtown Memphis will cost about $25; to East Memphis it will cost about $20. There are usually plenty of taxis around, but if you can't find one, call **Yellow/Checker Cab** (✆ **901/577-7777**) or **City Wide Cab Company** (✆ **901/324-4202**). The first mile is $3.20; after that, it's $1.50 per mile. Each additional passenger is 50¢ extra.

International visitors should note that insurance and taxes are almost never included in quoted rental-car rates in the U.S. Be sure to ask your rental agency about additional fees for these. They can add a significant cost to your car rental.

By Car

Nashville is a hub city intersected by three interstate highways. **I-65** runs north to Louisville, Kentucky, and south to Birmingham, Alabama. **I-40** runs west to Memphis and east to Knoxville, Tennessee. **I-24** runs northwest toward St. Louis and southeast toward Atlanta. Downtown Nashville is the center of the hub, encircled by interstates 40, 65, and 265. Briley Parkway on the east, north, and west and I-440 on the south form a larger "wheel" around this hub.

Here are some driving distances from selected cities: Atlanta, 250 miles; Chicago, 442 miles; Cincinnati, 291 miles; Memphis, 210 miles; New Orleans, 549 miles; and St. Louis, 327 miles.

If you're heading into downtown Nashville, follow the signs for I-65/24 and take either exit 84 or exit 85. If you're headed to Music Valley (Opryland Resort), take I-40 east to the Briley Parkway exit and head north. If your destination is the West End/Music Row area, take I-40 around the south side of downtown and get off at the Broadway exit.

To limit frustration, try to avoid hitting the interstates around either city at morning or afternoon rush hour. Traffic tie-ups and lengthy delays are becoming increasingly common, especially in Nashville. Ongoing freeway construction and renovation projects further congest the roadways. To find out about lane closures and other headaches, call the **Tennessee Department of Transportation**'s construction hotline at ✆ **800/858-6349.** Snow and ice storms may also make road conditions hazardous. For updates, call the state's inclement weather/road closure

Tuneful Tidbit

There is no richer, more illuminating showcase of musical roots in the country than in this 220-mile stretch of highway.

—Esteemed rock music critic Robert Hilburn of the *Los Angeles Times*, describing the 3-hour drive between Nashville and Memphis along I-40.

hotline (✆ **800/342-3258;** www.tdot.state.tn.us/tdotsmartway).

Memphis lies at the southwestern tip of Tennessee, bordering Mississippi and Arkansas. Interstate 40 connects Memphis with Nashville to the east and Little Rock, Arkansas, to the west. Interstate 55 connects Memphis with Mississippi to the south, and St. Louis to the north. Both interstates intersect with I-240, which loops around the city's north, east, and southern suburbs. The western edge of downtown Memphis is the Mississippi River.

For Memphis, here are some driving distances from other cities: Atlanta, 390 miles; Chicago, 534 miles; Little Rock 135 miles; New Orleans, 395 miles; St. Louis, 284 miles.

If you are a member of the **American Automobile Association (AAA)** and your car breaks down, call ✆ **800/222-4357** for 24-hour emergency road service. The **local AAA office** in Nashville is at 2501 21st Ave. S., Ste. 1 (✆ **615/297-7700**), and is open Monday to Friday 8:30am to 5:30pm and Saturday 9am to 1pm.

The speed limit is 70 mph for much of the stretch between Nashville and Memphis, which also offers access to clean rest stops and dozens of service stations and restaurants. For travel information at any time, dial ✆ **511** on your cell phone.

If you're visiting from abroad and plan to rent a car in the United States, keep in mind that foreign driver's licenses are usually recognized in the U.S., but you should get an international one if your home license is not in English.

Check out **Breezenet.com,** which offers domestic car-rental discounts with some of the most competitive rates around.

There is no plane service between Nashville and Memphis. You will have to rent a car and drive the 3-hour distance between the two cities. Interstate 40, also known as "The Music Highway," has several interesting diversions along the way.

By Bus

Greyhound (✆ **800/231-2222;** www.greyhound.com) is the sole nationwide bus line. International visitors can obtain information about the **Greyhound North American Discovery Pass.** The pass, which offers unlimited travel and stopovers in the U.S. and Canada, can be obtained from foreign travel agents or through www.discoverypass.com.

Greyhound offers service to Nashville from around the country. These buses operate along interstate corridors or local routes. The fare between New York and Nashville is about $66 one-way and $132 round-trip; the fare between Chicago and Nashville is about $45 one-way and $90 round-trip. The Greyhound bus station is on the south side of downtown Nashville at 200 Eighth Ave. S.

Greyhound service between New York and Memphis costs about $77 one-way and $154 round-trip; the fare between Chicago and Memphis is $54 one-way and $88 round-trip. The Greyhound bus station is in downtown Memphis, at 203 Union Ave.

From Atlanta, Georgia, round-trip fares are $78 to Memphis and $56 to Nashville.

By Train

Amtrak (✆ **800/872-7245;** www.amtrak.com) serves Memphis (but not Nashville) with a route that goes from Chicago through Memphis (about 11 hours' travel time) en route to New Orleans (about 8 hours) on the *City of New Orleans.* If you arrive in Memphis on an Amtrak train, you'll find yourself at **Central Station,** 545 S. Main St. (✆ **901/526-0052**), near Calhoun Street. This historic railway station has been completely renovated into a combination transportation center with public bus and Main Street Trolley connections and retail complex. However, the neighborhood around the station remains quite run-down. The area is not safe on foot, especially after dark. If arriving by train, you should take a cab or the Main Street Trolley to your hotel.

International visitors planning to visit several U.S. cities can buy a **USA Rail Pass,** good for 5, 15, or 30 days of unlimited travel on **Amtrak** (✆ **800/USA-RAIL** [872-7245]; www.amtrak.com). The pass is available online or through many overseas travel agents. See Amtrak's website for the cost of travel within the western, eastern, or northwestern United States. Reservations are generally required and should be made as early as possible. Regional rail passes are also available.

GETTING AROUND NASHVILLE

By Car

As mentioned earlier, driving between Nashville and Memphis is the only practical way to see both cities. Interstate 40 connects the two.

Because Nashville and its many attractions are quite spread out, the best way to get around is by car. It's surprisingly easy to find your way around the city and to find parking, even downtown. But bring plenty of cash. Parking can cost a few coins in the meter or upwards of $15 during special events. Some self-service lots also accept credit cards. For helpful downtown-parking information, check out **www.parkitdowntown.com**. The only time driving is a problem is during morning and evening rush hours. At these times, streets leading south and west out of downtown can get quite congested.

RENTAL CARS All the major rental-car companies and several independent ones have offices in Nashville. Fortunately, most of the companies have desks conveniently located on the lower level at the Nashville International Airport. Major car-rental companies in Nashville include **Alamo Rent-A-Car,** at the airport (✆ 800/327-9633 or 615/340-6546; www.alamo.com); **Avis Rent-A-Car,** at the airport (✆ 800/831-2847 or 615/361-1212; www.avis.com); **Budget Rent-A-Car,** at 1816 Church St., 1525 N. Gallatin Pike, and the airport (✆ 800/763-2999 or 615/366-0822; www.budget.com); **Dollar Rent-A-Car,** at the airport (✆ 800/800-4000 or 615/367-0503; www.dollar.com); **Enterprise Rent-a-Car,** at the airport (✆ 800/325-8007 or 615/275-0011; www.enterprise.com); **Hertz,** at the airport (✆ 800/654-3131 or 615/361-3131; www.hertz.com); **National Car Rental,** at the airport (✆ 800/227-7368 or 615/361-7467; www.nationalcar.com); and **Thrifty Car Rental,** 1201 Briley Pkwy., at Vultee Boulevard, and at the airport (✆ 800/367-2277 or 615/361-6050; www.thrifty.com).

PARKING In downtown Nashville, there are a variety of parking lots, ranging from $6 to more than $10 per day. Drop your money into the self-service machine at the end of the parking lot. Downtown parking is also available in other municipal and private lots and parking garages.

When parking on the street, be sure to check the time limit on parking meters.

Also be sure to check whether you can park in a parking space during rush hour (4–5:30pm), or your car may be ticketed and towed. On-street parking meters are free after 6pm on weekdays, after noon on Saturday, and all day Sunday. For more downtown-parking information, check out the new website www.parkit downtown.com.

DRIVING RULES A right turn at a red light is permitted after coming to a full stop, unless posted otherwise, but drivers must first yield to vehicles that have a green light or pedestrians in the walkway. Children under 4 years of age must be in children's car seats or other approved restraints when in the car.

Tennessee has a very strict DUI (driving under the influence of alcohol) law, and has a law that states a person driving under the influence with a child under 12 years of age in the vehicle may be charged with a felony.

By Bus

Although Nashville is served by the extensive and efficient **Metropolitan Transit Authority (MTA)** bus system, it is generally not practical for tourists to get around this way. Call the Customer Service Center (✆ **615/862-5950**), which is open Monday to Friday 6:30am until 6pm. The MTA information center and ticket booth, located at 400 Charlotte Ave., is open Monday to Friday 6:30am to 6:30pm and on Saturday 8am to 1pm. MTA bus stops are marked with blue-and-white signs; in the downtown area, signs include names and numbers of all the routes using that stop. All express buses are marked with an X following the route number.

Adult **bus fares** are $1.60 ($2.10 for express buses); children under 4 ride free. Exact change is required. You can purchase a weekly pass, good for unlimited local rides from Sunday to Saturday, for $22 per adult or $10 for ages 19 and under; a picture ID is required. Seniors and riders with disabilities qualify for an 80¢ fare with an MTA Golden Age, Medicare, TenneSenior, or Special Service card. Call ✆ **615/862-5950** to register for this discount. For more information, visit **www.nashvillemta.org**.

By Trolley

For a quick way to get around downtown during weekdays, look for the LunchLINE shuttles. As a convenience to downtown workers, the Central Business Improvement District and Nashville Downtown Partnership offer a free trolley that loops through the heart of downtown, weekdays from 11am to 1:30pm. Riders may hop on or off at any of the nine stops. A shuttle picks up at each stop every 10 minutes. No tickets are required. Just look for the yellow LunchLINE signs.

The **downtown route** passes by many points of interest in downtown Nashville and is a good way to get acquainted with the city. For more information and downloadable maps, log on to **www.nashville downtown.com**.

By Taxi

For quick cab service, call **Music City Taxi** (✆ 615/262-0451), **Checker Cab** (✆ 615/256-7000), **United Cab** (✆ 615/228-6969), or **Yellow Cab** (✆ 615/256-0101). The flag-drop rate is $3; after that it's $2 per mile, plus $1 for each additional passenger. There is a flat-fare triangle between the airport, downtown, and Opryland. Between any two points in the triangle, the fare is set at $25 for up to four passengers.

On Foot

With the exception of the quaint, strollable Germantown neighborhood just north of downtown, the heart of downtown Nashville is the only area where you're likely to do much walking around. In this area, especially around lower Broadway, you can visit attractions, do some shopping, have a good meal, and even go to a club, all without having to get in your car. The suburban strips can't make that claim.

GETTING AROUND MEMPHIS

By Car

Memphis is a big sprawling city, and the best—and worst—way to get around is by car. A car is nearly indispensable for traveling between downtown and East Memphis, yet traffic congestion can make this trip take far longer than you'd expect (45 min. isn't unusual). Avenues running east–west and almost any road in East Memphis at rush hour are the most congested. Parking downtown is not usually a problem, but stay alert for tow-away zones and watch the time on your meter. Out in East Memphis, there is usually no parking problem. When driving between downtown and East Memphis, you'll usually do better to take the interstate.

CAR RENTALS All the major car-rental companies and several independent companies have offices in Memphis. Some are located near the airport only, and some have offices near the airport and in other areas of Memphis. Be sure to leave yourself plenty of time for returning your car when you head to the airport to catch your return flight. None of the companies have an office in the airport itself, so you'll have to take a shuttle van from the car drop-off point to the airport terminal.

Major car-rental companies in Memphis include **Avis,** 2520 Rental Rd. (✆ **800/577-1521** or 901/345-6129; www.avis.com); **Budget Rent-A-Car,** 2650 Rental Rd. (✆ **800/527-0700;** www.budget.com); **Dollar Rent-A-Car,** 2600 Rental Road (✆ **866/434-2226;** www.dollar.com); **Enterprise Rent-a-Car,** 2909 Airways Blvd. (✆ **866/799-7965** or 901/396-3736; www.enterprise.com); **Hertz,** 2560 Rental Rd. (✆ **800/654-3131** or 901/345-5680; www.hertz.com); and **Thrifty Car Rental,** 2680 Rental Rd. (✆ **877/283-0898** or 901/345-0170; www.thrifty.com).

PARKING Parking in downtown Memphis is a lot more expensive than it used to be. There are plenty of parking lots behind the Beale Street clubs; these charge big bucks. Metered parking on downtown streets is becoming increasingly scarce; if you're lucky enough to snag a spot close to your destination, be sure to check the time limit on the meter. Downtown parking is also available in municipal and private lots and parking garages. Again, most require a stiff fee. The good news is, many of the automated parking kiosks now accept credit and debit cards for payment, eliminating the need to carry a lot of change.

In Midtown, where parking is rarely a problem, there is a free lot in Overton Square, between Madison Avenue and Monroe Avenue.

DRIVING RULES A right turn at a red light is permitted after coming to a full stop, unless posted otherwise, but drivers must first yield to vehicles proceeding through a green light or to pedestrians in the walkway. Children under 4 years of age must be in a child's car seat or other approved child restraint when in the car.

By Bus

The **Memphis Area Transit Authority (MATA;** ✆ **901/274-MATA** [6282]; www.matatransit.com) operates citywide bus service, but I do not recommend it for tourists. Public transportation here is poor and does not offer convenient connections between most hotels and tourist sites. Bus stops are indicated by green-and-white signs. For schedule information, ask a bus driver or call the MATA number above. The standard fare is $1.50, and exact change is required. Transfers from bus to bus cost 10¢, but there's no transfer fee to the trolley (see below). MATA offers a

Fun Facts Nashville on the Rise

For the past few years, Nashville has been awash in ambitious new construction projects. With the recent downturn in the U.S. economy, however, some of those projects have stalled. As of late 2009, among the skyscraper survivors are:

- The Encore, an $80-million residential and retail high-rise, at Third Avenue and Demonbreun
- The Pinnacle, a $110-million, 35-story residential building, between Second and Third avenues.

50% discount for travelers with disabilities and senior citizens with ID cards. (***Note:*** To qualify for the discounted fare, however, you need to show a Medicare card or obtain a MATA ID card by bringing two forms of identification to the MATA Customer Service Center at 444 N. Main St., open Mon–Fri 7am–7pm.)

By Trolley

The **Main Street Trolley** (✆ **901/577-2640**) operates renovated 1920s trolley cars (and modern reproductions) on a circular route that includes Main Street from the Pyramid to the National Civil Rights Museum and Central Station, and then follows Riverside Drive, passing the Tennessee State Visitors Center. It's a unique way to get around the downtown area. The fare is $1 each way, with a special lunch-hour rate of 50¢ between 11am and 1:30pm. An all-day pass is $3.50; exact change is required, and passengers may board at any of the 20 stations along Main Street. Trolleys are wheelchair accessible.

By Taxi

For quick cab service, call **Checker/Yellow Cab** (✆ **901/577-7777**) or **City Wide Cab Company** (✆ **901/324-4202**), or have your hotel or motel call one for you. The first mile is $3.80; after that, it's $1.80 per mile. Each additional passenger is $1 extra.

On Foot

Downtown Memphis is walkable, though the only areas that attract many visitors are the Beale Street area and Main Street from the National Civil Rights Museum north to the Pyramid. The rest of the city is not walkable.

4 MONEY & COSTS

Frommer's lists exact prices in the local currency. The currency conversions quoted above were correct at press time. However, rates fluctuate, so before departing consult a currency exchange website such as **www.oanda.com/convert/classic** to check up-to-the-minute rates.

The Value of the U.S. Dollar vs. Other Popular Currencies

US$	Can$	UK£	Euro (€)	Aus$	NZ$
$1	C$1.05	£.61	.68€	A$1.09	NZ$1.38

What Things Cost in Nashville & Memphis	
Cup of coffee	$1.50
Taxi from airport to downtown	$25.00
Moderate 3-course dinner for one, without alcohol	$30.00
A night in a moderately priced hotel room	$150.00
Self-guided tour of the Ryman Auditorium	$12.50
Admission to Country Music Hall of Fame Museum and Historic RCA Studio	$30.00
Graceland Mansion Tour	$30.00

It's always advisable to bring money in a variety of forms on a vacation: a mix of cash and credit cards. You should also exchange enough petty cash to cover airport incidentals, tipping, and transportation to your hotel before you leave home, or withdraw money upon arrival at an airport ATM.

Nashville and Memphis are moderately priced, compared with larger U.S. cities such as New York and Atlanta. While rapid growth and developments caused costs for downtown parking, hotels, and restaurants to spike in both cities in recent years, the recent U.S. economic recession has led many of these destinations to offer discounted rates or added perks to entice travelers.

ATMs are prevalent in Nashville and Memphis. Debit cards are widely accepted.

5 HEALTH

WHAT TO DO IF YOU GET SICK AWAY FROM HOME

If you need a doctor in Nashville, call **TriStar Medline** at ✆ **800/265-8624** or 615/342-1919; or contact the **Vanderbilt Medical Group Physician Referral Service** at ✆ **615/322-3000.**

In Memphis, call **Methodist Healthcare,** at 1211 Union Ave. (✆ **901/5176-7000**), or the **Regional Medical Center/ Elvis Presley Trauma Center,** at 877 Jefferson Ave. (✆ **901/545-7100**).

If you have dental problems in either city, a nationwide referral service, known as 1-800-DENTIST (✆ **800/336-8478**), will provide the name of a nearby dentist or clinic.

You may want to ask the concierge at your hotel to recommend a local doctor—even his or her own. This will probably yield a better recommendation than any toll-free number would.

You can also try the emergency room at a local hospital. Many hospitals also have walk-in clinics for emergency cases that are not life threatening; you may not get immediate attention, but you won't pay the high price of an emergency room visit.

If you suffer from a chronic illness, consult your doctor before your departure. Pack prescription medications in your carry-on luggage, and carry them in their original containers, with pharmacy labels—otherwise they won't make it through airport security. Visitors from outside the U.S. should carry generic names of prescription drugs. For U.S. travelers, most reliable health-care plans provide coverage if you get sick away from home. Foreign visitors may have to pay all medical costs upfront and be reimbursed later.

We list additional **emergency numbers** under "Fast Facts: Nashville & Memphis," on p. 255.

6 SAFETY

Nashville is a friendly city where travelers can feel safe both downtown and in outlying neighborhoods. Cautious tourists may want to be aware that the nightlife along Broadway downtown can become rowdy after dark.

Although it, too, is full of friendly people, Memphis also has a serious crime problem, with rampant gang activity and one of the highest violent crime rates in the U.S. Although tourists aren't necessarily targeted, neither are they immune. Avoid walking or driving in unpopulated or inner-city areas alone, especially after dark. Be mindful of your surroundings, and take prudent precautions to avoid becoming a victim, such as keeping valuables hidden and your car locked.

7 SPECIALIZED TRAVEL RESOURCES

In addition to the destination-specific resources listed below, please visit Frommers.com for additional specialized travel resources.

GAY & LESBIAN TRAVELERS

While lacking the vibrancy of many larger U.S. cities, both Nashville and Memphis have much to offer gay travelers. Church Street near downtown is the most well known gay district in Nashville. To find out more about the Nashville gay and lesbian community, contact **OutLoud! Book Store,** 1703 Church St. (© **615/340-0034;** www.outloudonline.com). Nashville also has several gay and lesbian newspapers, including the entertainment weekly ***Xenogeny*** (© **615/831-1806**).

In Memphis, volunteers staff the **Memphis Gay and Lesbian Community Center,** 892 S. Cooper (© **901/278-4297**) nightly. The Cooper-Young neighborhood is widely regarded as the most gay-friendly area of town. For more information, look for the Memphis *Triangle Journal,* a free weekly newspaper that's available at local bookstores, libraries, and other locations.

TRAVELERS WITH DISABILITIES

Most disabilities shouldn't stop anyone from traveling in the U.S. There are more options and resources out there than ever before.

Almost all hotels and motels in Nashville offer wheelchair-accessible accommodations, but when making reservations be sure to ask. Additionally, the MTA public bus system in Nashville either has wheelchair-accessible regular vehicles or offers special transportation services for travelers with disabilities. To find out more about special services, call **Access Ride** (© **615/880-3970**).

The **Disability Information Office,** 25 Middleton St. (© **615/862-6492**), provides a referral and information service for visitors with disabilities. The ***Nashville City Vacation Guide,*** available either through this office or the Nashville Convention & Visitors Bureau, includes information on accessibility of restaurants, hotels, attractions, shops, and nightlife around Nashville. Similarly, the **Memphis Center for Independent Living,** 1633 Madison Ave. (✆ **901/726-6404;** www.mcil.org), is a consumer-oriented organization that helps people with disabilities.

Wheelchair Getaways of Memphis, Tennessee (✆ **888/245-9944;** www.wheelchair-getaways.com), rents specialized vans with wheelchair lifts and other features for the disabled.

FAMILY TRAVEL

To locate accommodations, restaurants, and attractions that are particularly kid-friendly, refer to the "Kids" icon throughout this guide.

MULTICULTURAL TRAVELERS

Because Tennessee is so rich in African-American heritage, the convention and visitors bureaus in both cities offer free, specialized resources for travelers in black history and multicultural heritage.

For general information, contact the **Nashville Black Chamber of Commerce** (✆ **615/876-9634**), or the **Nashville Area Hispanic Chamber of Commerce** (✆ **615/216-5737**).

For further suggestions and direction, contact **Authentic Tours of Historic Black Nashville and Beyond** (✆ **615/299-5626;** www.tnvacations.com). Trained historians offer sightseeing tours and act as step-on guides.

Memphis visitors can contact the **Black Business Association** (✆ **901/525-2357;** http://bbamemphis.blogspot.com).

For customized tours for visitors from overseas, contact **Germania Travel Tour Guide** (✆ **901/794-0347;** www.germaniatraveltourguide.com).

STUDENT TRAVEL

There are many universities and colleges in the Nashville area, but the main ones are **Vanderbilt University,** on West End Ave. (✆ **615/322-7311**), a private 4-year research-oriented university; **Tennessee State University,** 3500 John A. Merritt Blvd. (✆ **615/963-5000**), a public 4-year university; **Belmont University,** 1900 Belmont Blvd. (✆ **615/460-6000**), a Baptist liberal arts university; and **Fisk University,** 1000 17th Ave. N. (✆ **615/329-8500**), a private 4-year African-American university.

There are about a dozen major colleges and universities in the Memphis area. The most prominent are **Rhodes College,** 2000 North Pkwy. (✆ **901/726-3000**), which has a Gothic-style campus located opposite Overton Park; and the **University of Memphis,** on Central Avenue between Highland and Goodlett streets (✆ **901/678-2000**), located on a large campus in Midtown Memphis.

8 SUSTAINABLE TOURISM

Being environmentally conscious isn't the main concern of most music fans visiting Nashville and Memphis, yet Tennessee has begun taking steps to change that. After all, it is the home state of former U.S. Vice President Al Gore, whose bestseller, *Earth in the Balance,* launched intense scrutiny of global warming.

Increasingly, hotel chains in Nashville and Memphis are trying to be more environmentally friendly, by giving guests the option of requesting fresh linens and towels on a nightly basis. For example, the new **Hutton Hotel,** in Nashville, is a pioneer in sustainable luxury. See p. 54.

General Resources for Green Travel

In addition to the resources for Nashville and Memphis listed above, the following websites provide valuable wide-ranging information on sustainable travel. For a list of even more sustainable resources, as well as tips and explanations on how to travel greener, visit www.frommers.com/planning.

- **Responsible Travel** (www.responsibletravel.com) is a great source of sustainable travel ideas; the site is run by a spokesperson for ethical tourism in the travel industry. **Sustainable Travel International** (www.sustainable travelinternational.org) promotes ethical tourism practices, and manages an extensive directory of sustainable properties and tour operators around the world.
- In the U.K., **Tourism Concern** (www.tourismconcern.org.uk) works to reduce social and environmental problems connected to tourism. The **Association of Independent Tour Operators** (**AITO;** www.aito.co.uk) is a group of specialist operators leading the field in making holidays sustainable.
- In Canada, **www.greenlivingonline.com** offers extensive content on how to travel sustainably, including a travel and transport section and profiles of the best green shops and services in Toronto, Vancouver, and Calgary.
- In Australia, the national body that sets guidelines and standards for ecotourism is **Ecotourism Australia** (www.ecotourism.org.au). **The Green Directory** (www.thegreendirectory.com.au), **Green Pages** (www.thegreen pages.com.au), and **Eco Directory** (www.ecodirectory.com.au) offer sustainable travel tips and directories of green businesses.
- **Carbonfund** (www.carbonfund.org), **TerraPass** (www.terrapass.org), and **Carbon Neutral** (www.carbonneutral.org) provide info on "carbon offsetting," or offsetting the greenhouse gas emitted during flights.
- **Greenhotels** (www.greenhotels.com) recommends green-rated member hotels around the world that fulfill the company's stringent environmental requirements. **Environmentally Friendly Hotels** (www.environmentally friendlyhotels.com) offers more green accommodation ratings. The **Hotel Association of Canada** (www.hacgreenhotels.com) has a Green Key Eco-Rating Program, which audits the environmental performance of Canadian hotels, motels, and resorts.
- **Sustain Lane** (www.sustainlane.com) lists sustainable eating and drinking choices around the U.S.; also visit **www.eatwellguide.org** for tips on eating sustainably in the U.S. and Canada.
- For information on animal-friendly issues throughout the world, visit **Tread Lightly** (www.treadlightly.org). For information about the ethics of swimming with dolphins, visit the **Whale and Dolphin Conservation Society** (www.wdcs.org).
- **Volunteer International** (www.volunteerinternational.org) has a list of questions to help you determine the intentions and the nature of a volunteer program. For general info on volunteer travel, visit **www.volunteer abroad.org** and **www.idealist.org**.

Perhaps most noticeably, green living begins with what people eat. Restaurants, such as Nashville's **tayst** (p. 80)—the city's first green-certified eatery—are drawing kudos for their efforts and encouraging other restaurants to take similar measures.

In both Nashville and in Memphis, chefs and restaurant owners are beginning to emphasize organic and/or locally grown and raised produce, cheese, and meat sources for their menu items. Both cities also have vibrant farmers' markets, allowing residents and tourists alike to shop for the fresh foods and ingredients.

In the pork-barbecue-loving cities of Nashville and Memphis, it's not always easy to avoid eating greasy, meat-heavy meals. But the situation is light-years better than it used to be. An abundance of ethnic eateries can be found in both cities, and vegetarian options at mainstream restaurants are much more common than they were, say, a decade ago.

Increasingly, coffee houses such as Bongo Java in Nashville feature fair-trade coffees in their own, distinctive blends.

9 SPECIAL-INTEREST TRIPS & ESCORTED GENERAL-INTEREST TOURS

SPECIAL-INTEREST TRIPS

Most large tour operators, including **Sweet Magnolia** (see below, under "Escorted General-Interest Tours"), tailor some of their trip offerings to music guests. Others have options for Civil War buffs, including tours of historic battlegrounds and plantations. African-American history tours include sites related to the American Civil Rights movement.

FOOD TRIPS

If you're more interested in barbecue and turnip greens cooked in "pot likker" than you are in Tennessee's music attractions, you probably already know about the **Southern Foodways Alliance,** P.O. Box 1848 University, MS 38677 (✆ **662/915-5993;** www.southernfoodways.com). Based at the University of Mississippi in Oxford, about an hour's drive south of Memphis, the fun-loving and highly regarded nonprofit organization specializes in culinary tourism. Special events, field trips, and symposia often sell out, so check their website for special activities that may be scheduled when you plan to visit the area.

ESCORTED GENERAL-INTEREST TOURS

For travel planning to Memphis, Northwest Airlines, which has a hub in Memphis, offers convenient packages. (From Europe, KLM airlines offers direct flights from Amsterdam to Memphis.) For travel to Nashville, Southwest Airlines offers similar packages into Nashville from major U.S. cities.

The convention and visitors bureaus' websites in Nashville and Memphis allow tourists to book vacation packages that include hotel and attractions options. For example, the Nashville Nights "Honky Tonk Heaven" package includes 2 hotel nights, and tours to Ryman Auditorium, the Tennessee State Capitol, Historic Second Avenue, the Wildhorse Saloon, and the Hard Rock Cafe. All packages can be customized online, allowing you to book additional nights and add attractions to your itinerary.

Sweet Magnolia Tours (www.sweetmagnoliatours.com) is one of the few tour operators in Tennessee with offices in both Nashville and Memphis. In 2008, the company began offering specific vacation packages that combine the best of both cities. The land-only packages include hotel and attractions. For more information, call ✆ **800/235-5295** or 615/646-0030 in Nashville, and ✆ **901-369-9838** in Memphis.

For European travelers interested in touring Tennessee as well as Atlanta and New Orleans, check out the following website: www.deep-south-usa.de.

For more information on escorted general-interest tours, including questions to ask before booking your trip, see www.frommers.com/planning.

10 STAYING CONNECTED

INTERNET & E-MAIL

Most coffee shops and hotels, along with many restaurants and bookstores in Nashville and Memphis, have free Wi-Fi access. Nashville was at the forefront of the connectivity trend a few years ago, when its Centennial Park, in the city's affluent West End, became one of the first in the nation to offer free Wi-Fi.

Throughout this book, I've indicated which hotels offer Wi-Fi and high-speed Internet access.

4

Suggested Nashville Itineraries

Nashville is spread out, with pockets of interesting neighborhoods, entertainment districts, and shopping areas scattered throughout the metro area, so having a car is important if you want to experience the breadth of all the city has to offer. However, the downtown area is relatively compact, making it feasible to hit several of Music City's high points right off the bat on your first day in town—and without too much driving. As with any destination, your interests will dictate what you choose to do and see. The itineraries below focus primarily on country music, fine arts, history and culture, and shopping and entertainment. These suggestions can be experienced during any season and regardless of most weather conditions.

NEIGHBORHOODS IN BRIEF

While there are plenty of neighborhoods throughout the city, few are of real interest to most visitors. There are, however, named areas of the city that you'll want to be familiar with. There are also several outlying bedroom communities that may be of interest.

Downtown With the state capitol, the Tennessee State Museum, the Tennessee Center for the Performing Arts, the Tennessee Convention Center, and the Ryman Auditorium, downtown Nashville is a surprisingly vibrant area for a small Southern city. However, this is still almost exclusively a business and government district, and after dark the streets empty out, with the exception of the area known as the District.

The District With restored buildings housing interesting shops, tourist restaurants, nightclubs, and bars, this downtown historic district (along Second Ave. and Broadway) is the center of Nashville's nightlife scene. With each passing year, it becomes a livelier spot; pickup trucks and limousines jockey for space at night along Second Avenue. On Friday and Saturday nights, the sidewalks are packed with partiers who roam from dive bar to retro-disco to line-dance hootenanny.

Germantown A few blocks northwest of downtown lies the charming historic community of Germantown. Named for the European immigrants who first started settling here in the mid–19th century, the 18 square blocks are bounded by Jefferson Street to the north, Rosa Parks Boulevard on the west and Third Avenue North on the east. On the National Register of Historic Places, the once-blighted area has become a benchmark for urban redevelopment in recent years, with new loft condos, cafes, shops, and professional offices.

Love Can Build a Bridge

Or at least it can restore it. The **Shelby Street Bridge** is a case in point. Dating back to 1909, the unique, multispan truss bridge is one of several over the Cumberland River connecting downtown Nashville with East Nashville. Closed to vehicles in 1998, the bridge was to be demolished, but historians and architects fought for its conversion to a pedestrian bridge. Refurbished at a cost of $15 million, the bridge is now a National Historic Landmark. In addition to its extensive use as a pedestrian and bike route, the Shelby Street Bridge has become a favorite backdrop for country music videos shot in Nashville, including Big & Rich's "Save a Horse (Ride a Cowboy)."

Jefferson Street and Fisk University Next to Germantown, stretching west along Jefferson Street, is an area known for some of the city's best soul food spots and African-American–owned businesses. This section of Nashville is home to historic Fisk University as well as Tennessee State University. Front-yard tailgating before college football games is a popular past-time here.

The Gulch Just south of downtown lies this once-abandoned industrial area that's become the hottest real estate in Nashville. Old warehouses are being razed and revamped, and gleaming high-rise condos and lofts are being developed, as upscale new hotels, restaurants, and clubs compete for space here.

Eighth Avenue South Just south of downtown and the Gulch, Eighth Avenue is an emerging district lined with antiques shops, corner cafes, and family-friendly eateries. If you're into leisurely bargain-shopping or are on a hunt for a one-of-a-kind antique, this no-frills, nontouristy area is great for browsing.

12th Avenue South What would have been unthinkable only a few years ago has come to pass. A once-blighted area south of downtown and the Gulch is enjoying a renaissance. Idealists, entrepreneurs, and young adults with dreams have been buying up and restoring old houses to set up shop. As a result, an interesting, off-the-beaten-path array of quirky boutiques and happening restaurants and night spots now dot the area roughly bordered by Linden and Kirkwood avenues.

Music Row Recording studios and record companies make this neighborhood, located around the corner from 16th Avenue South and Demonbreun Street (pronounced "De-*mon*-bree-in"), the center of the country-music recording industry. Driving down the tree-lined boulevards, you'll see stately homes converted into the offices of country music publishers, public-relations agents, and the occasional gated recording studio. Although Music Row is a distinct district, the general area between the edge of downtown and the West End is also sometimes referred to as midtown.

The West End While tourists and barflies congregate in the District, the moneymakers and musicians of the Nashville scene gather in the West End, referred to by locals as the intellectual side of town. Located adjacent to Vanderbilt and

Belmont universities, this upscale neighborhood is home to many small shops, lots of excellent (and often expensive) restaurants, and several hotels. Also known as **Hillsboro Village,** the area has a lively late-night dining scene fueled by the college crowd and well-heeled locals looking to see and be seen. At the edge of the West End is the affluent **Belle Meade** community. Mansions abound in Belle Meade, and country stars own many of them. Two such historic mansions—Belle Meade Plantation and Cheekwood—are open to the public.

East Nashville Across the Cumberland River from downtown Nashville is this laid-back enclave of bars, coffee shops, and funky boutiques. Many homes in the area, which date back to the early 1900s, are being preserved and renovated by young families attracted to the area. Increasingly, culturally diverse East Nashville is also home to some of the locals' best-loved restaurants, such as Marché Artisan Foods (p. 84).

Music Valley This area on the east side of Nashville is where you'll find the Opryland Resort, the Grand Ole Opry House, Opry Mills shopping center, and numerous other country-themed tourist attractions. There are very few decent restaurants in the area (except within Opry Mills and the Gaylord Opryland Resort itself).

Green Hills, South Nashville, and Berry Hill Upscale shopping, chain restaurants, and affluent residential areas define the suburban enclave of Green Hills. Among Nashvillians, Green Hills is considered to be a lively, desirable neighborhood. Tourists might visit the Mall at Green Hills, the go-to, shop-'til-you-drop spot that anchors the area. The famed Bluebird Cafe (p. 130), home to up-and-coming songwriters, is also out in this neck of the woods.

1 THE BEST OF NASHVILLE IN 1 DAY

The day begins with a crash-course in the origins of American popular music, but it's a history lesson most pop-culture enthusiasts will love. The Country Music Hall of Fame and Museum is an endlessly entertaining and informative experience that will help you grasp Nashville's importance as a songwriting and recording mecca. A few blocks away is the hallowed hall where it all began: the Ryman Auditorium. Soak up the spirits of Hank Williams and Patsy Cline, and then stroll the lively strip along Broadway. Your afternoon continues with a visit to Nashville's best art museum, the Frist Center for the Visual Arts. The evening is yours to barhop or boot-scoot at the Wildhorse Saloon, Tootsie's Orchid Lounge, B. B. King's Blues Club, or any other nightspot that strikes your fancy. ***Start:*** *Country Music Hall of Fame and Museum.*

❶ Country Music Hall of Fame and Museum ★★

Start your day downtown at the acclaimed Country Music Hall of Fame and Museum. It's chock-full of colorful exhibits and music, and seeing this will help you get your bearings for later exploration. See p. 88.

Walk north 4 blocks until, on your right, you see:

❷ Ryman Auditorium ★★

This sacred concert hall was a magnet for the so-called hillbilly and country music

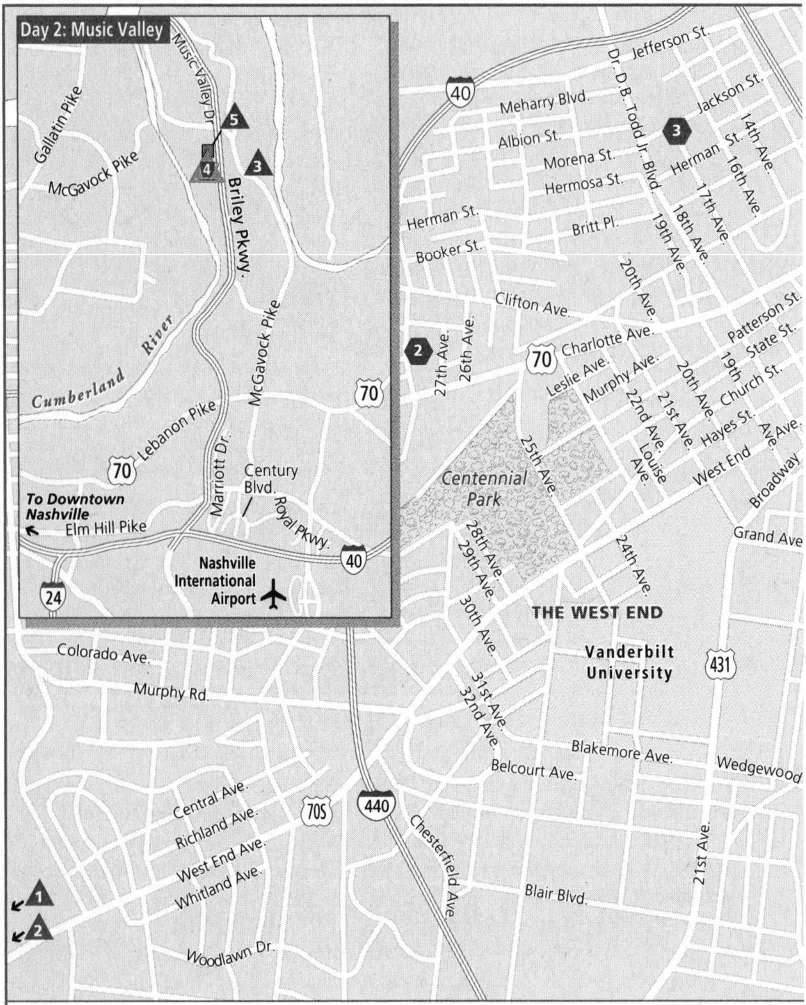

DAY ONE

1 Country Music Hall of Fame and Museum
2 Ryman Auditorium
3 Hatch Show Print
4 Jack's Bar-B-Que
5 Frist Center for the Visual Arts
6 The District

DAY TWO

1 Belle Meade Plantation
2 Cheekwood Botanical Garden & Museum of Art
3 Opry Mills
4 Rainforest Cafe
5 *Grand Ole Opry*

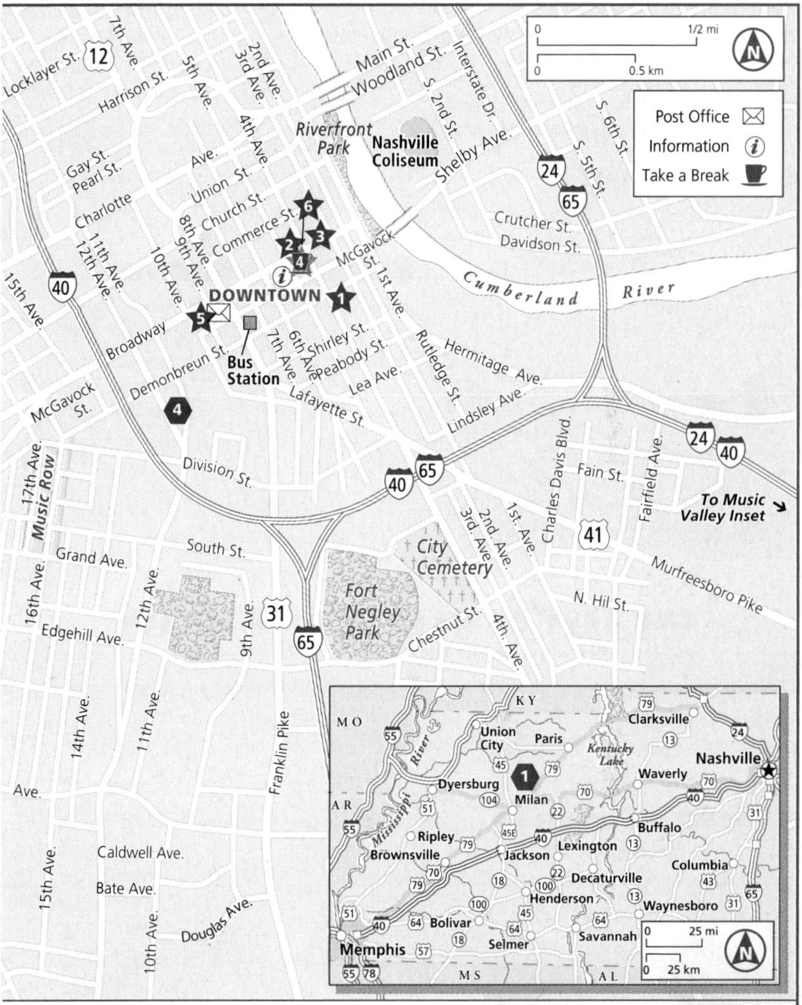

Post Office
Information
Take a Break

DAY THREE

1 The Hermitage

2 Swett's

3 Fisk University

4 Station Inn

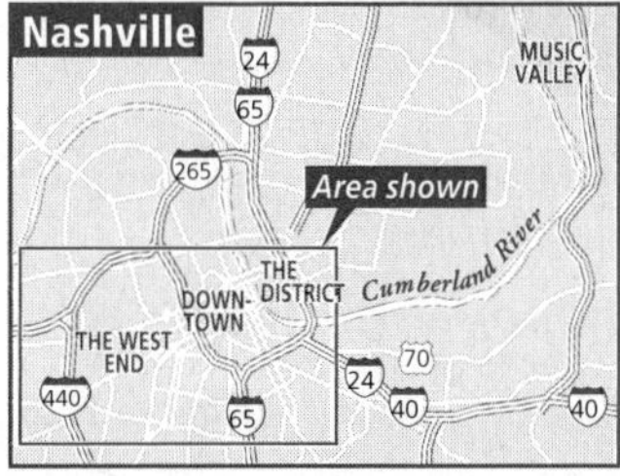

boom back in the 1940s and '50s. And because you're going to attend a performance of the *Grand Ole Opry* while you're here, it will be nice to see the modest venue where it all began. See p. 95.

Walk south back to Broadway, and then turn left and continue past the honky-tonks almost to Third Ave. On your left, you'll see:

❸ Hatch Show Print

Take a trip back in time and get lost in the nostalgic aura of this long-time print shop, where posters of live concerts by virtually all of country music's greatest stars were created. See p. 116.

> **4 JACK'S BAR-B-QUE**
> Slip in here and grab a Coke or a shredded-pork sandwich and some greasy fries. Jack's is a basic, no-frills dive. Make yourself at home. 416 Broadway. ✆ **615/254-5715.** www.jacksbarbque.com. See p. 85.

❺ Frist Center for the Visual Arts ★★★

Drive a few blocks west on Broadway to this outstanding museum, housed in a historic post-office building. First-rate exhibitions from throughout the world are shown here. The permanent ArtQuest Gallery is a wondrous, hands-on creativity center where children and adults alike can experiment with their own artwork. See p. 99.

❻ Barhopping in the District

After a bit of rest and a bite to eat, browse the bars and colorful nightlife along Broadway and the surrounding area. You can hear live music most anywhere, from Tootsie's Orchid Lounge to B. B. King's Blues Club. See chapter 10, "Nashville After Dark."

2 THE BEST OF NASHVILLE IN 2 DAYS

On your first day in town, follow the itinerary outlined above. Today you're enjoying an antebellum plantation and a botanical garden before heading out to Music Valley for a performance of the *Grand Ole Opry*. ***Start:*** *Belle Meade Plantation.*

❶ Belle Meade Plantation ★★

Take a tour of this elegant Greek Revival home, built in 1853 on 30 tree-shaded acres. After you've traipsed through the antiques-laden formal house, saunter the grounds of this former horse farm to find the log cabin, creamery, and carriage house. A highly anticipated new restaurant, named Belle, has just opened on the premises, too. (If you're visiting around lunchtime, you may want to make a reservation beforehand.) See p. 96.

❷ Cheekwood Botanical Garden & Museum of Art ★★

A bit farther toward the western outskirts of town, near Percy Warner Park, you'll find this mansion and museum set amid a lush, 55-acre park. If you didn't have lunch at Belle Meade, you can have it here at the cozy Pineapple Room. Then enjoy exploring the wooded walking trails, landscaped gardens, and outstanding collections of American art and decorative furnishings from around the world. See p. 99.

❸ Opry Mills

Head to the Opryland area to get in a bit of shopping before tonight's performance. Check out the vast selection of stores while browsing for everything from books and boots to bass fishing boats. See p. 120.

4 RAINFOREST CAFE ★★★
Especially if you're traveling with kids, have dinner with the monkeys, elephants, and tropical birds that spring to life at the Rainforest Cafe. Sure, it's kitschy, yet somehow the Disney-esque mood of this place fits right in with all the other commercial excesses of Opryland. 353 Opry Mills Dr. ✆ **615/514-3000.** www.rainforestcafe.com. See p. 84.

5 *Grand Ole Opry ★★★*
This is the ultimate for country music fans. Be prepared for a patriotic, toe-tappin' time and plenty of corny jokes. It's all part of the tradition here, where big-name acts share the stage with fading stars of yesteryear and new up-and-coming talents. See p. 129.

3 THE BEST OF NASHVILLE IN 3 DAYS

For Days 1 and 2, follow the itineraries above. History, African-American heritage, and old-time bluegrass music make today's itinerary sort of a multicultural sightseeing stew. You'll start with a tour of President Andrew Jackson's plantation home, just east of town, before heading back to the city. Grab some soul food at Swett's before spending the afternoon touring the impressive campus of Fisk University. In the evening, head to the West End for dinner at one of the scads of great restaurants here; there are plenty of options for all tastes and budgets. Tonight it's a performance of live bluegrass music in the Gulch landmark known as the Station Inn. ***Start:*** *From downtown, take Interstate 40 east to exit 221A (The Hermitage exit).*

1 The Hermitage ★
Andrew Jackson's stately Southern plantation home offers a fascinating glimpse into the former U.S. President's life here in Tennessee. Originally built in the Federal style in 1821, it was expanded and remodeled in 1831, and acquired its current appearance in 1836. Tours include all areas of the main house, as well as the kitchen, the smokehouse, the garden, Jackson's tomb, an original log cabin, the spring house (a cool storage house built over a spring), and, nearby, the Old Hermitage Church and Tulip Grove mansion. See p. 97.

2 SWETT'S ★★★
This cafeteria, specializing in Southern soul food, is the city's oldest minority-owned restaurant, in business since 1954. Try the fried chicken, collard greens, sweet potatoes, and cornbread. Don't even think about this one: Choose the banana pudding for dessert. 2725 Clifton Ave. ✆ **615/329-4418.** www.swettsrestaurant.com. See p. 74.

3 Fisk University
Founded in 1866 as a liberal arts institution committed to educating newly freed slaves, Fisk University is still a vibrant university in the heart of Nashville. Stroll the lovely campus to admire the Victorian Gothic architecture and to learn about the world-renowned Fisk Jubilee Singers. In a neo-Romanesque former church that dates back to 1888, the Carl Van Vechten Gallery showcases masterworks of art by Picasso and Cezanne. See p. 101.

❹ Station Inn

This battered-looking, unpretentious little music hall has been around for many years. Aside from the Ryman (and its summer bluegrass series), this is the year-round venue of choice for top-tier bluegrass acts. Local country swing favorites The Time Jumpers are currently the hottest ticket in town, but don't be surprised if other local stars, such as Vince Gill, show up to exercise their mandolin-playing chops. See p. 128.

Getting to Know Music City

Getting your bearings in a new city is often the hardest part of taking a trip, but in the following pages you'll find everything you need to know to get settled in after you arrive in town. This is the sort of nuts-and-bolts information that will help you familiarize yourself with Nashville.

1 NASHVILLE ORIENTATION

VISITOR INFORMATION

On the baggage-claim level of Nashville International Airport, you'll find the **Airport Welcome Center** (✆ **615/275-1675**), where you can pick up brochures, maps, and bus information, and get answers to any questions you may have about touring the city. This center is open daily from 6:30am to midnight. In downtown Nashville, you'll find the **Nashville Convention & Visitors Bureau Visitors Center,** Fifth Avenue and Broadway (✆ **800/657-6910** or 615/780-9401; www.visitmusiccity.com), the main source of information on the city and surrounding areas. The information center offers free Wi-Fi service and is located at the base of the radio tower of the Sommet Center (open daily during daylight hours). Signs on interstate highways around the downtown area will direct you to the arena. Information is also available from the main office of the **Chamber of Commerce/Nashville Convention & Visitors Bureau,** in the lower level of the US Bank building at the corner of Fourth Avenue North and Commerce (✆ **615/259-4730**). The office is open Monday to Friday 8am to 5pm.

For information on the state of Tennessee, contact the **Tennessee Department of Tourism Development,** P.O. Box 23170, Nashville, TN 37202 (✆ **615/741-2158;** www.state.tn.us).

CITY LAYOUT

Nashville was built on a bend in the Cumberland River; this and other bends in the river have defined the city's expansion over the years. The area referred to as **downtown** is located on the west side of the Cumberland and is built in a grid pattern. Numbered avenues run parallel to the river on a northwest–southeast axis. Streets perpendicular to

Did You Know?

Nashville has the largest U.S. population of Kurds. With 8,000 ex-patriots living in Music City, it has earned the nickname "Little Kurdistan."

War-Torn Cathedral Still Stands

Interesting architecture and history make the gentrified Germantown neighborhood just north of downtown a nice place for an afternoon stroll. Alongside expensive new condos and professional office buildings are 19th-century mansions, shotgun houses, and such unexpected gems as the **Church of the Assumption of the Blessed Virgin Mary** (1227 Seventh Ave. N.). The cathedral was only a few years old when, in 1864, it was pillaged by soldiers during the Civil War. Beautifully restored, the Catholic church remains an active parish today.

the river are named. Though the grid pattern is interrupted by I-40, it remains fairly regular until you get to Vanderbilt University, in the **West End** area.

For the most part, Nashville is a sprawling modern city. Though there are some areas of downtown that are frequented by pedestrians, the city is primarily oriented toward automobiles. With fairly rapid growth in recent years, the city's streets and highways have been approaching their carrying capacity, and rush hours see plenty of long backups all around the city. The most important things to watch out for when driving around Nashville are the numerous divisions of the interstate highways that encircle the city. If you don't pay very close attention to which lane you're supposed to be in, you can easily wind up heading in the wrong direction.

MAIN ARTERIES & STREETS The main arteries in Nashville radiate from downtown, like spokes on a wheel. **Broadway** is the main artery through downtown Nashville and leads southwest from the river. Just after crossing I-40, Broadway forks, with the right fork becoming **West End Avenue.** West End Avenue eventually becomes **Harding Road** out in the Belle Meade area. If you stay on Broadway (the left fork), the road curves around to the south, becoming **21st Avenue** and then **Hillsboro Pike.**

Eighth Avenue is downtown's other main artery and runs roughly north–south. To the north, Eighth Avenue becomes **Rosa Parks Boulevard;** to the south, it forks, with the right fork becoming **Franklin Pike** and the left fork becoming **Lafayette Road** and then **Murfreesboro Pike.**

There are also several roads that you should become familiar with out in the suburbs. **Briley Parkway** describes a large loop that begins just south of the airport, runs up the east side of the city through the area known as Music Valley, and then curves around to the west, passing well north of downtown. On the south side of the city, **Harding Place** connects I-24 on the east with Belle Meade on the west. Don't confuse Harding Place with Harding Road.

FINDING AN ADDRESS Nashville's address-numbering system begins downtown, at Broadway and the Cumberland River, and increases as you move away from this point. In the downtown area, and out as far as there are numbered avenues, avenues include either a north or south designation. The dividing line between north and south is the Broadway and West End Avenue corridor.

STREET MAPS You can get a map of the city from the **Nashville Convention & Visitors Bureau Visitors Center,** Fifth Avenue and Broadway (✆ **615/780-9401**), which is located below the radio tower of the Sommet Center. Maps can also be obtained

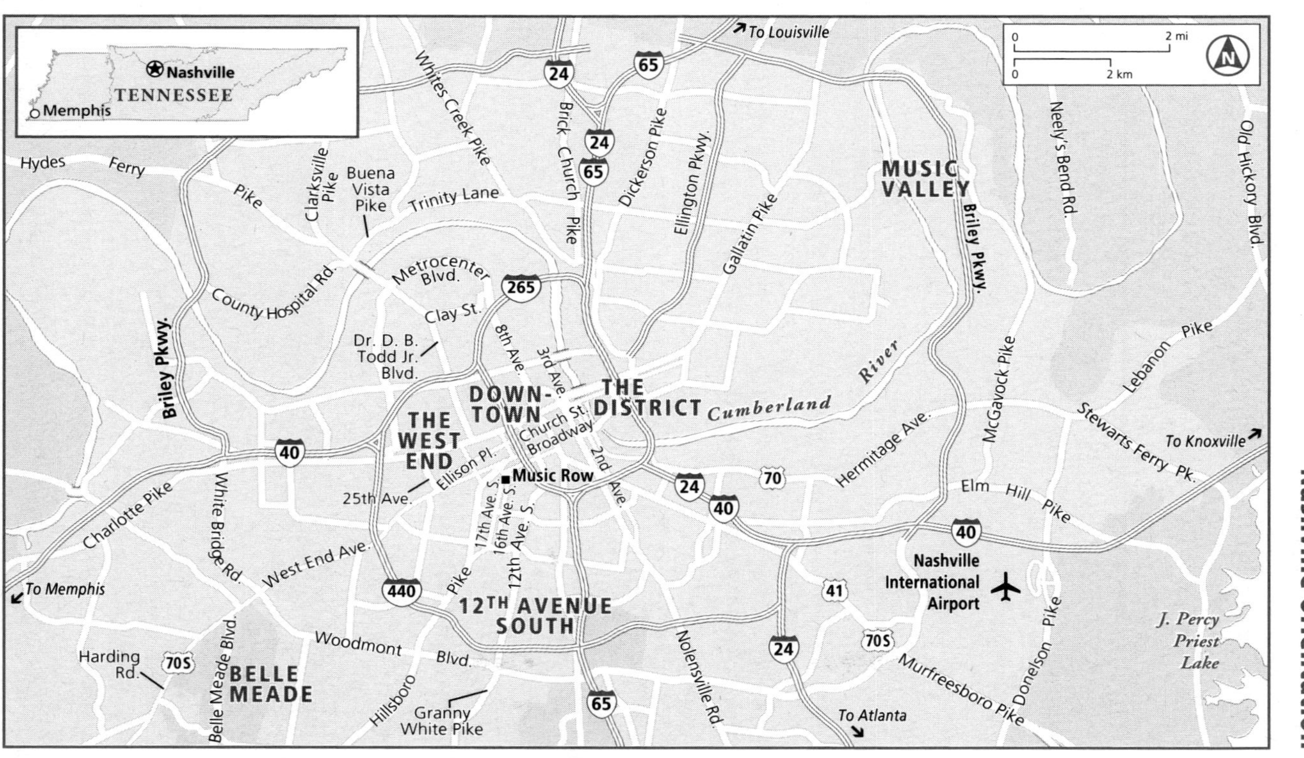

Nashville
TENNESSEE
Memphis
To Louisville
0
2 mi
0
2 km
N
Whites Creek Pike
Brick Church Pike
Dickerson Pike
Ellington Pkwy.
Gallatin Pike
MUSIC VALLEY
Briley Pkwy.
Neely's Bend Rd.
Old Hickory Blvd.
Hydes Ferry Pike
Clarksville Pike
Buena Vista Pike
Trinity Lane
County Hospital Rd.
Metrocenter Blvd.
Clay St.
Dr. D. B. Todd Jr. Blvd.
8th Ave.
3rd Ave.
Briley Pkwy.
DOWN-TOWN
THE DISTRICT
Cumberland River
THE WEST END
Church St.
Broadway
2nd Ave.
Ellison Pl.
Music Row
25th Ave.
17th Ave. S.
16th Ave. S.
12th Ave. S.
McGavock Pike
Lebanon Pike
Stewarts Ferry Pk.
To Knoxville
Hermitage Ave.
Elm Hill Pike
Charlotte Pike
White Bridge Rd.
West End Ave.
To Memphis
Pike
12TH AVENUE SOUTH
Nashville International Airport
J. Percy Priest Lake
Harding Rd.
Belle Meade Blvd.
BELLE MEADE
Woodmont Blvd.
Hillsboro
Granny White Pike
Nolensville Rd.
To Atlanta
Murfreesboro Pike
Donelson Pike
24
65
265
40
440
70
41
70S

Fun Facts **The King**

Elvis Presley may be more closely identified with Memphis than with Nashville, but the King did indeed make his mark on the Music City. Elvis recorded more than 200 of his songs, including Christmas carols, at Historic RCA Studio B, on Music Row.

in many hotel lobbies and at the **Airport Welcome Center** (© **615/275-1675**), on the baggage-claim level at the Nashville International Airport.

If you happen to be a member of **AAA,** you can get free maps of Nashville and Tennessee from your local AAA office or from the Nashville office at 2501 Hillsboro Rd., Ste. 1 (© **615/297-7700**). They're open Monday to Friday 8:30am to 5:30pm and Saturday 9am to 1pm.

6

Where to Stay in Nashville

Nashville caters to tens of thousands of country music fans each year and so has an abundance of inexpensive and moderately priced hotels. Although prices have risen in recent years to match Nashville's rise as a tourist and convention destination, you'll likely find a hotel that's both convenient and fits your budget. If you're used to expensive downtown hotels, you'll be pleasantly surprised to learn that rooms in downtown Nashville are, for the most part, reasonably priced, although that is rapidly changing. With the frenzied construction of swank condo and loft complexes around every corner, downtown is being transformed into a more chic city center with ever-escalating prices for everything from hotel rooms to parking. Beyond downtown, new and moderately priced hotel chains are the norm in all the metropolitan area's major tourist areas, especially near the airport along Elm Hill Pike, and in Music Valley, off Briley Parkway, northeast of downtown. Stay here if you're looking for more affordable simplicity, and if you're not looking for skyline views. However, if you want to be close to the city's best restaurants, trendiest nightspots, and wealthier neighborhoods, by all means book a room in the West End.

Although last-minute discounts aren't out of the question, long gone are the days when you could easily nab a decent hotel room for under $100. Nashville is growing in popularity, and prices reflect that. When big events such as music festivals and conventions bring lots of tourists to the city, rates spike and rooms can be sold out all over town—even at those otherwise more moderately priced chain properties in outlying areas.

If you do want to splurge, consider a luxury hotel such as the Hermitage, Hutton, or Loews. However, for sheer visual impact, you can't beat the massive Opryland Resort, which is shedding some of its Southern, Bible Belt clichés to appeal to more sophisticated tastes. A night here in a basic room will run you about $250 on average.

The rates quoted below are, for the most part, the published rates, sometimes called "rack rates" in hotel-industry jargon. At expensive business and resort hotels, rack rates are what you are most likely to be quoted if you walk in off the street and ask what a room will cost for that night. However, it's often not necessary to pay this high rate if you plan ahead or ask for a discount. It's often possible to get low corporate rates even if you aren't visiting on business. Many hotel and motel chains now have frequent-guest and other special programs that you can join. These programs often provide savings off the regular rates.

Virtually all hotels now offer nonsmoking rooms (in fact, most properties are going entirely smoke-free), and rooms equipped for guests with disabilities. When making a reservation, be sure to request the type of room you need. While multiline telephones are often the norm, charges for telephone calls vary widely. Some offer free local calls, while others do not. Another welcome trend is the inclusion of standard, in-room amenities such as flatscreen TVs and Wi-Fi. Internet fees range from free access to about $12 per day. Increasingly, hotels have public computers in the their lobbies—a nice perk if you don't travel with a laptop.

If you'll be traveling with children, always check into policies on children staying for free. Some hotels let children under 12 stay free, while others set the cutoff age at 18. Still others charge you for the kids, but let them eat for free in the hotel's restaurant.

The rates quoted here don't include the Tennessee sales tax (9.25%) and state and city room taxes, which altogether will add 16.25% onto your room bill. Keep this in mind when you're searching for rates, because most quotes will not include these taxes. And if you're driving to Nashville, don't overlook the cost of parking your car, which can cost up to $25 a night at downtown and West End hotels. I have used the following rate definitions for price categories in this chapter (rates are for double rooms): **very expensive,** more than $200; **expensive,** $150 to $200; **moderate,** $100 to $150; **inexpensive,** under $100.

1 THE BEST HOTEL BETS

- **Best Green Hotel: Hutton Hotel,** 1808 West End Ave. (✆ **615/340-9333;** www.huttonhotel.com), sets a new standard of excellence for sustainability, from the decor, which features reclaimed wood and bamboo furnishings, to its use of biodegradable cleaning products and energy-saving lighting, plumbing, and elevators. Even the hotel's two luxury courtesy vehicles are hybrid SUVs. See p. 54.
- **Best Place to Splurge with Your Pet:** Not only is the posh **Hermitage Hotel,** 231 Sixth Ave. N. (✆ **888/888-9414** or 615/244-3121; www.thehermitagehotel.com), one of the classiest and most romantic hotels in Tennessee, it also will accept—and even pamper—your pet. See below.
- **Best for Business Travelers:** The **Nashville Airport Marriott,** 600 Marriott Dr. (✆ **800/228-9290** or 615/889-9300; www.marriott.com), is designed specifically with business travelers in mind, offering the tools to make any stay productive while offering a warm environment that makes it easy for those road warriors to unwind. Close to the airport and easy to find, the hotel is also renowned throughout the city for its bountiful breakfast buffet. See p. 60.
- **Most Like a Cruise Ship:** With the *Grand Ole Opry* and numerous theaters showcasing live country music nearby, an endless array of restaurants, bars, shops, and a world-class spa, the gargantuan **Gaylord Opryland Resort,** 2800 Opryland Dr. (✆ **888/777-OPRY** [6779] or 615/889-1000; www.gaylordhotels.com), is a cocoon of comfort and entertainment. See p. 59.

2 DOWNTOWN AREA, MUSIC ROW & THE WEST END

VERY EXPENSIVE

The Hermitage Hotel ★★★ Moments This historic downtown hotel, built in 1910 in the classic Beaux Arts style, is Nashville's grand hotel. Still fresh from an $18-million restoration, this is the city's top choice if you crave both space and elegance. The lobby, with its marble columns, gilded plasterwork, and stained-glass ceiling, is the most magnificent in the city. Afternoon tea is served here Thursday through Saturday. Guest rooms have been recently upgraded and are spacious and comfortable, with down-filled duvets and pillows on the beds. All rooms feature large windows and marble-floored bathrooms with double vanities. Ask the staff to draw you a warm bath with a sprinkling of rose petals. North-side rooms have good views of the capitol. In the lower level, you'll find the **Capitol Grille** (p. 68), which, with its vaulted ceiling, has the feel of a wine cellar. Also in the basement is a dark and woody lounge with an ornate plasterwork ceiling.

231 Sixth Ave. N., Nashville, TN 37219. ✆ **888/888-9414** or 615/244-3121. Fax 615/254-6909. www.thehermitagehotel.com. 122 units. $249–$439 suite; $1,500–$2,500 and up for Presidential Suite. AE, DC, DISC, MC, V. Valet parking $25, plus tax; no self-parking. Pets allowed ($50 daily fee). **Amenities:** Restaurant and lounge; babysitting; concierge; room service. *In room:* A/C, TV/DVD, CD player, hair dryer, MP3 docking station, umbrella, Wi-Fi (free).

Hilton Nashville Downtown ★★ One of Nashville's newer hotels boasts a bustling downtown location, with a palm-lined and Wi-Fi-equipped atrium lobby. Booking a room here is a good bet if you plan to spend time at LP Field (where the Tennessee Titans play) or the Country Music Hall of Fame and Museum, both of which are within short walking distance of the Hilton. Each suite comes equipped with a pullout sofa and two TVs, making the Hilton a comfy-but-sophisticated place to hang your hat while in Music City. Rooms include pillowtop mattresses, Egyptian cotton sheets, and curved shower curtains.

121 Fourth Ave. S., Nashville, TN 37201. ✆ **800/HILTONS** (445-8667) or 615/620-1000. Fax 615/620-2050. www.nashvillehilton.com. 330 units (all suites). $219–$459 suite. AE, DC, DISC, MC, V. Valet parking $22; no self-parking. **Amenities:** 3 restaurants; 2 lounges; health club; indoor pool; valet service. *In room:* A/C, TV w/pay movies, fridge, hair dryer, microwave, Wi-Fi ($12 per 24 hr.).

Loews Vanderbilt Hotel ★★★ This high-rise across the street from Vanderbilt University maintains an air of quiet sophistication, which makes it the poshest West End hotel. European tapestries and original works of art adorn the travertine-floored lobby. The hotel also houses the upscale Kraus commercial art gallery. The lower guest rooms, with angled walls that slope inward, are among the hotel's most charming, with a wall of curtains lending a romantic coziness. Service is gracious and attentive. Concierge-level rooms are more spacious and upscale and include complimentary breakfast and evening hors d'oeuvres in an elegant lounge with a view of the city. One level below the lobby, you'll find a Ruth's Chris Steakhouse.

2100 West End Ave., Nashville, TN 37203. ✆ **800/23-LOEWS** (235-6397) or 615/320-1700. Fax 615/320-5019. www.loewsvanderbilt.com. 340 units. $199–$349 double; $800–$1,600 suite. AE, DC, DISC, MC, V. Valet parking $24; self-parking $21. Pets allowed; no deposit required if paying by credit card, although guests are liable for damage caused by pets. **Amenities:** 2 restaurants; babysitting; concierge; concierge-level rooms; exercise room & spa; room service; shoe-shine service; valet service; Wi-Fi (free, in lobby and restaurant). *In room:* A/C, TV, CD player, fax, minibar, hair dryer, Internet ($9.95 per 24 hr.), umbrella.

EXPENSIVE

Courtyard Nashville Downtown ★ This clean, inviting, and smoke-free hotel is within easy walking distance of The Ryman and other downtown attractions, yet far enough away from the rowdy night-life of Broadway to offer a more peaceful environment. Rooms and public spaces are done in cheerful bright blues and pale yellows. The staff goes

Nashville Accommodations: Downtown Area, Music Row & the West End

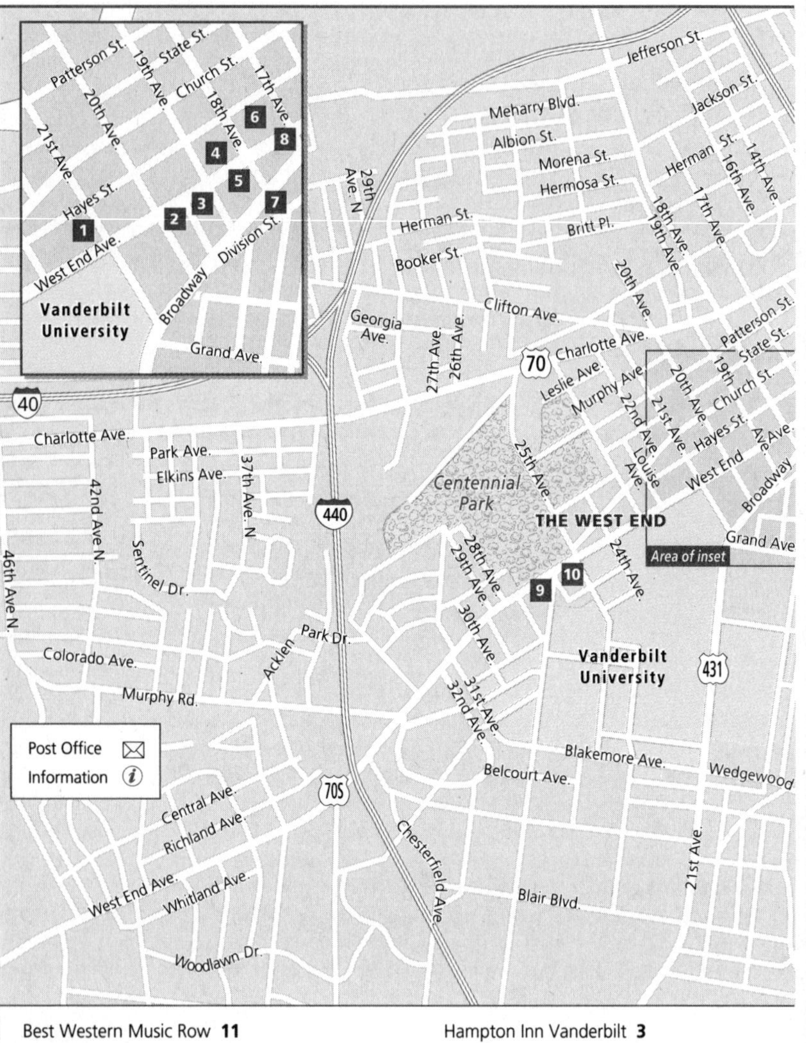

Best Western Music Row **11**
Comfort Inn Downtown–Music Row **12**
Courtyard Nashville Downtown **19**
Courtyard Vanderbilt **2**
Days Inn Vanderbilt/Music Row **4**
Doubletree Hotel Nashville **20**
Embassy Suites Nashville at Vanderbilt **7**
Hampton Inn and Suites Downtown **17**
Hampton Inn Vanderbilt **3**
The Hermitage Hotel **21**
Hilton Garden Inn Nashville Vanderbilt **8**
Hilton Nashville Downtown **16**
Holiday Inn Express Nashville Downtown **15**
Holiday Inn Select Vanderbilt **9**
Homewood Suites Hilton Downtown **14**
Hotel Indigo West End **6**

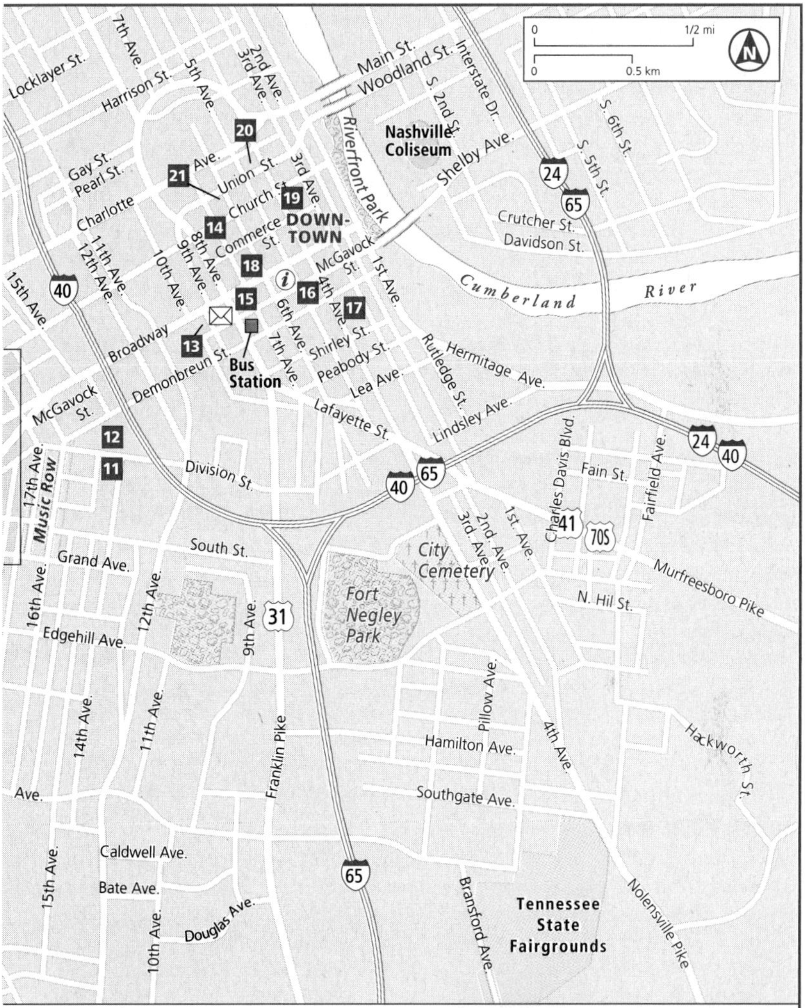

Hutton Hotel **5**
Loews Vanderbilt Plaza Hotel **1**
Nashville Marriott at Vanderbilt **10**
Renaissance Nashville Hotel **18**
Union Station: A Wyndham Historic Hotel **13**

out of its way to offer friendly service. All guest rooms have new bedding, free high-speed Internet access, spacious work desks and task chairs, and multiline telephones.

170 Fourth Ave. N. Nashville, TN 37219. ✆ **888/687-9377** or 615/256-0900. Fax 615/256-0901. www.marriott.com. 192 units. $169–$209 double; $224 and up for suites. AE, DC, DISC, MC, V. Valet parking $22; no self-parking. **Amenities:** Restaurant. *In room:* A/C, TV w/pay movies, fridge, hair dryer, Internet (free, in standard rooms), microwave, Wi-Fi (free, in King Suites).

Doubletree Hotel Nashville ★★ Of the high-rise hotels in downtown Nashville, this is one of the best choices if you're here on vacation. This Hilton property has a less hectic atmosphere than the Renaissance, for example, which is often crowded with convention-goers. Warm, contemporary decor features maple-colored wood paneling and comfy seating in the elegant, second-floor lobby, where there's a full-service Starbucks cafe. Perks include fresh-baked cookies upon your check-in. Located a few blocks from the District, this hotel is also convenient for anyone in town on state government business. The corner rooms, with their sharply angled walls of glass, are the most appealing units in the hotel.

315 Fourth Ave. N., Nashville, TN 37219. ✆ **800/222-TREE** (8733) or 615/244-8200. Fax 615/747-4894. www.nashvilledoubletree.com. 338 units. $109–$189 double; from $199 suite. AE, DC, DISC, MC, V. Valet parking $24; off-site self-parking $18. **Amenities:** Restaurant; lounge; concierge; exercise room; indoor pool; room service, Wi-Fi (free, in lobby). *In room:* A/C, TV w/pay movies, hair dryer, Wi-Fi ($9.95 per 24 hr.).

Embassy Suites Nashville at Vanderbilt ★★ (Finds) In the city's fashionable West End/Vanderbilt University district, this property combines gracious service and impeccable decor. A sunny garden atrium features lush plants, cascading waterfalls, and overstuffed furniture arranged in cozy nooks. The spacious, tastefully appointed suites have comfy pullout sofas, easy chairs, work desks, and lamps. With value-added touches, including a free shuttle service (within a 2-mile radius of the hotel), this is a good choice for those who want to feel pampered without paying an arm and a leg. Downstairs is an Omaha Steak House.

1811 Broadway, Nashville, TN 37203. ✆ **800/362-2779** or 615/320-8899. Fax 615/320-8881. www.embassysuites.com. 208 units (all suites). $149–$239 suite. Rates include cooked-to-order breakfast. AE, DC, DISC, MC, V. Valet parking $19; self-parking $15. **Amenities:** Restaurant; lounge; exercise room; room service; sauna. *In room:* A/C, TV w/pay movies, kitchenette (microwave, minibar, and sink), hair dryer, Wi-Fi ($6 per 24 hr.).

Hutton Hotel ★★ Unpretentious yet stylish, this independent boutique hotel set a new standard in sustainable luxury when it opened in 2009. Architecturally stunning, the contemporary property touts many green initiatives, including biodegradable cleaning products, decor made from reclaimed wood, and bamboo flooring and furnishings. Rooms are well appointed with sumptuous bedding and bathrobes. The marble bathrooms include environmentally-friendly fixtures, including walk-in showers with programmable temperature controls. Each suite has a large work desk, sofa, chair and 42-inch high-definition TVs. Seven of the suites are equipped with in-room cardio-equipment.

1808 West End Ave., Nashville, TN 37203. ✆ **615-340-9333.** Fax 615-340-0010. www.huttonhotel.com. 248 units. $189–$199 double; $249 suite. AE, DC, DISC, MC, V. Valet parking $24; self-parking $20. Pets allowed with $50 deposit. **Amenities:** Restaurant; concierge; exercise room; room service. *In room:* A/C, TV, hair dryer, minibar, Wi-Fi (free).

Hampton Inn and Suites Downtown ★ Built in 2007, this user-friendly property is a bit off the beaten path—a block south of the Country Music Hall of Fame and

Museum. Appealing to independent travelers who want convenience and style, the six-story redbrick inn offers relative proximity to area restaurants and clubs downtown and the nearby Gulch. Continental breakfast is served in the open, contemporary lobby, where there's plenty of natural sunlight and free Wi-Fi. Clean, modern rooms are equipped with comfy beds and crisp linens, as well as flatscreen TVs and wet bars.

310 Fourth Ave. S., Nashville, TN 37201. ✆ **800/HAMPTON** (426-7866) or 615/277-5000. Fax 615/564-1700. www.hamptoninn.com. 154 units. $189–$359 double; $259 and up suite. AE, DC, DISC, MC, V. Free self-parking. **Amenities:** Fitness room; indoor pool; whirlpool. *In room:* A/C, TV w/pay movies, fridge, hair dryer, microwave, Wi-Fi (free).

Holiday Inn Express Nashville Downtown ★ With an inviting, spacious lobby and simple yet elegant furnishings, this above-ordinary property offers a slightly less expensive alternative to the historic Union Station Hotel across the street. In fact, rooms with westward views of the Union Station's Gothic beauty are an added plus—and though you'll still be able to see and hear the trains rumbling down the railroad tracks, they're not right outside your window as they are at Union Station. This hotel is across the street from the Frist Center for the Arts and a short hike (about 5 blocks straight down Broadway) to bars and nightclubs in the District. Rooms are bright, clean, and reasonably spacious.

920 Broadway, Nashville, TN 37203. ✆ **800/258-2466** or 615/244-0150. Fax 615/244-0445. www.holiday-inn.com. 287 units. $149–$179 double; $244–$319 suite. Rates include continental breakfast. AE, DISC, MC, V. Self-parking $15. **Amenities:** Exercise room; outdoor pool. *In room:* A/C, TV, fridge and microwave (in suites and in all rooms on the 6th and 7th floors), hair dryer, Wi-Fi (free).

Homewood Suites Hilton Downtown Staying here may make you feel as if you have your own downtown apartment. The new property, located within a historic building, has become increasingly popular with business travelers and those planning extended stays. Spacious studios and suites with one or two bedrooms have furnished kitchens with full-sized refrigerators, stoves, and dishwashers. Large work desks, two TVs, and two phones are included. You can even bring your pet; the hotel offers cat and dog beds, treats, and other accessories.

706 Church St., Nashville, TN 37203. ✆ **800-445-8667** or 615/742-5550. Fax 615-742-9949. www.nashvilledowntown.homewoodsuites.com. 113 units. $149–$189 double. AE, DISC, MC, V. Valet parking $20; self-parking (off site) $9. Pets allowed ($100 nonrefundable fee). **Amenities:** Exercise room. *In-room:* hair dryer, Internet (free), kitchenette.

Hotel Indigo West End ★ If an on-site sushi restaurant, contemporary decor, and individualized attention from staff appeal to your senses, you'll love the Indigo, a trendy boutique hotel owned by the InterContinental Hotels chain. The angular 11-story—and, yes, deep blue—building has an ideal location, about halfway between downtown and the West End. East-facing upper rooms and the eighth-floor outdoor patio have great views of the Nashville skyline. Indigo's Zen-like theme of promising guests "peace and serenity" is highlighted in framed leaf and seashell prints, chartreuse and plum-colored walls, and black-and-white photo murals. Rooms feature plush bedding and are surprisingly spacious, with polished wood-laminated floors, throw rugs, and comfy chairs and work desks. A second location, featuring 96 rooms, is scheduled to open soon in the historic American Trust Building at Third Avenue North and Union Street.

1719 West End Ave., Nashville, TN 37303. ✆ **877/270-1396** or 615-329-4200. Fax 615/3294205. www.hotelindigo.com. 139 units. $128–$234 double. Pets accepted ($75 per night). Valet parking $23; self-parking $19. AE, DISC, MC, V. **Amenities:** Lounge, fitness center. *In room:* A/C, TV, hair dryer, Wi-Fi (free).

 Family-Friendly Hotels

Embassy Suites Nashville (p. 62) With an indoor pool and a garden atrium, there is plenty to keep the kids distracted here. The two-room suites also provide kitchenettes and lots of space, including a separate bedroom for parents.

Gaylord Opryland Resort (p. 59) The kids can wander all over this huge hotel's three tropical atria, exploring waterfalls, hidden gardens, fountains, whatever, and then head for one of the pools. There are also enough restaurants under this one roof (the property encompasses nine under glass) to keep everyone in the family happy.

GuestHouse Inn & Suites Music Valley (p. 62) A budget-friendly hotel that is very popular with vacationing families, this clean, comfortable hotel across the street from Opryland is convenient to the interstate and area attractions.

Hyatt Place Opryland (p. 63) Teens and tweens can appreciate a place with huge, in-room plasma TVs with plug-and-play capability. This completely refurbished property also offers spacious rooms with beds as well as comfy leather ottomans and pull-out sofas so the family can spread out.

Nashville Airport Marriott (p. 60) Lower-level rooms are perfect for families whose kids want to spend time in the large indoor/outdoor pool.

Nashville Marriott at Vanderbilt ★★ This rose-colored high-rise hotel rivals the nearby Loews for elegance and sophistication. Upper rooms at the 11-story property offer bird's-eye views of both the Vanderbilt football stadium and the Parthenon, in nearby Centennial Park. The location is ideal for those who want to be in the thick of things. It's within a corner of an upscale shopping complex and close to all the West End action. (The downside is that during peak dinner hours and weekends, the hotel parking lot and garage can become a tangled traffic jam.) Guests visiting here on business will appreciate the spacious rooms, decorated in soothing cream colors, with well-lighted work desks and multiline phones.

2555 West End Ave., Nashville, TN 37203. ✆ **800/228-9290** or 615/321-1300. Fax 615/321-1400. www.marriott.com. 307 units. $149–$359 double; $350–$459 suite. AE, DC, DISC, MC, V. Valet parking $22; self-parking $19. **Amenities:** Restaurant; lounge; concierge; health club; indoor pool; room service; valet service. *In room:* A/C, TV w/pay movies, hair dryer, Wi-Fi ($9.95 per 24 hr.).

Renaissance Nashville Hotel ★★ Because it's connected to the Nashville Convention Center, this large, modern hotel is usually filled with convention-goers and consequently can feel crowded and chaotic. However, it does offer all the expected luxuries. The king rooms (especially the corner kings, which have slightly larger bathrooms) are a better choice than rooms with two beds, which are a bit cramped. Whichever style room you choose, you'll have a comfortable chair in which to relax, and walls of glass let in plenty of light. The upper floors (24th and 25th) offer additional amenities, including a concierge, private lounge, bathrobes, express checkout, complimentary continental breakfast and evening hors d'oeuvres, and evening turndown service. There's a Starbucks in the lobby, as well as several lounges and restaurants. Although the hotel is smoke-free, you'll likely have to walk through a gauntlet of smokers once you step outside the front lobby.

611 Commerce St., Nashville, TN 37203. ✆ **800/327-6618** or 615/255-8400. Fax 615/255-8202. www.renaissancehotels.com. 673 units. $169–$229 double; $300–$500 suite. AE, DC, DISC, MC, V. Valet parking $25; self-parking $6. **Amenities:** 2 restaurants; 2 bars; concierge; exercise room; indoor pool & whirlpool; room service; sauna; sundeck; valet service. *In room:* A/C, TV w/pay movies, hair dryer, Wi-Fi ($12 per 24 hr.).

Union Station: A Wyndham Historic Hotel ★ **Moments** Built in 1900 and housed in the Romanesque Gothic former Union Station railway terminal, this hotel is a grandly restored National Historic Landmark. Following a $10-million renovation, completed in 2007, all guest rooms and public spaces have been updated. The lobby is the former main hall of the railway station and has a vaulted ceiling of Tiffany stained glass. In contrast to the historic atmosphere, decor in the public spaces such as the lobby is contemporary. Although guest rooms offer exterior views, some also have the disadvantage of overlooking the railroad tracks, a plus for railroad buffs but perhaps less endearing to those who can't sleep with the clang-and-roar that continues day and night. Be sure to take advantage of the hotel's valet parking; self-parking is inconvenient and down several flights of outdoor stairs (and it's more expensive).

1001 Broadway, Nashville, TN 37203. ✆ **800/996-3426** or 615/726-1001. Fax 615/248-3554. www.wyndham.com. 125 units. $169–$239 double; $349–$499 suite. AE, DC, DISC, MC, V. Valet parking $20; self-parking $22. **Amenities:** Restaurant and lounge; exercise room; limited room service. *In room:* A/C, TV w/pay movies, hair dryer, Wi-Fi ($12 per 24 hrs.).

MODERATE

Courtyard Vanderbilt ★ This seven-story hotel on West End Avenue fills the price and service gap between the Loews Vanderbilt Plaza and the less-expensive motels listed below. Guest rooms are none too large, but units with king-size beds are well suited to business travelers. For the most part, what you get here is a good location, close to Music Row, at prices only slightly higher than those at area motels. A breakfast buffet is available daily ($6.95 plus tax).

1901 West End Ave., Nashville, TN 37203. ✆ **800/245-1959** or 615/327-9900. Fax 615/327-8127. www.marriott.com. 223 units. $99–$169 double; $199–$239 suite. AE, DC, DISC, MC, V. Valet parking $14; self-parking $12. **Amenities:** Lounge; exercise room; outdoor pool; whirlpool. *In room:* A/C, TV, hair dryer.

Hampton Inn Vanderbilt This reliable chain is just 1 block from Vanderbilt University and 6 blocks from both Music Row and the Parthenon. Open while undergoing a top-to-bottom renovation, this property reportedly ranks as one of the Hampton chain's busiest in the country. Guest rooms are modern and comfortable. You'll find the

Fun Facts **Nashville Notables**

Music stars such as Amy Grant and Vince Gill aren't the only celebrities who hang their hats in Nashville. Other superstar locals include Jack White, Kid Rock, Reese Witherspoon, Sheryl Crow, Ashley Judd, Peter Frampton, Michael McDonald, Kirk Whalum, Donna Summer, and Nicole Kidman and Keith Urban. Among the city's best-known former residents are Oprah Winfrey, former U.S. Vice President Al Gore, and Fred Thompson, the Tennessee-senator-turned-actor *(Law and Order).*

king rooms particularly spacious. There are quite a few good restaurants within walking distance.

1919 West End Ave., Nashville, TN 37203. ✆ **800/HAMPTON** (426-7866) or 615/329-1144. Fax 615/320-7112. www.hampton-inn.com. 171 units. $99–$189 double. Rates include cooked breakfast. AE, DC, DISC, MC, V. Free parking. **Amenities:** Exercise room; outdoor pool; valet service. *In room:* A/C, TV, hair dryer, Wi-Fi (free).

Hilton Garden Inn Nashville Vanderbilt Ergonomic Herman Miller chairs, premium bedding, and work-efficient guest rooms are highlights of this hotel, which opened in 2009. Just a few doors down from the larger Embassy Suites, the Hilton Garden Inn is a bit less expensive. Clean, comfortable rooms come equipped with 36-inch high-definition TVs. A cheerful, ground-floor cafe looks out into the tree-lined street. An added bonus for guests is the complimentary shuttle service within a 5-mile radius of the hotel.

1715 Broadway, Nashville, TN 37203. ✆ **866-538-6194** or 615-369-5900. Fax 615/369-5901. www.hiltongardeninn.com. 194 units. $129–$159 double; $159–$164 suite. AE, DC, DISC, MC, V. Valet parking $23; self-parking $18. **Amenities:** Restaurant; health club; indoor pool, whirlpool. *In-room:* Fridge, hair dryer, microwave.

Holiday Inn Select Vanderbilt With the Vanderbilt University football stadium right outside this 12-story hotel's back door, it isn't surprising that this is a favorite with Vanderbilt alumni and football fans. Guests are also right across the street from Centennial Park and the Parthenon, making it a good option for families with children. Couples and business travelers will do well to ask for a king room. If you ask for a room on the park side of the hotel, you may be able to see the Parthenon from your room. All units here have small private balconies.

2613 West End Ave., Nashville, TN 37203. ✆ **800/HOLIDAY** (465-4329) or 615/327-4707. Fax 615/327-8034. www.holiday-inn.com. 300 units. $109–$179 double. AE, DC, DISC, MC, V. Free parking. **Amenities:** Restaurant; lounge; concierge; outdoor pool. *In room:* A/C, TV w/pay movies, hair dryer, Wi-Fi (free).

INEXPENSIVE

Best Western Music Row ★ This casual, no-frills motel stays booked most of the time with cost-conscious tourists who appreciate affordability and easy access to both downtown and Music Row. Bargain-priced rooms are standard, although the suites offer significantly more space for a few extra dollars; and all rooms offer free local calls. Live music is performed nightly (except Sun) in the lounge.

1407 Division St., Nashville, TN 37203. ✆ **800/228-5151** or 615/242-1631. Fax 615/244-9519. www.bestwestern.com. 103 units. $70–$130 double. Rates include continental breakfast. AE, DC, DISC, MC, V. Free parking. Pets accepted up to 25 pounds ($10 per day). **Amenities:** Lounge; outdoor pool. *In room:* A/C, TV, fridge, hair dryer, microwave, Wi-Fi (free).

Comfort Inn Downtown–Music Row ★ If you want to stay right in the heart of Music Row and near downtown, try this popular motel. In the lobby, you'll find walls covered with dozens of autographed photos of country music stars who have stayed here in years past. The rooms are fairly standard, though all are quite clean and comfortable. The seven suites all have whirlpool tubs. Local calls are free here.

1501 Demonbreun St., Nashville, TN 37203. ✆ **800/552-4667** or 615/255-9977. Fax 615/242-6127. www.comfortinnnashville.com. 144 units. $79–$89 double; $119–$149 suite. Rates include continental breakfast. AE, DC, DISC, MC, V. Free parking (mobile-home and bus spaces available). Pets accepted ($10 per day). **Amenities:** Nearby golf course; outdoor pool; nearby lighted tennis courts. *In room:* A/C, TV, fridge, hair dryer (on request), microwave, whirlpool (in suites), Wi-Fi (free).

Days Inn Vanderbilt/Music Row If you're looking for a decent room and a bargain, consider this motel that dates back to the 1960s. Rooms are refurbished every few years, but prices have remained modest by Nashville standards. Music Row and Vanderbilt University are both within walking distance, and the hotel has free shuttle service to the nearby medical center. Local calls are free.

1800 West End Ave., Nashville, TN 37203. ✆ **800/329-7466** or 615/327-0922. Fax 615/327-0102. www.daysinn.com. 151 units. $65–$109 double. Rates include continental breakfast. AE, DC, DISC, MC, V. Free parking. **Amenities:** Exercise room; outdoor pool; complimentary shuttle to nearby medical center. *In room:* A/C, TV, hair dryer, Wi-Fi (free).

3 MUSIC VALLEY & THE AIRPORT AREA

If you plan to spend any amount of time at either the Gaylord Opryland Resort or the Opry Mills mall, staying in the Music Valley area will be your best bet. It will also be much more convenient if you plan to attend the *Grand Ole Opry,* where the second of two nightly shows can sometimes extend past midnight. After a night of all that barn-raising music, who wants to drive across town to their hotel?

VERY EXPENSIVE

Gaylord Opryland Resort & Convention Center ★★ Kids What Graceland is to Memphis, Opryland is to Nashville. Whether you're into country music or not, a tour of this palatial property, with its 85-foot water fountains, tropical foliage, and winding "rivers," has become almost obligatory. The Opryland has the look and feel of a cruise ship, and it does attract thousands of visitors daily (on top of those who are actually staying at this massive hotel). The most impressive of the hotel's numerous areas is the Cascade Conservatory, which consists of two linked atria. Waterfalls splash across rocky outcroppings, and fountains dance with colored lights and lasers. Bridges and meandering paths and a revolving gazebo bar add a certain quaint charm. Elsewhere at Opryland, the Magnolia lobby resembles an elegant antebellum mansion, with its classically proportioned double staircase worthy of Tara itself.

The hotel's spa, **Relâche,** provides an extensive array of salon and fitness services. Scented candles flicker and soothing music wafts through the dim corridors and 12 treatment rooms, where guests can indulge in raw-earth stone pedicures, warming sugar-spice facials, and pink-pearl firming body massages. Also here are a 25-meter indoor pool (in addition to outdoor pools) and a state-of-the-art fitness center with an arsenal of cardio machines and other exercise equipment.

Opryland's standard guest rooms, while not overly spacious, are comfortable and convenient. All the guest rooms have been updated with new furnishings, including queen beds with pillowtop mattresses and fine linens. Rooms with atrium views ($75 extra) are charming, but musical events in the lobby below might not be as quaint if you want to hit the sack early. Gift shops, cafes, and food specialty stores are scattered throughout Opryland. From family-style Italian dining and a build-your-own burger joint to upscale steak and seafood restaurants—there's something here for all tastes and budgets. And don't be too cheap to unscrew the water bottles in your room. Opryland has recently begun charging overnight hotel guests an additional $15 per day resort fee, which includes the H_20 (two bottles per day, plus Wi-Fi).

Tips Boots Made for Walking

If you're staying at the Gaylord Opryland Resort, comfortable walking shoes are a must. Even if you opt for the valet parking, the distances between drop-off points and your room can be daunting. Each member of the bell staff at Opryland walks an average of 12 miles a day.

2800 Opryland Dr., Nashville, TN 37214. ✆ **888/777-OPRY** (6779) or 615/889-1000. Fax 615/871-5728. www.gaylordhotels.com. 2,881 units. $199–$274 double; $319–$3,500 suite. AE, DC, DISC, MC, V. Valet parking $25, plus tax; self-parking $18, plus tax. **Amenities:** 14 restaurants and lounges; concierge; off-premises children's daycare; golf club; health club; 2 outdoor pools and 1 indoor pool; room service; spa. *In room:* A/C, TV w/pay movies, fridge (in some units), hair dryer, kitchen or kitchenette (in suites), minibar (in some units), Wi-Fi (included in resort fee).

EXPENSIVE

Nashville Airport Marriott ★★ Kids This is one of the airport area's most resort-like hotels, which includes a spacious indoor/outdoor pool. If you want to stay in shape while you're away from home, this is an excellent choice. All fitness equipment was replaced in late 2009. The hotel grounds cover 17 landscaped and wooded acres, though the proximity to the highway means it's rather noisy. Traffic sounds are not a problem if you book an upper-level room. All the guest rooms were recently updated with contemporary decor and flatscreen TVs. For business travelers, there are large work desks and a concierge level. Families may like the lower-level poolside rooms; for extra space, try one of the corner units, which are 30% larger than standard rooms. The casual restaurant serves a wide range of pasta, poultry dishes, and generous salads, and has a pleasant view of the woods outside.

600 Marriott Dr., Nashville, TN 37214-5010. ✆ **800/228-9290** or 615/889-9300. Fax 615/889-9315. www.marriott.com. 398 units. $105–$189 double; $450–$650 suite. AE, DC, DISC, MC, V. Free parking. **Amenities:** Restaurant; lounge; free airport shuttle; babysitting; concierge; health club; indoor/outdoor pool; room service; sauna; valet service; whirlpool; Wi-Fi (free, in lobby). *In room:* A/C, TV w/pay movies, hair dryer, Wi-Fi ($15 per 24 hr.).

Sheraton Music City ★★ Big, elegant, and set on 23 acres in a modern business park near the airport, this large convention hotel (second in size only to Gaylord Opryland) has a commanding vista of the surrounding area. Classic Georgian styling sets the tone and evokes an antebellum mansion. In the elegant lobby, you'll find marble floors and burnished paneling and free computer access with color printers. Comfortable guest rooms feature sleigh beds, work desks, and three telephones. The hotel reserves 20 rooms on the ground-floor level specifically for pet owners.

777 McGavock Pike, Nashville, TN 37214-3175. ✆ **800/325-3535** or 615/885-2200. Fax 615/231-1134. www.sheratonmusiccity.com. 410 units. $109–$189 double; $300–$600 suite. AE, DC, DISC, MC, V. Valet parking $7; self-parking free. Pets up to 80 pounds accepted ($200 cleaning fee). **Amenities:** Restaurant; lounge; free airport shuttle; concierge; health club w/whirlpool; indoor pool; outdoor pool in quiet central courtyard; valet service. *In room:* A/C, TV, hair dryer, Internet ($9.95 per 24 hr.).

MODERATE

Doubletree Guest Suites Nashville Airport If your flight plans have you taking a red-eye in or out of Nashville, consider staying here—the only hotel in the area offering

Nashville Accommodations: Music Valley & the Airport Area

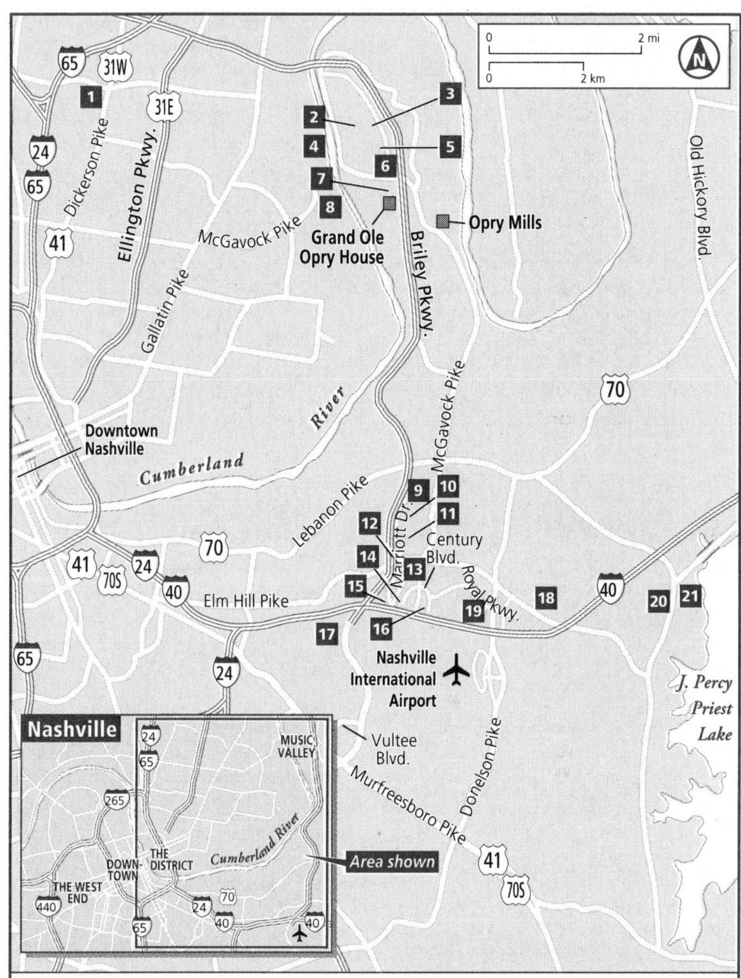

Alexis Inn and Suites **9**
Best Western Airport Inn **21**
Comfort Inn **3**
Days Inn **20**
Doubletree Guest Suites Nashville Airport **10**
Embassy Suites Nashville **14**
Fairfield Inn Opryland **4**
Gaylord Opryland Resort & Convention Center **7**
GuestHouse Inn & Suites Music Valley **5**
Holiday Inn Select Music Valley **8**
Holiday Inn Select Opryland Airport **12**
Hotel Preston **17**
Hyatt Place Opryland **2**
La Quinta Inn Nashville-Briley Parkway **11**
Nashville Airport Marriott **15**
Radisson Hotel at Opryland **6**
Red Roof Inn-Nashville East **19**
Residence Inn Airport **13**
Sheraton Music City **16**
Sleep Inn Nashville **1**
Springhill Suites by Marriott **18**

free 24-hour shuttle service. The spacious suites include separate sleeping and living room areas that include newly furnished sleeper sofas. Rooms have everything you might need, from a work desk and two telephones to a refrigerator and microwave.

2424 Atrium Way, Nashville, TN 37214. ✆ **615/889-8889.** Fax 615/883-7779. www.doubletree.com. 138 units (all suites). $89–$124 suite. AE, DC, DISC, MC, V. Free parking. **Amenities:** Restaurant, free airport shuttle, exercise room, indoor/outdoor pool. *In-room:* A/C, TV, fridge, hair dryer, microwave, Wi-Fi (free).

Embassy Suites Nashville ★ Kids This all-suite hotel makes a great choice and a good value for families, as well as for business travelers. These two-room suites are spacious, modern, and tastefully decorated in warm colors. The centerpiece of the hotel is its large atrium, which is full of tropical plants, including palm trees. A rocky stream runs through the Wi-Fi–accessible atrium, and caged tropical songbirds add their cheery notes to the pleasant atmosphere.

10 Century Blvd., Nashville, TN 37214. ✆ **800/EMBASSY** (362-2779) or 615/871-0033. Fax 615/883-9987. www.embassysuites.com. 296 units (all suites). $99–$179 suite. Rates include cooked-to-order breakfast and evening manager's reception. AE, DC, DISC, MC, V. Free parking. **Amenities:** Restaurant; bar; free airport shuttle; exercise room; hot tub; indoor pool; room service. *In room:* A/C, TV w/pay movies, fridge, hair dryer, microwave, wet bar, Wi-Fi ($9.95 for 24 hr.).

Fairfield Inn Opryland ★★ One of my favorite affordable hotels when I'm traveling alone on business is this consistently clean, top-notch hotel with a spacious indoor pool and a small but recently updated exercise room. Rooms are set up for productivity and relaxation—with big work desks and large-screen TVs. Bathrooms are modest in size but serviceable, with granite vanities. Staff members are especially welcoming and helpful.

211 Music City Circle, Nashville, TN 37214. ✆ **888-236-2427** or 615/872-8939. Fax 615/872-7230. www.fairfieldinn.com. 109 units. $89–$114 double; suites from $124. Rates include continental breakfast. AE, DISC, MC, V. Free parking. **Amenities:** Exercise room; indoor pool. *In room:* A/C, TV, hair dryer, Wi-Fi (free).

GuestHouse Inn & Suites Music Valley Kids Especially popular with vacationing families, this four-story redbrick hotel is within walking distance of the Gaylord Opryland Resort & Convention Center, but a free shuttle will take you there, so you don't have to dodge the traffic on foot. Suites feature pullout sofas in addition to king-size beds. Four larger family suites have two queen-size beds and two full-size sleeper sofas, in addition to two vanity areas and kitchenettes.

2420 Music Valley Dr., Nashville, TN 37214. ✆ **800/214-8378** or 615/885-4030. Fax 615/329-4890. www.guesthouseintl.com. 184 units. $99–$129 double. Rates include continental breakfast. AE, DC, DISC, MC, V. Free self-parking, including in covered garage. Pets accepted free. **Amenities:** Lounge; free airport and Opryland shuttle; exercise room; hot tub; indoor pool. *In room:* A/C, TV, hair dryer, Wi-Fi (free).

Holiday Inn Select Opryland Airport If you're looking for someplace convenient to the airport, this Holiday Inn, just off the Briley Parkway, is a good bet. The lobby features two back-to-back atria, one of which houses the reception desk, a car-rental desk, and a couple of seating areas, while the other contains a swimming pool, lobby/lounge area, and terraced restaurant. Guest rooms are fairly standard, with big TVs and plenty of counter space in the bathrooms. The king rooms have a bit more space and are designed with business travelers in mind. On the 14th-floor executive level, you'll receive a complimentary breakfast and other upgraded amenities.

2200 Elm Hill Pike, Nashville, TN 37214. ✆ **800/HOLIDAY** (465-4329) or 615/883-9770. Fax 615/391-4521. www.holiday-inn.com. 382 units. $109–$140 double. AE, DC, DISC, MC, V. Free parking. **Amenities:** Restaurant; lounge; free airport shuttle; exercise room; hot tub; indoor pool; room service; sauna; valet service. *In room:* A/C, TV w/pay movies, fridge and microwave (available by request), hair dryer, Wi-Fi (free).

Holiday Inn Select Music Valley ★★ A large indoor swimming pool with beautiful wooded views is one of the standouts of this brand-new hotel, which opened in late 2009. Farther away from the interstate, and a bit more secluded than the other budget-friendly chain hotels that have started mushrooming in this suburban area around Music Valley, it offers everything you'd expect: a great lobby and dining area, free parking, and personable service. Crisply appointed guest rooms feature comfortable beds and small kitchenettes with dining room tables under decorative, hanging light fixtures. You'll feel at home here.

2461 McGavock Pike, Nashville, TN 37214. ✆ **800/HOLIDAY** (465-4329) or 615/829-7777. Fax 615/829-7799. www.holiday-inn.com. 113 units. $109–$129 double. Rates include cooked breakfast. AE, DISC, MC, V. Free parking. **Amenities:** 24-hour exercise room, indoor pool. *In room:* A/C, TV, hair dryer, microwave, Wi-Fi (free).

Hotel Preston One of the busy airport area's more unique properties is this 11-story boutique hotel that takes pride in offering quirky perks such as in-room lava lamps, pet fish, rubber duckies, and art kits. Although some floors are designated smoke-free, the ventilation system doesn't quite do the trick; those sensitive to second-hand smoke may want to book elsewhere. Guest rooms are furnished with pillowtop mattresses on the beds (and a menu of pillows from which to choose), comfy chairs, and well-lighted work desks. Aveda bath products and in-room Starbucks coffee and Tazo teas are other nice touches.

733 Briley Pkwy., Nashville, TN 37217. ✆ **877/361-5500** or 615/361-5900. Fax 615/367-4468. www.hotelpreston.com. 196 units. $129–$159 double; $169 suite. AE, DC, DISC, MC, V. Free parking. Pets allowed ($50 nonrefundable fee). **Amenities:** Restaurant and lounge; free airport and Opryland-area shuttle; outdoor pool; valet service. *In room:* A/C, TV w/pay movies, CD player, hair dryer, Wi-Fi ($9 per day).

Hyatt Place Opryland ★ Kids This midrise hotel is located just off Music Valley Drive and is your most comfortable choice in the area if you aren't willing to splurge on the Gaylord Opryland Resort. With the look and feel of a contemporary boutique hotel, this inviting property offers standard rooms that are larger and less expensive than those at nearby Opryland. Cushy pullout sofas and wet bars mean you can stretch out and make yourself at home in front of 42-inch-screen plasma TVs with plug-and-play capability. Beyond the lobby, a sunny breakfast kitchen area features morning cereals, pastries and breads, served on white china with real silverware. Continental breakfast with freshly brewed Starbucks coffee is complimentary each morning, with hot-cooked entrees and picnic items, such as sandwiches, available for purchase.

220 Rudy's Circle, Nashville, TN 37214. ✆ **888-HYATTHP** (492-8847) or 615/872-0422. Fax 615/872-9283. www.hyatt.com. 123 units. $99–$189 double. Rates include continental breakfast. AE, DISC, MC, V. Free parking. **Amenities:** Exercise room; small outdoor pool. *In room:* A/C, TV, hair dryer, kitchenette, Wi-Fi (free).

Residence Inn Airport ★ This sprawling, extended-stay Marriott property feels more like a suburban apartment complex than a chain hotel. Studios are a real bargain, considering they include a queen-size bed, pullout sofa, and full kitchens, which, in 2010, are being upgraded with new stainless-steel appliances (refrigerators and stoves). For a few dollars more, you can book a two-story loft with two bedrooms. The property is also in the process of upgrading its televisions to high-definition sets. As with all Marriott properties, rooms are smoke free.

2300 Elm Hill Pike, Nashville, TN 37214. ✆ **800/331-3131** or 615/889-8600. Fax 615/871-4970. www.marriott.com. 168 units. $109–$159 double. Rates include cooked breakfast. AE, DC, DISC, MC, V. Free parking. Pets accepted ($50 1–3 nights; $100 4 nights or more). **Amenities:** Exercise room; outdoor pool; valet service. *In room:* A/C, TV w/pay movies, hair dryer, Internet (free).

Radisson Hotel at Opryland ★ The next-best thing to staying at the Opryland Resort during your visit to Nashville may be to hang your hat here—across the street. This modest but welcoming property is owned by the same company. Offering complimentary shuttle service to the resort, Opry Mills, and downtown tourist attractions, it's a more affordable alternative, too.

2401 Music Valley Dr. Nashville, TN 37214. ✆ **800/333-3333** or 615/889-0800. Fax 615/883-1230. www.radisson.com/nashvilletn. 302 units. $119–$129 double. Rates include continental breakfast. AE, DISC, MC, V. Free self-parking. **Amenities:** Free shuttle to Opryland and other attractions; indoor pool, sauna. *In room:* A/C, TV, hair dryer, Internet (in exterior rooms; free); Wi-Fi (in interior rooms; free).

INEXPENSIVE

A number of national and regional chain motels, generic but dependable, can be found in the area (see "Fast Facts," p. 255, for many toll-free reservation numbers), including **Alexis Inn and Suites,** 600 Ermac Dr. (✆ **615/889-4466**), charging $69 to $79 for a double; **Best Western Airport Inn,** 701 Stewart's Ferry Pike (✆ **615/889-9199**), charging $60 to $70 for a double; **Comfort Inn,** 2516 Music Valley Dr. (✆ **615/889-0086**), charging $75 to $90 for a double; and **Days Inn,** 2460 Music Valley Dr. (✆ **615/889-0090**), charging $50 to $90 double (with an outdoor pool and an adjacent miniature-golf course).

Other affordable options include **La Quinta Inn Nashville-Briley Parkway,** 2345 Atrium Way (✆ **615/885-3000**), charging $59 to $69 for a double; **Red Roof Inn–Nashville East,** 510 Claridge Dr. (✆ **615/872-0735**), charging $50 to $60 for a double; **Sleep Inn Nashville,** 3200 Dickerson Pike (✆ **866-538-0187**), with rates starting at $55 per night; and **Springhill Suites by Marriott,** 1100 Airport Center Dr. (✆ **615/884-6111**), charging $72 to $119 for a double.

7

Where to Dine in Nashville

The rest of the country may make fun of Southern cooking, with its fatback and chitlins, collard greens, and fried everything, but there is much more to Southern food than these tired stereotypes. You'll find that Southern fare, in all its diversity, is a way of life here in Nashville. This is not to say that you can't get good Italian, French, German, Japanese, Chinese, or even Thai—you can. However, as long as you're below the Mason-Dixon Line, you owe it to yourself to try a bit of country cookin'. Barbecue and fried catfish are two inexpensive staples well worth sampling (see "Barbecue & Hot Chicken" and "Music Valley & East Nashville" sections later in this chapter for restaurants serving these specialties). If you enjoy good old-fashioned American food, try a "meat-and-three" restaurant, where you get your choice of three vegetables with your meal. However, to find out what Southern cooking is truly capable of, try someplace serving New Southern or New American cuisine. This is the equivalent of California cuisine, but made with traditional, and not-so-traditional, Southern ingredients.

Nashville is well represented by scores of popular chain restaurants, including a disproportionate number of upscale steakhouses: **Morton's of Chicago,** 641 Church St. (✆ **615/259-4558**); **Fleming's Prime Steakhouse and Wine Bar,** 2525 West End Ave. (✆ **615/342-0131**); **Ruth's Chris Steak House,** 2100 West End Ave. (✆ **615/320-0163**); and **Stoney River Legendary Steaks,** 3015 West End Ave. (✆ **615/340-9550**).

I prefer to find worthy independent places to recommend. Happily, Nashville is bursting at the seams with them. In this chapter, I've only been able to scratch the surface.

For these listings, I have classified restaurants in the following categories (estimates do not include beer, wine, or tip): **expensive,** if a complete dinner would cost $40 or more; **moderate,** where you can expect to pay between $20 to $40 for a complete dinner; and **inexpensive,** where a complete dinner can be had for less than $20.

1 THE BEST DINING BETS

- **Best Spot for a Business Lunch: Capitol Grille,** 231 Sixth Ave. N. (✆ **615/345-7116;** www.thehermitagehotel.com), at the Hermitage Hotel, is very popular with the downtown business set. Why? It could be the prime spot next to the state capitol, or the traditional ambience, or perhaps the secret is in the exclusive wine list, grilled steaks, and espresso fudge cake.
- **Best for Kids:** It's not everywhere that you get to eat in a restaurant next to a full-size trolley car, and anyway, isn't spaghetti one of the major food groups? For less than most restaurants charge for a round of drinks, the whole family can eat at **The Old**

Spaghetti Factory, 160 Second Ave. N. (✆ **615/254-9010;** www.osf.com), in the heart of the District. See p. 73.

- **Best for Big Families:** You'll think it's Sunday dinner at Grandma's when you enter the cozy Victorian home that houses **Monell's,** 1235 Sixth Ave. N. (✆ **615/248-4747**), downtown. You'll share a big table with family and fellow travelers, passing dishes of old-fashioned Southern staples such as fried chicken, mashed potatoes, and greens. See p. 75.
- **Best Southern Soul Food:** One of Nashville's oldest minority-owned restaurants, **Swett's,** 2725 Clifton Ave. (✆ **615/329-4418;** www.swettsrestaurant.com), is still the benchmark for home-style comfort foods such as pork chops, slow-simmered green beans, cornbread, and macaroni and cheese. That first bite of banana pudding may bring tears to your eyes.

2 RESTAURANTS BY CUISINE

American

Elliston Place Soda Shop ★ (West End, $, p. 80)
German Town Café ★ (Germantown, $$, p. 75)
Harper's (Jefferson Street, $, p. 75)
Margot Café & Bar ★★ (East Nashville, $$$, p. 82)
Pancake Pantry (West End, $, p. 81)
Paradise Park Trailer Resort (Downtown, $, p. 73)
Rainforest Cafe ★ (Music Valley, $$, p. 84)
Tin Angel ★ (West End, $$, p. 80)
The Yellow Porch ★★ (Southwest, $$, p. 80)

Barbecue

Bar-B-Cutie ★ (Airport area, $, p. 85)
Jack's Bar-B-Que ★★ (Downtown, $, p. 85)
Mary's Old-Fashioned Bar-B-Q ★ (Jefferson Street, $, p. 85)
Whitt's Barbecue (various locations, $, p. 86)

Breakfast/Brunch

Allium (East Nashville, $$, p. 84)
Chappy's on Church ★ (West End, $$$, p. 68)
German Town Café ★ (Germantown, $$, p. 75)
Loveless Cafe ★ (Southwest, $$, p. 78)
Marché Artisan Foods ★★ (East Nashville, $$, p. 84)
Margot Café & Bar ★★ (East Nashville, $$$, p. 82)
Monell's ★★ (Germantown, $$, p. 75)
Noshville ★★ (Music Row & the West End, $, p. 81)
Pancake Pantry (West End, $, p. 81)
Tin Angel ★ (West End, $$, p. 80)

Burgers

Blackstone Restaurant & Brewery (West End, $$, p. 77)
Bobbie's Dairy Dip ★ (West End, $, p. 80)
PM (West End, $$, p. 79)
Rotier's Restaurant (West End, $, p. 81)

Cajun/Creole

Chappy's on Church ★ (West End, $$$, p. 68)

Caribbean

Couva Calypso Cafe (various locations, $, p. 87)
Rainforest Cafe ★ (Music Valley, $$, p. 84)

Delicatessen

Noshville ★★ (Music Row & the West End, $, p. 81)
Savarino's Cucina (West End, $, p. 86)

Key to Abbreviations: $$$$ = Very Expensive $$$ = Expensive $$ = Moderate $ = Inexpensive

French

Allium (East Nashville, $$, p. 84)
Marché Artisan Foods ★★ (East Nashville, $$, p. 84)
Margot Café & Bar ★★ (East Nashville, $$$, p. 82)
Miro District Food & Drink (West End, $$, p. 79)

Fusion

Mambu (West End, $$$, p. 77)
Mirror ★ (12th Avenue South, $$, p. 72)
PM (West End, $$, p. 79)

German

Gerst Haus ★★ (Downtown, $$, p. 72)

Hot Dogs

Hot Diggity Dogs (Downtown, $, p. 73)

Ice Cream

Bobbie's Dairy Dip ★ (West End, $, p. 80)
Elliston Place Soda Shop ★ (West End, $, p. 80)
Las Paletas ★ (12th Avenue South, $, p. 73)

Italian

City House ★ (Germantown, $$, p. 74)
The Old Spaghetti Factory ★ (Downtown, $, p. 73)

Japanese

Goten (West End, $$, p. 78)

Mediterranean

Kalamatas ★ (Green Hills/Southwest, $, p. 81)

Mexican

Cantina Laredo (the Gulch, $$, p. 69)
Las Paletas ★ (12th Avenue South, $, p. 73)
Taqueria La Hacienda ★★ (Southwest, $$, p. 79)

New American/ New Southern

The Acorn (West End, $$$, p. 75)
Blackstone Restaurant & Brewery (West End, $$, p. 77)
Bound'ry (West End, $$$, p. 76)
Cabana ★ (West End, $$, p. 78)
Capitol Grille ★★★ (Downtown, $$$, p. 68)
F. Scott's Restaurant & Jazz Bar ★★★ (Green Hills/Southwest, $$$, p. 76)
The Mad Platter (Germantown, $$$, p. 74)
The Merchants ★ (Downtown, $$$, p. 68)
Midtown Cafe ★ (West End, $$$, p. 77)
Miro District Food & Drink (West End, $$, p. 79)
Sunset Grill ★★ (West End, $$$, p. 77)
tayst Restaurant & Wine Bar ★★ (West End, $$, p. 80)
Watermark ★★ (the Gulch, $$$, p. 69)

Pizza

City House ★ (Germantown, $$, p. 74)
DaVinci's Gourmet Pizza ★ (West End, $$, p. 78)
MAFIAoZA's (12th Avenue South, $, p. 73)

Seafood

Aquarium (Music Valley, $$$, p. 82)
Caney Fork Fish Camp (Music Valley, $$, p. 84)
Chappy's On Church ★ (Downtown, $$$, p. 68)
Cock of the Walk (Music Valley, $$, p. 84)
South Street (West End, $$, p. 79)

Southern

Arnold's Country Kitchen ★★ (Downtown, $, p. 73)
Bailey & Cato Family Restaurant ★ (East Nashville, $, p. 85)

Cock of the Walk (Music Valley, $$, p. 84)
Harper's (Jefferson Street, $, p. 75)
Loveless Cafe ★ (Southwest, $$, p. 78)
Monell's ★★ (Germantown, $$, p. 75)
Prince's Hot Chicken Shack ★ (north of downtown, $$$, p. 85)
South Street (West End, $$ p. 79)
Swett's ★★★ (Downtown, $, p. 74)

Steaks

Jimmy Kelly's (West End, $$$, p. 76)
Old Hickory Steakhouse ★★★ (Music Valley, $$$, p. 82)
The Palm Restaurant (Downtown, $$$, p. 69)
Stock-Yard Restaurant (Downtown, $$$, p. 69)

3 DOWNTOWN, THE GULCH & 12TH AVENUE SOUTH

EXPENSIVE

Capitol Grille ★★★ NEW AMERICAN/NEW SOUTHERN Chef Tyler Brown is maintaining the high standards at the posh Hermitage Hotel's Capitol Grille, a lower-level dining room brimming with politicians, power-lunchers, and theatergoers from the nearby Tennessee Performing Arts Center. Grilled grouper, Niman Ranch pork chops, and Kobe beef short ribs are cooked to perfection. Pair them with your choice of a la carte sides, including truffle mac-and-cheese, fried green tomatoes, or honeyed carrots with thyme. Starters include crab cakes, pâtés, interesting soups such as the sweet onion bisque with bacon and chives, and grilled cheese made with brie. Befitting such a prestigious hotel, service is expectedly polished yet unpretentious. A nice combination for well-traveled diners with high expectations.

In the Hermitage Hotel, 231 Sixth Ave. N. ✆ **615/345-7116.** www.thehermitagehotel.com. Reservations recommended. Main courses $24–$36. AE, DC, DISC, MC, V. Daily 5:30–10pm; Mon–Sat 6:30–10:30am and 11:30am–2pm; Sun 6:30–10am and 11am–2pm.

Chappy's on Church ★ CAJUN/CREOLE/SEAFOOD/BRUNCH Mississippi Gulf Coast restaurateur John Chapman lost his 20-year-old restaurant, Chappy's, during Hurricane Katrina. Relocating to Nashville, he set up shop in this yellow-brick corner building on Church Street in 2006. An old New Orleans vibe, with French streetlamps and stained glass, pervades the romantic, two-tiered restaurant and bar. Creole soups, seafood, grits, and bread pudding are among Chef Chapman's signature dishes. Elevate your spirits with the Sunday-morning champagne brunch, which features live Southern gospel music. Live jazz is offered most Friday and Saturday nights.

1721 Church St. ✆ **615/322-9932.** www.chappys.com. Reservations recommended. Main courses $19–$32. AE, DISC, MC, V. Mon–Fri 11am–2pm and 5–10pm; Sat–Sun 11am–10pm (brunch until 3pm).

The Merchants ★ NEW AMERICAN/NEW SOUTHERN Housed in a restored brick building amid the rowdy bars of lower Broadway, this classy restaurant is another favorite power-lunch spot and after-work hangout for the young executive set. The restaurant's first floor is a cafe and bar (The Grille menu includes a smattering of burgers, salads, and sandwiches in the $10–$12 price range), while the upstairs is a more formal dining room. Lunch or dinner here might begin with shrimp-and-lobster fondue. From there, you could move on to pan-seared, pecan-crusted trout with chive butter, or perhaps a pork tenderloin with smoked cheddar and chorizo polenta. The Merchants also boasts an extensive wine list.

401 Broadway. ✆ **615/254-1892.** www.merchantsrestaurant.com. Reservations recommended. Main courses $21–$39. AE, DC, DISC, MC, V. Mon–Thurs 11am–10pm; Fri–Sat 11am–11pm; Sun 5–9pm.

The Palm Restaurant STEAKS Currently the "in" place to see and to be seen, the Palm is an upscale enclave, located within the cushy confines of the Hilton Suites downtown. Conspicuous consumption is a hallmark here, where a 36-oz. New York strip for two comes with a $60 price tag. Chops include thick cuts of lamb, pork, and veal, while beef eaters may opt for everything from prime rib to aged porterhouse. Salads, pasta, chicken, and fish dishes should appease diners who don't do beef. String beans, creamed spinach, mashed potatoes, and other sides are served family style. Celebs favor the private dining rooms, though if you keep your eyes peeled, you may see a Tennessee Titan or two, or the occasional country-music star.

1140 Fifth Ave. S. ✆ **615/742-7256.** www.thepalm.com. Reservations recommended. Main courses $15 lunch, $18–$38 dinner. AE, DC, DISC, MC, V. Mon–Fri 11am–11pm; Sat 5–11pm; Sun 5–10pm.

Stock-Yard Restaurant STEAKS If The Palm seems too pompous, head a few blocks uptown to the old Nashville Union Stockyard building, where local old-money types have gathered to slice slabs of beef for decades. It's where Dad comes for Father's Day, or Son on his graduation. Prime rib, porterhouse, rib-eyes, and surf-and-turf combos are available in small, medium, and large portions. If you're not a steak eater but still would like to visit this Nashville tradition, you'll find several seafood, pork, and chicken dishes, as well as a few pasta plates. Although there's plenty of free parking on-site, the restaurant offers a free shuttle to hotels within a 15-mile radius. Call ahead for a space on the buses, which seat between 14 and 45 people.

901 Second Ave. N. ✆ **615/255-6464.** http://stock-yardrestaurant.com. Reservations highly recommended. Main courses $21–$45. AE, DC, DISC, MC, V. Mon–Thurs 5–10pm; Fri–Sat 5–11pm; Sun 5–9pm.

Watermark Restaurant ★★ NEW AMERICAN/NEW SOUTHERN/SOUTHERN When Executive Chef Joe Shaw, a protégé of Birmingham's renowned Frank Stitt, opened this fine-dining spot in the Gulch in late 2005, Nashvillians had high expectations. Shaw delivered, but his departure 2 years later did little to dampen Watermark's immense appeal. The sophisticated urban dining room and bar is a sleek, modern space, done in blacks and whites. Exquisite preparations of Southern-influenced delicacies include Low Country oyster stew with roasted leeks, bacon, and sherry; and wood-grilled quail, swordfish, and lamb-loin entrees. Local and regional products, such as artisanal cheeses and farm-fresh produce, enliven the flavors brought to the table by experienced waitstaff. Be sure to save room for a dessert wine or the fancy s'mores—a marshmallow-y Jack Daniel's soufflé with graham streusel and chocolate ganache.

507 12th Ave. S. ✆ **615/254-2000.** www.watermark-restaurant.com. Reservations recommended. Main courses $18–$42. AE, DISC, MC, V. Mon–Thurs 5:30–9pm; Fri–Sat 5:30–10pm.

MODERATE

Cantina Laredo MEXICAN A spacious, upscale dining room done in warm woods and metals sets the stage for the newest eatery in the Gulch. The restaurant specializes in plentiful portions of gourmet Mexican food. Everything from the enchiladas, chile rellenos, and carnitas to the fajitas and tacos are fresh and first rate. The guacamole that's made tableside may be gimmicky, but it tastes good. Creamy flan or chocolate cake might seem like good dessert options, but consider the crepes instead. They're apple-filled thin pancakes with cajeta sauce, Kahlúa, and Grand Marnier, topped with candied pecans and vanilla ice cream.

Nashville Dining: Downtown Area, Music Row & the West End

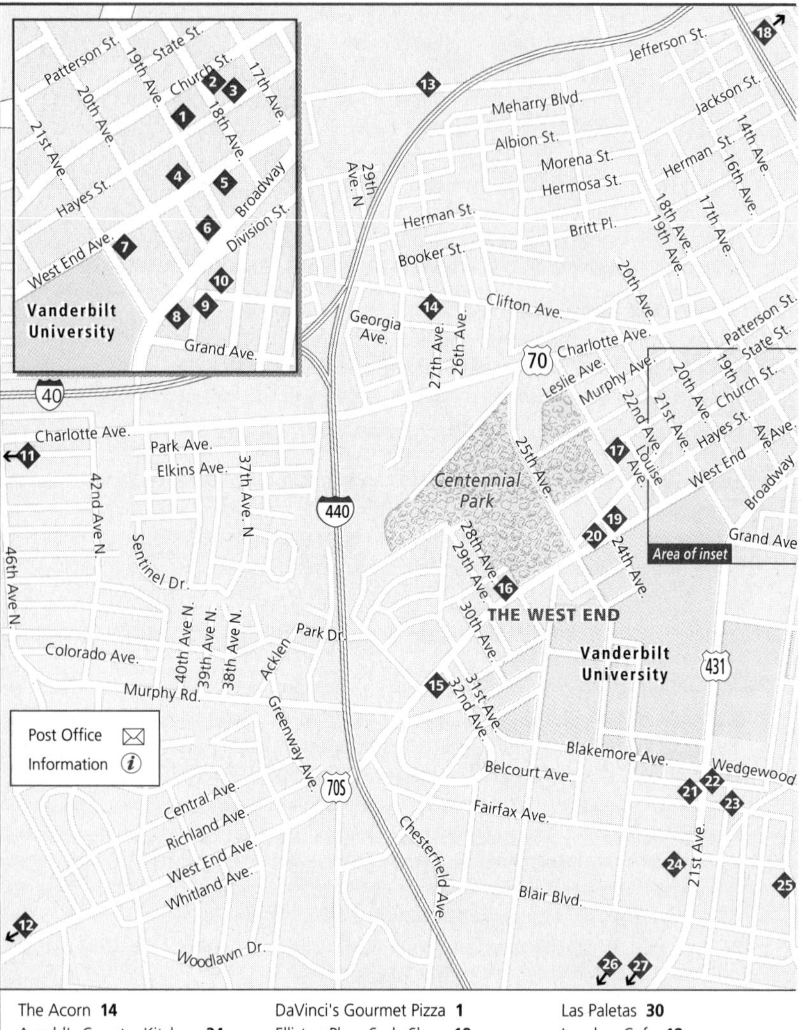

The Acorn **14**
Arnold's Country Kitchen **34**
Blackstone Restaurant and Brewery **4**
Bobby's Dairy Dip **11**
Bound'ry **8**
Cabana **21**
Cantina Laredo **33**
Capitol Grille **40**
Chappy's on Church **2**
City House **46**
DaVinci's Gourmet Pizza **1**
Elliston Place Soda Shop **19**
F. Scott's Restaurant & Jazz Bar **27**
German Town Café **47**
Gerst Haus **43**
Goten **7**
Harper's **13**
Hot Diggity Dogs **35**
Jack's Bar-B-Que **39**
Jimmy Kelly's **17**
Kalamata's **26**
Las Paletas **30**
Loveless Cafe **12**
The Mad Platter **45**
MAFIAoZA's **29**
Mambu **3**
Mary's Old-Fashioned Bar-B-Q **18**
The Merchants **38**
Midtown Café **5**
Miro District Food & Drink **10**
Mirror **28**

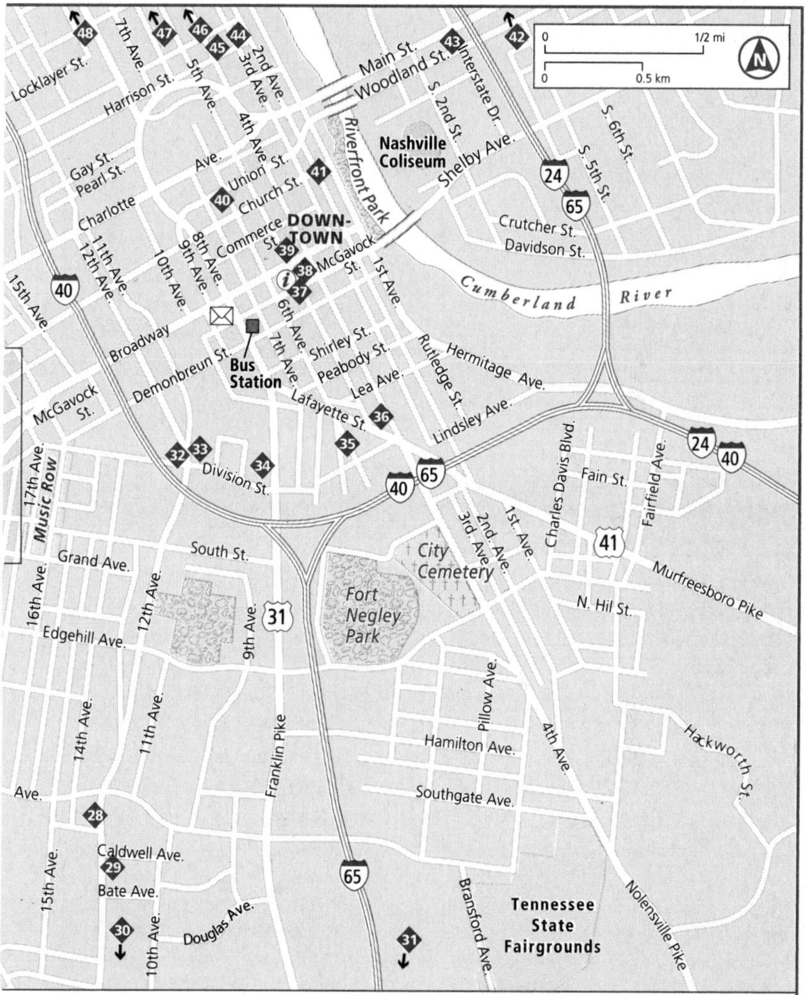

Monell's **48**
Nashville Farmers' Market **48**
Noshville **6**
The Old Spaghetti Factory **41**
The Palm Restaurant **36**
Pancake Pantry **22**
Paradise Park Trailer Resort **37**
PM **25**
Prince's Hot Chicken Shack **42**
Rotier's Restaurant **20**
South Street **9**
Stock-Yard Restaurant **44**
Sunset Grill **23**
Swett's **14**
Tayst Restaurant & Wine Bar **24**
Tin Angel **15**
Watermark Restaurant **32**
The Yellow Porch **31**

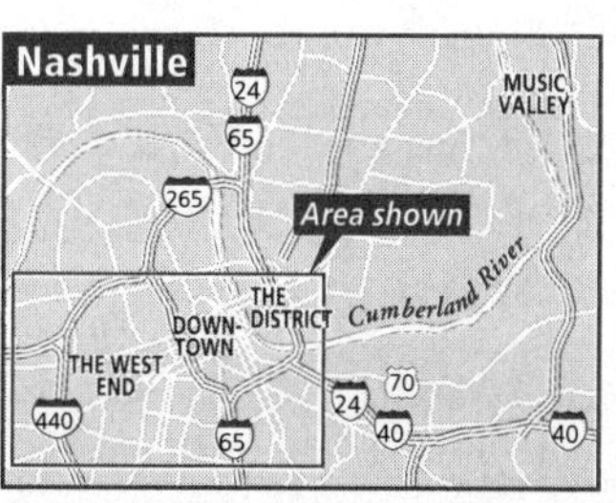

Family-Friendly Restaurants

Aquarium (p. 82) Kids love eating around the 20,000-gallon aquarium filled with tropical fish.

Elliston Place Soda Shop (p. 80) Old-fashioned ice-cream desserts and even fried baloney sandwiches are on the menu at this authentic soda shop in the West End, where you can wax nostalgic with the kids about what hanging out was like before fast-food restaurants.

The Old Spaghetti Factory (p. 73) A winning combination of simplicity and novelty make this downtown pasta place an affordable option for families. What kid wouldn't want to eat spaghetti and meatballs in a real trolley car?

Rainforest Cafe (p. 84) For an over-the-top theatrical mealtime experience, this junglelike dining room is king. Elephants, monkeys, and tropical birds appear to come to life, and families can eat their way through sudden thundershowers, all of which makes for big fun at Opry Mills.

592 12th Ave. S. ✆ **615/259-9282.** www.cantinalaredo.com. Reservations recommended. Main courses $12–$27. AE, DISC, MC, V. Mon–Thurs 11am–10pm; Fri–Sat 11am–11pm; Sun 11am–9pm.

Gerst Haus ★★ GERMAN Since 1955, this beloved Nashville landmark has been best known for its beer-hall atmosphere and classic German food. From its plum perch across the street from LP Field (home of the NFL's Tennessee Titans), chances are the Gerst Haus will be endearing new fans of hearty Bavarian fare for generations to come. Hearty platters include the crowd-pleasing wiener schnitzel (breaded-and-fried veal) and the tender and tangy sauerbraten (wine-braised lean beef). Sausages and brats also abound on the menu. Red cabbage, rye bread, and handmade spaetzle are savory sides.

301 Woodland St. ✆ **615/244-8886.** www.gersthaus.com. Main courses $13–$19. AE, MC, V. Daily 11am–11pm.

Mirror ★ FUSION Mirror serves one of the best vodka cucumber martinis in town, a feat that befits this underrated restaurant in the 12th Avenue South district. Metallic furniture, pale-blue walls, and gauze curtains define the casual, chic setting. Spanish sherry is a must when ordering from the extensive tapas menu, which include olives and tuna ceviche (raw fish marinated in citrus juice and spices). Entrees include homemade pastas including ravioli and fettuccini—try the latter with lemon-cream sauce—and a few unexpected finds: Crispy pork cutlets are served with a white-corn soufflé and chipotle barbecue sauce. Another fun entree is the "drunken chicken casserole," an herb-smoked chicken poached in beer and layered with potatoes, turnip greens, and tomato pesto.

2317 12th Ave. S. ✆ **615/383-8330.** www.eatdrinkreflect.com. Tapas $1–$3.50; main courses $14–$18. AE, MC, V. Mon–Wed 5–10pm; Thurs–Sat 5–11pm.

INEXPENSIVE

In addition to the restaurants listed here, you can get quick, inexpensive meals at the **Nashville Farmers' Market,** 900 Eighth Ave. N. (✆ **615/880-2001**), adjacent to the Bicentennial Capitol Mall State Park. It's open daily from 9am to 6pm year-round, except winter, when it closes at 5pm.

Arnold's Country Kitchen ★★ SOUTHERN Plan to arrive early to grab a parking spot in the cracked and busted lot next to Arnold's, a soul-food landmark for more than 2 decades. Be prepared to stand in line and to share a table with strangers too, if you plan to eat your buffet meal on the premises. But don't worry; over fried green tomatoes, barbecued pork, fried chicken, and knee-weakening mashed potatoes, you're always among friends.

605 Eighth Ave. S. ✆ **615/256-4455.** Main courses $6.50. MC, V. Mon–Fri 10:30am–2:30pm.

Hot Diggity Dogs (Finds) HOT DOGS Hot dogs and bratwursts come dressed with sauerkraut, coleslaw, mustard, pickles, or dozens of other combinations at this rickety-looking house just south of downtown. It's a small, cramped diner where you order the minute you open the door. Snag a stool by the window or venture to the outdoor deck to enjoy a beer, a dog, and a side of fries. And in your wildest weenie dreams, I'll bet you couldn't have guessed that they also offer vegetarian dogs too. But they do.

614 Ewing Ave. ✆ **615/255-3717.** www.hotdiggitydogstn.com. Hot dogs $2.75, bratwursts $5.75. MC, V. Mon–Fri 10:30am–4:30pm; Sat 11am–4:30pm.

Las Paletas ★ ICE CREAM/MEXICAN Sweet indulgences such as these *paletas* (traditional Mexican popsicles) are sublime when they're both delicious *and* wholesome—made fresh daily without preservatives or syrupy artificial additives. The small, unmarked storefront at the edge of the 12th Avenue South corridor offers several dozen flavors on any given day: Rose-petal, hibiscus, tamarind, watermelon, and prune are delicate tastes, while jalapeño and chili-cucumber are bright and bold on the palate. At only $2.50 a pop, you can afford to try more than one.

2907 12th Ave. S. ✆ **615/386-2101.** Popsicles $2.50. MC, V. Tues–Sat noon–6pm. Hours are seasonal; call ahead.

MAFIAoZA's PIZZA With a toasty fire crackling in the pizza ovens and the dim roar of a lively cocktail crowd, this pizzeria in the trendy 12th Avenue South district has built a loyal following. An outdoor patio gives patrons a great place to hang while throwing back a few beers or bottles of vino. Skip the soggy, tomato-laden bruschetta, but try the meaty pasta dishes and thin-crust pizzas, sold by the slice or whole pie.

2400 12th Ave. S. ✆ **615/269-4646.** www.mafiaozas.com. Main courses $6.75–$25. AE, DISC, MC, V. Tues–Fri 4pm–3am; Sat–Sun 11am–3pm.

The Old Spaghetti Factory ★ (Value) (Kids) ITALIAN With its ornate Victorian elegance, you'd never guess that this restaurant was once a warehouse. Where boxes and bags were stacked, diners now sit surrounded by burnished wood. There's stained and beveled glass all around, antiques everywhere, and plush seating in the waiting area. The front of the restaurant is a large and very elegant bar. Now if they'd just do something about that trolley car someone parked in the middle of the dining room. A complete meal—including a salad, bread, spumoni ice cream, and a beverage—will cost you less than a cocktail in many restaurants. Where else can you opt for gluten-free pasta dishes and order an Oreo milkshake for dessert? A great spot to bring the family, this is one of the cheapest places to get a good meal downtown.

160 Second Ave. N. ✆ **615/254-9010.** www.osf.com. Main courses $9–$12. AE, DISC, MC, V. Mon–Fri 11:30am–2pm; Mon–Thurs 5–10pm; Sat noon–11pm; Sun noon–10pm.

Paradise Park Trailer Resort AMERICAN Funny how fried bologna and Spam-and-cheese sandwiches taste so mighty good with Guns N' Roses blaring in the background.

But they do at this cheap, 24-hour diner that looks and feels like a trailer park in the wrong part of town. The could-care-less staff wear T-shirts reading "Best Mullet in Town," a thought for you to ponder as you sink back into your plastic lawn chair and decide whether to cap off your paper-plate meal with the Twinkie or the Moon Pie, both of which are on the menu. Paradise Park also serves bacon and eggs and pancakes for breakfast.

411 Broadway. ✆ **615/251-1515.** www.paradiseparkonline.com. Main courses $6–$9. MC, V. Daily 24 hours.

Swett's ★★★ SOUTHERN Southern soul food is doled out, cafeteria style, in the city's oldest minority-owned restaurant, which has been in business since 1954. Fresh-cooked collard greens, sweet potatoes, buttered corn, pork-laden green beans, and crumbly cornbread keep the place packed from lunchtime until after supper. Entrees include juicy fried chicken as well as beef, pork, and fish dishes, but I can make a meal of the wicked macaroni and cheese. Wash it down with sweet iced tea—and save room for banana pudding.

2725 Clifton Ave. ✆ **615/329-4418.** www.swettsrestaurant.com. Main courses $5.75. AE, DISC, MC, V. Daily 11am–8pm.

4 GERMANTOWN & JEFFERSON STREET

For restaurants in this section, see "Nashville Dining: Downtown Area, Music Row & the West End" map, on p. 70.

EXPENSIVE

The Mad Platter NEW AMERICAN/NEW SOUTHERN For many years now, the Mad Platter has been one of Nashville's trendiest restaurants. Located in an old brick corner store in a historic neighborhood of restored Victorian houses, the Mad Platter feels like a cozy upscale library, with bookshelves crammed with knickknacks and old copies of *National Geographic.* The ambience is reserved, not pretentious, and service is personable, if a bit slow at times. The menu, including vegetarian options, changes daily. Appetizers might include a Gorgonzola-and-asparagus Napoleon, as well as a prosciutto roulade stuffed with truffle mousse. Recent entrees have included grilled duck breast basted with a pomegranate molasses and a rack of lamb *moutarde.* Don't leave without trying the best-named dessert in all of Nashville: Chocolate Elvis, is an obscenely rich, fudgy cake that, put simply, takes the cake.

1239 Sixth Ave. N. ✆ **615/242-2563.** www.themadplatterrestaurant.com. Reservations recommended. Main courses $18–$29. AE, DC, DISC, MC, V. Mon–Fri 11am–2pm; Tues–Sat 5:30–11pm; Sun 5–9pm.

MODERATE

City House ★ ITALIAN/PIZZA Antipasto, pizza, and pasta are plentiful at this new rustic Italian restaurant in the Germantown neighborhood. But City House's hallmark is its charcuterie, including house-cured meats, salami, terrines, and meatballs. Menus change frequently to reflect the whims and creative pursuits of the restaurant's young chefs. House-made sausages with cabbage, cannellini beans and horseradish will stick to your ribs, while cornmeal-crusted catfish is a tad lighter, served with baby butter beans, lemon, parsley, and chilies. An extensive wine collection includes a variety of dessert wines, and the restaurant's screened-in wood porch makes a great place to linger.

1222 Fourth Ave. North. ✆ **615/736-5838.** www.cityhousenashville.com. Main courses $15–$25. AE, DISC, MC, V. Mon 5–10pm; Wed–Sat 5–10pm; Sun 5–9pm.

German Town Café ★ AMERICAN/BRUNCH For a stunning view of the Nashville skyline at sunset, stake out a dinner table at this pristine bistro in the Germantown neighborhood, just north of downtown. Sip a cocktail and pore over the eclectic menu, which includes artful interpretations of crab cakes, French onion soup, and even fried green tomatoes with goat cheese. Grilled fish entrees, such as the herb-crusted skate, are excellent, as are the tasso-stuffed chicken and the substantial mustard-marinated pork tenderloin served with a savory plum sauce. As for side dishes, the garlic mashed potatoes are out of this world. Service is polished and gracious.

1200 Fifth Ave. N. ✆ **615/242-3226.** www.foodbusinessrestaurants.com. Reservations recommended. Main courses $9–$20 dinner, $5–$13 lunch. AE, DC, DISC, MC, V. Mon–Sat 11am–2pm and 5–11pm; Sun brunch 10:30am–2pm.

Monell's ★★ Finds Kids BRUNCH/SOUTHERN Dining out doesn't usually involve sitting at the same table with total strangers, but be prepared for just such a community experience at Monell's. Housed in a restored brick Victorian home dating back to 1905, this traditional boardinghouse-style lunch spot feels as if it has been around for ages, which is just what the proprietors want you to think. A meal at Monell's is meant to conjure up family dinners at Grandma's house, so remember to say "please" when you ask for the mashed potatoes or peas. The food is good, old-fashioned home cookin' most of the year, and everything is all-you-can-eat. Feast on fried chicken, meatloaf, and sliced beef roast with gravy. Kids eat for about half-price, and ages 4 and under eat free.

1235 Sixth Ave. N. ✆ **615/248-4747.** Reservations not accepted. Main courses $13 lunch, $15–$18 dinner. MC, V. Mon–Fri 10:30am–2pm; Tue–Fri 5–8:30pm; Sat 8:30am–1pm and 5–8:30pm; Sun 8:30am–4pm.

INEXPENSIVE

Harper's Finds AMERICAN/SOUTHERN If the thought of slow-simmered turnip greens, crispy fried chicken, tender sweet potatoes, and fluffy yeast rolls makes your mouth water, wipe off your chin and immediately head to the Jefferson Street district for Nashville's best soul food. Be sure to save room for a slice of pie or a heaping bowl of banana pudding. Popular with white-collar professionals and blue-collar laborers alike, Harper's attracts a friendly, diverse clientele. Unlike seamier soul-food haunts, this immaculate cafeteria accepts credit cards and (thankfully) does not allow smoking.

2610 Jefferson St. ✆ **615/329-1909.** Main courses $4–$7. AE, DISC, MC, V. Mon–Fri 6am–8pm; Sat–Sun 11am–6pm.

5 MUSIC ROW, THE WEST END & AREAS SOUTHWEST

For restaurants in this section, see "Nashville Dining: Downtown Area, Music Row & the West End" map, on p. 70.

EXPENSIVE

The Acorn NEW AMERICAN/NEW SOUTHERN In a tree-shaded neighborhood near Centennial Park, Acorn offers evocative lighting, contemporary artwork, and a treehouse-view patio. Though a tad overpriced, the food is first-rate. The restaurant's top-selling entree is a chorizo- and potato-crusted halibut, served with a Jack Daniel's cream sauce. Other standouts include grilled pork tenderloin as well as the crispy, braised lamb shank. Appetizers include the scrumptious acorn-squash-stuffed ravioli with cream sauce, and the crab cake BLT with tomato jam.

114 28th Ave. N. ✆ **615/320-4399.** www.theacornrestaurant.com. Reservations recommended. Main courses $18–$32. AE, DC, DISC, MC, V. Daily 5pm–midnight.

Bound'ry NEW AMERICAN/NEW SOUTHERN With its colorful murals and chaotic angles, this Music Row eatery is popular with young adults and the cocktail crowd. The eclectic menu features tapas such as pork egg rolls with chipotle-juniper barbecue sauce and fried calamari served with anchovy aioli. Bound'ry's signature salad combines endive and radish relish with crispy ham, tomatoes, and black-eyed peas. Large platter entrees include vegetarian dishes such as polenta stacked with eggplant, Portobello mushrooms, and cheeses, as well as meaty pork chops and steaks, including the 16-oz. porterhouse. Wine and beer choices are quite extensive here.

911 20th Ave. S. ✆ **615/321-3043.** www.pansouth.net. Reservations recommended; not accepted Fri–Sat after 6:30pm. Tapas $4.75–$11; main courses $15–$30. AE, DC, DISC, MC, V. Restaurant daily 5pm–1am; bar daily 4pm–2:30am.

F. Scott's Restaurant & Jazz Bar ★★★ Finds NEW AMERICAN/NEW SOUTHERN Chic and urbane, F. Scott's is an unexpected gem tucked amid the shopping center hinterlands surrounding the Green Hills area. The classic movie-palace marquee out front announces, in no uncertain terms, that this place is different. Inside, everything is tastefully sophisticated yet comfortable and cozy. The restaurant's seasonally inspired menu is among the most creative in the city. Although the menu changes frequently, you might start with an appetizer of Pernod-cured salmon carpaccio, or try the mache with garlic croutons and camembert in phyllo. Sophisticated entrees are executed with care and precision. For example, the pan-seared lemon sole is paired with crab and potato hash, with dandelion greens and a lemon-butter sauce. The roasted duck breast is served with caramelized onion comfit and fresh corn pancake. Sorbets and crème brûlée are on the dessert line-up, as are such unusual creations as roasted Carolina peaches with grilled angel food cake, basil oil, and mascarpone. Live nightly jazz in the lounge provides another incentive to keep sophisticates coming back. There's also free valet parking.

> **Tips Curbside Service**
>
> If you're planning to drive and dine in the West End, carry some cash for valet parking. Most restaurants offer the complimentary service, but tips are expected.

2210 Crestmoor Rd. ✆ **615/269-5861.** www.fscotts.com. Reservations recommended. Main courses $28–$30. AE, DC, DISC, MC, V. Sun 11am–2pm and 5:30–9pm; Mon–Thurs 5:30–10pm; Fri–Sat 5:30–11pm.

Jimmy Kelly's STEAKS Tradition is the name of the game at Jimmy Kelly's, so if you long for the good old days of gracious Southern hospitality, be sure to schedule a dinner here. The restaurant is in a grand old home with neatly trimmed lawns and a valet-parking attendant (it's free) waiting out front. Inside you'll almost always find the dining rooms and bar bustling with activity as waiters in white jackets navigate from the kitchen to the tables and back. Though folks tend to dress up for dinner here, the several small dining rooms are surprisingly casual. The kitchen turns out well-prepared traditional dishes such as chateaubriand in a burgundy-and-mushroom sauce and blackened catfish (not too spicy, to accommodate the tastes of middle Tennessee). Whatever you have for dinner, don't miss the cornbread—it's the best in the city.

217 Louise Ave. ✆ **615/329-4349.** www.jimmykellys.com. Reservations recommended. Main courses $18–$36. AE, DC, MC, V. Mon–Sat 5–11pm.

Mambu FUSION Chefs Corey Griffith and Anita Hartel co-own this quirky restaurant that's like a secluded hideaway, located in an old blue house behind the new Hutton Hotel. Each dining room in the cluttered Victorian is chock-full of kitschy decor, from fake flowers to found-object folk art. The menu is a mish-mash too, blending Asian influences and Mediterranean flavors with plain-old American fare. For instance, you could begin a meal with the spinach and watermelon salad or the arugula with mango, walnuts, and goat cheese; or nibble on crab cakes, hummus, or pot stickers while deciding what entree to order. The herb-crusted rack of lamb is a sure bet. However, tasting a bit less inspired than its name might imply, the pan-seared garam masala salmon over red potatoes with curry-drizzled veggies and tzatziki sauce is slightly ho-hum.

1806 Hayes St. ✆ **615/329-1293.** www.eatdrinkmambu.com. Reservations recommended. Main courses $22–$39. AE, DC, MC, V. Mon–Sat 5–10pm.

Midtown Cafe ★ NEW AMERICAN/NEW SOUTHERN Located just off West End Avenue, this small, upscale restaurant conjures up a very romantic atmosphere with indirect lighting and bold displays of art. The design has been pulling in Nashvillians for years. Rich and flavorful sauces are the rule here, with influences from all over the world. The dinner tasting menu is a good way to sample the fare. Be sure to start a meal here with the lemon-artichoke soup, which is as good as its reputation around town. From there, consider moving on to crab cakes served with cayenne hollandaise, and available either as an appetizer or an entree. Lunches here are much simpler than dinners, with lots of sandwiches on the menu. However, a few of the same dishes from the dinner menu are available, including the crab cakes.

102 19th Ave. S. ✆ **615/320-7176.** www.midtowncafe.com. Dinner reservations recommended. Main courses $19–$30. AE, DC, DISC, MC, V. Mon–Fri 11am–2:30pm; daily 5–10pm.

Sunset Grill ★★ NEW AMERICAN/NEW SOUTHERN In the West End neighborhood of Hillsboro Village, the Sunset Grill is that rare breed of restaurant that's both critically acclaimed in the national press and an enduring favorite with the locals. The decor is minimalist and monochromatic with original paintings to liven things up a bit. The menu changes daily, with an emphasis on seafood preparations. After all these years, I still can't resist the Sonoma Salad, a scrumptious combination of mixed field baby greens, tart apples, almonds, and blue cheese in a pink wine-garlic vinaigrette. Others may prefer the ostrich carpaccio, spicy voodoo pasta, or Szechuan duck. Desserts, such as coconut sushi or butterscotch-habanero bread pudding, show creative panache. On Sundays, Sunset offers half-price wine specials. With more than 300 varieties by the bottle and more than 100 by the glass, you have plenty of choices.

2001 Belcourt Ave. ✆ **615/386-FOOD** (3663). www.sunsetgrill.com. Reservations recommended. Main courses $12–$33. AE, DC, DISC, MC, V. Mon 4:45–10pm; Tues–Thurs 11am–10pm; Fri 11am–midnight; Sat 4:45pm–midnight; Sun 4:45–11pm.

MODERATE

Blackstone Restaurant & Brewery BURGERS/NEW AMERICAN/NEW SOUTHERN At this glitzy brewpub, brewing tanks in the front window silently crank out half a dozen different beers ranging from a pale ale to a dark porter. Whether you're looking for a quick bite of pub grub (pizzas, soups, pub-style burgers) or a more formal dinner (a meaty pork loin well complemented by apple chutney and a smidgen of rosemary, garlic, and juniper berries), you'll be satisfied with the food here, especially if you're into good microbrews. Fish and chips can't be beat, especially when washed down by a St. Charles Porter ale. This place is big, and you'll have the option of dining amid a pub atmosphere or in one of the sparsely elegant dining areas.

1918 West End Ave. ✆ **615/327-9969.** www.blackstonebrewpub.com. Sandwiches, pizza, and main courses $8–$20. AE, DC, DISC, MC, V. Mon–Thurs 11am–midnight; Fri–Sat 11am–1am; Sun noon–10pm.

Cabana ★ NEW AMERICAN/NEW SOUTHERN Ultracool Cabana boasts one of the liveliest after-dark scenes of all the West End's restaurant/lounges. Co-owned by restaurateur Randy Rayburn (Midtown Cafe, Sunset Grill), Cabana has a sprawling, 2,900-square-foot outdoor patio that's in use year-round. Gorgeous young people hover at the bar or mingle in chic private cabanas equipped with flatscreen TVs. Food here is affordable and, above all, fun. Nosh on homemade potato chips with Gorgonzola dipping sauce. Then dive into top-notch interpretations on Tennessee sliders (miniature fried-ham sandwiches) or the childlike chicken-wing lollipops, and frosty root beer floats with freshly baked cookies on the side.

1910 Belcourt Ave. ✆ **615/577-2262.** www.cabananashville.com. Reservations accepted. Main courses $6–$12. AE, DISC, MC, V. Mon–Sat 4pm–3am; Sun 4pm–2am.

DaVinci's Gourmet Pizza ★ PIZZA Frequently voted the best pizza in Nashville, this casual neighborhood place is in a renovated brick house in a nondescript neighborhood. As you step through the front door, you'll likely be hit with the overpowering aromas of fragrant pizzas baking in the oven. The pizzas here are all made from scratch and include some very interesting creations. The oysters-Rockefeller pizza is made with smoked oysters, while the Southwestern comes with salsa, roasted chicken, and cilantro. With such offerings as potato pizza, vegetarians are catered to as well. To wash your pizza down, there are lots of imported and domestic beers. In the summer, there's outdoor seating in the flower-dotted front yard.

1812 Hayes St. (at 19th Ave., 1 block off West End Ave.). ✆ **615/329-8098.** Pizzas $6.50–$22. AE, DC, DISC, MC, V. Mon–Fri 11am–2pm; Sun–Thurs 4:30–9pm; Fri–Sat 4:30–10pm.

Goten JAPANESE Glass-brick walls and a high-tech Zen-like elegance set the mood at this West End Japanese restaurant, across the street from Vanderbilt University. The valet parking is a clue that this restaurant is slightly more formal than other Japanese restaurants in Nashville. Don't come here expecting watery bowls of miso soup and a few noodles. Hibachi dinners are the specialty, with the menu leaning heavily toward steaks, which are just about as popular in Japan as they are in Texas. However, if you prefer sushi, don't despair; the sushi bar here is Nashville's best, and you can get slices of the freshest fish in town.

1719 West End Ave. ✆ **615/321-4537.** www.gotennashville.com. Reservations recommended. Main courses $10–$20. AE, DC, DISC, MC, V. Mon–Fri 11am–2pm; Sun–Thurs 5–10pm; Fri–Sat 5–11pm.

Loveless Cafe ★ **Moments** BREAKFAST/SOUTHERN For some of the best country cooking in the Nashville area, take a trip out past the city's western suburbs to this old-fashioned roadhouse and popular Nashville institution. People rave about the cooking here—and with good reason. The country ham with red-eye gravy, Southern fried chicken, and homemade biscuits with homemade fruit jams are made just the way Granny used to make them back when the Loveless opened nearly 40 years ago. This restaurant may be a little out of the way, but it's well worth it if you like down-home cookin'—and if you're prepared to endure a long wait to get one of the few available tables inside.

8400 Tenn. 100, about 7½ miles south of Belle Meade and the turnoff from U.S. 70 S. ✆ **615/646-9700.** www.lovelesscafe.com. Reservations recommended. Main courses $7–$17. AE, DISC, MC, V. Daily 7am–9pm.

Miro District Food & Drink FRENCH/NEW AMERICAN/NEW SOUTHERN One of the prettiest new dining rooms in Nashville, Miro is elegant in its simplicity, with floor-to-ceiling windows, framed mirrors, flickering wall sconces, and dark woods. When the restaurant opened in 2009, it was more of a French bistro than it has since become, with the arrival of a new chef who specializes in American Southern cuisine. Thus, you get menu items ranging from French onion soup to chicken-and-andouille sausage gumbo, and entrees including a classic goat-cheese tart, and Carolina shrimp-and-grits. Service is a bit erratic but well-meaning. It remains to be seen whether or not this split culinary personality will affect the restaurant's longevity. However, given the lasting popularity of its sister location, Watermark Restaurant (which opened a few years ago in the Gulch), Miro should have staying power.

1922 Adelicia St. ✆ **615/320-1119.** www.mirodistrictnashville.com. Reservations accepted. Main courses $8–$20. AE, DISC, MC, V. Mon–Fri 11am–3pm; Fri–Sat 5–10pm.

PM BURGERS/FUSION Surprise! Noted Thai-American chef Arnold Myint's casual East-meets-West bistro serves up one of the best burgers in Nashville. It's true; just ask the locals, who consistently vote it tops in various polls. The hefty, juicy hamburgers are nothing fancy—just perfectly cooked and simply delicious. PM's wildly eclectic menu reflects international cuisines, including Latin American and Asian. Try the rice bowls, sushi, chicken skewers, or wraps. Service has slipped in recent years, but the food at this spacious old Belmont College hang-out is consistent. Next door, Myint has recently opened a more upscale restaurant, ChaCha.

2017 Belmont Blvd. ✆ **615/297-2070.** pmnashville.com. Reservations not necessary. Main courses under $10; burgers $7. MC, V. Mon–Sat 11am–1am; Sun 4pm–1am.

South Street SEAFOOD/SOUTHERN The flashing neon sign proclaiming "authentic dive bar," a blue-spotted pink cement pig, and an old tire swing out front should clue you in that this place doesn't take itself too seriously. In fact, this little wedge-shaped eatery is as tacky as an episode of *Hee Haw,* but with Harleys often parked out front. On the menu, you'll find everything from fried pickles to handmade nutty buddies (candy bars). However, the mainstays are crispy catfish, pulled pork barbecue, smoked chicken, ribs, and steaks with biscuits. If you're feeling flush, you can opt for the $43 crab-and-slab dinner for two (two kinds of crab and a "slab" of ribs).

907 20th Ave. S. ✆ **615/320-5555.** www.pansouth.net. Main courses $9–$13. AE, DC, DISC, MC, V. Mon–Sat 11am–3am; Sun 11am–midnight.

Taqueria La Hacienda ★★ MEXICAN Ethnic eateries and Mexican restaurants have flooded the outskirts of Nashville in recent years, but this former taco stand rises above the rest. Now a family-friendly, full-service restaurant, it's adorned with rustic handmade wood tables and oversized chairs, as well as colorful wall murals. Crisp, hot tortilla chips, potent salsa, and chunky guacamole are exceptional, as are the enchiladas, flautas, rice, and refried beans. The menu includes tasty little crisp tacos with a long list of fillings, including chorizo and beef tongue. There are also fajitas with chicken, beef, or shrimp. You can get Salvadoran *pupusas* (corn tortillas), and just about everything comes with fresh house-made tortillas. Wash it all down with a glass of *tamarindo.*

2615 Nolensville Rd. ✆ **615/256-6142.** www.lahaciendainc.com. Main courses $7–$20. AE, DISC, MC, V. Mon–Thurs 10am–9pm; Fri–Sat 9am–10pm; Sun 9am–9pm.

tayst Restaurant & Wine Bar ★★ NEW AMERICAN/NEW SOUTHERN Nashville's first and only green-certified restaurant is also a destination for foodies. The menu is organized into three sections, or first, second, and third "tastes." A handful of choices in each category manage to cover all the culinary bases, from meats, game, and poultry to pastas, salads, and vegetarian options. Each course is paired with a recommended wine selection, but budget-conscious connoisseurs shouldn't feel intimidated to order without the wine pairings. Inventive preparations of common dishes are a delight, from the trout with stone-ground grits and pickled ramps, to the roasted lamb with garlic bread pudding, mint, and peas.

2100 21st Ave. ✆ **615/383-1953.** www.taystrestaurant.com. Reservations recommended. Main courses $9.50–$26. AE, DC, MC, V. Tues–Thurs 5–10pm; Fri–Sat 5–11pm.

Tin Angel ★ AMERICAN/BRUNCH A mainstay in the West End, Tin Angel is a well-kept secret among locals and college students. The pressed-tin ceiling, dark wood paneling, and crackling fireplace lend a hearth-worthy warmth to the bistro that's known for its soups, fresh salads, and pasta dishes. If you're looking to avoid (other) tourists, it's also a pleasant place to enjoy a leisurely Sunday brunch, with service that's unfrenzied and friendly.

3201 West End Ave. ✆ **615/298-3444.** www.tinangel.net. Reservations recommended. Main courses $14–$21. AE, DISC, MC, V. Mon–Thurs 11am–10pm; Fri 11am–11pm; Sat 5–11pm; Sun 11am–3pm.

The Yellow Porch ★★ AMERICAN In the cute Berry Hill neighborhood south of Nashville, next to a gas station and just across a busy, multilane highway, lies this irresistible little bistro. Look for the rocking chair garden planter out front. Service is cordial, and the atmosphere is casual. Salads are excellent. Try the port-poached, sun-dried cherry salad with baby greens, spiced walnuts, and balsamic vinaigrette. Also tempting is the antipasti plate with Genoa salami, Tennessee prosciutto, cheeses, hummus, sun-dried tomato pesto, and Greek olives. Steaks include a tequila-marinated porterhouse with poblano skillet corn, tomatillo salsa, and mole sauce, while myriad vegetarian options include Mediterranean vegetarian lasagna.

734 Thompson Lane. ✆ **615/386-0260.** www.theyellowporch.com. Main courses $13–$25. AE, DISC, MC, V. Mon–Sat 11am–3pm and 5–10pm.

INEXPENSIVE

Bobbie's Dairy Dip ★ BURGERS/ICE CREAM Scrumptious black-bean veggie burgers with guacamole and salsa may be the most unexpected find at this nostalgic, pink-and-green neon, drive-in ice-cream stand that's been around for decades. Beefy burgers, sloppy chili dogs, and greasy, fresh-cut fries are also preferred preludes to creamy, hand-dipped milkshakes, hot-fudge sundaes, and other cool treats.

5301 Charlotte Pike. ✆ **615/463-8088.** Main courses $7–$9. AE, DISC, MC, V. Daily 11am–10pm (open seasonally; call ahead).

Elliston Place Soda Shop ★ Kids AMERICAN/ICE CREAM One of the oldest eating establishments in Nashville, the Elliston Place Soda Shop has been around since 1939, and it looks it. The lunch counter, black-topped stools, and signs advertising malted milks and banana splits all seem to have been here since the original opening. It's a treat to visit this time capsule of Americana, with its red-and-white tiled walls, old beat-up Formica tables, and individual booth jukeboxes. The soda shop serves plate lunches of an entree and veggies, with four different specials of the day. Of course, you can also get club sandwiches, steaks, and hamburgers, and the best chocolate shakes in town.

2111 Elliston Place. ✆ **615/327-1090.** Main courses $2–$6. MC, V. Mon–Fri 7am–7pm; Sat 7am–5pm.

Kalamatas ★ MEDITERRANEAN Risk the road rage that usually comes with a traffic-choked drive out to the Green Hills neighborhood for this oasis of sumptuous Mediterranean cuisine. Its setting may be a nondescript suburban shopping center, but the food is consistently fresh and flavorful. Leafy green salads are flecked with feta cheese and olives, while the creamy hummus—laced with a drizzle of olive oil—is out of this world when dipped alongside soft pita bread and crispy falafel.

3764 Hillsboro Rd. ✆ **615/383-8700.** www.eatatkalamatas.com. Main courses $5–$12. AE, DISC, MC, V. Mon–Thurs 11am–8pm; Fri–Sat 11am–9pm.

Noshville ★★ BREAKFAST/DELICATESSEN There's only so much fried chicken and barbecue you can eat before you just have to have a thick, juicy Reuben or a bagel with hand-sliced lox. When the deli craving strikes in Nashville, head for Noshville. The deli cases in this big, bright, and antiseptic place are filled to overflowing with everything from beef tongue to pickled herring to corned beef to chopped liver. Make mama happy: Start your meal with some good matzo-ball soup. Then satisfy the kid inside you by splurging on a hefty, two-fisted chocolate-and-vanilla-iced shortbread cookie.

1918 Broadway. ✆ **615/329-NOSH** (6674). www.noshville.com. Main courses $6–$16. AE, DC, DISC, MC, V. Mon 6:30am–2:30pm; Tues–Thurs 6:30am–9pm; Fri 6:30am–10:30pm; Sat 7:30am–10:30pm; Sun 7:30am–9pm.

Pancake Pantry Overrated AMERICAN/BREAKFAST The *New York Times, Bon Appetit,* and long lines (even in all kinds of foul weather) attest to the immense popularity of this satisfying but otherwise unextraordinary eatery in Nashville's West End. College students, country-music stars, NFL players, tourists, and locals alike queue up outside the redbrick building for the chance to sit inside and sip a cup of coffee and cut into a stack of steamy flapjacks. With such varied wait times, it's worth noting that the Pancake Pantry also includes lunch items among its extensive breakfast menu.

1796 21st Ave. S. ✆ **615/383-9333.** Main courses $5–$15. AE, DC, DISC, MC, V. Mon–Fri 6am–3pm; Sat–Sun 6am–4pm.

Tired of Waiting?

The Pancake Pantry may be a breakfast-lover's first choice, but the daunting lines can aggravate appetites as well as patience. Across the street, the brew pub **Boscos** (p. 134) and bakery **Provence** (p. 86) both do a delectable brunch. Next door, barflies looking for hangover relief flock to laid-back **Jackson's in the Village** (1800 21st Ave. S., at Belcourt Ave.; ✆ **615/385-9968**]), for Bloody Marys and fried eggs.

Rotier's Restaurant BURGERS If you're a fan of old-fashioned diners, don't miss Rotier's. This little stone cottage is surrounded by newer buildings but has managed to remain a world unto itself. Sure, it looks like a dive from the outside, and the interior doesn't seem to have been upgraded in 40 years, but the food is good and the prices great. The cheeseburger here is said to be the best in the city, and the milkshakes are pretty good, too. For bigger appetites, there is that staple of Southern cooking—the "meat-and-three." You get a portion of meat (minute steak, pork chops, fried chicken, whatever) and three vegetables of your choice. They also do daily blue-plate specials and cheap breakfasts.

2413 Elliston Place. ✆ **615/327-9892.** www.rotiers.com. Sandwiches/main courses $4.25–$16. MC, V. Mon–Fri 10:30am–10pm; Sat 9am–10pm.

6 MUSIC VALLEY & EAST NASHVILLE

Music Valley includes the Gaylord Opryland Resort and Opry Mills, both of which offer a plethora of eateries—from food-court buffets to sit-down restaurants. While the airport area is mostly devoid of recommendable places to grab more than a quick bite, the flourishing East Nashville neighborhood has excellent bars, bistros, and cafes.

EXPENSIVE

Aquarium (Kids) SEAFOOD The novelty of dining amid 20,000 gallons of water teeming with tropical fish ensures family traffic at this Opry Mills eatery-as-entertainment venue. While the overpriced menu includes burgers, sandwich wraps, soups, and salads, specialties are platters of seafood (broiled, grilled, blackened, or fried). Despite its fun atmosphere, service can be so-so.

516 Opry Mills Dr. ✆ **615/514-3474.** www.nashvilleaquarium.com. Main courses $13–$32. AE, DISC, MC, V. Mon–Thurs 11am–10pm; Fri 11am–11pm; Sat 10:30am–11pm; Sun 10:30am–9pm.

Margot Café & Bar ★★ AMERICAN/BREAKFAST/FRENCH Chef-owner Margot McCormack's cozy brick cafe in East Nashville is a charmer, especially during Sunday brunch, when diners with prized reservations queue up to sip mimosas or the coffee that's served in individual French-press carafes. On the menu are mouthwatering breads, pastries, and breakfast dishes such as the creamy chicken-artichoke casserole. Tables and banquettes are close together, creating a convivial atmosphere among the clientele, which ranges from upscale professionals to casually clad coeds. Service is exceedingly friendly and efficient.

1017 Woodland St. ✆ **615/227-4668.** www.margotcafe.com. Reservations highly recommended. Main courses $18–$26. AE, MC, V. Tues–Sat 6–10pm; Sun 11am–2pm.

Old Hickory Steakhouse ★★★ STEAKS Opryland is in the process of revamping all of its restaurants, including the seafood restaurant Cascades and the family-style Italian place, Volare Ristorante. No changes were needed at the Old Hickory Steakhouse, which is the property's best fine-dining restaurant. Its antebellum mansion decor, replete with a library lounge serving single-malt whiskeys and rare cognacs, reflects Old South grandeur. The menu is much more cosmopolitan than the setting implies, however. Delicious steaks, including certified Angus beef and lean bison cuts, are grilled perfectly to diners' specifications. Succulent Atlantic salmon with bacon ravioli is the best non-steak entree. A tantalizing array of sheep, cow, and goat cheese from throughout the U.S. and Western Europe is served tableside, from a glass-encased cart, along with plump fresh fruits. Service is impeccable, making Old Hickory worth the drive to Music Valley from wherever you might be.

2800 Opryland Dr. ✆ **615/871-6848.** www.gaylordopryland.com. Reservations recommended. Main courses $23–$40. AE, DISC, MC, V. Sun–Thurs 5–10pm; Fri–Sat 5–11pm.

Nashville Dining: Music Valley & East Nashville

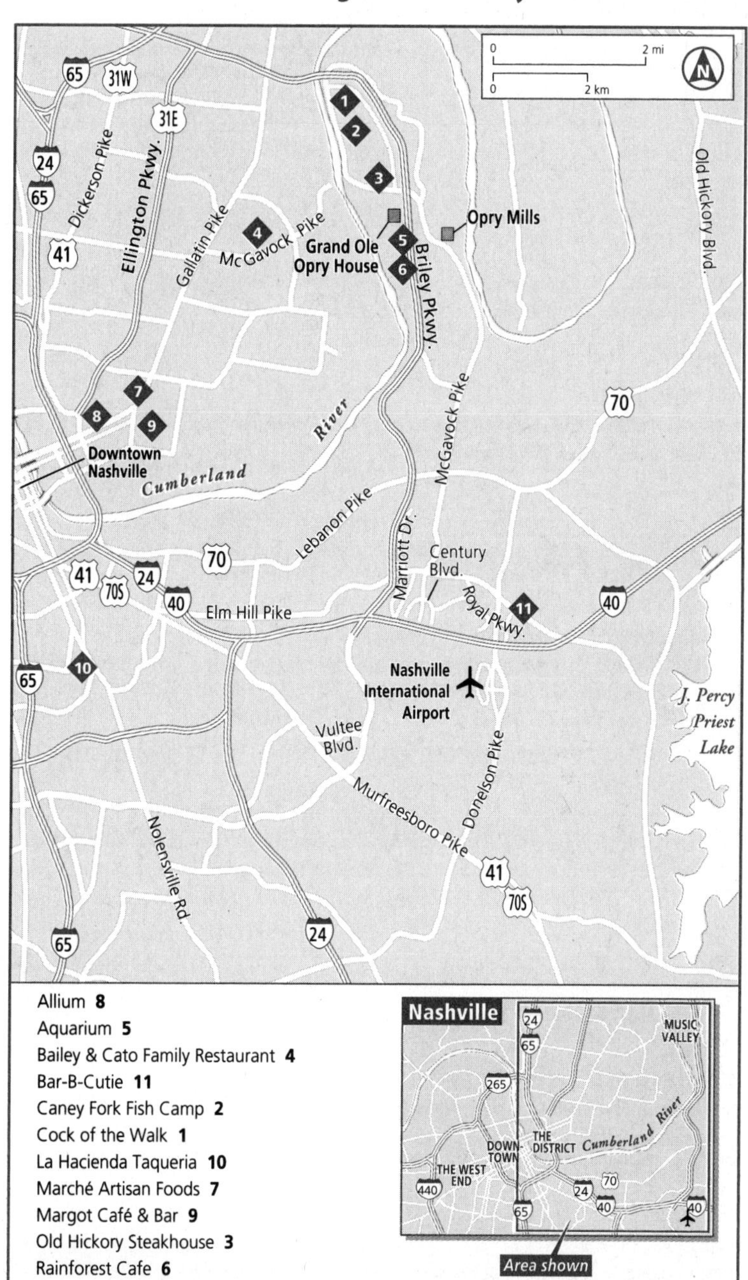

MODERATE

Allium BRUNCH/FRENCH Good news for fans of German Town Café. The owners have recently opened a sister restaurant, called Allium, in another burgeoning neighborhood—East Nashville. Located at Fifth and Main (just across the Cumberland River from downtown), the French bistro named for the garlic bulb plant does the classics. Sample the savory roast chicken, scallops Parisienne, and steak frites at dinner, or try the quiche at brunch. Muted colors decorate the contemporary dining room, which offers rarely seen, west-facing views of the Nashville skyline. There's also a full bar.

501 Main St. ✆ **615/242-3522.** www.alliumnashville.com. Reservations accepted. Main courses $12–$22. MC, V. Tue–Fri 11am–2pm; Tue–Sat 5pm–close (about 9pm); Sun brunch 10:30am–2pm.

Caney Fork Fish Camp SEAFOOD Two-fisted fried catfish sandwiches, barbecued pork ribs, and comfort-food favorites such as meatloaf and mashed potatoes fill the bill at this cavernous, log cabin/lodgelike restaurant near Opryland. Fireplaces, a waterfall and small pond, and big-screen TVs augment the outdoorsy camp decor, with fishing nets, rods, lures, and an old 1939 pick-up truck adding visual interest.

2400 Music Valley Dr. ✆ **615/724-1200.** www.caneyforkfishcamp.com. Main courses $8–$18. AE, DISC, MC, V. Sun–Thurs 11am–10pm; Fri–Sat 11am–11pm.

Cock of the Walk SEAFOOD/SOUTHERN No, roosters aren't on the menu. The restaurant takes its unusual name from an old flatboatman's term for the top boatman. This big, barnlike eatery near the Opryland Resort is well known around Nashville for having the best seafood in town. Like the catfish filets and dill pickles on the menu, the shrimp and chicken are also fried in peanut oil. Rounding out the hearty platters are such sides as beans and turnip greens, brought to the table in big pots.

2624 Music Valley Dr. ✆ **615/889-1930.** www.cockofthewalkrestaurant.com. Reservations accepted for groups of 20 or more. Main courses $9–$12. AE, DISC, MC, V. Mon–Thurs 5–9pm; Fri–Sat 5–10pm; Sun 11am–9pm.

Marché Artisan Foods ★★ BRUNCH/FRENCH Part market, part bistro and deli, this vegetarian-friendly restaurant serves breakfast, lunch, and dinner. A sunny spot with big picture windows for people-watching, the cafe is owned by Margot McCormack, of Margot Café (see above), right around the corner. McCormack's attention to detail and freshness is evident in every aspect of the meals served here, from the fresh-cut summer zinnias in glass jars on the marble tables, to artisanal breads and crisp biscotti, fluffy omelets, luscious salads, and creamy quiches. Before you feast, sip coffee or champagne as you browse the edible goods that abound: Imported olive oils, pestos, and pastas are artfully displayed around wooden farmhouse tables.

1000 Main St. ✆ **615/262-1111.** www.marcheartisanfoods.com. Reservations not accepted for lunch. Main courses $12–$15. AE, DISC, MC, V. Tues–Fri 7am–7pm; Sat 8am–5pm; Sun 9am–4pm.

Rainforest Cafe ★ Kids AMERICAN/CARIBBEAN Lush waterfalls, live birds, and brilliantly colored fish in floor-to-ceiling aquariums provide a feast for the senses at this popular theme restaurant. Indulge in huge platters of oversized burgers, fish sandwiches, and rich entrees such as pasta Alfredo. Then save room for the flaming chocolate-volcano dessert, which is sure to turn heads when the safari-clad waitstaff parade it to your table.

353 Opry Mills Dr. ✆ **615/514-3000.** www.rainforestcafe.com. Reservations recommended. Main courses $10–$30. AE, DC, DISC, MC, V. Mon–Thurs 11am–9:30pm; Fri–Sat 10:30am–10:30pm; Sun 10:30am–8:30pm.

INEXPENSIVE

Bailey & Cato Family Restaurant ★SOUTHERN The weathered-looking, faded pink cottage in the Inglewood section of East Nashville might not look like much from the street, but trust me: You want to go inside. This family-owned soul-food restaurant opened in 2009, and the buzz spread quickly that it was the real deal. Bailey & Cato serves up such mouthwatering comfort food as barbecued ribs, oxtails in a brown gravy, meatloaf and mashed potatoes, and crispy fried chicken like Grandma used to make. Southern sides include turnip greens, cooked cabbage, sweet potatoes, and golden cornbread. A list of the day's homemade cakes, pies, and puddings are posted near the steam table. Order it for take-out, or try to nab one of the few tables inside. Service is friendly, the place is clean, and you might get the added bonus (like I did, on a recent visit) of hearing gospel music wafting from the kitchen.

1307 McGavock Pike. ✆ **615/227-4694.** Main courses under $10. MC, V. Tues–Wed 11am–10pm; Thurs–Sat 11am–11pm; Sun noon–10pm.

7 BARBECUE & HOT CHICKEN

INEXPENSIVE

Bar-B-Cutie ★BARBECUE If you're out by the airport and have an intense craving for barbecue, head to Bar-B-Cutie. Just watch for the sign with the bar-b-doll cowgirl in short shorts. Bar-B-Cutie has been in business since 1948 and, while there is mesquite-grilled chicken available, you'd be remiss if you didn't order the pork shoulder or baby-back ribs. There's another Bar-B-Cutie at 5221 Nolensville Rd. (✆ **615/834-6556**), on the south side of town.

501 Donelson Pike. ✆ **888/WE-BAR-B-Q** (932-2727) or 615/872-0207. www.bar-b-cutie.com. Full meals $5–$10. AE, DC, MC, V. Sun–Thurs 10am–9pm; Fri–Sat 10am–10pm.

Jack's Bar-B-Que BARBECUE When the barbecue urge strikes you downtown, don't settle for cheap imitations; head to Jack's, where you can get pork shoulder, Texas beef brisket, St. Louis ribs, and smoked turkey, sausage, and chicken. There's another Jack's, at 334 W. Trinity Lane (✆ **615/228-9888**), in north Nashville.

416 Broadway. ✆ **615/254-5715.** www.jacksbarbque.com. Main courses $3–$9.50. AE, DISC, MC, V. Summer Mon–Sat 10:30am–10pm; winter Mon–Wed 10:30am–3pm, Thurs–Sat 10:30am–10pm, Sun during Tennessee Titans home games.

Mary's Old-Fashioned Bar-B-Q ★ BARBECUE Succulent pork short-ribs and cornmeal-dusted fried fish sandwiches are served on white bread at this Jefferson Street landmark. Ask for hot sauce, onions, and pickles, if you like.

1108 Jefferson St. ✆ **615/256-7696.** Meals $5–$7. MC, V. Mon–Thurs 8am–midnight; Fri–Sat 8am–2am; Sun 2–10pm.

Prince's Hot Chicken Shack ★SOUTHERN Grease will soak through the brown paper bag in which your fiery, deep-fried chicken is unceremoniously served. That's to be expected here at this proud but run-down joint in a dicey part of town. Line up at the counter with the diverse local clientele to pick your poison—mild, medium, or extra-hot sauce? If you need a cool-down, pray you've got enough change for the Coke machine.

123 Ewing Dr. ✆ **615/226-9442.** Meals $6.50–$8. No credit cards. Tues–Thurs noon–midnight; Fri–Sat noon–4am.

Whitt's Barbecue BARBECUE Walk in, drive up, or get it delivered. Whitt's serves some of the best barbecue in Nashville. There's no seating here, so take it back to your hotel or plan a picnic. You can buy barbecue pork, beef, and even turkey by the pound, or order sandwiches and plates with the extra fixin's. The pork barbecue sandwiches, topped with zesty coleslaw, gets my vote for best in town. Among the many other locations are those at 2535 Lebanon Rd. (✆ **615/883-6907**), and at 114 Old Hickory Blvd. E. (✆ **615/868-1369**).

5310 Harding Rd. ✆ **615/356-3435.** www.whittsbarbecue.com. Meals $3–$8; barbecue $6.60 per pound. AE, DC, DISC, MC, V. Mon–Sat 10:30am–8pm.

8 CAFES, DELIS, BAKERIES & PASTRY SHOPS

When you just need a quick pick-me-up, a rich pastry, or some good rustic bread for a picnic, there are several good cafes, coffeehouse, and bakeries scattered around the city. Downtown, in the sunny lobby of the Country Music Hall of Fame and Museum, you can order cocktails or coffee with lunch at **SoBro Grill,** 222 Fifth Ave. S. (✆ **615/254-9060;** www.sobrogrill.com). The stretch of 12th Avenue South is where you'll find the funky **Frothy Monkey,** 2509 12th Ave. S. (✆ **615/292-1808;** www.frothymonkeynashville.com), a bungalow with hardwood floors and a skylight, not to mention free Wi-Fi. **Portland Brew,** 2605 12th Ave. S. (✆ **615/292-9004**), and 1921 Eastland (✆ **615/262-9088;** www.portlandbrewcoffee.com), is another locally owned spot whose owners were inspired by coffee shops they encountered in Oregon.

Trendy tea houses have opened and closed with regularity in recent years. Survivors include the **Savannah Tea Company,** 2206 Eighth Ave. S. (✆ **615/383-1832**), which doubles as a cafe and wedding-cake shop in Germantown.

Bongo Java, 2007 Belmont Blvd. (✆ **615/385-JAVA** [5282]; www.bongojava.com), located near Belmont University, is located in an old house on a tree-lined street. It has good collegiate atmosphere, but parking during peak hours can pose a challenge. Nearby in the West End, where coffee shops and cafes are ubiquitous, two of my favorites are **Grins** (pronounced "greens") **Vegetarian Café,** at 25th Avenue and Vanderbilt Place (✆ **615/322-8571**); and **Fido,** 1812 21st Ave. S. (✆ **615/385-7959**), an arty former pet shop and current musicians' hangout that is one of the friendliest Wi-Fi spots in the neighborhood. You can link to both places through Bongo Java's website, listed above.

Across the street from Fido you'll find **Provence Breads & Café** ★, 1705 21st Ave. S. (✆ **615/386-0363;** www.provencebreads.com), a European-style coffeehouse that bakes crusty French baguettes along with the most delectable tarts and cookies in town. Gourmet sandwiches and salads, along with brunch items, are on the extensive menu. Provence also has a stylish bistro in the downtown library, 601 Church St. (✆ **615/644-1150**). Also in this area is the new, New York City–style Italian deli, **Savarino's Cucina;** it's at 2121 Belcourt Ave. (✆ **615/460-9878**).

Cupcakes are all the rage these days in cities across the country. Nashville gets its due with **Gigi's Cupcakes,** 1816 Broadway (✆ **615/342-0140;** www.gigiscupcakesusa.com), where you can choose from more than two dozen flavors of cake beneath a hefty blob of buttercream frosting. **Sweet 16th—A Bakery,** 311 N. 16th St. (✆ **615/226-8367;** www.sweet16th.com), is a charming bakery anchoring a trendy residential neighborhood in East Nashville. Heavenly aromas fill the cheerful, immaculate shop, which has a few

Best Tennessee-Based Eateries

All three of these homegrown Tennessee chains have multiple locations throughout the state and beyond.

Back Yard Burgers: More prevalent in Memphis than in Nashville, this fast-food chain specializes in home-style grilled burgers, spicy seasoned fries, and hand-dipped milkshakes. Founded in Cleveland, Mississippi, in 1987, today, it's a publicly traded, Memphis-based company with more than 200 locations nationwide. Burgers are big, juicy, and meaty (they also serve substantial hot dogs), but my favorite drive-through indulgence is the savory grilled chicken sandwich, and an extra-thick chocolate milkshake. ✆ **800/333-9566;** www.backyardburgers.com.

Cracker Barrel Old Country Store: A sure bet on any road trip through Tennessee, Cracker Barrels are ubiquitous along interstates. You'll recognize them by the rows of wooden rocking chairs on the brown buildings' wide porches. The restaurant chain, based in Lebanon, Tennessee, is the real McCoy, serving hearty portions of consistently good, home-style food at breakfast, lunch, and dinner. Chock full of old farm equipment, kitchen gadgets, and other antiques, the eateries all have crackling stone fireplaces that are especially welcoming in cold winter weather. You can also browse for old-fashioned candy in the gift stores, and even rent audio books for your travels.

There are more than 570 restaurants in 41 states, including multiple locations in Memphis and Nashville. Best breakfast bet: fried ham, biscuits and gravy, scrambled eggs, and Southern-style grits swimming in butter. ✆ **800/333-9566;** www.crackerbarrel.com.

J. Alexander's: Based in Nashville, J. Alexander's operates contemporary, full-service American restaurants in more than a dozen central U.S. states, with two locations in Nashville and one in Memphis. Unlike Back Yard Burgers and Cracker Barrel, J. Alexander's has a relaxing yet upscale atmosphere and offers a full bar with wines available by the glass or bottle. Signature dishes: baby back ribs, prime beef, and cilantro shrimp. My choice: rattlesnake pasta.

In Nashville: 2609 West End Ave. (✆ **615/340-9901**), and 3401 West End Ave. (✆ **615/269-1900**). In Memphis: 2670 N. Germantown Parkway, Cordova (in the suburbs, near Wolfchase Galleria mall; ✆ **901/381-9670;** www.jalexanders.com).

window seats for those who like to savor their pastries over coffee. From fresh scones and iced éclairs to festive cookies and decadent brownies, this sweet spot has it all.

And, finally, **Couva Calypso Cafe,** 2424 Elliston Place (✆ **615/321-3878;** www.calypsocafe.com), is an inexpensive local chain with multiple locations that features Caribbean-inspired salads and sandwiches, including good vegetarian options such as Boca burgers. There is also a location at 5101 Harding Pike (✆ **615/356-1678**).

8

Exploring Nashville

Nashville, Music City, the Country Music Capital of the World. There's no question why people visit Nashville. But you may be surprised to find that there's more to see and do here than just chase country stars. Sure, you can attend the ***Grand Ole Opry,*** linger over displays at the **Country Music Hall of Fame,** take a tour past the homes of the country legends, and hear the stars of the future at any number of clubs. However, the state capital of Tennessee also has plenty of museums and other attractions that have nothing to do with country music. The city has many other enriching cultural attractions, including the impressive **Frist Center for the Visual Arts, Cheekwood Botanical Garden & Museum of Art,** and **Van Vechten Art Gallery at Fisk University**—not to mention Nashville's full-size reproduction of the **Parthenon.**

So even if you could care less about Toby Keith and Taylor Swift, you'll find something to keep you busy while you're in town. However, if you can't wait for the next Kenny Chesney or Sugarland release, you'll be in hog heaven on a visit to Nashville.

1 ON THE MUSIC TRAIL

For information on the *Grand Ole Opry* and other country music performance halls, theaters, and clubs, see chapter 10, "Nashville After Dark." For information on country music gift shops, see chapter 9, "Shopping in Nashville." If you want to drive by some houses of the country stars, pick up a copy of the "Homes of the Stars" map, sold at the **Ernest Tubb Record Shop,** 417 Broadway (✆ **615/255-7503**), and at other country music souvenir shops around town. But consider yourself forewarned: The reality is that most of today's superstars live in ultraexclusive, gated enclaves, so your chances of driving by a mansion to catch Tim McGraw mowing his grass are slim to none.

At the **Visitors Center** in the **Sommet Entertainment Center,** you can also get a booklet with more information on the homes of the stars. With celebrity books all the rage these days, it's not surprising that **Davis-Kidd Booksellers,** 2121 Green Hills Village Dr. (inside the Mall at Green Hills; ✆ **615/385-2645**), brings in country music stars for book-signings several times a year. Call them for a schedule.

Cooter's Place "Breaker! Breaker!" Actor Ben Jones, who starred as Cooter in the late-1970s TV show *The Dukes of Hazzard,* owns this "good-ol'-boys" hang-out, where you can buy Confederate flags and other Southern knickknacks. A museum dedicated to the cult TV hit displays props, records, costumes, posters, and scripts related to the show and its stars. Allow 20 to 30 minutes to tour the museum and have your picture taken in front of the General Lee—a bright orange 1969 Dodge Charger.

2613 McGavock Pike. ✆ **615/872-8358.** www.cootersplace.com. Free admission. Daily 9am–7pm. Take McGavock Pkwy to Music Valley Dr.

Country Music Hall of Fame & Museum ★★ Although it's more Patsy Montana than Carrie Underwood, country music fans should not miss this wonderfully entertaining museum. Here you can immerse yourself in the deep roots of country music. Savvy

Who Was Patsy Montana?

No, she wasn't the godmother of contemporary teen idol Miley Cyrus/Hannah Montana—even though Miley's real-life dad is Billy Ray ("Achy-Break Heart") Cyrus. Patsy Montana was one of the first bona fide, female country-music stars. Her Depression-era radio hit, "I Want to Be a Cowboy's Sweetheart," made her the first non-pop female singer ever to sell a million records. Born in a log cabin in the Ozark Mountains near Hope, Arkansas, in 1908, Patsy Montana was an icon of her day—known as much for her yodeling and fringed cowgirl outfits and wholesome, girl-next-door good looks. Montana died in 1996, the same year she was inducted into the Country Music Hall of Fame. You can learn more about Patsy Montana's colorful career at the Country Music Hall of Fame & Museum.

exhibits let visitors absorb bluegrass, country swing, rockabilly, Cajun, honky-tonk, and contemporary country music through what seems like miles of individual CD listening posts, interactive jukeboxes, and eye-catching multimedia displays.

Elvis's gold-leafed Cadillac (a gift from Priscilla) is a top draw, but on my many return visits here, I always relish revisiting these artifacts: a crude banjo made of hand-split oak and groundhog hide; black-and-white film footage of comic Stan Laurel mugging with the Cumberland Ramblers in 1935; Jimmie Rodgers's guitar and trademark railroad brakeman's cap; and Bill Monroe's walking cane, personal Bible (with a joker playing-card bookmark tucked inside), and his beloved 1923 Gibson F-5 mandolin. And, as if all of this wasn't more than a visitor could stand, the museum also showcases such down-home objets d'art as the kitschy cornfield from TV's *Hee Haw*—complete with Junior Samples's denim overalls and Lulu Roman's plus-size gingham dress. Because of its vast repository of materials, the museum's core exhibit, "Sing Me Back Home: A Journey Through Country Music," is continually refreshed with new artifacts and audio/video. So chances are, if you've been there before, you'll find something new on a return trip. Special themed exhibits also draw big crowds. Due to popular demand, the Hank Williams exhibit, "Family Tradition: The Williams Family Legacy," has been extended 2 years beyond its initial run, until December 2011.

If you want to arrange a visit to the old RCA recording studio (see "Historic RCA Studio B," below), where Elvis and other greats laid down a few hits, you'll need to sign up here at the Hall of Fame. The studio itself is located in the Music Row area of Nashville. Allow 2 to 3 hours.

222 Fifth Ave. S. (at Demonbreun). ✆ **800/852-6437** or 615/416-2001. www.countrymusichalloffame.com. Admission $20 adults; $18 seniors 60 and up, college students, and military; $15 children 6–17; free for children 5 and under. (Platinum Package tickets, which include the Historic RCA Studio B Tour, are a bargain at $30 for adults and $22 for youth.) Daily 9am–5pm. Closed major holidays and Tues Jan–Feb.

Grand Ole Opry Museum ★ Adjacent to the Grand Ole Opry House, these exhibits are tributes to the performers who have appeared on the famous radio show over the years: Patsy Cline, Hank Snow, George Jones, Jim Reeves, Marty Robbins, and other longtime stars of the show. There are also about a dozen other exhibits on more recent performers such as Martina McBride, Reba McEntire, and Clint Black. These museums are best visited in conjunction with a night at the *Opry,* so you might want to arrive early. Allow 20 to 30 minutes (just right for browsing prior to attending a performance of the *Grand Ole Opry*).

Nashville Attractions: Downtown Area & Music Row

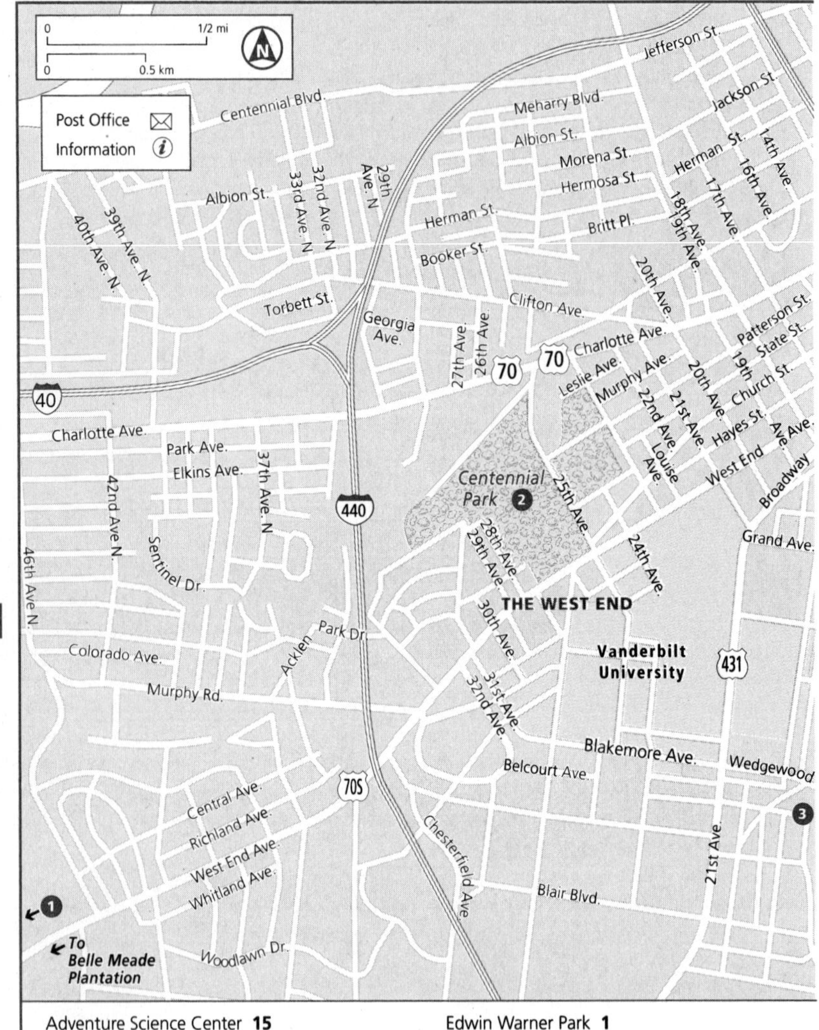

Adventure Science Center **15**
Belle Meade Plantation **1**
Belmont Mansion **3**
Bicentennial Capitol Mall State Park **4**
Centennial Park **2**
Cheekwood Botanical Garden & Museum of Art **1**
Country Music Hall of Fame and Museum **12**
Edwin Warner Park **1**
Fort Nashborough **7**
The Frist Center for the Visual Arts **11**
Historic RCA Studio B **14**
Lane Motor Museum **16**
Musicians Hall of Fame and Museum **13**
Nashville Coliseum **8**
Nashville Zoo at Grassmere **17**
The Parthenon **2**

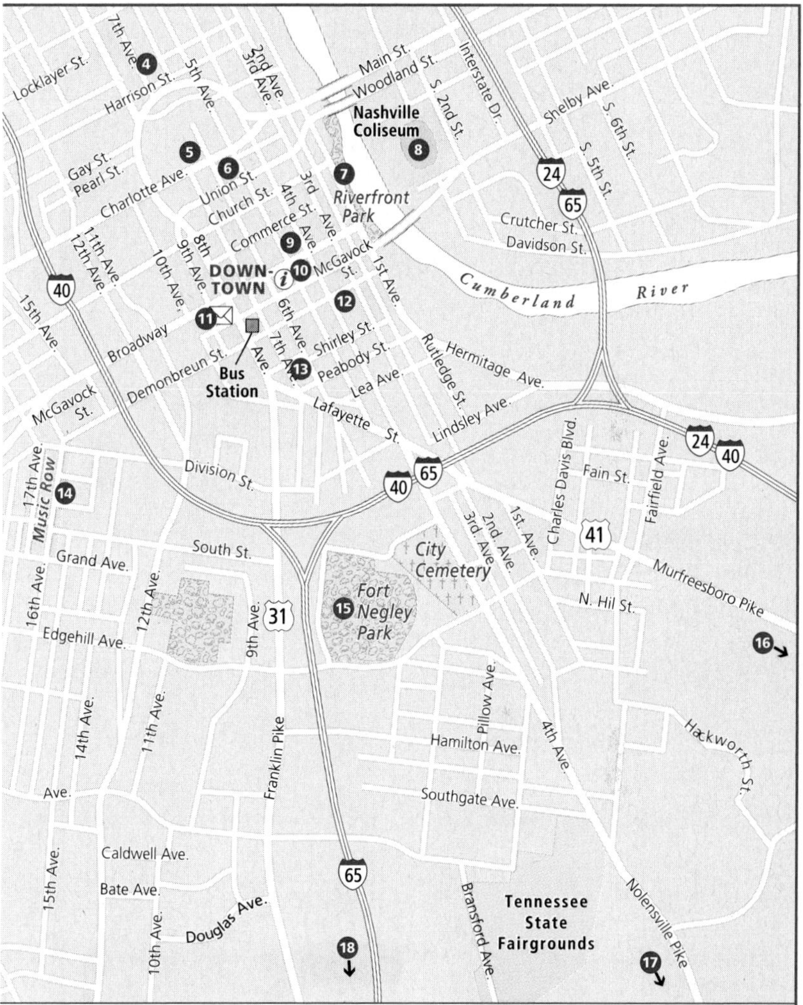

Locklayer St.
7th Ave.
4
Harrison St.
5th Ave.
2nd Ave.
3rd Ave.
Main St.
Woodland St.
Interstate Dr.
S. 2nd St.
Nashville Coliseum
8
Shelby Ave.
S. 6th St.
S. 5th St.
24
65
Gay St.
Pearl St.
5
6
Charlotte Ave.
Union St.
Church St.
3rd Ave.
4th Ave.
Commerce St.
7
Riverfront Park
Crutcher St.
Davidson St.
11th Ave.
12th Ave.
10th Ave.
9th Ave.
8th Ave.
9
DOWN-TOWN
10
McGavock St.
1st Ave.
Cumberland River
40
15th Ave.
11
12
Broadway
6th Ave.
7th Ave.
Shirley St.
Peabody St.
Rutledge St.
Hermitage Ave.
Demonbreun St.
Bus Station
13
Lea Ave.
McGavock St.
Lafayette St.
Lindsley Ave.
Charles Davis Blvd.
Fairfield Ave.
24
40
Fain St.
17th Ave.
Music Row
14
Division St.
40
65
2nd Ave.
3rd Ave.
1st Ave.
41
Grand Ave.
South St.
City Cemetery
Murfreesboro Pike
16th Ave.
12th Ave.
9th Ave.
31
15
Fort Negley Park
N. Hil St.
Edgehill Ave.
16
14th Ave.
11th Ave.
Franklin Pike
Pillow Ave.
Hamilton Ave.
4th Ave.
Hackworth St.
Ave.
Southgate Ave.
15th Ave.
Caldwell Ave.
Bate Ave.
65
Douglas Ave.
10th Ave.
18
Bransford Ave.
Tennessee State Fairgrounds
Nolensville Pike
17

Percy Warner Park **1**
Ryman Auditorium & Museum **9**
Sommet Center **10**
Tennessee State Capitol **5**
Tennessee State Museum **6**
Travellers Rest Historic House Museum **18**

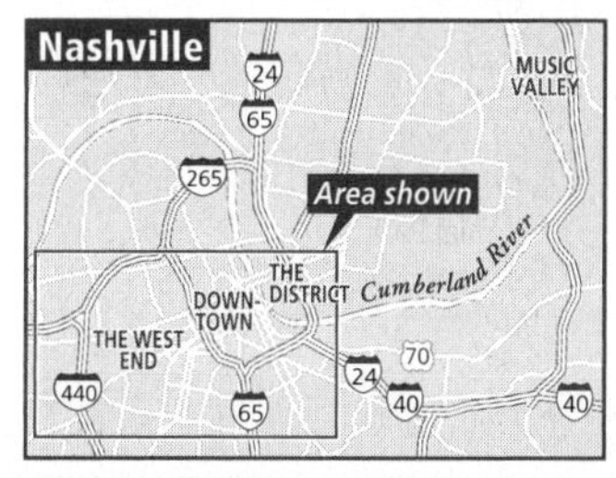

Nashville Attractions: Music Valley

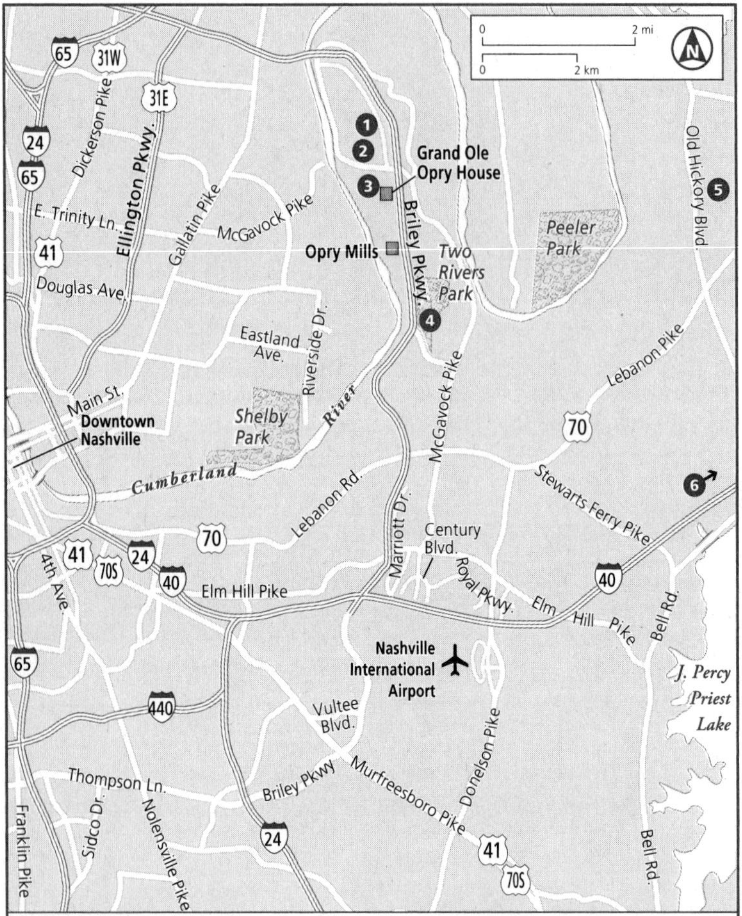

Cooter's Place **2**
General Jackson Showboat at Opryland Resort **3**
Grand Old Golf & Games **1**
Grand Ole Opry Museum **3**
The Hermitage **5**
Nashville Shores **6**
Opryland Resort **3**
Wave Country and Skatepark **4**
Willie Nelson & Friends Museum & General Store **2**

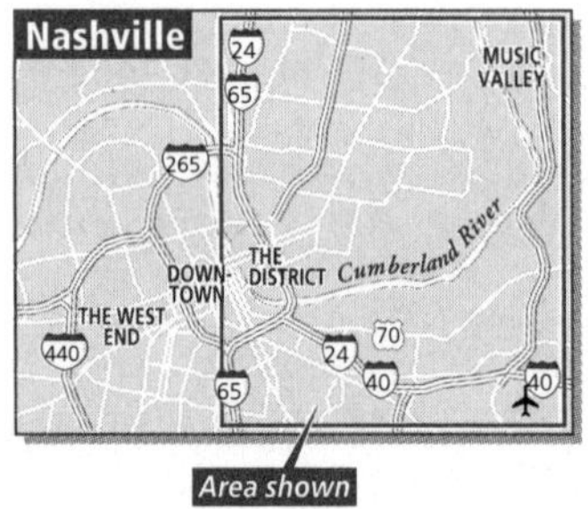

Fun Facts **Symbolism in the Architecture of the Country Music Hall of Fame & Museum**

Architecture	Symbol
Dark windows	Piano keys
Upward arch of roof	Fin of a 1950s Cadillac
Spire	Country's WSM radio tower
Tiered rotunda	Vinyl 78s, 45s, and CDs
From overhead	Museum resembles a bass clef

2804 Opryland Dr. ✆ **615/871-OPRY** (6779). www.gaylordopryland.com. Free admission. Daily 10am to varied closing hours, depending on performance schedule. Closes for special events; call ahead. At the Grand Ole Opry House (it's within the same complex).

Historic RCA Studio B ★ Dubbed "Home of 1,000 Hits," this humble building on Music Row was a hotbed of recording activity from the time it opened in 1957 until the early 1970s (it closed in 1977). Guided tours include vintage film footage, photo displays, and a lingering look inside the legendary studio where Elvis recorded his immortal "Are You Lonesome Tonight?" Other hits cut here include The Everly Brothers' "All I Have to Do is Dream"; Roy Orbison's "Only the Lonely"; and Dolly Parton's "I Will Always Love You." Tours are available only through the Country Music Hall of Fame and Museum (see above), which shuttles visitors between the downtown museum and the Music Row recording studio. Allow about an hour and a half.

Music Row (departures from Country Music Hall of Fame & Museum, 222 Fifth Ave. S.) ✆ **800/852-6437** or 615/416-2001. www.countrymusichalloffame.com. Admission $13 adults, $11 children 6–17. (Combination tickets available for both museum and studio tour.) Daily 9am–5pm.

Musicians Hall of Fame & Museum **Finds** Ever wonder who was behind the haunting steel-guitar hook on Bob Dylan's "Lay Lady Lay"? Nashville's newest music museum answers that mystery and many others, as it pays tribute to the back-up musicians behind the stars. Its displays are more old-school than those of the nearby Country Music Hall of Fame. No sensory overload here—just low-tech exhibit cases chock-full of fascinating music trivia. For example, see candid pics of Paul and the late Linda McCartney living on a Nashville farm with their young children in the early 1970s. So whether you crave details on the bio of Jimi Hendrix's bass player, or you want to see the autographed snare drum used on the Red Hot Chili Peppers' *Mothers' Milk* and *Blood Sugar Sex Magik,* this is the place. Allow about an hour for a visit here.

301 Sixth Ave. S. ✆ **615/244-3263.** www.musicianshalloffame.com. Admission $15 adults; $12 seniors, students, and military; $9.95 children 7–12; free for children 6 and under. Mon–Thurs 10am–6pm; Fri–Sat 10am–5pm. Closed major holidays.

Gaylord Opryland Resort ★ **Moments** Hotels aren't usually tourist attractions, but this one is an exception. With 2,881 rooms, the place is beyond big, but what makes it worth a visit are the three massive atria that form the hotel's three main courtyards. Together these atria are covered by more than 8 acres of glass to form vast greenhouses full of tropical plants. There are rushing streams, roaring waterfalls, bridges, pathways, ponds, and fountains. There are also plenty of places to stop for a drink or a meal. In the evenings, live music and a laser light show can be seen in the Cascades Atrium.

Notable Songs & Albums Recorded in Music City

YEAR	ARTIST	SONG/ALBUM
1956	**Elvis Presley**	"Heartbreak Hotel"
1957	**The Everly Brothers**	"Bye Bye Love"
1958	**Brenda Lee**	"Rockin' Around the Christmas Tree"
1964	**Roy Orbison**	"Oh, Pretty Woman"
1966	**Bob Dylan**	*Blonde on Blonde*
1967	**Robert Night**	"Everlasting Love"
1971	**Joan Baez**	"The Night They Drove Old Dixie Down"
1978	**Kansas**	"Dust in the Wind"
1987	**R.E.M.**	*Document*
1992	**Vanessa Williams**	"Save the Best for Last"
2000	**Matchbox Twenty**	*Mad Season*
2001	**India.Arie**	*Acoustic Soul*
2006	**The Raconteurs**	*Consolers of the Lonely*
2004	**Jimmy Buffett**	*License to Chill*
2007	**Alison Krauss and Robert Plant**	*Raising Sand*
2007	**Bon Jovi**	*Lost Highway*
2007	**Kid Rock**	*Rock N Roll Jesus*
2007	**White Stripes**	*Icky Thump*
2008	**Kings of Leon**	*Only By the Night*

The largest of the three atria here is the Delta, which covers 4½ acres and has a quarter-mile-long "river," a 110-foot-wide waterfall, an 85-foot-tall fountain, and an island modeled after the French Quarter in New Orleans. On this island are numerous shops and restaurants, which give the hotel the air of an elaborate shopping mall. You can take boat rides on the river and, at night, catch live music in a nightclub on the island. Allow 20 to 30 minutes.

2800 Opryland Dr. ✆ **615/889-1000.** www.gaylordopryland.com. Free admission. Daily 24 hours. Parking $10. Take I-40 to exit 215 and take Briley Pkwy. (155 North) to exit 12; turn left at the second traffic light into the Gaylord Opryland complex.

Willie Nelson & Friends Museum& General Store Overrated Less a museum than a souvenir shop with a few dusty exhibits in a big back room, this tourist site for die-hard Willie fans features many of his old guitars, gold and platinum records, movie posters, and even his pool table. It's a hodgepodge that includes areas devoted to fellow Outlaws Waylon Jennings, Johnny Cash, and Kris Kristofferson, as well as an extensive collection of B-movie Western star Audie Murphy's

Fun Facts **Music Row**

Nashville's Music Row has lots of high-profile recording studios and music publishing offices representing big-name country artists as well as others. Music Row clients have run the gamut from Harry Connick, Jr., and Sheryl Crow to Matchbox Twenty and Yo-Yo Ma.

Traveling Between Downtown and Music Valley

A cab ride from downtown to the Opryland Resort costs about $25. A trolley serves Music Valley attractions, but a car is really the best way to get around. If you're staying as a guest at Opryland, you'll have access to daily, round-trip shuttle service to downtown tourist sites, including the Wildhorse Saloon and the Ryman Auditorium.

memorabilia. Unexpected finds, such as a ticket stub from Elvis Presley's final concert, can be jarring. The museum displays are tucked behind saloonlike doors of a gift shop that hawks everything from shot glasses, T-shirts, and swizzle sticks to feathery dream catchers and dolphin figurines. Allow 20 to 30 minutes.

2613A McGavock Pike. ✆ **615/885-1515.** www.willienelsongeneralstore.com. Admission $5 adults, $4.50 seniors, $3 children 6–12, free for children under 6. Mon–Thurs 9am–7pm; Fri–Sat 9am–8pm; Sun 9am–6pm. Closed Dec 25 and Jan 1. Take McGavock Pkwy. to Music Valley Dr.

IN THE DISTRICT

All downtown attractions are accessible from the downtown trolley.

Ryman Auditorium ★★ If you're as enamored of music history as I am, you could devote several hours to a self-guided tour of this National Historic Landmark, where you're free to stand onstage—even belt out a few bars if the spirit moves you—or sit in the hardwood "pews," and wander the halls upstairs and down, looking at memorabilia in glass showcases. However, the typical tourist may be satisfied with a quick walk through the stately redbrick building. In either case, the best way to experience the Ryman is to attend a performance here. The site of the Grand Ole Opry from 1943 to 1974, the Ryman Auditorium is known as the "Mother Church of Country Music," the single most historic site in the world of country music. Originally built in 1892 as the Union Gospel Tabernacle by riverboat captain Tom Ryman, this building served as an evangelical hall for many years. By the early 1900s, the building's name had been changed to honor its builder and a stage had been added. That stage, over the years, saw the likes of Enrico Caruso, Katharine Hepburn, Will Rogers, and Elvis Presley. The *Grand Ole Opry* began broadcasting here in 1943. For the next 31 years, the Ryman Auditorium was host to the most famous country music radio show in the world. However, in 1974, the *Opry* moved to the then new *Grand Ole Opry* House in the Music Valley area. Since its meticulous renovation in 1994, the Ryman has regained its prominence as a temple of bluegrass and country music. Its peerless acoustics make it a favored venue of rock's best singer-songwriters and classical musicians, as well. Acts as diverse as Yo-Yo Ma, Coldplay, and Keith Urban have performed here. In 2005, director Jonathan Demme filmed Neil Young's performance for the concert film *Prairie Wind.* Allow at least an hour for a self-guided tour.

116 Fifth Ave. N. (btw. Commerce and Broadway) ✆ **615/458-8700** or 615/889-3060. www.ryman.com. Self-guided tours admission $13 adults, $6.25 children 4–11, free for children 3 and under. Daytime tour plus guided backstage tour tickets $16 adults, $10 children 4–11. ***Note:*** Backstage tours are subject to cancellation due to concerts and special events. Daily 9am–4pm. Closed Thanksgiving, Dec 25, and Jan 1.

"Tricky Dick" Tickled the Ivories

In 1974, when the *Grand Ole Opry* moved from its former home at the Ryman downtown to its new state-of-the-art theater in present-day Music Valley, U.S. President Richard Nixon was onstage for the first radio broadcast. A proficient pianist, the president performed "God Bless America."

2 MORE ATTRACTIONS

HISTORIC BUILDINGS

Belle Meade Plantation ★★ Belle Meade was built in 1853 after this plantation had become famous as a stud farm that produced some of the best racehorses in the South. Today, the Greek Revival mansion is the centerpiece of the affluent Belle Meade region of Nashville and is surrounded by 30 acres of manicured lawns and shade trees. A long driveway leads uphill to the mansion, which is fronted by six columns and a wide veranda. Inside, the restored building has been furnished with 19th-century antiques that hint at the elegance and wealth that the Southern gentility enjoyed in the late 1800s.

Tours led by costumed guides follow a theme (for example, holidays, aspects of plantation life, and so on) that changes every 3 months. These themed tours provide fascinating glimpses into the lives of the people who once lived at Belle Meade. Also on the grounds are a large carriage house and stable that were built in 1890 and that now house a large collection of antique carriages. During your visit, you can also have a look inside a log cabin, a smokehouse, and a creamery that are here on the grounds. Belle Meade's parklike grounds make it a popular site for festivals throughout the year.

In fall 2009, a new cafe opened next door to the mansion, replacing the popular Martha's at the Plantation. Allow a full morning or afternoon to soak up everything here. 5025 Harding Rd. ✆ **800/270-3991** or 615/356-0501. www.bellemeadeplantation.com. Admission $15 adults, $13 seniors, $7 children 6–12, free for children 5 and under. Family rate: $45 (includes 2 adults and up to 4 children). Mon–Sat 9am–5pm; Sun 11am–5pm. (Last tour starts at 4pm.) Closed Thanksgiving, Dec 25, Jan 1, and Easter. Take 70 South to Belle Meade Blvd. to Deer Park Drive, and follow the signs.

Belmont Mansion ★ Built in the 1850s by Adelicia Acklen, then one of the wealthiest women in the country, this Italianate villa is the city's most elegant historic home open to the public, and its grand salon is one of the most elaborately decorated rooms in any antebellum home in Tennessee. Belmont Mansion was originally built as a summer home, yet no expense was spared in its construction. On your tour of the mansion, you'll see rooms filled with period antiques, artwork, and marble statues.

Fun Facts Make Mine a Shower

Portly President Howard Taft once got stuck in a bathtub at Belle Meade Plantation while visiting Nashville. The subsequent installation of a shower at Belle Meade prompted Taft to have a shower installed at the White House.

Tips Shutterbugs, Take Note

Unlike at many museums and historic mansions, photography *is* permitted inside the Belmont Mansion. So click away!

New updates include the restoration of the master bedroom suite, which has never been open to the public. Tentatively scheduled to open by the end of 2010, the suite will be the mansion's most elaborate, with original furniture and wallpaper, featuring a French scenic of Telemachus on the island of Calypso. This museum also has an excellent gift shop full of reproduction period pieces. Allow at least 90 minutes to tour the mansion.

1900 Belmont Blvd. ✆ **615/460-5459.** www.belmontmansion.com. Admission $10 adults, $9 seniors, $3 children 6–12, free for children 5 and under. Mon–Sat 10am–4pm; Sun 1–4pm. (Last tour starts at 3:15pm.) Closed all major holidays. Take Wedgewood Ave. off 21st Ave. S. (an extension of Broadway), turn right on Magnolia Ave., left on 18th Ave. S., then left on Acklen.

Fort Nashborough Though it's much smaller than the original, this reconstruction of Nashville's first settlement includes several buildings that faithfully reproduce what life in this frontier outpost was like in the late 18th century. The current fort looks oddly out of place in modern downtown Nashville, but if you're interested in Tennessee's early settlers, this site is worth a brief look. Allow 30 minutes or more if you've got kids who want to play here.

170 First Ave. N. (btw. Church and Commerce). No phone. Free admission. Daily 9am–4pm. At the edge of Riverfront Park, on the banks of the Cumberland River.

The Hermitage ★ Though you may not know it, you probably see an image of one of Nashville's most famous citizens dozens of times every week. Whose face pops up so frequently? It's Andrew Jackson's. His visage appears on the $20 bill, and he's the man who built The Hermitage, a stately Southern plantation home. Jackson moved to Tennessee in 1788 and became a prosecuting attorney. He served as the state's first congressman and later as a senator and judge. However, it was during the War of 1812 that he gained his greatest public acclaim as the general who led American troops in the Battle of New Orleans. His role in that battle helped Jackson win the presidency in 1828 and again in 1832. Though the Hermitage now displays a classic Greek Revival facade, this is its third incarnation. Originally built in the Federal style in 1821, it was expanded and remodeled in 1831, and acquired its current appearance in 1836. Recordings that describe each room and section of the grounds accompany tours through the mansion and around it. In addition to the main house, you'll also visit the kitchen, the smokehouse, the garden, Jackson's tomb, an original log cabin, the spring house (a cool storage house built over a spring), and, nearby, the Old Hermitage Church and Tulip Grove mansion. You can tour the museum and grounds in a few hours—or linger here for an entire day.

Old Hickory Blvd., Nashville. ✆ **615/889-2941.** www.thehermitage.com. Admission $17 adults, $14 seniors, $11 students 13–18; $7 children 6–12, free for children 5 and under. Apr–Oct 15 daily 8:30am–5pm; Oct 16–Mar 9am–4:30pm. Closed Thanksgiving, Dec 25, and 3rd week of Jan. Take I-40 east to exit 221, then head north 4 miles.

The Parthenon Centennial Park, as the name implies, was built for the Tennessee Centennial Exposition of 1897, and this full-size replica of the Athens Parthenon was the exposition's centerpiece. The original structure was only meant to be temporary, however, and, by 1921, the building, which had become a Nashville landmark, was in an advanced state of deterioration. In that year, the city undertook reconstruction of its Parthenon, and, by 1931, a new, permanent building stood in Centennial Park. The building now duplicates the floor plan of the original Parthenon in Greece. Inside stands the 42-foot-tall statue of Athena Parthenos, the goddess of wisdom, prudent warfare, and the arts. Newly gilded with 8 pounds of gold leaf, she is the tallest indoor sculpture in the country.

In addition to this impressive statue, there are original plaster castings of the famous Elgin marbles—bas-reliefs that once decorated the pediment of the Parthenon. Inside the air-conditioned galleries, you'll find an excellent collection of 19th- and 20th-century American art. The Parthenon's two pairs of bronze doors, which weigh in at 7½ tons per door, are considered the largest matching bronze doors in the world. Allow about 30 minutes.

Centennial Park, West End Ave. (at West End and 25th aves.). © **615/862-8431.** www.nashville.gov/parthenon. Admission $6 adults, $3.50 seniors and children 4–17, free for children 3 and under. Tues–Sat 9am–4:30pm (Apr–Sept also Sun 12:30–4:30pm, except Sun after Labor Day.)

Tennessee State Capitol The Tennessee State Capitol, completed in 1859, is a classically proportioned Greek Revival building that sits on a hill on the north side of downtown Nashville. The capitol is constructed of local Tennessee limestone and marble that slaves and convict laborers quarried and cut. Other notable features include the 19th-century style and furnishings of several rooms in the building, a handful of ceiling frescoes, and many ornate details. President and Mrs. James K. Polk are both buried on the capitol's east lawn. You can pick up a guide to the capitol at the Tennessee State Museum. It won't take long to admire it from the outside.

Charlotte Ave. (btw. Sixth and Seventh aves.). © **615/741-2692.** Free admission. Mon–Fri 9am–5pm. Closed all state holidays.

Travellers Rest Plantation & Museum Built in 1799, Travellers Rest, as its name suggests, once offered gracious Southern hospitality to travelers passing through a land that had only recently been settled. Judge John Overton (who, along with Andrew Jackson and General James Winchester, founded the city of Memphis) built Travellers Rest. Overton also served as a political advisor to Jackson when he ran for president. Among the period furnishings you'll see in this restored Federal-style farmhouse is the state's largest public collection of pre-1840 Tennessee-made furniture. Allow an hour to tour the museum, more if you want to wander the grounds and outbuildings.

Going to Church

With more than 700 churches, dozens of seminaries, and numerous Christian-music-publishing companies based in Nashville, it's easy to see how Music City got its other best-known nicknames: "The Buckle of the Bible Belt" and "The Protestant Vatican." Among the organizations with headquarters here are the Southern Baptist Convention, the United Methodist Church, the National Baptist Convention, the National Association of Free Will Baptists, the Gideons International, the Gospel Music Association, and Thomas Nelson, the world's largest producer of Bibles.

636 Farrell Pkwy. ✆ **615/832-8197.** www.travellersrestplantation.org. Admission $10 adults, $9 seniors, $5 students 13–18, $3 children 6–12, free for children 5 and under. Mon–Sat 10am–4pm; Sun 1–4pm. Closed Sun in Mar and Easter, Thanksgiving, Dec 24–25, and Dec. 31. Take I-65 to exit 78B (Harding Place West), go west to Franklin Pike, turn left, and then follow the signs.

MUSEUMS

Adventure Science Center Kids It's hard to say which exhibit kids like the most at the Center. There are just so many fun interactive displays to choose from in this modern, hands-on museum. Though the museum is primarily meant to be an entertaining way to introduce children to science, it can also be fun for adults. Kids of all ages can learn about technology, the environment, physics, and health as they roam the museum pushing buttons and turning knobs. The latest craze is the BLUE MAX, a flight-simulator thrill-ride that lets riders perform daring aerial maneuvers from the safety of a cockpit. In the **Sudekum Planetarium,** there are regular shows that take you exploring through the universe. Allow 2 hours.

800 Ft. Negley Blvd. ✆ **615/862-5160.** www.adventuresci.com. Admission $11 adults, $9 seniors and children 3–12, free for children 2 and under. BLUE MAX rides cost an additional $5. Mon–Sat 10am–5pm (till 7pm Fri–Sat Memorial Day–Labor Day); Sun 12:30–5:30pm. Closed Thanksgiving, Dec 25, and Jan 1. Fourth Ave. S. to Oak St., to Bass St. to Fort Negley.

Cheekwood Botanical Garden & Museum of Art ★★ Kids In celebration of its 50th anniversary, Cheekwood will host a blockbuster exhibition through October 2010, "Chihuly at Cheekwood." The work of world-renowned glass artist Dale Chihuly will feature thousands of hand-blown glass sculptures on display throughout Cheekwood's botanical gardens and ponds. Once a private estate, Cheekwood is situated in a 55-acre park that's divided into several formal gardens and naturally landscaped areas. The museum itself is housed in a Georgian-style mansion, with such features as a lapis lazuli fireplace mantel. Within the building are collections of 19th- and 20th-century American art, Worcester porcelains, antique silver serving pieces, Asian snuff bottles, and a good deal of period furniture. The grounds are designed for strolling, and there are numerous gardens, including Japanese, herb, perennial, as well as greenhouses full of orchids. Kids will enjoy romping around the grassy meadows on the museum grounds. Don't miss the glass bridge that rewards hikers along the wooded sculpture trail. You'll also find a gift shop and good restaurant, The Pineapple Room, on the grounds. Allow a couple of hours to tour the museum, or up to a full day if you plan to explore the grounds and garden.

1200 Forrest Park Dr. (8 miles southwest of downtown). ✆ **615/356-8000.** www.cheekwood.org. Admission $10 adults, $8 seniors, $5 college students and children 6–17, free for children 5 and under; household ticket $30. Tues–Sat 9:30am–4:30pm (also Memorial Day and Labor Day Mon); Sun 11am–4:30pm. Closed Thanksgiving, Dec 25, Jan 1, and 2nd Sat in June. Take West End Ave. to Belle Meade Blvd. and turn left; then left at Page Road and left on Forrest Park Dr.

Frist Center for the Visual Arts ★★★ Kids Opened in 2001, the Frist Center for the Visual Arts brings world-class art exhibits to the historic downtown post office building. The nonprofit center does not maintain a permanent collection but rather presents exhibitions from around the globe. Upcoming exhibits include "The Birth of Impressionism: Masterpieces from the Musée d'Orsay," with paintings by Cezanne, Monet, Renoir, and others (Oct 15, 2010–Jan 23, 2011). In addition, world-renowned glass artist Dale Chihuly will be the focus of an exhibition opening May 14, 2010, and running until January 2, 2011. Upstairs, the Martin **ArtQuest Gallery** ★ encourages visitors to

Fun Facts Planes, Trains & Automobiles

Constructed during the Depression, Nashville's main post office is home to the Frist Center for the Visual Arts. Classical and Art Deco architectural styles are prominent within the marble and gray-pink granite building, which is on the National Register of Historic Places. Intricate grillwork celebrates icons of American progress: an airplane, a locomotive, a ship, and an automobile. Among other achievements represented in the icons: scientific research (microscope, test tube, and flask), harvesting (sheaf of wheat and sickle), industry (cogwheels), publishing (book press), sowing (hand plow), metalwork (hammer and anvil), the pursuit of knowledge (lamp of learning resting on books), and nautical endeavors (dolphin and propeller).

explore a range of art experiences through more than 30 interactive multimedia stations. Creative kids and likeminded adults could spend hours here.

The Frist is free to visitors 18 and under, making it an excellent value. Seniors get half-price admission the third Monday of each month, when musical activities such as singalongs are held. And on Thursday and Friday nights, college students are admitted free.

919 Broadway. ✆ **615/244-3340.** www.fristcenter.org. Admission $8.50 adults, $7.50 seniors, free for children 18 and under. (Admission prices may change for special exhibitions.) Mon–Wed 10am–5:30pm; Thurs–Fri 10am–9pm; Sat 10am–5:30pm; Sun 1–5:30pm. Closed Thanksgiving, Dec 25, and Jan 1. Btw. Ninth and 10th Aves. next to the Union Station Hotel.

Lane Motor Museum Housed in a former large bakery building, this unexpected find features about 150 unusual cars, including amphibious, alternative-fuel and military vehicles, minicars, and motorcycles. Most are European vehicles from the 1950s through the 1970s. Cars are arranged by country (Austria, Germany, Great Britain, Italy, Japan, and Sweden, among others). The museum boasts the largest collection of Czechoslovakian cars outside of Europe. Whatever the vehicles' country of origin, mechanics and car buffs alike will enjoy ogling the candy-colored Citroëns and one-of-a-kind prototypes, such as a 1928 Martin Aerodynamic Car, and a 1946 Hewson Rocket. More than just pretty to look at, the Lane also has a practical mission: to keep all the cars in its collection, from Fiats to Lamborghinis, in good running order. Give yourself about an hour and a half here.

702 Murfreesboro Pike ✆ **615/742-7445.** www.lanemotormuseum.com. Admission $7 adults, $5 seniors, $2 children 6–17, free for children 5 and under. Thurs–Mon 10am–5pm. Closed Thanksgiving, Dec 25, and Jan 1.

Tennessee State Museum Kids Kids always rush to find the 3,000-year-old Egyptian mummy on display, but along the way maybe they will gain a better understanding of Tennessee history during a visit to this museum beneath the Tennessee Performing Arts Center. The museum showcases Native American artifacts as well as objects from 18th-century century pioneer life. You'll see Daniel Boone's rifle and a powder horn that once belonged to Davy Crockett, along with exhibits on presidents Andrew Jackson and James K. Polk.

Visitors may view pre–Civil War artifacts, including full-scale replicas of old buildings and period rooms, a log cabin, a water-driven mill, a woodworking shop, an 18th-century print shop, and an 1855 parlor. Although the lower level of the museum is devoted mostly to the Civil War and Reconstruction, exhibits change; visitors are advised to call ahead to see what is currently on display. One block west, on Union Street, you'll find the museum's Military Museum, which houses displays on Tennessee's military activity from the Spanish-American through Vietnam wars. Allow 2 to 3 hours.

Fifth Ave. (btw. Union and Deaderick Sts.). ✆ **800/407-4324** or 615/741-2692. www.tnmuseum.org. Free admission; donations encouraged. Tues–Sat 10am–5pm; Sun 1–5pm (except Military Museum). Closed Easter, Thanksgiving, Dec 25, and Jan 1.

PARKS, PLAZAS & BOTANICAL GARDENS

To celebrate the 200th anniversary of Tennessee statehood, Nashville constructed the impressive **Bicentennial Capitol Mall State Park** (✆ **615/741-5280**), north of the state capitol. The mall, which begins just north of James Robertson Parkway and extends (again, north) to Jefferson Street between Sixth and Seventh avenues, is a beautifully landscaped open space that conjures up the countryside with its limestone rockeries and plantings of native plants. As such, it is a very pleasant place for a leisurely stroll. The western edge of the park offers fantastic views of the capitol.

However, this mall is far more than just a park. It is also a 19-acre open-air exhibition of Tennessee history and geography and a frame for the capitol, which sits atop the hill at the south end of the mall. Also at the south end of the mall is a 200-foot-long granite map of the state, and behind this are a gift shop/visitor center, a Tennessee rivers fountain, and an amphitheater used for summer concerts. Along Sixth Avenue, you'll find a walkway of Tennessee counties, with information on each county (beneath the plaques, believe it or not, are time capsules). Along Seventh Avenue is the Pathway of History, a wall outlining the state's 200-year history. Within the mall, there are also several memorials.

Fun Facts African-American Heritage

Fisk University was founded in 1866 as a liberal arts institution committed to educating newly freed slaves. Prominent 20th-century cultural figures, such as educator W. E. B. DuBois, artist Aaron Douglas, and poet Nikki Giovanni, attended the school. Fisk is perhaps best known for its Jubilee Singers, an African-American singing group that preserved spirituals, or slave songs, from extinction. The choir's 1873 tour of the U.S. and Europe helped finance the construction of Fisk University. **Jubilee Hall,** one of the oldest structures on the campus, is a Victorian Gothic gem listed on the register of National Historic Landmarks. Now used as a dormitory, the building houses a floor-to-ceiling portrait of the original Jubilee Singers, commissioned by Queen Victoria of England as a gift to Fisk. In another building, a neo-Romanesque former church that dates back to 1888, is the **Carl Van Vechten Gallery,** which includes the prestigious Alfred Stieglitz Collection of modern American and European art. Works by Picasso, Cezanne, Renoir, Toulouse-Lautrec, and O'Keeffe are among the unexpected treasures here. The museum is generally open every day (closed Sun and school holidays), but call ahead to be sure. For more information, contact **Fisk University Galleries,** 1000 17th Ave. N. (✆ **615/329-8720;** galleries@fisk.edu).

Known together as "The Warner Parks" (✆ **615/370-8051;** www.nashville.gov), Edwin Warner Park and Percy Warner Park offer beautiful scenery, miles of hiking and equestrian trails, picnic areas, and outdoor recreation sites. **Percy Warner Park** (2500 Old Hickory Blvd.) is the crown jewel of Nashville green spaces. Named for Percy Warner, a local businessman and avid outdoorsman, the wooded hills and rolling meadows extend for more than 2,000 acres. Though popular with bicyclists, be aware that they must share the winding, paved roads with vehicular traffic. Perfect for picnics and other outdoor pursuits, the park offers clean shelters, restrooms, and even a 27-hole golf course. **Edwin Warner Park,** 50 Vaughn Rd. (on Old Hickory Blvd., near Hwy. 100), also has lovely picnic areas, scenic overlooks, and a dog park.

After visiting this park, it seems appropriate to take a stroll around **Centennial Park,** located on West End Avenue at 25th Avenue. This park, built for the 1896 centennial celebration, is best known as the site of the Parthenon, but also has many acres of lawns, colorful playground equipment, 100-year-old shade trees, and a small lake.

See also the entry for **Cheekwood Botanical Garden & Museum of Art** on p. 99.

NEIGHBORHOODS

The District

The District, encompassing several streets of restored downtown warehouses and other old buildings, is ground zero for the Nashville nightlife scene. It's divided into three areas. Second Avenue between Broadway and Union Street, the heart of the District, was originally Nashville's warehouse area and served riverboats on the Cumberland River. Today, most of the old warehouses have been renovated and now house a variety of restaurants, nightclubs, souvenir shops, and other shops. Anchoring Second Avenue at the corner of Broadway is the **Hard Rock Cafe,** and a few doors up the street is the **Wildhorse Saloon,** a massive country music dance hall. Along Broadway between the Cumberland River and Fifth Avenue, you'll find several of country music's most important sites, including the **Ryman Auditorium** (home of the ***Grand Ole Opry*** for many years), **Tootsie's Orchid Lounge** (where Opry performers often dropped by for a drink), **Gruhn Guitars,** and the **Ernest Tubb Record Shop.** Along this stretch of Broadway, you'll also find **Robert's Western World,** the entrance to the **Gaylord Entertainment Center,** and the **Nashville Convention & Visitors Bureau Visitors Center.** The third area of the District is Printer's Alley, which is off Church Street between Third and Fourth avenues. Though not as lively as it once was during the days of Prohibition and speakeasies, the alley is an interesting place for an afternoon or early-evening stroll. At night, a few clubs still offer live music.

Music Row

Located along 16th and 17th avenues, between Demonbreun Street and Grand Avenue, Music Row is the very heart of the country music recording industry and is home to dozens of recording studios and record-company offices. The neighborhood is a combination of old restored homes and modern buildings that hint at the vast amounts of money generated by the country music industry. This is one of the best areas in town for spotting country music stars, so keep your eyes peeled. Anchoring the Music Row "turnaround" (a circular

Long Live Vinyl

United Record Pressing, a vinyl pressing plant in downtown Nashville, is one of only four remaining vinyl manufacturers in the nation. It opened in 1949.

roadway at the entrance to the area) is ***Musica.*** The 40-foot-tall bronze sculpture of nine nude figures was considered a bit shocking when it was unveiled in the fall of 2003. After all, Nashville is considered "the buckle of the Bible Belt."

The Gulch

The Gulch is a rapidly growing area just south of downtown that's being developed at a furious pace. An increasing cluster of buzz-worthy restaurants, such as **Watermark Restaurant** (p. 69) and **Cantina Laredo** (p. 69), have ramped up the area's cachet with the in-crowd. Construction of $250,000 condominium and loft towers and other mixed-use high-rises is proceeding at breakneck pace. Retail has followed, with new eateries, clothing stores, and nightspots adding to the Gulch's urban appeal.

Eighth Avenue South & 12th Avenue South

While Eighth Avenue boasts the biggest cluster of antiques shops and consignment stores in the area just south of downtown, a few blocks away lies another unique neighborhood that's off the beaten tourist track. Known as 12th Avenue South, the area has undergone a refurbishment over the past decade, as home owners have moved in and spruced up their cute bungalows and established a real community presence here. The area, roughly bounded by Linden and Kirkwood avenues, is also home to several commendable restaurants and boutiques. There are a couple of clothing stores, including **Serendipity Emporium** and **Katy K's Ranch Dressing.** Start your sojourn into 12th Avenue South with a bite to eat at **Mirror** (p. 72) or **MAFIAoZA's** (p. 73), browse the boutiques, and end the trip with a gourmet Popsicle from **Las Paletas** (p. 73).

East Nashville

If you're looking for an antidote to the West End's pricey restaurants, college crowds, and frenetic social scene, look east. Across the Cumberland River from downtown Nashville lies the endearing community of East Nashville. A bit more affordable and a lot more laid back, East Nashville is a friendly and diverse neighborhood beloved for its bistros and bars, including **Margot Café & Bar** (p. 82), **Family Wash** (p. 133), and **Lipstick Lounge** (p. 134). From downtown, take the Woodland Street bridge east and follow it a mile or so to reach the heart of the area.

Music Valley

The **Gaylord Opryland Resort** (p. 59) is a destination unto itself. Book a stay here, and you might never venture beyond the acres of parking lots surrounding the massive hotel complex. Opryland and the adjacent Opry Mills mall are the anchors for this entire geographic area, collectively known as Music Valley. However, aside from these two megaplexes, there is not much variety here. A few country-music souvenir shops and a couple of live-music venues are interspersed between chain hotels and restaurants. Increasingly, Music Valley seems to be attracting an older clientele—including escorted tour-bus groups. The area caters to this demographic. Music Valley has its advantages if you just want to shop and to wander the vast corridors of the Gaylord Opryland Resort. If the urge strikes, from here you can book tours to other Nashville attractions, including the Wildhorse Saloon and Ryman Auditorium downtown, and the *General Jackson* Showboat.

A DAY AT THE ZOO

Nashville Zoo at Grassmere (Kids) This 80-acre zoo just south of downtown has it all, from giraffes, elephants, and alligators to meerkats, rainbow-colored lorikeets, and

African wild hogs. In the naturalistic habitats, you'll see river otters, bison, elk, black bear, gray wolves, bald eagles, and cougars, as well as other smaller animals. In the past 2 years, the zoo has added Eurasian lynx, African-crested porcupines, and giant anteaters. A new flamingo exhibit is also in the works. In the park's aviary, you can walk among many of the state's songbirds, and at the Cumberland River exhibit expect to see fish, reptiles, and amphibians. Kids can ride wood-carved cougars and other critters on the zoo's colorful new carousel, and frolic under a new water feature in the Jungle Gym playground. Allow 2 to 3 hours. ***Tip:*** To beat the crowds, try visiting the zoo during off-peak times of the day. Best bets are any weekday around 1pm, or Sunday morning at 9am.

3777 Nolensville Pike. ✆ **615/833-1534.** www.nashvillezoo.org. Admission $14 adults, $12 seniors, $9 children 3–12, free for children 2 and under. Parking $2. Mar 15–Oct 15 daily 9am–6pm; Oct 16–Mar 14 daily 9am–4pm. Closed Thanksgiving, Dec 25, and Jan 1. Follow Fourth Ave. south to Nolensville Pike to U.S. 11 and turn on Zoo Rd.

3 ESPECIALLY FOR KIDS

Even if your child is not a little Tim McGraw or Faith Hill in training, Nashville is full of things for kids to see and do. In addition to the attractions listed below, see also the listings in this chapter for **Cheekwood Botanical Garden & Museum of Art** (p. 99), **Adventure Science Center** (p. 99), the **Frist Center for the Visual Arts** (p. 99), the **Nashville Zoo at Grassmere** (p. 103), and the **Tennessee State Museum** (p. 100).

Grand Old Golf & Games/Valley Park GoKarts With three miniature-golf courses, a go-kart track, and family game room, this place, located near the Gaylord Opryland Resort, is sure to be a hit with your kids. You can easily spend the whole day here.

2444 Music Valley Dr. ✆ **615/871-4701.** www.grandoldgolf.net. Fees 1 course $7.50, 2 courses $8.50, 3 courses $9.50; rates for children 10 and under are $3.50, $4, and $4.50. Fees for go-karts $7 for single seat, $8 for double seat. May–Sept Mon–Thurs 10am–10pm, Fri–Sat 10am–11pm, Sun noon–11pm; Oct–Nov daily noon–9pm; Dec–Feb daily noon–5pm; Mar–Apr daily 11am–10pm. All open hours are weather-permitting. Closed Thanksgiving, Dec 25, and Jan 1. Take Briley Pkwy. to McGavock Pike to Music Valley Dr.

Nashville Shores Tucked on the pristine shores of Percy Priest Lake, about 10 miles outside Nashville, this massive water park and family recreation destination offers white-sand beaches, jet-ski and boat rentals, eight water slides, and even kayaking areas. In the summer, Dive-In Movies are a popular way to stay cool; you float in a lagoonlike pool while watching action on a 40-foot inflatable screen. Other activities include lake cruises, miniature golf, volleyball, basketball, and horseshoes. Allow 3 to 4 hours here.

Fun Facts Sand-Castle Nirvana

Not only does Nashville Shores boast what it dubs the world's largest free-style slide—it's four stories (170 feet) high—but the outdoor recreation attraction also has an 8,000-square-foot beach-style sandbox. The critical issue of sand wetness is constantly monitored, ensuring the best possible texture and consistency for building sand castles.

Tips Picnic It

To reserve a picnic shelter in any of Nashville's city parks, call ✆ **615/862-8408.**

4001 Bell Road. ✆ **615/889-7050.** www.nashvilleshores.com. Mon–Sat 10am–6pm; Sun 11am–6pm. Admission $25 adults 48 inches and taller; $18 for 47 inches and shorter, seniors 55 and older, and military; children 2 and under free. After 3pm, general admission is half price. Parking $5.

Wave Country and Skatepark Skate, bike, or speed-slide in the water. It's your choice at these two parks, operated by the Nashville Parks and Recreation Department. Located just off Briley Parkway at Two Rivers Park and Golf Course, Wave Country has a huge freshwater wave pool as well as a wave-free pool, three water flumes, and two speed slides. The Skatepark allows skateboards, in-line skates, and pegged BMX bikes; helmets are required, and protective knee pads are recommended. So pick your park, pack a picnic, and make an afternoon of it.

2320 Two Rivers Pkwy. (off Briley Pkwy.). ✆ **615/885-1052.** www.nashville.gov. Wave Country Mon–Thurs 10am–5pm (till 6pm Memorial Day–Labor Day); Fri–Sat 10am–6pm; Sun 11am–6pm. Admission $12 adults, $10 children 5–12, free for children 4 and under; half price for children after 4pm.

4 STROLLING AROUND NASHVILLE

If you'd like a bit more information on some of these sites or would like to do a slightly different downtown walk, pick up a copy of the *Nashville City Walk* brochure at the Visitors Center in the Gaylord Entertainment Center. This brochure, produced by the Metropolitan Historical Commission, outlines a walk marked with a green line painted on downtown sidewalks. Along the route are informational plaques and green metal silhouettes of various characters from history.

WALKING TOUR DOWNTOWN NASHVILLE

Start: Riverfront Park at the intersection of Broadway and First Avenue. (There's a public parking lot here.)

Finish: Printer's Alley.

Time: Anywhere from 3 to 8 hours, depending on how much time you spend in the museums, shopping, or dining.

Best Times: Tuesday through Friday, when both the Tennessee State Museum and the Tennessee State Capitol are open to the public.

Worst Times: Sunday, Monday, and holidays, when a number of places are closed. Or anytime the Titans have a home football game, which makes traffic and parking a mess.

Though Nashville is a city of the New South and sprawls in all directions with suburbs full of office parks and shopping malls, it still has a downtown where you can do a bit of exploring on foot. Within the downtown area are the three distinct areas that make up the District, a historic area containing many late-19th-century commercial buildings that have been preserved and now house restaurants, clubs, and interesting shops. Because Nashville is the state capital, the downtown area also has many impressive government office buildings.

Start your tour at the intersection of Broadway and First Avenue, on the banks of the Cumberland River, at:

❶ Riverfront Park

The park was built as part of Nashville's bicentennial celebration, and it's where the Nashville trolleys start their circuits around downtown and out to Music Row. If you grow tired of walking at any time during your walk, just look for a trolley stop and ride the free trolley back to the park.

Walk north along the river to:

❷ Fort Nashborough

This is a reconstruction of the 1780 fort that served as the first white settlement in this area.

Continue up First Avenue to Union Street and turn left. Across the street is the:

❸ Metropolitan Courthouse

This imposing building, which also houses the Nashville City Hall, was built in 1937. It incorporates many classic Greek architectural details. Of particular interest are the bronze doors, the etched-glass panels above the doors, and the lobby murals. At the information booth in the lobby, you can pick up a brochure detailing the building's many design elements.

If you now head back down Second Avenue, you'll find yourself in the:

❹ Second Avenue Historic District

Between Union Avenue and Broadway are numerous Victorian commercial buildings, most of which have now been restored. Much of the architectural detail is near the tops of the buildings, so keep your eyes trained upward.

TAKE A BREAK

Second Avenue has several excellent restaurants where you can stop for lunch or a drink. **The Old Spaghetti Factory,** 160 Second Ave. N. (✆ **615/254-9010**), is a cavernous place filled with Victorian antiques. There's even a trolley car parked in the middle of the main dining room. A couple of doors down is **B. B. King's Blues Club,** at 152 Second Ave. N. (✆ **615/256-2727**), a bluesy bar with a juke-joint atmosphere where you can sample Southern food or grab a burger.

Note: There are several interesting antiques and crafts stores along Second Avenue.

A few doors down from The Old Spaghetti Factory you'll find:

❺ Wildhorse Saloon

This is Nashville's hottest country nightspot. In the daylight hours, you can snap a picture of the comical, cowboy-booted horse statue near the front entrance.

Also along this stretch of the street is the:

❻ Market Street Emporium

The emporium holds a collection of specialty shops.

At the corner of Second Avenue and Broadway, turn right. Between Third and Fourth avenues, watch for:

❼ Hatch Show Print

The oldest poster shop in the United States still prints its posters on an old-fashioned letterpress printer. The most popular posters are those advertising the *Grand Ole Opry.*

Cross Fourth Avenue and you'll come to:

❽ Gruhn Guitars

This is the most famous guitar shop in Nashville; it specializes in used and vintage guitars.

Walk up Fourth Avenue less than a block and you will come to the new main entrance of:

❾ Ryman Auditorium

The *Grand Ole Opry* was held here from 1943 to 1974. The building was originally built as a tabernacle to host evangelical revival meetings, but because of its good acoustics and large seating capacity, it became a popular setting for theater and music performances.

After leaving the Ryman Auditorium, walk back down to the corner of Broadway and Fourth Avenue.

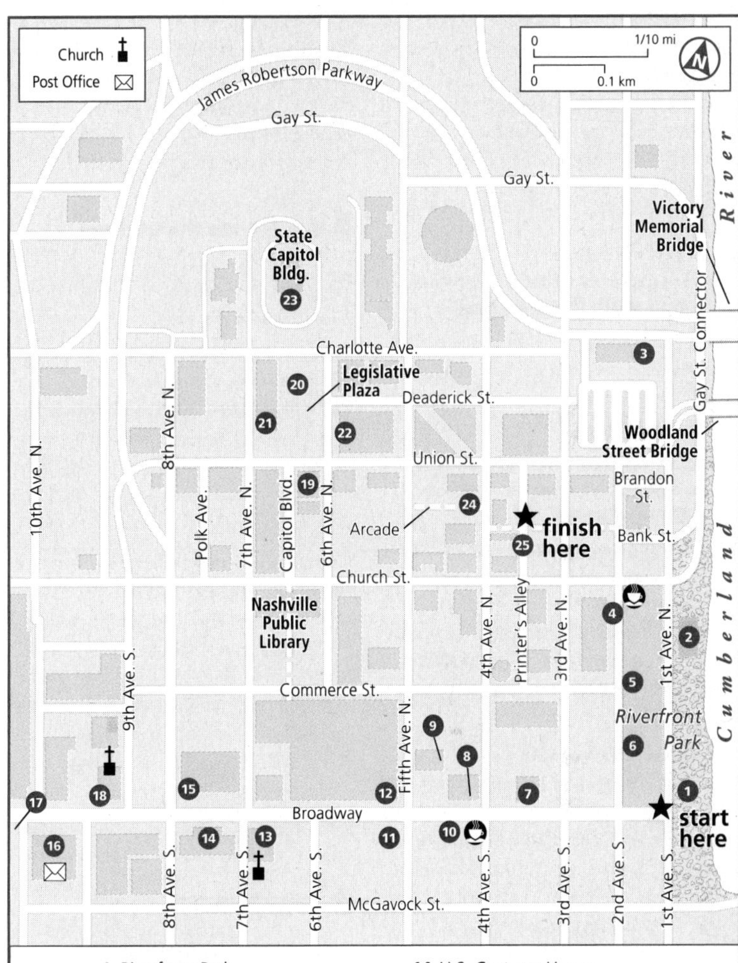

1 Riverfront Park
2 Fort Nashborough
3 Metropolitan Courthouse
4 Second Avenue Historic District
5 Wildhorse Saloon
6 Market Street Emporium
7 Hatch Show Print
8 Gruhn Guitars
9 Ryman Auditorium
10 Ernest Tubb Record Shop
11 Sommet Center
12 Tootsie's Orchid Lounge
13 First Baptist Church
14 U.S. Customs House
15 Hume-Fogg High School
16 Frist Center for the Visual Arts
17 Union Station–A Wyndham Historic Hotel
18 Christ Episcopal Church
19 Hermitage Hotel
20 Legislative Plaza
21 War Memorial Building
22 Tennessee State Museum
23 Tennessee State Capitol
24 Nashville Arcade
25 Printer's Alley

TAKE A BREAK
If you didn't stop for lunch on Second Avenue, now would be a good time. On the opposite side of the street from the Ryman, at Fourth and Broadway, is **The Merchants** restaurant, at 401 Broadway (✆ **615/254-1892**), a favorite Nashville power-lunch spot. The atmosphere is sophisticated and the cuisine is New American and New Southern.

In the same block as The Merchants, you'll find the:

⑩ Ernest Tubb Record Shop

This store was once the home of the *Midnite Jamboree,* a country music radio show that took place after the *Grand Ole Opry* was over on Saturday nights.

Continue up the block to the corner of Fifth Avenue and you'll come to the main entrance of the new:

⑪ Sommet Center

The Sommet Center is a sports and entertainment venue that also houses the Nashville Convention & Visitors Bureau Visitors Center. If you haven't already stopped in for information or to check out the gift shop or pick up a map, now would be a good time.

Back across Broadway, you'll find:

⑫ Tootsie's Orchid Lounge

Grand Ole Opry musicians used to duck in here, one of the more famous bars in Nashville, before, during, and after the show at the Ryman. There's live country music all day long at Tootsie's.

From this corner, head up Broadway, and at the corner of Seventh Avenue, you'll find the:

⑬ First Baptist Church

This modern building incorporates a Victorian Gothic church tower built between 1884 and 1886. The church's congregation wanted a new church but didn't want to give up the beautiful old tower. This is the compromise that was reached.

Across Seventh Avenue is the:

⑭ U.S. Customs House

Now leased as private office space, this Victorian Gothic building was built in 1877 and displays fine stonework and friezes. The imposing structure, with its soaring tower and arched windows, could be in any European city.

Directly across the street is:

⑮ Hume-Fogg High School

Built between 1912 and 1916, the building incorporates elements of English Tudor and Gothic design.

Two blocks farther up Broadway, you'll see a decidedly different style of architecture, the:

⑯ Frist Center for the Visual Arts

This breathtaking art museum is housed in the historic U.S. Post Office building, designed with elements of both neoclassical and Art Deco architectural styling.

The post office shares a parking lot with:

⑰ Union Station Hotel

This Victorian Romanesque Revival building was built in 1900 as Nashville's main passenger railroad station, but, in 1986, it was renovated and reopened as a luxury hotel. The stone exterior walls incorporate many fine carvings, and the lobby is one of the most elegant historic spaces in Nashville.

Head back the way you came and cross over to the opposite side of Broadway at Ninth Avenue. Here you'll find:

⑱ Christ Episcopal Church

Constructed between 1887 and 1892, the building is in the Victorian Gothic style and is complete with gargoyles. This church also has Tiffany stained-glass windows.

Continue back down Broadway and, at Seventh Avenue, turn left and walk up to Union Street and turn right. In 1 block, you'll come to the:

⑲ Hermitage Hotel

This is Nashville's last grand old hotel The lobby exudes Beaux Arts extravagance, with a stained-glass skylight and marble columns and floor.

Across Union Street from the Hermitage Hotel is:

20 Legislative Plaza

This large public plaza is a popular lunch spot for downtown office workers.

Fronting this plaza is the:

21 War Memorial Building

This neoclassical building was built in 1925 to honor soldiers who died in World War I. The centerpiece is an atrium holding a large statue titled *Victory.* This building also houses the Tennessee State Museum Military Branch.

On the opposite side of the plaza is the:

22 Tennessee State Museum

In the basement of the same building that houses the Tennessee Performing Arts Center, this museum contains an extensive and well-displayed collection of artifacts pertaining to Tennessee history.

Returning to the Legislative Plaza and continuing to the north across Charlotte Street will bring you to the:

23 Tennessee State Capitol

This Greek Revival building was built between 1845 and 1859. Be sure to take a look inside, where you'll find many beautiful architectural details and works of art.

If you walk back across the Legislative Plaza and take a left on Union Street and then a right on Fifth Avenue (cross to the far side of the street), you'll come to the west entrance of the:

24 Nashville Arcade

This covered shopping arcade was built in 1903 and is modeled after an arcade in Italy. Only a few such arcades remain in the United States, and, unfortunately, no one has yet breathed new life into this one. Still, you can mail a letter here or buy a bag of fresh-roasted peanuts.

Walk through the arcade and continue across Fourth Avenue. The alley in front of you leads to:

25 Printer's Alley

For more than a century, this has been a center for evening entertainment. Today, things are much tamer than they once were, but you can still find several nightclubs featuring live music.

5 ORGANIZED TOURS

CITY & HOMES-OF-THE-STARS TOURS

Gray Line Nashville, 2416 Music Valley Dr. (✆ **800/251-1864** or 615/883-5555; www.graylinenashville.com), offers more than half a dozen different tours ranging in length from 3½ hours to a full day. On the popular 3½-hour tour of the stars' homes, you'll ride past the current or former houses and mansions of such chart-toppers as Hank Williams, Dolly Parton, Trisha Yearwood, Martina McBride, and Alan Jackson. Other themed tours focus exclusively on historical sites, honky-tonks, and nightlife. Adult tour prices range from $40 for the "Homes of the Country Stars" bus tour to $90 for a dinner cruise on the *General Jackson* Showboat.

Johnny Walker Tours, 2416 Music Valley Dr. (✆ **800/722-1524** or 615/834-8585; www.johnnywalkertours.com), has merged with Gray Line Tours. However, the company still sells group tours and individual vacation packages.

For a fun and campy tour of Nashville aboard a gaudy pink bus, try **Nash-Trash Tours** (✆ **800/342-2132** or 615/226-7300; www.nashtrash.com), narrated by the spandex-clad "Jugg" sisters. Sheri Lynn and Brenda Kay dish the dirt on all your favorite country stars. Throw in a few risqué jokes, plenty of music, and a policy that allows passengers to bring aboard coolers (with alcohol, if desired), and it all makes for a trashy good time in Music City. Because the 90-minute tours can become rowdy, they're not advised for

Nashville Name Game

Can you identify these country stars and legends by their real first/last names?

Birth Name	Stage Name
Audrey Faith Perry	Faith Hill
Alvis Edgar	Buck Owens
Virginia Pugh	Patsy Cline
Eileen Regina Edwards	Shania Twain
Floyd Elliot Wray	Collin Raye
Waylon Albright	Shooter Jennings
Sarah Ophelia Colley Cannon	Minnie Pearl
Patricia Lynn	Trisha Yearwood
Maurice Woodward	Tex Ritter
Ernest Jennings Ford	Tennessee Ernie Ford
William Neal Browder	T. G. Sheppard
Anthony Graham	T. Graham Brown
Randy Bruce Traywick	Randy Travis
Patricia Lee Ramey	Patty Loveless
Ruby Blevins	Patsy Montana
Lonnie Melvin	Mel Tillis
Loretta Webb	Loretta Lynn
Loretta Lynn Morgan	Lorrie Morgan
James Cecil Dickens	Little Jimmy Dickens
Eileen Muriel Deason	Kitty Wells
Kathleen Alice	Kathy Mattea
Louis Marshall	Grandpa Jones
Troyal Brooks	Garth Brooks
Virginia Patterson Hensley	Patsy Cline
Brenda Gail Webb Gatzimos	Crystal Gayle

Bonus question: Which country star's middle name is also his wife's maiden name? **Answer:** Vince Grant Gill, who married Amy Grant.

Double bonus question: Which singer/songwriter named one of her daughters after Minnie Pearl? **Answer:** Amy Grant, who named her daughter Sarah Cannon Chapman.

young children (those under 13 are not allowed.) Hours vary, but generally speaking, tours are offered Tuesday through Saturday. Call in advance for current times and to make reservations, which are required. Tickets, which cost $32 for adults, $30 for seniors and ages 13 to 18, include tip for the bus driver but not 9.25% sales tax. (Rates are discounted in January). Bring plenty of extra cash if you want to buy any of the commemorative souvenirs the sisters hawk. ***Note:*** The bus is not wheelchair-accessible.

For groups such as family reunions, churches, and students who would like to learn more about the African-American history of Nashville, contact Bill Daniel at **Nashville Black Heritage Tours,** in nearby Smyrna, TN (✆ **615/890-8173**).

RIVERBOAT TOURS

The Gaylord Opryland Resort, 2800 Opryland Dr. (✆ **615/883-2211;** www.generaljackson.com), operates the paddle-wheeler—the ***General Jackson*** **Showboat** (✆ **615/458-3900**)—on the Cumberland River. Tours depart from a dock near the Gaylord Opryland Resort. At 300 feet long, the *General Jackson* Showboat recalls the days when riverboats were the most sophisticated way to travel. You go on this cruise for the paddle-wheeler experience, not necessarily for the food (not so great) and entertainment that go along with it. Choose from comedy-variety acts to those with live country music. During the summer, the Southern Nights Cruise offers a three-course dinner and dancing under the stars to live bands. Fares for this trip cost $73 for adults. Midday cruises are also available mid-April to mid-October and cost $45 for adults. Discounted rates are available for cruise only, or cruise and buffet only, without entertainment. In addition, special-event cruises with such themes as Valentine's Day, Mardi Gras, Tennessee Titans tailgating, and the holidays are offered year-round. Prices vary. Call for details.

6 OUTDOOR ACTIVITIES

BOAT RENTALS In the summer, pontoon boats can be rented at **Four Corners Marina,** on Percy Priest Lake, 4027 Lavergne Couchville Pike, Antioch (✆ **615/641-9523**). The grocery store sells bait but no longer sells tackle or fishing licenses. The gorgeous lake, only a few miles east of downtown, is surrounded by a series of parks, trees, and natural beauty.

At Kingston Springs, about 20 miles west of Nashville off I-40, you can rent canoes from **Tip-a-Canoe,** 1279 U.S. 70, at Harpeth River Bridge (✆ **800/550-5810** or 615/254-0836; www.tip-a-canoe.com), or bring your own. Canoe trips of varying lengths, from a couple of hours up to 5 days, can be arranged. Rates, which include paddles, life-jackets, cushions and the shuttle upriver to your chosen put-in point, start at $45 per canoe and go up to $125 for a 5-day trip. The Harpeth River is a meandering, scenic river of mostly Class I water with some Class II—and a few spots where you'll have to carry the canoe.

GOLF For many golfing visitors, Opryland's **Gaylord Springs Golf Links,** 18 Springhouse Lane (✆ **615/458-1730;** www.gaylordsprings.com), is a highlight. This par-72, 18-hole course is set on the bank of the Cumberland River. The course boasts not only challenging links, but also an antebellum-style clubhouse that would have made Rhett Butler feel right at home. Greens fees range from $35 to $75 for 18 holes. For the most serious enthusiasts, the Golf Institute at Gaylord Springs offers high-tech analysis of golfers' swings, two indoor hitting bays for year-round instruction, and on-site customized club fittings and repair workshop.

HORSEBACK RIDING If you want to go for a ride through the Tennessee hills, there are a couple of nearby places where you can rent a horse. **A Cowboy Town,** 3665 Knight Rd., Whites Creek, 7 miles north of downtown Nashville, is a Western-style family theme park. Admission, which is $38 per day for adults, includes stage shows, such as gunfights, hiking, hayrides, and horseback riding. The park is open only on weekends from May 1 through October 31. To make reservations by phone on weekdays, call ✆ **615/242-6201;** on weekends, call ✆ **615/876-1029.** Also visit www.acowboytown.com.

JuRo Stables, 735 Carver Lane, Mt. Juliet (✆ **615/773-7433;** www.jurostables.com), is located about 15 minutes from Nashville on I-40 east, at the Mt. Juliet exit, and charges $22 an hour ($44 for sunset and evening rides). In business for more than 2 decades, JuRo Stables is open daily, year-round.

SWIMMING Though most of the hotels and motels listed in this book have pools, if you'd rather go jump in a lake, head for **Percy Priest Lake.** You'll find this large man-made reservoir just east of downtown Nashville, at exit 219 off I-40. Stop by the information center to get a map showing the three designated swimming areas.

7 SPECTATOR SPORTS

AUTO RACING The **Music City Raceway,** 3302 Ivy Point Rd., Goodlettsville (✆ **615/876-0981;** www.musiccityraceway.com), is the place to catch National Hot Rod Association (NHRA) drag-racing action. The drag strip, known as Nashville's "Playground of Power," has races on Tuesdays, Fridays, Saturdays, and some Sundays between March and October. Admission ranges from $5 to $10.

BASEBALL The **Nashville Sounds** (✆ **615/242-4371;** www.nashvillesounds.com), a Triple-A team affiliate of the Milwaukee Brewers, play at Greer Stadium, 534 Chestnut St., off Eighth Avenue South. Admission ranges from $6 to $12 (advance-purchase tickets $10 reserved seats, $6 for general admission; day-of-game tickets $12 reserved seats, $8 general admission). ***Note:*** There are no children's prices, and all kids need to have a ticket.

FOOTBALL Having made numerous play-off appearances, the **Tennessee Titans** draw loyal crowds to the 68,000-seat LP Field on the banks of the Cumberland River. The stadium is at 1 Titans Way, Nashville, TN 37213 (✆ **615/565-4200;** www.titansonline.com).

GOLF TOURNAMENTS Vanderbilt Legends Club (✆ **615/791-8100**) hosts an annual LPGA event each spring. Call for prices and dates.

HOCKEY Nashville's own NHL hockey team, the **Nashville Predators** (✆ **615/770-PUCK** [7825]; http://predators.nhl.com), plays at the Sommet Center on lower Broadway in downtown Nashville—or "Smashville," as the sport's brawny fans like to brag. Ticket prices range from $10 to $95.

HORSE SHOWS Horse shows are important events on the Nashville area's calendar. The biggest and most important horse show of the year is the annual **Tennessee Walking Horse National Celebration** (✆ **931/684-5915;** www.twhnc.com). This show takes place 40 miles southeast of Nashville in the town of Shelbyville and is held each year in late August. Advance reserved ticket prices range from $7 to $60, while general-admission tickets are $5 to $12.

The city's other big horse event is the annual running of the **Iroquois Steeplechase** (✆ **615/591-2991;** www.iroquoissteeplechase.org), on the second Saturday in May. This is one of the oldest steeplechase races in the country and is held in Percy Warner Park in the Belle Meade area. Proceeds from the race benefit the Vanderbilt Children's Hospital. General admission tickets are $12 at the gate or $10 in advance.

Shopping in Nashville

Nashville is a great shopping city, so be sure to bring your credit cards. Whether you're looking for handmade stage outfits costing thousands of dollars or a good deal on a pair of shoes at a factory-outlet store, you'll find plenty of spending opportunities in Nashville.

1 THE NASHVILLE SHOPPING SCENE

As in most cities of the South, the shopping scene in Nashville is spread out over the width and breadth of the city. Most of the city's best shopping can be found in the many large new shopping malls scattered around the newer suburbs. However, there are also many interesting and exclusive shops in the West End area. In downtown Nashville, you'll find gift and souvenir shops, antiques stores, and musical instrument and record stores that cater to country musicians and fans.

Country music buffs will appreciate plenty of opportunities to shop for Western wear. There are dozens of shops specializing in the de rigueur attire of country music. You probably can't find a better selection of cowboy boots anywhere outside Texas, and if your tastes run to sequined denim shirts or skirts, you'll find lots to choose from.

Hours vary, but most businesses in Nashville are open daily, with some exceptions on Sunday. It's best to call ahead.

2 NASHVILLE SHOPPING A TO Z

ANTIQUES

For the best antiques browsing, drive just south of downtown to the corner of Eighth Avenue South and Douglas Street, where several large antiques shops are clustered.

ART & HOME FURNISHINGS

The Arts Company Many of Nashville's most promising artists, working divergent media such as painting, sculpture, and photography, display and sell their pieces at this prominent downtown gallery. 415 Fifth Ave. N. ✆ **615/254-2040.** www.theartscompany.com.

Cumberland Art Gallery With an emphasis on regional artists, this well-regarded gallery deals in sculptures, paintings, photographs, and works on paper in a wide variety of styles. 4107 Hillsboro Circle. ✆ **615/297-0296.** www.artnet.com/cumberland.html.

Curious Heart Emporium ★ Quirky gifts such as offbeat refrigerator magnets, photography books, stuffed animals, children's toys, whimsical folk art, and arty home decor create an eclectic mix at this unusual shop. There are two locations, including one near the Loveless Cafe southwest of town at 8414 Hwy. 100. Berry Hill, 2832 Bransford Ave. ✆ **615/298-7756.** www.curiousheartemporium.com.

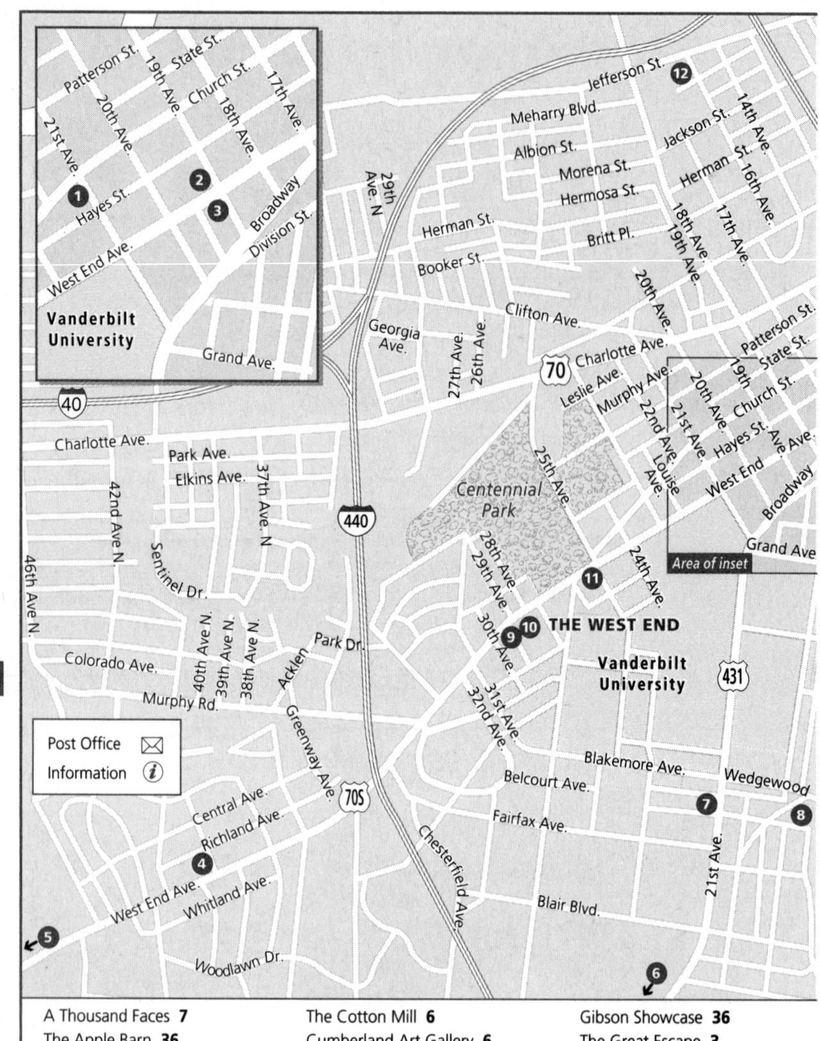

A Thousand Faces **7**
The Apple Barn **36**
The Arts Company **15**
Betty Boots **22**
BookMan BookWoman **7**
Boot Country **19**
Borders **11**
Boutique Bella **9**
Coco **5**
The Cocoa Tree **14**
Cotten Music Center **7**
The Cotton Mill **6**
Cumberland Art Gallery **6**
Curious Heart Emporium **32**
Davis-Kidd Booksellers **6**
Dillard's **6**
Elder's Bookstore **1**
Ernest Tubb Record Shop **23**
Finer Things Gallery **34**
Fire Finch **7**
Flavour **25**
Fork's Drum Closet **28**
Gibson Showcase **36**
The Great Escape **3**
Grimey's **29**
Gruhn Guitars **18**
Hatch Show Print **19**
International Market and Restaurant **8**
Jamie **4**
Johnston & Murphy Outlet **35**
Katy K's Ranch Dressing **27**
Lazzaroli Pasta **14**

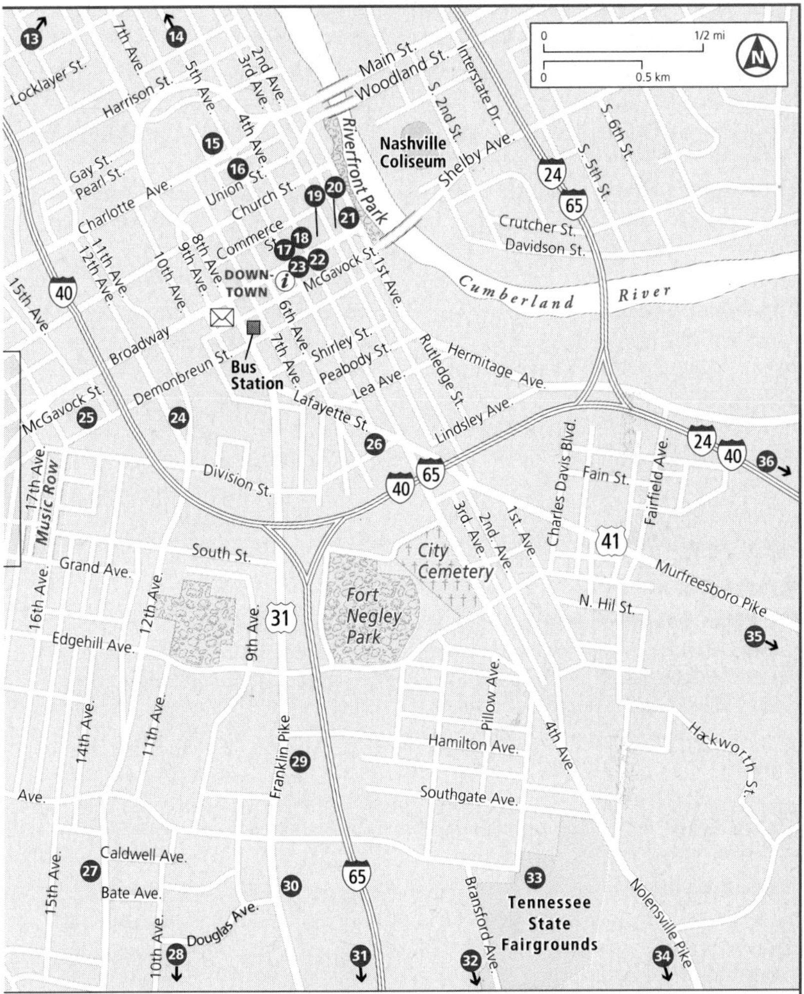

Local Color Gallery **2**
Macy's **31**
Nashville Cowboy **21**
Nashville Farmers' Market **13**
Opry Originals **19**
Pangaea **7**
The Peanut Shop **17**
Posh Boutique **7**
Prime Outlets **36**
Rymer Gallery **16**
Savannah Tea Company **30**
Scarlett Begonia **10**
Social Graces **10**
Ten Thousand Villages **6**
Tennessee State Fairgrounds Flea Market **33**
Trail West **20**
Urban Outfitters **24**
Woodcuts **12**

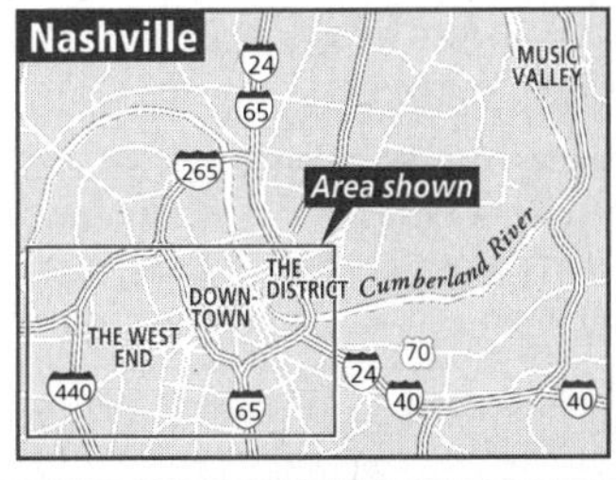

Finer Things Gallery It's a short drive from downtown, but if you have an appreciation of unusual and highly imaginative fine contemporary art, consider Finer Things. It's an eclectic gallery that also sells a few antiques, primitives, and other pieces of folk art. 1898 Nolensville Rd. ✆ **615/244-3003.** www.finerthingsgallery.com.

Hatch Show Print This is the oldest letterpress poster print shop in the country, and not only does it still design and print posters for shows, but it also sells posters to the public. Reprints of old circus, vaudeville, and *Grand Ole Opry* posters are the most popular. 316 Broadway. ✆ **615/256-2805.** www.hatchshowprint.com.

Local Color Gallery Tennessee artists—mostly watercolorists and other painters—are showcased in this aptly named gallery. Landscapes, still lifes, and portraits are among the most common genres represented. 1912 Broadway. ✆ **615/321-3141.** www.localcolornashville.com.

The Rymer Gallery Conveniently located in downtown Nashville, this vibrant art gallery has an extensive roster of artists working in an array of different media, from bronze sculpture and oil paintings to abstract ink-jet prints mounted on aluminum. Regarded as one of the top galleries in the area, this one is definitely worth a look. 233 Fifth Ave. N. ✆ **615/752-6030.** www.therymergallery.com.

Woodcuts If you're interested in artworks by African-American artists, this is the place to visit in Nashville. Prints, posters, note cards, and greeting cards make up the majority of the offerings here, though they also do framing. The shop is adjacent to Fisk University. 1613 Jefferson St. ✆ **615/321-5357.**

BOOKS

BookMan/BookWoman ★ Widely regarded (and rightfully so) as Nashville's best used-book bookstore, this Vandy-area favorite has tens of thousands of books, including hardcover and collectors' editions. Their inexpensive paperbacks encompass nearly every genre, including mysteries, science fiction, photography, and children's books. 1713 21st Ave. S. ✆ **615/383-6555.** www.bookmanbookwoman.com.

Borders This multilevel bookstore, part of a national chain, dominates a busy intersection near the Vanderbilt University campus. Thousands of books, CDs, and an extensive selection of DVDs draw shoppers, as do frequent author book signings. 2501 West End Ave. ✆ **615/327-9656.** www.borders.com.

Davis-Kidd Booksellers ★ For the best and biggest selection of books in Nashville, go to the Green Hills area, where you'll find this welcoming, well-stocked, and locally owned store. With an active roster of book signings and other community-oriented events, a good second-floor cafe, and an array of unique gift items, Davis-Kidd gets my pick as the best bookstore chain in Tennessee. (Other locations are in Memphis and Jackson.) 4007 Hillsboro Pike. ✆ **615/385-2645.** www.daviskidd.com.

Elder's Bookstore This dusty old shop looks as if some of the antiquarian books on sale were stocked back when they were new. Every square inch of shelf space is jammed full of books, and there are more stacks of books seemingly everywhere you turn. This place is a book collector's dream come true. And who needs a fancy, in-store Starbucks cafe when you've got the retro Elliston Soda Shop right next door? 2115 Elliston Place. ✆ **615/327-1867.** www.eldersbookstore.com.

CRAFTS

Pangaea ★★ From hand-carved soaps and South American textiles to one-of-a-kind Elvis icons, this eclectic boutique in Nashville's trendy Hillsboro Village area has interesting gifts to suit a variety of tastes, if not budgets. (They also sell cool clothes.) Items are on the pricey side, but for a unique shopping experience adjacent to scores of hip coffee shops and galleries, even window-shopping at Pangaea is time well spent. 1721 21st Ave. S. ✆ **615/269-9665.** www.pangaeanashville.com.

Ten Thousand Villages ★ Fair-trade gift items, including jewelry, crafts, home decor, and more, fill this colorful store, located in an otherwise nondescript shopping center between the West End and the Green Hills area. 3900 Hillsboro Pike, ✆ **615/385-5814.** www.tenthousandvillages.com.

DEPARTMENT STORES

Dillard's Dillard's is recognized as one of the nation's leading department stores. They carry many leading brands and have stores at several malls around Nashville: **Mall at Green Hills,** 2126 Abbott Martin Rd. (✆ **615/297-0971**); **RiverGate Mall,** 1000 RiverGate Pkwy., Goodlettsville (✆ **615/859-2811**); and **Cool Springs Galleria,** 1800 Galleria Blvd. (✆ **615/771-7101**).

Macy's Anchoring many of the major shopping malls in Nashville is this well-known national chain, noted for its wide selection of fine lines. **Cool Springs Galleria,** 1800 Galleria Blvd., in Franklin (✆ **615/771-2100**); **Mall at Green Hills,** 2126 Abbott Martin Rd. (✆ **615/383-3300**); **Hickory Hollow Mall,** 917 Bell Rd. (✆ **615/731-5050**); and **RiverGate Mall,** 1000 RiverGate Pkwy., Goodlettsville (✆ **615/859-5251**).

DISCOUNT SHOPPING

Johnston & Murphy Outlet Located across the road from the airport, this outlet mall offers good shopping for all kinds of discounted shoes. Genesco Park, 1415 Murfreesboro Rd. ✆ **615/367-4443.** www.johnstonmurphy.com.

Prime Outlets Well worth the hour-long drive from Nashville, the Prime Outlets, in Lebanon, Tennessee, are the mother lode of brand-name merchandise at bargain prices. The massive orange and yellow outdoor mall is clean and well-maintained, and offers substantial discounts on Coach, Bath & Body Works, Nike, Aeropostale, The Children's Place, Tommy Hilfiger, and dozens of other well-known brands. From downtown Nashville, take I-40 east to exit 238. One Outlet Village Blvd., Lebanon, TN. ✆ **615/444-0433.** www.primeoutlets.com.

FASHIONS

See also "Western Wear," below.

Boutique Bella If you're looking for a Splendid T or Kooba handbag, this West End shop will fit the bill. Although its men's apparel shop closed in late 2009, ladies can find dozens of denim brands including 7 for All Mankind and Humanity. In the Park Place Shopping Center. 2817 West End Ave. ✆ **615/467-1471.** www.boutiquebella.com.

Coco This ladies' boutique sells designer sportswear, dresses, and accessories, and features such lines as Ellen Tracy and Emmanuel. Both the fashions and the clientele tend to be upscale. 4239 Harding Rd. ✆ **615/292-0362.**

The Cotton Mill Discriminating fashionistas looking for the latest from Marc Jacobs, See by Chloe, Milly, Alice & Olivia, and Badgley Mischka look to this Green Hills–area boutique. 4009 Hillsboro Circle. © **615/298-2188.** www.thecottonmillnashville.com.

Flavour A go-to spot for the coolest jeans and fresh looks for both men and women, this boutique is your best shopping bet if you want to stay in the downtown/midtown area. Brands ranging from True Religion and Morphine Generation to Da-Nang, Cha Cha, and Alice & Trixie are just a few of those offered at this Music Row retailer. 1522-B Demonbreun. © **615/254-2064.** www.flavourclothing.com.

Jamie One of Nashville's most elite women's boutiques, Jamie exudes luxury. Deep-pocketed shoppers looking for just the right look from Prada or Versace, Donna Karan or Vera Wang will likely find it here, along with the jewelry and shoes to match. 4317 Harding Rd. © **615/292-4188.** www.jamie-nashville.com.

Posh Boutique Trendy clothes and footwear by the likes of Prophetik (a Nashville-based sustainable clothing line getting big buzz), Diesel, Boyfriend, J Brand Jeans, and MM Couture attract a young, affluent clientele. That's not to say you can't scour the place for occasional bargains. There's a second location at the Hill Center, 4027 Hillsboro Pike, Ste. 705 (© **615/269-6250**). 1801 21st Ave. S. © **615/383-9840.** www.poshonline.com.

Scarlett Begonia Ethnic fashions, jewelry, and fine crafts from around the world prove that there is life beyond country Nashville. The emphasis here is on South American clothing, and the quality is much higher than you'll find in the average import store. 2805 West End Ave. © **615/329-1272.** www.scarlettbegonia.com.

Urban Outfitters With the opening of this stylish store in the Gulch, downtown dwellers finally have hope that other desirable retail chains will follow. Although the store also sells a bit of contemporary furniture, wall art, and pop-culture collectibles, Urban Outfitters' core merchandise is casual clothing for both men and women. Graphic T-shirts and tank tops, jackets, jumpers, shirts, shoes, and accessories are part of the mix. 405 12th Ave. S. © **615/254-3339.** www.urbanoutfitters.com.

FINE GIFTS/SOUVENIRS

Nashville abounds in shops purveying every manner of country-themed souvenirs. The greatest concentrations of these shops are in the Music Row and Music Valley (Opryland Resort) areas, where several of the stores specialize in particular country music performers. Several of the gift shops, including Cooter's and the Willie Nelson Museum on McGavock Pike (Music Valley), also have backroom museums where you can see music memorabilia. But these museums are really just an excuse to get you into the big souvenir shop out front, though if you're a fan, you'll enjoy touring the exhibits and maybe picking up a souvenir. See "On the Music Trail," p. 88, for further information.

A Thousand Faces ★ Beautifully crafted one-of-a-kind gifts including jewelry, artwork, and home decor are packed inside every square inch of this vibrant West End boutique that's perfect for leisurely browsing. 1720 21st Ave. S. © **615/298-3304.** www.athousandfaces.com.

Fire Finch Eclectic, primitive-style artwork and other interesting, upscale gift items are sold in this atmospheric store. And, yes, you might see a finch or two. A second location opened in 2007 in Printer's Alley, downtown. It's at 305 Church St. (© **615/942-5271**). 1818 21st Ave. S. © **615/385-5090.** www.firefinch.net.

Social Graces Designer stationery sets, invitations, handmade paper, and an assortment of luxurious writing gifts and accessories are lavishly displayed here. As part of a full day of shopping, the relatively quiet, contemplative atmosphere at this store makes a nice change of pace from some of the West End's livelier shops. 1704 21st Ave. S. ✆ **615/383-1911.** www.socialgracesonline.com.

FLEA MARKETS

Tennessee State Fairgrounds Flea Market This huge flea market is held the fourth weekend of every month (except Dec, when it's the third weekend), attracting more than 1,000 vendors selling everything from cheap jeans to handmade crafts to antiques and collectibles. You'll find the fairgrounds just a few minutes south of downtown. Tennessee State Fairgrounds, Fourth Avenue. ✆ **615/862-5016.** www.tennesseestatefair.org.

FOOD

The Apple Barn Cider Mill & General Store Promising an authentic, Smoky Mountain tradition, this replica of an old-timey general store specializes in freshly baked apple pies, apple butter, juices, and cider. Other edible merchandise includes country hams and bacon, and home-style jams and jellies. Inside Opry Mills (see below, under "Malls/Shopping Centers"). ✆ **615/514-6000.** www.applebarncidermill.com.

The Cocoa Tree Truffles, toffee, cakes, and other confections are decadent splurges at this quaint little chocolate shop that just opened in historic Germantown. Locally owned by a passionate chocolatier, the store sells its artisan chocolates and desserts by the piece, by the pound, or by the slice. While you're trying to decide, you can linger at the cafe over a cup of Mayan hot chocolate. 1200 Fifth Ave. N., Ste. 104. ✆ **615/255-5060.** www.thecocoatree.com.

International Market and Restaurant Open daily until 9pm, this one-of-a-kind find in the Belmont University neighborhood offers lots of Asian-imports on items ranging from chopsticks and rice to specialty culinary ingredients and fine teas. A buffet line at one end of the market brims with freshly prepared, hot Thai dishes, including satays and noodles. 2010 Belmont Blvd. ✆ **615/297-4453.**

Lazzaroli Pasta Fresh pastas, including homemade ravioli and sauces, and take-and-bake meals are mainstays at this new Germantown market. Whether you want traditional egg noodles or hand-cut pappardelle, you'll find it here, along with gourmet pantry items, cheeses, and classic Italian desserts such as tiramisu and fresh-filled cannoli. They also carry local company Olive & Sinclair–brand chocolates. 1314 Fifth Ave. N. ✆ **615/291-9922.** www.lazzaroli.com.

Savannah Tea Company English Earl Grey, orange-blossom oolong, and rosebud-and-petals herb teas are among the delightful choices at this Germantown tea house. More than 100 different types of loose-leaf teas include more than two dozen flavors of black tea alone. Wedding cakes are also sold at the cute shop, which doubles as a dainty cafe serving afternoon tea replete with fresh scones and clotted cream and jam. (Advance reservations are required.) 707 Monroe St. ✆ **615/383-1832.** www.savannahteacompany.com.

Nashville Farmers' Market ★ Located across the street from the Bicentennial Mall, this large indoor farmers' market has 100 farm stalls, as well as 100 flea-market stalls. There are also more than a dozen prepared-food vendors and gourmet- and imported-food stalls, selling everything from Jamaican meat patties to hundreds of different hot sauces. The market is open daily 8am to 7pm in summer, 9am to 6pm the rest of the year. 900 Eighth Ave. N. ✆ **615/880-2001.** www.nashvillefarmersmarket.org.

The Peanut Shop If you've been trudging around downtown Nashville all day and need a quick snack, consider a bag of fresh-roasted peanuts. This tiny shop in the Arcade (connecting Fourth Ave. N. and Fifth Ave. N.) has been in business since 1927 and still roasts its own peanuts. In fact, there are more styles of peanuts sold here than you've probably ever seen in one place. A true Nashville institution. 19 Arcade. ✆ **615/256-3394.** www.nashvillenut.com.

MALLS/SHOPPING CENTERS

Cool Springs Galleria A 15-minute drive south of Nashville off I-65 (at the Moore's Lane exit) is one of the city's newest shopping malls. Although it is more convenient to affluent locals and tourists in the Brentwood suburb than it is for most tourists to downtown Nashville, this is a top-tier mall that has it all. 1800 Galleria Blvd. ✆ **615/771-2128.** www.coolspringsgalleria.com.

Hickory Hollow Mall Familiar mall stores such as Aeropostale, Claire's, Payless Shoes, and Lane Bryant are among the scores of specialty shops at this retail venue west of the Nashville area, in Antioch. There's also a food court and two major department stores, Macy's and Sears. You'll find the mall southwest of downtown off I-24 east, at exit 60. 5252 Hickory Hollow Pkwy., Antioch ✆ **615/731-3500.** www.hickoryhollowmall.com.

The Mall at Green Hills Locals love The Mall at Green Hills, making it Nashville's busiest. In this congested area surrounded by other good shopping centers, the Mall caters to shoppers with discriminating tastes. Here, you'll find Sephora, Crabtree & Evelyn, Tiffany & Co., Brooks Brothers, Ann Taylor Loft, Chico's, and Pottery Barn, along with anchor stores Macy's and Dillard's. But the really big retail news is that Nordstrom's has announced plans to locate its first Nashville-area store there in early 2010. 2126 Abbott Martin Rd. ✆ **615/298-5478.** www.themallatgreenhills.com.

Opry Mills (Kids) Miles of retail sales, not to mention live music during special events, await customers at Nashville's premier shopping mall, a vast extravaganza of department stores, specialty boutiques, restaurants, and entertainment venues that's laid out in an oval, racetrack formation. At this mall, you can try your hand at rock climbing, see a first-run movie, or visit the IMAX 3-D Theatre, and top it all off with a chocolate soda at Ghirardelli's old-time ice-cream parlor. Among Opry Mills' 200 tenants are anchors Bass Pro Shops Outdoor World, Barnes & Noble, Off Broadway Shoe Warehouse, Old Navy, and Rainforest Cafe. If you want to shop 'til you drop, this is the place to do it. 433 Opry Mills Dr. ✆ **615/514-1000.** www.oprymills.com.

Fun Facts The One & Only Other E.T.

Ernest Tubb was one of Nashville's earliest country recording stars. This native Texan, known to friends as "E.T.," scored a big hit with "Walkin' the Floor Over You" in 1941. The beloved entertainer, who in gratitude to his audiences had the word "Thanks" emblazoned on the back of his guitar, earned a slew of industry awards, played Carnegie Hall, and was inducted into the Country Music Hall of Fame. After a long and successful career as one of the pioneers in country music, he died in Nashville in 1984.

Kids' Stuff

Don't overlook music attractions as shopping sources. For instance, in addition to an extensive selection of books and CDs, the **Country Music Hall of Fame and Museum** (p. 88) features a wondrous kids' corner, with hundreds of goodies, from kazoos and coin purses to rooster-headed pencil sharpeners and cowboy-hatted rubber duckies.

RiverGate Mall If you're looking for shopping in northern Nashville, head up I-65 North to exit 95 or 96. The RiverGate Mall includes four department stores and scores of boutiques and specialty shops. 1000 RiverGate Pkwy., Goodlettsville ✆ **615/859-3456.** www.rivergate-mall.com.

MUSIC

Ernest Tubb Record Shop ★ Moments Whether you're looking for a reissue of an early Johnny Cash album or the latest from Kenny Chesney, you'll find it at Ernest Tubb. These shops sell exclusively country music recordings on CD, cassette, and a handful of vinyl records by the likes of Loretta Lynn and Jimmie Davis. There's another location out near Opryland, at 2416 Music Valley Dr. (✆ **615/889-2474**); this is where the Midnite Jamboree is held each Saturday night at midnight. 417 Broadway. ✆ **615/255-7503.** www.ernesttubb.com.

The Great Escape This old store adjacent to the Vanderbilt campus caters to the record and comic book needs of college students and other collectors and bargain-seekers. The used records section has a distinct country bent, but you can also find other types of music as well. This is a big place with a great selection, including records, CDs, comic books, video games, and so on. There are five locations throughout the city. 1925 Broadway. ✆ **615/327-0646.** www.thegreatescapeonline.com.

Grimey's ★★ New and "preloved" (don't call them used) CDs are bought and sold at this independently owned record store and community clearinghouse for all things related to the local music scene. You can buy T-shirts, posters, concert memorabilia, and other cool stuff, and get a leg up on everything that's going on around town. 1604 Eighth Ave. S. ✆ **615/254-4801.** www.grimeys.com.

MUSICAL INSTRUMENTS

Cotten Music Center High-end acoustic stringed instruments have kept this West End music store in business since 1961. Acoustic guitars and mandolins, new and vintage electric guitars, and accessories, including strings, straps, cases, and gig bags, are sold here. Check the Backroom Bargains for great deals. The shop offers lessons, repair service, and special orders, too. 1815 21st Ave. S. ✆ **615/383-8947.** www.cottenmusic.com.

Fork's Drum Closet Drums and other percussion instruments fill this large shop near the far end of 12th Avenue South. It's also a great place to hang—in hopes of networking with other working musicians. 2701 12th Ave. S. ✆ **615/383-8343.** www.forksdrumcloset.com.

Nashville in the Movies

Nashville's most celebrated power couple, Nicole Kidman and Keith Urban, would've been perfect for this. Alas, another Academy Award–winning actress, Gwyneth Paltrow, and one of Music City's top country superstars, Tim McGraw, are co-starring in a movie that began filming in Nashville not long before this book went to press, in early 2010.

Paltrow, who will do her own singing for the film, plays a fallen country singer, and McGraw co-stars as her husband/manager. Other juicy additions to the cast include hot celeb Leighton Meester, of TV's *Gossip Girl,* as a beauty queen, and Garrett Hedlund, from the movie *Friday Night Lights,* as a promising star whose career is on the rise.

Gibson Showcase Nightly music is offered at this combination performance stage and retail store, where Gibson-brand guitars are sold, and where the company's bluegrass stringed instruments, including dobros, mandolins, and banjos, are crafted and shipped worldwide. Free bluegrass jams are open to all comers beginning at 7pm Mondays and Wednesdays. Tuesday is Songwriters' Night. Local bands usually perform Thursdays and Fridays. Call for a schedule. In Opry Mills, 161 Opry Mills Dr. ✆ **615/514-2233.** www.gibsonshowcase.com.

Gruhn Guitars Nashville's biggest guitar dealer (and one of the largest in the world) stocks classic used and collectible guitars as well as reissues of musicians' favorite instruments. If you're in the market for a 1953 Les Paul or a 1938 Martin D-28, this is the place to hit. 400 Broadway. ✆ **615/256-2033.** www.gruhn.com.

WESTERN WEAR

In addition to places listed below, you can pick up clothing at the Wildhorse Saloon and other shops in the District. There are also clothing stores in Music Valley and on Music Row.

Betty Boots Looking for the perfect pair of cowgirl boots or a sexy Stetson? One of downtown's newest Western-wear shops caters to the ladies. In addition to Nashville-inspired gear, you'll find flip-flops, purses, and a few souvenirs. 321 Broadway. ✆ **615/736-7698.**

Boot Country Cowboy boots, more cowboy boots, and still more cowboy boots. That's what you'll find at this boot store. Whether you want a basic pair of work boots or some fancy python-skin showstoppers, you'll find them here. 304 Broadway. ✆ **615/259-1691.**

Katy K's Ranch Dressing ★★ Finds Head south of downtown to find this hot boutique with the shapely cowgirl cutout on the building's stone facade. For more than a decade, this trendsetting shop has sold everything from spangled gowns by Nudie's of Hollywood to corsets and crinolines. Western wear includes designer boots, belts, buckles, hats and shirts, but you can also get sexy vintage dresses and even irreverent—but cute—baby clothes. It's a kick. 2407 12th Ave. S. ✆ **615/297-4242.** www.katyk.com.

Nashville Cowboy You can smell the leather a block away from this new downtown store. A staggering collection of boots, belts, hats, and buckles are on display. Coats come in all sizes and styles, from the simple to the fringed-suede and lambskin-lined varieties. 132 Second Ave. N. ✆ **615/259-8922.** www.nashvillecowboy.com.

Opry Originals: The Shop On Broadway Manuel, Nashville's legendary clothier to the country-music stars, opened in the heart of downtown Nashville's famed lower Broadway area in 2009. Here you'll find Opry-brand jackets, shirts, jeans, and boots. Gifts, souvenirs, home furnishings, and food products are also part of the mix. 300 Broadway. ✆ **615/259-9777.**

Trail West For all your Western-wear needs, this store is hard to beat. They handle the Brooks & Dunn Collection plus all the usual brands of hats, boots, and denim. There are other locations at 2416 Music Valley Dr., across from the Gaylord Opryland Resort (✆ **615/883-5933**), and at 219 Broadway (✆ **615/255-7030**). 214 Broadway. ✆ **615/255-7030.**

10 Nashville After Dark

Live music surrounds you in Nashville. Not only are there dozens of clubs featuring live country and bluegrass music, as you'd expect, but there's also a very lively rock scene. Jazz, blues, and folk clubs are also part of the mix, as are nightclubs and songwriters' showcases. And, of course, there's the granddaddy of them all, the long-running country music radio broadcast known as the *Grand Ole Opry.*

Some of this music can be found in unexpected places: street corners, parking lots, parks, or hotel lounges. Like Memphis, the city overflows with talented musicians who play where they can, much to the benefit of visitors to Nashville.

If I've given you the impression that Nashville is a city of live popular music only, let me point out the city's well-rounded, if lesser known, performing arts organizations. Nashville boasts a vibrant symphony orchestra, opera company, ballet company, the state's largest professional theater company, and several smaller community theaters.

The ***Nashville Scene*** is the city's arts-and-entertainment weekly. It comes out on Thursday and is available at restaurants, clubs, convenience stores, and other locations. Just keep your eyes peeled. Every Friday, the ***Tennessean,*** Nashville's morning daily, publishes the *Opry* lineup, and on Sunday it publishes a guide to the coming week's entertainment. Nashville nightlife happens all around town but predominates in two main entertainment areas—the District and Music Valley. **The District,** an area of renovated warehouses and old bars, is the livelier of the two. Here you'll find the Wildhorse Saloon and two dozen other clubs showcasing bands on any given weekend night. On the sidewalks, people are shoulder to shoulder as they parade from one club to the next, and in the streets, stretch limos vie for space with tricked-out pickup trucks. Within the District, Second Avenue is currently the main drag—where you'll find the most impressive of the area's clubs. However, there was a time shortly after the Civil War when Printer's Alley was the center of downtown Nashville nightlife.

Within a few blocks of the District, you'll also find the **Tennessee Performing Arts Center** and several other clubs.

Music Valley offers a more family-oriented, suburban nightlife scene. This area on the east side of Nashville is where you'll find the Grand Ole Opry House, Nashville Palace, and Texas Troubadour Theatre, as well as the Opryland Resort, which has bars featuring live music. The neighborhood of East Nashville, just south of Music Valley, also has a growing number of excellent cafes and bars showcasing local talent.

Tickets to major concerts and sporting events can be purchased through **Ticketmaster** (✆ **800/745-3000;** www.ticketmaster.com), which maintains a desk at the Tennessee Performing Arts Center box office. A service charge is added to all ticket sales. Finally, for a comprehensive list of live music, performing arts, and sports events, visit **www.nowplayingnashville.com**.

1 THE COUNTRY MUSIC SCENE

IN THE DISTRICT & THE GULCH

In addition to the clubs mentioned here, you'll find several small bars along lower Broadway, in an area long known as **Honky-tonk Row** or **Honky-tonk Highway.** The teeming, 2-block strip between Fourth and Fifth avenues is a nostalgic neon hootenanny of country-music sights, sounds, and occasionally some good old-fashioned rabble-rousing.

Layla's Bluegrass Inn Pure hillbilly—and proud of it—Layla's is a stalwart of the strip here in downtown Nashville. In addition to hosting hillbilly and rockabilly acts, the cozy venue hosts country, Americana, and, of course, bluegrass and even progressive "newgrass" musicians. Its vintage cowgirl/cowboy decor and "howdy pardner" appeal hark back to Nashville's first big heyday in the 1940s and 1950s. 418 Broadway. ✆ **615/726-2799.** www.laylasbluegrassinn.com. No cover.

Legends Corner Value Today's starving artists are tomorrow's country music superstars, and this beloved dive in the District sets the stage for such happily-ever-after scenarios. Die-hard bar-hoppers insist that Legends Corner has downtown's best live local music and one of the friendliest staffs in all of Music City. Nostalgic memorabilia on the walls adds a quaint, down-home charm. And you can't beat the price: The tip jar gets passed around the room like a collection plate, enabling the rowdy crowds to help support the struggling pickers and grinners who've put Nashville on the map. Ages 21 and older only after 6pm. 428 Broadway. ✆ **615/248-6334.** www.legendscorner.com. No cover.

Douglas Corner Cafe Though it has the look and feel of a neighborhood bar, this is one of Nashville's top places for songwriters trying to break into the big time—it's the city's main competition for The Bluebird Cafe. The club also has occasional shows by established performers. It's located a few minutes south of downtown, near all the antiques shops. 2106 Eighth Ave. S. ✆ **615/298-1688.** www.douglascorner.com. Cover up to $7.

Robert's Western World ★ Located just a couple of doors down from the famous Tootsie's, this former Western-wear store helped launch the career of BR549. These days, Brazilbilly rocks the house most Friday and Saturday nights. 416 Broadway. ✆ **615/244-9552.** www.robertswesternworld.com. No cover.

Ryman Auditorium ★★ Moments Once the home of the *Grand Ole Opry,* this historic theater was renovated a few years back and is once again hosting performances with a country and bluegrass music slant. The Ryman was showcased in the documentary *Down From the Mountain,* a film version of the all-star bluegrass concert performed there featuring music from the movie soundtrack *O Brother, Where Art Thou?* In 2003, the venue was the site of a star-studded memorial concert for the late Johnny Cash. Today,

Did You Know?

BR549, the well-known country-rock band that hails from Nashville, took its name from Junior Samples's used-car-commercial skit on the old TV show *Hee Haw.* BR549 was the phone number to call for a great deal on a junker.

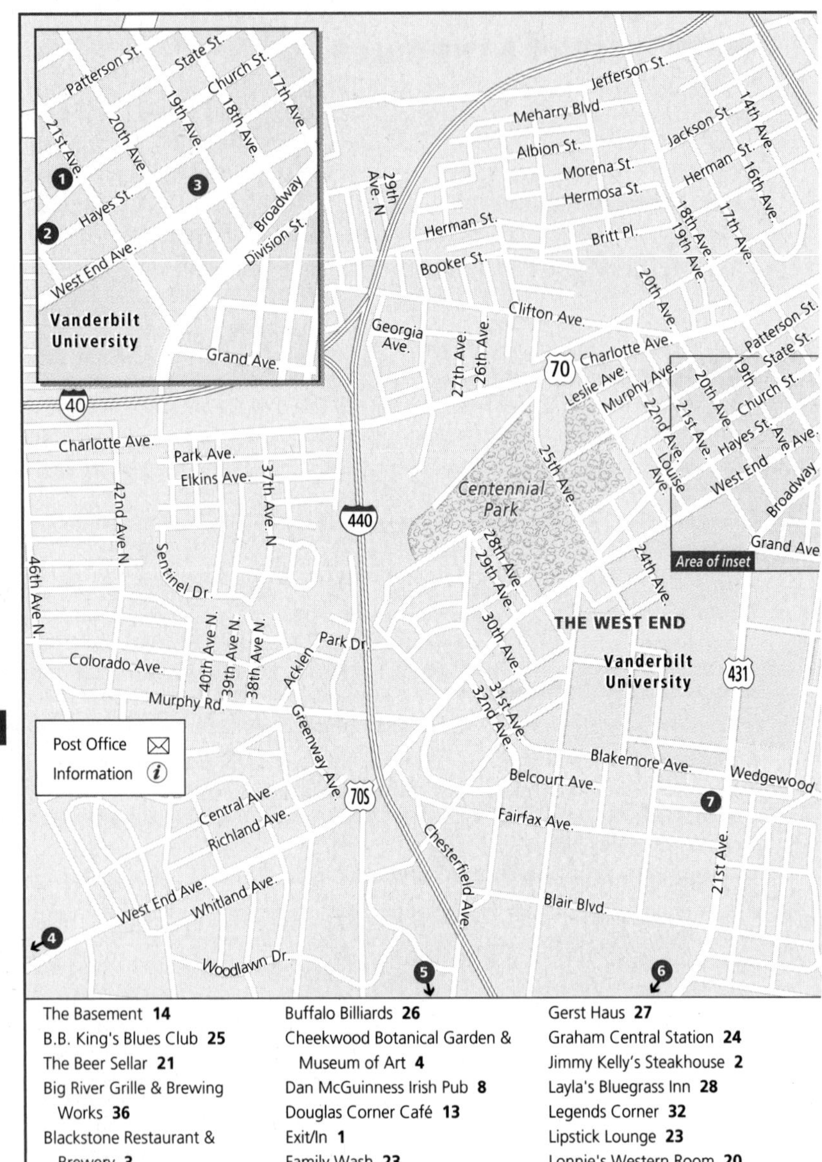

The Basement **14**
B.B. King's Blues Club **25**
The Beer Sellar **21**
Big River Grille & Brewing Works **36**
Blackstone Restaurant & Brewery **3**
Bluebird Cafe **5**
Boscos **7**
Bourbon Street Blues and Boogie Bar **29**
Buffalo Billiards **26**
Cheekwood Botanical Garden & Museum of Art **4**
Dan McGuinness Irish Pub **8**
Douglas Corner Café **13**
Exit/In **1**
Family Wash **23**
Flying Saucer Draught Emporium **17**
F. Scott's Restaurant & Jazz Bar **6**
Gerst Haus **27**
Graham Central Station **24**
Jimmy Kelly's Steakhouse **2**
Layla's Bluegrass Inn **28**
Legends Corner **32**
Lipstick Lounge **23**
Lonnie's Western Room **20**
Mercy Lounge/ Cannery Ballroom **16**
Mulligan's Pub **22**
The Muse **35**

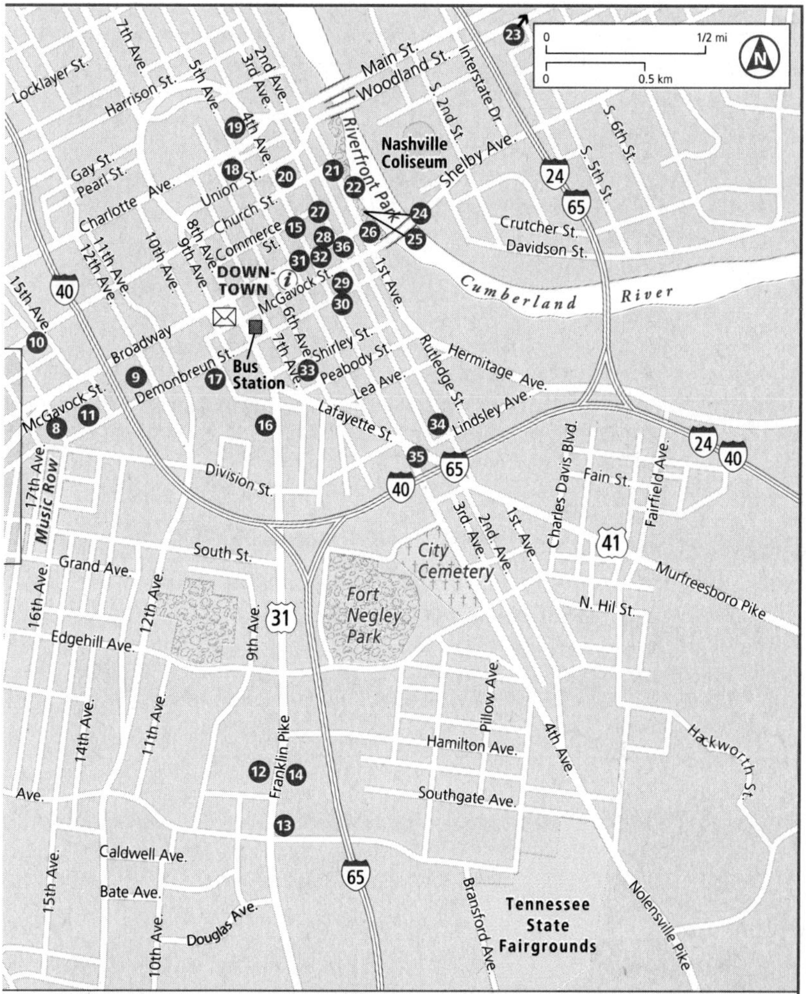

Nashville Municipal Auditorium **19**
Rippy's Smokin' Bar & Grill **31**
Robert's Western World **32**
Rocketown **33**
Ryman Auditorium **15**
Schermerhorn Hall **30**
Station Inn **21**
Tennessee Performing Arts Center **18**
3rd & Lindsley **34**
The Tin Roof **11**
Tootsie's Orchid Lounge **32**
Tribe **10**
Whiskey Kitchen **9**
Wildhorse Saloon **22**
Zanies Comedy Club **12**

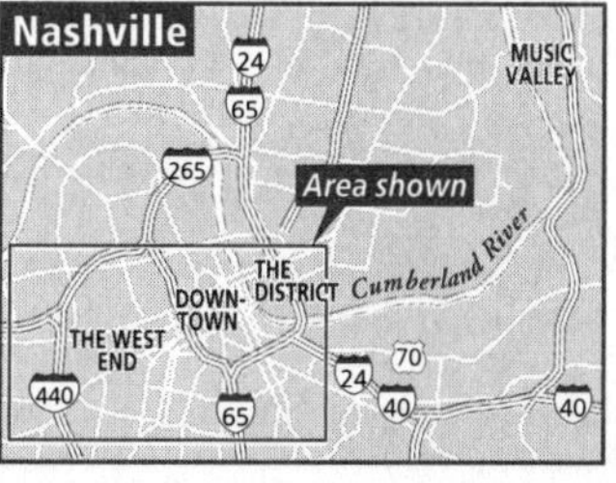

Know Before You Go

Opry bound? Be aware that not all country stars are members of the grand ol' gang. So if you're hoping to see, say, George Strait, Wynonna, or the Dixie Chicks, look elsewhere. Many fans might not realize that *Opry* members are invited performers who must agree to a certain number of *Opry* appearances. Consequently, due to scheduling conflicts or other concerns, not every country singer who's a household name is represented.

But plenty of them are. The *Opry*'s stellar roster includes Trace Adkins, Bill Anderson, Dierks Bentley, Clint Black, Garth Brooks, Jim Ed Brown, Roy Clark, John Conlee, Skeeter Davis, Diamond Rio, Little Jimmy Dickens, Joe Diffie, Holly Dunn, The Gatlin Brothers, Vince Gill, Billy Grammer, Tom T. Hall, Emmylou Harris, Jan Howard, Stonewall Jackson, Alan Jackson, George Jones, Hal Ketchum, Alison Krauss, Patty Loveless, Loretta Lynn, Martina McBride, Del McCoury, Reba McEntire, Montgomery Gentry, Lorrie Morgan, The Osborne Brothers, Brad Paisley, Dolly Parton, Charley Pride, Jeanne Pruett, Del Reeves, Riders In The Sky, Ricky Van Shelton, Jean Shepard, Ricky Skaggs, Ralph Stanley, Marty Stuart, Pam Tillis, Randy Travis, Travis Tritt, Carrie Underwood, Ricky Van Shelton, Steve Wariner, The Whites, and Trisha Yearwood.

musicians of all genres revere the intimate auditorium, where the acoustics are said to be better than Carnegie Hall's. In recent years, acts as diverse as Beck, Yo-Yo Ma, Coldplay, Al Green, and India.Arie have played to packed houses at this National Historic Landmark. 116 Fifth Ave. N. ✆ **615/254-1445** or 615/889-6611. www.ryman.com. Tickets $18–$43.

The Station Inn ★ For decades widely regarded as one of the best bluegrass venues around, this humble little dive still thrives in the shadow of the rapidly developing Gulch district south of Broadway in downtown. Live music is on tap 7 nights a week. Seating is first-come, first-served, so plan to arrive early, especially for such favorites as the Time Jumpers or the Grascals. A relatively more laid-back antidote to the boozy bars on Broadway, the Station Inn has a strict no-smoking policy. 402 12th Ave. S. ✆ **615/255-3307.** www.stationinn.com. Cover $7 Tues–Sat; free Sun.

Tootsie's Orchid Lounge ★ Value This rowdy country dive has been a Nashville tradition since the days when the *Grand Ole Opry* was still performing in the Ryman Auditorium around the corner. Back then, *Opry* stars used to duck into Tootsie's for a drink. Today, you can see signed photos of the many stars who have downed a few here. Free live country music spills out onto the sidewalks daily 10am to 3am, and celebrities still occasionally make the scene. 422 Broadway. ✆ **615/726-0463.** www.tootsies.net. No cover.

Wildhorse Saloon Run by the same company that gave Nashville the Opryland Resort and stages the *Grand Ole Opry,* this massive, three-story dance hall attracts everyone from country music stars to line-dancing senior-citizens groups. In recent years, the saloon has tried to reach beyond its boot-scootin' roots to a more mainstream crowd by booking rock bands such as Todd Rundgren and Styx. Because the club closes for private

parties from time to time, be sure to call first before you head out. 120 Second Ave. N.
✆ **615/251-1000.** www.wildhorsesaloon.com. Cover varies.

IN MUSIC VALLEY

General Jackson Showboat ★ If you'd like to combine some evening entertainment with a cruise on the Cumberland River, try the *General Jackson.* This huge reproduction paddle-wheeler brings back the glory days of river travel. Comedy and country music with a strong patriotic undercurrent keep the predominately bus-tour clientele happy. During the summer, the Southern Nights Cruise offers dancing under the stars to live bands; dinner is optional. Barbershop harmony ensembles are new in 2010. 2812 Opryland Dr. ✆ **615/889-6611,** ext. 1000. Tickets $20 night cruises, $52 dinner cruises. Louise Mandrell Christmastime dinner shows $67.

Grand Ole Opry ★★★ Moments The show that made Nashville famous, the *Grand Ole Opry* is the country's longest continuously running radio show and airs every weekend from a theater adjacent to the Gaylord Opryland Resort. Over the years, the *Opry* has had several homes, including the Ryman Auditorium in downtown Nashville. In late 2003, the 4,400-seat Grand Ole Opry House got its first major refurbishment since 1974, when the program was moved from the Ryman to its current home in the Music Valley. Through it all, the *Opry* remains a comforting mix of country music and gentle humor that has endured for nearly three-quarters of a century. Over the decades, the program has featured nearly all the greats of country music. There is an *Opry* show on Tuesday and Friday (at 7pm), and two performances on Saturday (7 and 9:30pm). Additionally, a new Opry Country Classics performance on Thursday nights shines the spotlight on classic country songs that have defined country music for generations of fans. 2804 Opryland Dr. ✆ **800/SEE-OPRY** (733-6779) or 615/871-OPRY (6779). www.opry.com. Tickets $28–$53.

Nashville Palace Remember Randy Travis and Ricky Van Shelton? These two country stars who first hit the charts in the late 1980s are among the former struggling musicians who got their starts at this Music Valley venue. Open nightly from 5pm to 1:30am for live country-and-western music and line-dancing, the Nashville Palace is especially popular with the tour-bus crowd. The Palace is easy to find, located directly opposite the Gaylord Opryland Resort entrance. 2400 Music Valley Dr. ✆ **615/889-1540.** www.nashville palace.net. Cover $5.

Texas Troubadour Theatre/Cowboy Church ★★ Although the original jamboree started at Ernest Tubb's downtown record shop on Broadway, the Music Valley location now hosts the weekly **Ernest Tubb *Midnite Jamboree.*** Recent headliners have included Bill Anderson, the Osborne Brothers, and Connie Smith; to find out who's

Tips Sitting Pretty

What's the difference between the *Grand Ole Opry* at Opryland and the Ryman Auditorium? Plenty, but the most practical piece of information is this: The long pews at the Opry are padded, while the ones at the Ryman are hard, well-worn wood. But don't despair over your derriere; inexpensive plastic seat cushions can be purchased at the Ryman's lobby gift shop.

Tips **Shhh!**

That's the slogan of **The Bluebird Cafe.** So save your hell-raising for elsewhere. Once the audition-winning songwriters step onstage, the Bluebird becomes pin-drop quiet. For musicians the world over, playing here is the country music equivalent of Carnegie Hall. Reserving one of the venue's 21 tables takes persistence. Weekend shows often sell out days in advance. The Bluebird advises patrons to start calling on Monday "and keep hitting the redial button until you get through!" If you can't get reservations, there's usually standing-room-only (on a first-come, first-served basis) at the bar or at benches.

scheduled during your visit, log onto the Ernest Tubb Record Shop's website at www.etrecordshop.com. If you're looking for a down-home dose of gospel music ministry the morning after, make it to the Cowboy Church on time: The old-timey, nondenominational services kick off Sundays at 10am sharp (✆ **615/859-1001;** www.nashvillecowboychurch.org). Come as you are or don your best Stetson and bolo tie. Either way, you'll fit right in with the eclectic, all-ages congregation of locals and tourists alike who pack the pews every week for a patriotic praise-and-worship service. Music Valley Village, 2416 Music Valley Dr. ✆ **615/889-2474.**

GREEN HILLS AREA

The Bluebird Cafe ★★ **Moments** For a quintessential Nashville experience, visit this unassuming 100-seat club that remains one of the nation's premier venues for up-and-coming as well as established songwriters. Surprisingly, you'll find the Bluebird not in the District or on Music Row but in a suburban shopping plaza across the road from the Mall at Green Hills. There are usually two shows a night. Between 6 and 7pm, there is frequently music in the round, during which four singer-songwriters play some of their latest works. After 9pm, when more-established acts take the stage, there's a cover charge. This is the place in Nashville to catch the music of people you'll be hearing from in coming years. Because the club is so small, reservations (taken noon–5pm) are recommended. 4104 Hillsboro Rd. ✆ **615/383-1461.** www.bluebirdcafe.com. No cover for early shows, but there is a minimum $7 order per person at tables. Cover fees vary ($8–$20) for late shows after 9pm.

2 ROCK, BLUES, JAZZ & MORE

The Basement This eclectic, live music venue hosts an array of alternative, rock, and indie artists. Look for it in the same unassuming little building that houses Grimey's New and Preloved Music, one of the best record stores in town. Like the Station Inn in the Gulch, this club has gone smoke-free (except for the outdoor patio). 1604 Eighth Ave. S. ✆ **615/254-8006.** www.thebasementnashville.com.

Exit/In Mercifully free of the glitz of the bigger nightspots in the District, this battered old building has long been a local favorite of alternative-rock and even the fast-growing alternative-country genre. Music ranges from rock to blues to reggae and a little country; there's usually live music 6 nights a week. 2208 Elliston Place. ✆ **615/321-3340.** www.exitin.com. Cover varies.

Graham Central Station Tucked in the middle of all the action on Second Avenue North, this entertainment complex includes four floors of music and seven different clubs under one roof (in fact, there is even a party on the roof when the weather's good). There are clubs devoted to Top 40 music and karaoke fun, as well as a South Beach–style lounge and a live music showcase. Basically, this place covers all the bases. 128 N. Second Ave. ✆ **615/251-9593.** www.grahamcentralstationnashville.com. Cover up to $14.

Mercy Lounge/Cannery Ballroom San Francisco rockers Third Eye Blind and Memphis act Lucero have done recent shows at this cool-again live-music venue, located just a few blocks off of Eighth Avenue South. A century after its beginnings as an 1883 flour mill, the multilevel warehouse began life as a live music venue, hosting acts such as Jane's Addiction and Midnight Oil. Today the ground-floor Cannery Ballroom can hold up to 1,000 people. Upstairs, the Mercy Lounge can hold 500 people. One Cannery Row. ✆ **615/251-3020.** www.mercylounge.com. Cover varies.

The Muse If you're looking for an edgier underground scene, take a dive into The Muse, Nashville's most cutting-edge performance space. Here, on any given night, you can catch punk and rap acts such as Unstoppable Death Machine, Sisters Grimm, K-Will, and The Screemin' Boweevils. 835 Fourth Ave. S. ✆ **615/251-0190.** www.themusenashville.com. Cover $6–$8.

JAZZ & BLUES

The **Tennessee Jazz & Blues Society** publishes a free monthly newsletter featuring news and event listings of interest to music buffs of these genres (www.jazzblues.org). If you're here in the summer, check to see who's playing at the society's concert series at Belle Meade Plantation (✆ **615/356-0501**).

B. B. King's Blues Club ★★ Nashville can consider itself lucky to have landed one of the legendary blues guitarist's few clubs. The original, launched in Memphis in 1991, has become Beale Street's crown jewel (satellite locations have since sprouted up in a few other U.S. cities). B. B. himself inaugurated the Music City spot with a sold-out, standing-room-only show in September 2003. Since then, locals and tourists craving another alternative to Nashville's pervasive country music bars have ensured this authentic blues bar has a solid future in the District. 152 Second Ave. ✆ **615/256-2727.** http://nashville.bbkingclubs.com. Cover $5–$7 (usually $50–$200 for B. B.'s increasingly infrequent, but always sold-out, concerts).

Fun Facts Music City Loves Jack White

Nashville's "cool quotient" has gone up considerably since the enigmatic musician/indie record producer Jack White started calling it home. The multitalented Detroit native recorded *Icky Thump* here with his band the White Stripes. Other recent releases have included bluegrass romps with the acoustic group The Raconteurs (featuring Ricky Skaggs), and White's latest dark-rock ensemble, the Dead Weather. White's new downtown Nashville recording studio is home to his **Third Man Records** imprint. It's a one-stop production house with a rehearsal and photo studio and darkroom. Curious? Drive by and take a look: 623 Seventh Ave. S. (www.thirdmanrecords.com).

Good, Godly Fun

Grammy-winning contemporary Christian music star Michael W. Smith founded **Rocketown** (401 Sixth Ave. S.; ✆ **615/843-4001;** www.rocketown.com) in 2003 to provide a place for kids, teens, and young adults to hang out and have fun in a safe, drug- and alcohol-free environment. A nonprofit outreach and entertainment complex spanning more than 40,000 square feet, Rocketown offers everything from a challenging skate park and coffeehouse to a fully equipped concert hall. Although many of the club's activities are geared toward adolescents and teens, concerts are all-ages events. The live-music venue, which has three stages, showcases many of today's top up-and-coming rock bands and singer-songwriters. Who knows? Maybe this is where the next Newsboys, Casting Crowns, or MercyMe will emerge.

Bourbon Street Blues and Boogie Bar If you're wandering around in the District wishing you could hear some wailing blues guitar, head over to Printer's Alley and check out the action at this club tucked within downtown's historic Printers Alley district. Live blues and a Cajun-American menu are on tap 7 nights a week. 220 Printers Alley. ✆ **615/242-5837.** www.bourbonstreetblues.com. Cover $5–$10.

F. Scott's Restaurant & Jazz Bar Live jazz is presented 6 nights a week at this classy restaurant/lounge that has been a standard-bearer for Nashville sophisticates since its opening in 1986. It offers a selection of more than 300 wines, an upscale dinner menu, and intimate bar. Arrive early if you want a seat at the 40-seat bar area for the jazz sets. Valet parking is an added perk at F. Scott's, located a stone's throw from The Mall at Green Hills. 2210 Crestmoor Rd. ✆ **615/269-5861.** www.fscotts.com. No cover.

3rd & Lindsley Bar and Grill Eight blocks south of Broadway, in a new office complex surrounded by old warehouses, you'll find Nashville's premier bar and grill. The atmosphere may lack the rough edges and smoke that you'd expect of a blues club, but the live music encompasses everything from Americana and soul to rock. Recent acts have included the Subdudes, Edwin McCain, and Jenny Gill with her dad, Vince. Good pub grub is available for lunch, dinner, and take-out. 818 Third Ave. S. ✆ **615/259-9891.** www.3rdandlindsley.com. Cover up to $20.

CELTIC

Dan McGuinness Irish Pub A lively pub atmosphere pervades this Music Row watering hole, where you can hear live music and succumb to cheap eats like the hearty "Pie and Pint" combo, a bowl of traditional shepherd's pie and a 20-ounce draft for $3. And, as expected, that includes Guinness. 1538 Demonbreun. ✆ **615/252-1991.** www.danmcguinnesspub.com. No cover.

Mulligan's Pub This small pub in the heart of the District is always packed at night and definitely has the feel of an Irish pub. There's good Irish food, cold pints, and live Irish and American folk music Thursday to Saturday nights. 117 Second Ave. N. ✆ **615/242-8010.** www.mulligansspubandrestaurant.com. No cover.

3 THE BAR & PUB SCENE

The Nashville bar scene, for the most part, is synonymous with the Nashville restaurant scene; an establishment has to serve food in order to serve liquor. So, in addition to the places listed below, if you want a cocktail, step into almost any moderately priced or expensive restaurant. The first thing you're likely to see is a bar.

BARS

Beer Sellar As the name implies, this downtown mainstay is all about the brew. By the bottle or on tap, there's a vast selection of beers that draws a rowdy crowd of fun-loving types. The dark but homey basement bar has a kickin' jukebox, too. 107 Church St. ✆ **615/254-9464.** www.beersellar.net.

Buffalo Billiards You might not dance by the light of the moon, but you can shoot pool, drink, and throw a few darts at this grungy warehouse located smack-dab in the middle of the District. 154 Second Ave. N. ✆ **615/313-7665.** www.buffalobilliards.com/nashville.

Family Wash A cozy former East Nashville Laundromat has become a landmark beer joint known for having the best pub grub in town. While chilling to the live nightly music, sample some hearty shepherd's pie or roasted chicken with mashed potatoes and gravy. 2038 Greenwood Ave. ✆ **615/226-6070.** www.familywash.com.

Gerst Haus Though ostensibly a German restaurant, this place is more like a lively beer hall than anything else. They serve their own amber lager, and on weekends there is a live polka band in the evenings. 228 Woodland St. ✆ **615/244-8886;** www.gersthaus.com.

Jimmy Kelly's Steakhouse Sip a sherry, smoke a cigar, and revel in the Old South splendor that pervades this decades-old local favorite. Jimmy Kelly's is primarily a steak-house, and the bar isn't very large, but you'll feel as though you're part of a Nashville tradition when you have a drink here. The place is always lively, and the clientele tends to be older and well-to-do. 217 Louise Ave. ✆ **615/329-4349.** www.jimmykellys.com.

Lonnie's Western Room Formerly known as the "Voodoo Room" in the 1960s and '70s, Lonnie's is a time-worn piano bar that's evolved into the college crowd's cult favorite for late-night karaoke. One of the liveliest nightspots in downtown's historic Printers Alley, Lonnie's also offers nightly open-mic sessions. 208 Printers Alley. ✆ **615/251-1122.** www.lonnieswesternroom.com.

Rippy's Smokin' Bar & Grill With its expansive, open-air patio, this barbecue-and-beer joint at Fifth and Broadway offers a rowdy good time—and the best people-watching

A Comedy Club

Nashville's oldest, if not only, comedy club, **Zanies Comedy Club** has shows Wednesday through Sunday nights. Most weekend headliners have TV and movie track records. Zanies is at 2025 Eighth Ave. S. (✆ **615/269-0221;** www.zanies.com). Cover $20 (cover slightly higher for big-name comedians; minimum of 2 drink or food orders in addition to cover charge).

within spitting distance of the honky-tonks across the street. Especially in good weather, this is a prime indoor/outdoor party spot. 429 Broadway. ✆ **615/244-7477.**

Tin Roof American pub fare, a casual atmosphere, and a thriving happy-hour scene make this Music Row bar a refreshing antidote to the crowded dives along Broadway downtown. Music industry execs, session musicians, and college kids frequent this club, where there always seems to be a party. 1516 Demonbreun St. ✆ **615/313-7103.** www.tinroofbars.com.

Whiskey Kitchen Opened in fall 2009, this fancified tavern at 12th Avenue South specializes in whiskeys, from single-malt, Scotch blends, and bourbons to American, rye, and wheat varieties. Beer, wine, and cocktails share the menu with burgers, pizzas, wraps, and British Isles–inspired entrees. You'll either love or hate the decor, which includes crocodile-leather wall coverings. The patio has a cozy brick fire pit. 118 12th Ave. S. ✆ **615/254-3029.** www.whiskeykitchen.com.

BREWPUBS

Big River Grille & Brewing Works With a weird, retro-contemporary atmosphere that harks back to a friendly '70s fern bar, this vast pub, part of a small Chattanooga-based chain, does a brisk food business. Handcrafted "boutique" beers include lagers, pilsners, and stouts, along with a seasonal brew that changes throughout the year. On weekends, this place stays packed. 111 Broadway. ✆ **615/251-4677.** www.bigrivergrille.com.

Blackstone Restaurant & Brewery Nashville's most upscale brewpub draws a lot of business travelers who are staying in nearby hotels. Casual comfort is the setting here, with cushioned chairs, a fireplace, and marbled bar. The food, including wood-fired pizzas and pretzels, is consistently good. But the beer is the main focus. Choose from a variety of brews including several that change with the seasons. There's also a six-pack sampler. 1918 West End Ave. ✆ **615/327-9969.** www.blackstonebrewery.com.

Boscos ★ With locations in Memphis and Nashville, Tennessee-based Boscos has built a reputation as the best brewpub around. Here in Music City, Boscos occupies a cavernous but congenial space in Hillsboro Village. Either inside the vivacious brew pub or outside on the lovely teakwood deck, patrons can wash down fresh fish dishes, gourmet pizzas, and stuffed mushrooms with a choice of more than half a dozen beers on tap. The bar sometimes serves cask-conditioned ales. 1805 21st Ave. S. ✆ **615/385-0050.** www.boscosbeer.com.

Flying Saucer Draught Emporium Beers from all over the world, as well as 75 beers on tap, make this a top pick for hops connoisseurs. In the shadow of the nearby Frist Center for the Arts, the Flying Saucer is housed in a rambling old building that used to be the baggage claim area for the historic Union train station. The bar's big, open-air porch is just made for socializing over soft pretzels and loaded brats. 1010 Demonbreun St. ✆ **615/259-7468.** www.beerknurd.com.

GAY & LESBIAN DANCE CLUBS AND BARS

The Lipstick Lounge ★ The periwinkle and cherry-red corner house in an East Nashville residential area entertains patrons with karaoke, trivia contests, Wii Wednesdays, and frequent live music. Along with a full breakfast menu, inventive cocktails, and an upstairs pool table, this is a beloved lesbian lounge where everyone can feel at home. 1400 Woodland St. ✆ **615/226-6343.** www.thelipsticklounge.com. Cover $3–$5.

More Nightlife

An ever-increasing array of nightspots keep Nashville jumping after dark. Redevelopment is bustling in the Gulch. Across the street from the venerable bluegrass venue the Station Inn is **Sambuca,** 601 12th Ave. S. (✆ **615/248-2888;** www.sambucarestaurant.com), a Dallas-based newcomer with an eclectic menu and nightly live music—with an emphasis on jazz. The upper-deck outdoor patio, with its cushy sofa seats and dazzling views of the Nashville skyline, make it a popular spot for a romantic date. Next door is another hipster hangout, **Ru San's,** 505 12th Ave. S. (✆ **615/252-8787;** www.ru-sans.com), a vibrant, ultramodern sushi bar.

A few blocks west of downtown, **Suzy Wong's House of Yum,** 1517 Church St. (✆ **615/329-2913;** www.suzywongsnashville.com), has just opened adjacent to Tribe, Nashville's best gay bar (see listing, above). Designer cocktails along the lines of the ginger-flecked "Lolita's Kiss" are all the rage, as is the late-night dining menu created by noted chef/restaurateur Arnold Myint. The new hot spot also has a smoke-free outdoor courtyard.

Farther south of downtown, **Rumours Wine Bar,** 2304 12th Ave. S. (✆ **615/292-9400;** www.rumourswinebar.com), is a cozy house converted into a festive bar that offers more than 50 by-the-glass wines along with tasty tapas, flat breads, and fish specialties. The arty patio, with its whimsical metal sculptures, is an unexpected find.

Meanwhile, in the West End, **Virago,** 1811 Division St. (✆ **615/320-5149;** www.viragosushi.com), is still the Vanderbilt University area's most sizzling sushi bar and a late-night gathering place.

Tribe ★ A cosmopolitan gay bar, Tribe attracts fashionable men and women. Music videos and a pool table provide diversions away from the dance floor, but the energetic crowds don't usually disperse until late into the night and early morning. Sunday evenings are dedicated to show tunes. 1517A Church St. ✆ **615/329-2912.** www.tribenashville.com. No cover.

4 THE PERFORMING ARTS

THE TENNESSEE PERFORMING ARTS CENTER (TPAC)

A major renovation completed in fall 2003 gave the drab, utilitarian **Tennessee Performing Arts Center (TPAC),** 505 Deaderick St. (✆ **615/782-4000;** www.tpac.org), a much-needed makeover. Glass walls and an electronic marquee now illuminate the formerly nondescript, concrete exterior of Nashville's premier performance facility. The center houses three theaters: the Andrew Johnson, the James K. Polk, and the Andrew Jackson, whose expanded lobby now dazzles patrons with a 30-foot waterfall and other aesthetic touches. The three spaces can accommodate large and small productions (ticket prices $10–$45). Resident companies based here include the **Nashville Ballet** (✆ **615/297-2966;** www.nashvilleballet.com), which each year stages two full-length ballets and two programs of selected pieces; and the **Nashville Opera** (✆ **615/832-5242;** www.nashvilleopera.org), which mounts four lavish productions annually.

TPAC, as locals know it, is also home to two theater companies. The **Tennessee Repertory Theatre** (✆ **615/244-4878;** www.tnrep.org) is the state's largest professional theater company. Its five seasonal productions run from September to May and include dramas, musicals, and comedies. TPAC's other resident theater company is **Circle Players** (✆ **615/332-PLAY** [7529]; www.circleplayers.net), Nashville's oldest nonprofit volunteer arts group. This company does six productions per season and seems to take more chances on lesser-known works than the Rep does.

In addition to productions by Nashville's main performing arts companies, TPAC also hosts various acts and an annual **"Broadway Series"** (✆ **615/782-4000**) that brings first-rate touring productions such as *My Fair Lady* and *Spamalot* to Nashville between October and June. Tickets to TPAC performances are available either at the TPAC box office or through **Ticketmaster** (✆ **615/255-9600;** www.ticketmaster.com).

The **Nashville Symphony** (✆ **615/783-1200;** www.nashvillesymphony.org), which presents a mix of classical and pops concerts, as well as a children's series, has a stunning new home in the **Schermerhorn Hall** (corner of Fourth Ave. S. at Demonbreun). The acoustically superior 1,872-seat venue features 30 soundproof overhead windows, making it the only major concert hall in the world featuring natural light.

OTHER VENUES & SERIES AROUND THE CITY

Looking beyond TPAC, you'll find a wide array of performances in the **Great Performances at Vanderbilt** series (✆ **615/322-2471;** www.vanderbilt.edu), which is staged at Vanderbilt University's Ingram Hall, Blair School of Music, 24th Avenue South at Children's Way (tickets $10–$26). Each year, this series includes more than a dozen internationally acclaimed performing arts companies from around the world. Recent acts have included Grupo Cultural AfroReggae, the Trey McIntyre Project, L.A. Theatre Works, and India's Nrityagram Dance Ensemble. The emphasis is on chamber music and modern dance, but touring theater productions are also scheduled.

The **Nashville Municipal Auditorium,** 417 Fourth Ave. N. (✆ **615/862-6390;** www.nashvilleauditorium.com), for many years, was the site of everything from circuses to revivals. Today the aging, dome-roofed venue plays host to everyone from Bob Dylan to Bob the Builder. Plus, there's always the occasional rodeo, boxing match, or monster-truck mash. A stone's throw away, the newly renamed **Sommet Center** (previously the Gaylord Entertainment Center), 501 Broadway (✆ **615/770-2000;** www.sommetcenter.com), is now the venue of choice for major rock and country music concerts, ice shows, the Arena Football League's Kats, and NHL hockey, courtesy of the Nashville Predators. Thanks to the recent purchase of the team by a group of Nashville investors, the Predators' future in Nashville seems secure.

The "Music City J.A.M. (Jazz and More)" festival is one of the premier live, outdoor music events. It takes place Saturday and Sunday over Labor Day weekend at downtown Nashville's **Riverfront Park.** Every Thursday night from June to August, Grammy-nominated jazz saxophonist Kirk Whalum serves as emcee for the all-star, family-oriented program, which includes gospel, jazz, soul, reggae, and blues acts. Admission is $25 for a 2-day pass or $15 for a single-day pass. For more information, call Ticketmaster outlets (✆ **615/255-3588**). The **Frist Center for the Arts** offers Frist Fridays on the last Friday of every month (May–Sept). Free admission includes live music and appetizers outside in the courtyard, along with entry into the Frist's galleries (5:30–9pm). For more information, call ✆ **615/244-3340.**

Farther away, the verdant grounds of **Cheekwood Botanical Garden & Museum of Art,** 1200 Forrest Park Dr. (✆ **615/356-8000;** www.cheekwood.org), are the site of annual summer concerts by the Nashville Symphony each June.

In addition, I highly recommend the **Belcourt Theatre,** 2102 Belcourt Ave. (✆ **615/383-9140;** www.belcourt.org), where you can catch the latest art-house film releases and other cinematic fare that's all but ignored by today's modern multiplexes. From October through December, the theater stages a weekend classics matinee series called "The Best Old Movies for Families." Neil Simon's *Rumors,* Noel Coward's *Blithe Spirit,* and the bluegrass musical *Smoke on the Mountain Reunion* were recently staged here. Live entertainment, including musical events and occasional lectures/discussions, are also staged occasionally at the Belcourt—fitting, as the venue was one of the early homes of the *Grand Ole Opry.*

If you enjoy dinner theater, you may want to check out **Chaffin's Barn Dinner Theatre,** 8204 Tenn. 100 (✆ **800/282-BARN** [2276] or 615/646-9977; www.dinnertheatre.com), housed in a big old Dutch-colonial barn 20 minutes outside Nashville (dinner and show $40 adults, $20 children 12 and under; show only $33 adults, $25 children). The dinner is an all-you-can-eat country buffet (think fried catfish, ham, green beans, and fruit cobblers and berry shortcakes). Recent stage shows have run the gamut from *Chicago* and *Lend Me a Tenor* to *Arsenic and Old Lace.* Performances are Tuesday through Saturday. Reservations are required and must be paid for 24 hours in advance. To reach Chaffin's Barn, take I-40 west to exit 199 (Old Hickory Blvd.) and head south to Old Harding Road (Tenn. 100), turn right, and continue for 4 miles.

11

Side Trips from Nashville

After you've had your fill of Nashville's country music scene, it may be time for a change of scenery—and a taste of the real country. Heading out in any direction from Nashville, you'll hit the Tennessee hills. These are the hills famous for their walking horses and sour-mash whiskey. They also hold historic towns and Civil War battlefields that are well worth visiting.

1 FRANKLIN, COLUMBIA & SCENIC U.S. 31

Franklin is 20 miles south of Nashville; Columbia is 46 miles south of Nashville.

South of Nashville, U.S. 31 leads through the rolling Tennessee hills to the historic towns of Franklin and Columbia. This area was the heart of the middle Tennessee plantation country, and there are still many antebellum mansions along this route. Between Nashville and Franklin, you'll pass by more than a dozen old plantation homes, with still more to the south of Franklin.

ESSENTIALS

GETTING THERE The start of the scenic section of U.S. 31 is in Brentwood, at exit 74 off I-65. Alternatively, you can take I-65 straight to Franklin (exit 65) and then take U.S. 31 back north to Nashville. From Columbia, you can head back north on U.S. 31, take U.S. 412/Tenn. 99 east to I-65, or head west on Tenn. 50 to the **Natchez Trace Parkway.** This latter road is a scenic highway administered by the National Park Service.

VISITOR INFORMATION In Franklin, stop in at the tiny **Williamson County Visitor Information Center,** 209 E. Main St. (✆ **615/591-8514**), open Monday to Friday 9am to 4pm, Saturday 9am to 5pm, and Sun 1 to 4pm; closed holidays.

EXPLORING HISTORIC FRANKLIN

At the visitor center—housed in a former doctor's office built in 1839—you can pick up information about various historic sites around the area, including a map to the historic homes along U.S. 31 and a self-guided walking-tour map of Franklin. A 15-block area of downtown and quite a few other buildings around town have been listed on the National Register of Historic Places. Today, nearly the entire town has been restored—both commercial buildings around the central square and residential buildings in surrounding blocks—giving the town a charming 19th-century air. The best thing to do in Franklin is just stroll around admiring the restored buildings, browsing through the many antiques stores and malls. In addition to downtown antiques malls, there are others at the I-65 interchange.

Franklin is best known in Tennessee as the site of the bloody Battle of Franklin during the Civil War. During this battle, which took place on November 30, 1864, more than

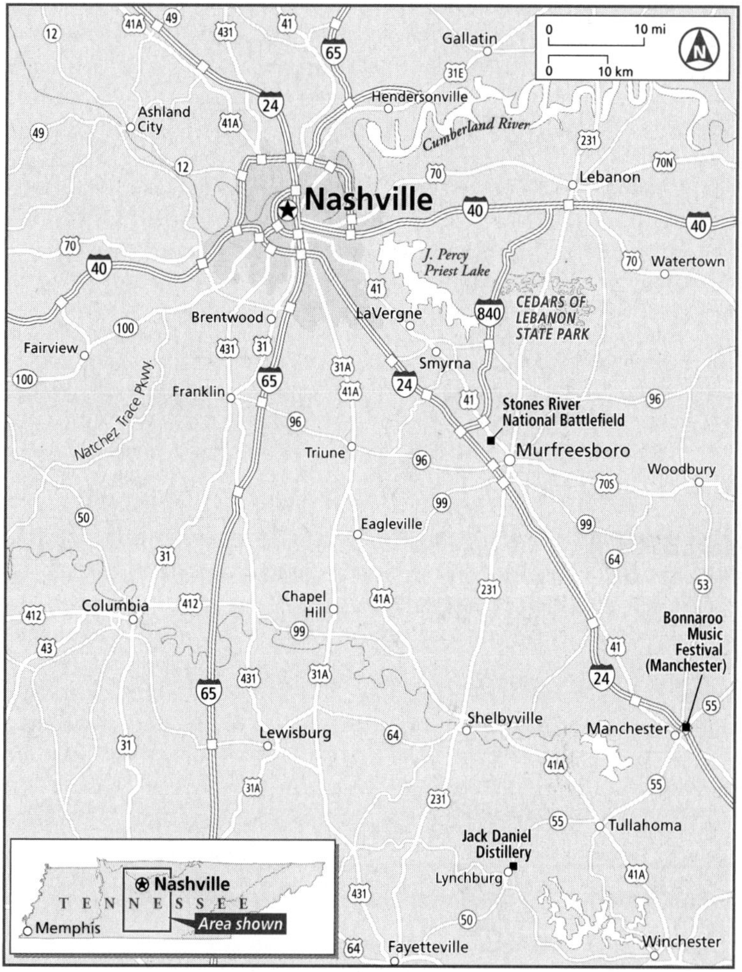

6,000 Confederate and 2,000 Union soldiers were killed. Each year on November 30, there are special activities here to commemorate the battle. Among the events are costumed actors marching through town and, after dark, a bonfire. Contact the Visitor Information Center for details.

To learn more about the town's Civil War history, visit the following historic homes.

Carnton Plantation & Battlefield ★ Recently, this somber tourist attraction gained greater visibility as the backdrop for Robert Hicks's best-selling historic novel, *The Widow of the South* (2006). Built in 1826 by Randal McGavock, a former mayor of Nashville, Carnton Plantation is a beautiful neoclassical antebellum mansion with a

Greek Revival portico. During the Battle of Franklin, one of the bloodiest battles of the Civil War, this plantation home served as a Confederate hospital, and today you can still see the blood stains on floors throughout the house. The interior of the stately old home is almost completely restored and houses many McGavock family pieces and other period furnishings. Two years after the battle, the McGavock family donated 2 acres of land to be used as a cemetery for Confederate soldiers who had died during the Battle of Franklin. There are almost 1,500 graves in the McGavock Confederate Cemetery, which makes this the largest private Confederate cemetery in the country.

1345 Carnton Lane. ✆ **615/794-0903.** www.carnton.org. Admission $10 adults, $9 seniors, $5 children 6–12. Mon–Sat 9am–5pm, Sun 1–5pm. Closed major holidays.

The Carter House Built in 1830, the Carter House served as the Union army command post during the Battle of Franklin. Throughout the bloody fight, which raged all around the house, the Carter family and friends hid in the cellar. Today, you can still see many bullet holes in the main house and various outbuildings on the property. In addition to getting a tour of the restored home, you can spend time in the museum, which contains many Civil War artifacts. A video presentation about the battle that took place here will provide you with a perspective for touring the town of Franklin.

1140 Columbia Ave. ✆ **615/791-1861.** www.carterhouse1864.com. Admission $12 adults, $10 seniors, $6 children 6–13. Apr–Oct Mon–Sat 9am–5pm, Sun 1–5pm; Nov–Mar Mon–Fri 9am–4pm, Sun 1–4pm. Closed major holidays.

COLUMBIA

Heading south from Franklin on U.S. 31 for about 26 miles will bring you to the town of Columbia. Along the way, you'll see a dozen or so historic antebellum homes, and in Columbia itself, more old homes and three districts listed on the National Register of Historic Places.

James K. Polk Home This modest home was where James K. Polk, the 11th president of the United States, grew up and where he lived when he began his legal and political career. Though Polk may not be as familiar a name as those of some other early presidents, he did achieve two very important goals while in office: Polk negotiated the purchase of California and settled the long-standing dispute between the United States

Full Speed at the National Corvette Museum

If the **Lane Motor Museum** (p. 100) in Nashville whets your appetite for more auto-centric sightseeing, head north on I-65 toward Bowling Green, Kentucky. Less than an hour's drive from Music City is the **National Corvette Museum** (✆ **800/53-VETTE** [538-3883] or 270/781-7973; www.corvettemuseum.com), devoted entirely to the car model that was first launched in 1953.

With its distinctive red-and-yellow spiral tower, the museum is an eye-catching oddity within clear view of the interstate. Inside, the museum's 110,000 square feet of displays, videos, photos, and memorabilia are enough to keep speed-enthusiasts salivating. Of course, the real showstoppers are the dozens of Corvette models and concept cars. Across the street is the Corvette Assembly Plant, which also offers tours.

and England over where to draw the border of the Oregon Territory. The house is filled with antiques that belonged to Polk's parents when they lived here and to Polk and his family during their time in the White House. There's even a lock of former U.S. President Andrew Jackson's hair.

301 W. Seventh St., Columbia. ✆ **931/388-2354.** www.jameskpolk.com. Admission $7 adults, $6 seniors, and $4 students 6–18 (maximum of $20 per family for parents with children under 18). Apr–Oct Mon–Sat 9am–5pm, Sun 1–5pm; Nov–Mar Mon–Sat 9am–4pm, Sun 1–5pm. Closed major holidays.

2 DISTILLERIES, HORSES & A BATTLEFIELD

Though Tennessee was last to secede from the Union, the Civil War came early to the state, and 3 years of being on the front lines left Tennessee with a legacy written in blood. More Civil War battles were fought here than in any other state except Virginia, and the bloodiest of these was the Battle of Stones River, which took place 30 miles south of Nashville, near the city of Murfreesboro. Today this battle is commemorated at the **Stones River National Battlefield.**

In the 2 decades that followed the war, Tennessee quickly recovered and developed two of the state's most famous commodities—Tennessee sippin' whiskey and Tennessee walking horses. Another 45 miles or so south of Murfreesboro, you can learn about both of these time-honored Tennessee traditions.

For those who are not connoisseurs of sour-mash whiskeys, Tennessee whiskey is *not* bourbon. This latter whiskey, named for Bourbon County, Kentucky, where it was first distilled, is made much the same way, but it is not charcoal-mellowed the way fine Tennessee sour-mash whiskey is.

Stones River National Battlefield On New Year's Eve 1862, what would become the bloodiest Civil War battle west of the Appalachian Mountains began just north of Murfreesboro, along the Stones River. Though by the end of the first day of fighting the Confederates thought they were assured a victory, Union reinforcements turned the tide against the rebels. By January 3, the Confederates were in retreat and 23,000 soldiers lay dead or injured on the battlefield. Today, 351 acres of the battlefield are preserved. The site includes a national cemetery and the Hazen Brigade Monument, which was erected in 1863 and is the oldest Civil War memorial in the United States. In the visitor center you'll find a museum full of artifacts and details of the battle.

3501 Old Nashville Hwy., Murfreesboro. ✆ **615/893-9501.** www.nps.gov/stri. Free admission. Daily 8am–5pm. Closed Dec 25. Take I-24 south from Nashville for about 30 miles to exit 78B.

Jack Daniel's Distillery ★ Old Jack Daniel (or Mr. Jack, as he was known hereabouts) didn't waste any time setting up his whiskey distillery after the Civil War came to an end. Founded in 1866, this is the oldest registered distillery in the United States and is on the National Register of Historic Places. It's still an active distillery; you can tour the facility and see how Jack Daniel's whiskey is made and learn how it gets such a distinctive earthy flavor. There are two secrets to the manufacture of Mr. Jack's famous sour-mash whiskey. The first of these is the water that comes gushing—pure, cold, and iron-free—from Cave Spring. The other is the sugar maple that's used to make the charcoal. In fact, it is this charcoal, through which the whiskey slowly drips, that gives Jack Daniel's its renowned smoothness.

After touring the distillery, you can glance in at the office used by Mr. Jack and see the safe that did him in. Old Mr. Jack kicked that safe one day in a fit of anger and wound up getting gangrene for his troubles. One can only hope that regular doses of Tennessee sippin' whiskey helped ease the pain of his last days. If you want to take home a bottle of Jack Daniel's, they can be purchased here at the distillery, but nowhere else in this county, which is another of Tennessee's dry counties. (No tastings at the end of the tour, I'm afraid.)

Note: It's easy to get here after visiting the Stones River National Battlefield (above). Continue on I-24 to exit 105, then drive southwest for 10 miles to Tullahoma and follow signs to the distillery in nearby Lynchburg.

182 Lynchburg Hwy, Lynchburg. ✆ **931/759-6319.** www.jackdaniels.com. Free admission. Daily 9am–4:30pm. Tours at regular intervals throughout the day. Reservations not accepted. Closed Thanksgiving, Dec 24–25, Dec 31, and Jan 1. Take Tenn. 55 off I-24 and drive 26 miles southwest to Lynchburg.

Tennessee Walking Horse Museum The Tennessee walking horse, named for its unusual high-stepping walking gait, is considered the world's premier breed of show horse, and it is here in the rolling hills of middle Tennessee that most of these horses are bred. Using interactive videos, hands-on exhibits, and other displays, this museum presents the history of the Tennessee walking horse. Though the exhibits here will appeal primarily to equine enthusiasts, there is also much for the casual visitor to learn and enjoy. The annual Tennessee Walking Horse National Celebration, held each August here in Shelbyville, is one of middle Tennessee's most important annual events. Tennessee walkers can also be seen going through their paces at various other annual shows in the Nashville area.

183 Main St., Lynchburg. ✆ **931/759-5747.** www.twhnc.com. Free admission. Tues–Sat 10am–noon and 1–4pm. Closed major holidays.

AN UNFORGETTABLE LUNCH STOP IN LYNCHBURG

Miss Mary Bobo's Boarding House Restaurant ★ SOUTHERN You'll feel as if you should be wearing a hoop skirt or top hat when you see this grand white mansion, with its columns, long front porch, and balcony over the front door (but casual,

Tennessee Jammin'

If you're a rock-and-roots music fan planning a Tennessee road trip, don't miss the **Bonnaroo Music & Arts Festival** in Manchester, about 60 miles southeast of Nashville. This wild, 4-day outdoor concert event—held every June and rapidly becoming one of the hottest live music events in the country—conjures up a laid-back, hippie vibe on a grassy, 700-acre farm not far from Jack Daniel's and George Dickel's noted whiskey distilleries (in Lynchburg and Tullahoma, respectively).

Bring your camping gear and sense of free-spirited abandon to Bonnaroo. In between sets by such diverse headliners such the Dave Matthews Band, Kings of Leon, Stevie Wonder, Jay-Z, Norah Jones, Jimmy Cliff, and Jeff Beck, browse the eccentric village scene for other entertaining diversions and eye-popping people-watching. For more information, visit www.bonnaroo.com.

contemporary clothes are just fine). Miss Mary Bobo's, housed in an antebellum-style mansion built slightly postbellum (in 1866), opened for business as a boardinghouse back in 1908, and though it no longer accepts boarders, it does serve the best lunch for miles around. Be prepared for filling portions of good Southern home cooking, and remember, lunch here is actually midday dinner. Miss Mary's is very popular, and you generally need to book a weekday lunch 2 to 3 weeks in advance; for a Saturday lunch, you'll need to make reservations at least 2 to 3 *months* in advance.

Main St., Lynchburg. ✆ **931/759-7394.** www.jackdaniels.co.uk/lynchburg/boarding.asp. Reservations required well in advance. Set menu $11 adults, $5 children 9 and under. No credit cards. Lunch seatings Mon–Fri 1pm; Sat 11am and 1pm.

12 The Best of Memphis

Memphis spawned several of the most important musical forms of the 20th century, yet Nashville stole the Tennessee limelight with its country music. Ask the average American what makes Memphis special, and he or she *might* be able to tell you that this is the city of Graceland, Elvis Presley's mansion.

What they're less likely to know is that Memphis is also the birthplace of the blues, rock 'n' roll, and soul music. Memphis is where W. C. Handy put down on paper the first written blues music, where The King made his first recording, and where Otis Redding and Al Green expressed the music in their souls.

Many fans of American music (and they come from all over the world) know Memphis. Walking down Beale Street today, sitting in the Sun Studio Cafe, or waiting to pass through the wrought-iron gates of Graceland, you're almost as likely to hear French, German, and Japanese as you are to hear English. British, Irish, and Scottish accents are all common in a city known throughout the world as the birthplace of the most important musical styles of the 20th century. For these people, a trip to Memphis is a pilgrimage. The Irish rock band U2 came here to pay homage and wound up infusing their music with Americana on the record and movie *U2: Rattle and Hum.* Lead singer Bono, when interviewed for the city's new Soulsville museum, called the city's musical heritage "extraordinary."

Pilgrims come to Memphis not only because Graceland, the second most-visited home in America (after the White House), is here, but they also come because Beale Street was once home to Handy—and later, B. B. King, Muddy Waters, and others—who merged the gospel singing and cotton-field work songs of the Mississippi Delta into a music called the blues. They come because Sun Studio's owner, Sam Phillips, in the early 1950s began recording several young musicians who experimented with fusing the sounds of "hillbilly" (country) music and the blues into an entirely new sound. This uniquely American sound, first known as rockabilly, would quickly become known as rock 'n' roll, the music that has written the soundtrack for the baby-boom generation.

1 FROMMER'S MOST UNFORGETTABLE TRAVEL EXPERIENCES

- **Remembering Reverend Martin Luther King from the Balcony of the Lorraine Motel:** Mournful gospel hymns play softly in the background as visitors approach the place where the civil rights leader was assassinated in 1968. This is the conclusion of a visit to the inspiring **National Civil Rights Museum,** 450 Mulberry St. (© **901/521-9699;** www.civilrightsmuseum.org), built on the site of this once-segregated motel. See p. 214.
- **Standing at the Sun Studio Microphone that Elvis Used for His First Recordings:** It's worth the tour admission price just to handle the microphone in this famed recording studio at 706 Union Ave. (© **800/441-6249;** www.sunstudio.com). It launched the

career of Elvis Presley and created a sound that would come to be called rock 'n' roll. See p. 211.

- **Getting Your First Glimpse of the "Jungle Room":** Sure, you've probably heard about the hideously gaudy decor inside Graceland mansion, 3734 Elvis Presley Blvd. (✆ **800/238-2000;** www.elvis.com), but nothing prepares you for that first face-to-faux-fur encounter in the green-and-gold den Elvis created to remind him of Hawaii. See p. 208.

2 THE BEST SPLURGE HOTELS

- **River Inn of Harbor Town,** 50 Harbor Town Square (✆ **877/222-1531** or 901/260-3333; www.riverinnmemphis.com): A small, European-style hotel tucked within an affluent community on the resortlike residential island of Harbor Town, this hotel is a hidden gem. With sumptuous furnishings, gourmet food, impeccable service, and beautiful walking trails just steps away on the bank of the Mississippi River, it is unlike any other property in Memphis. See p. 169.
- **The Peabody,** 149 Union Ave. (✆ **800/PEABODY** [732-2639] or 901/529-4000; www.peabodymemphis.com): Steeped in tradition and brimming with gracious hospitality, this is one of the most elegant hotels in the South. Of course, you'll also be sharing the lobby with the famous Peabody ducks. See p. 168.
- The **Madison Hotel,** 79 Madison Ave. (✆ **866/44-MEMPHIS** [446-3674] or 901/333-1200; www.madisonhotelmemphis.com): This sophisticated boutique hotel was built in a historic bank building downtown. Warm and intimate, it's a romantic retreat that offers spectacular sunsets from the rooftop garden. See p. 168.

3 THE BEST MODERATELY PRICED HOTELS

- **Elvis Presley's Heartbreak Hotel–Graceland,** 3677 Elvis Presley Blvd. (✆ **877/777-0606** or 901/332-1000; www.elvis.com): If you're an Elvis fan, this one's a no-brainer. Operated by Graceland and mere steps away from the King's mansion, this modest hotel has kitsch to spare. Elvis is everywhere, from the breakfast nook to the outdoor pool. See p. 180.
- **Sleep Inn–Downtown at Court Square,** 40 N. Front St. (✆ **877/424-6423** or 901/522-9700; www.choicehotels.com): With a terrific downtown location, between Court Square and the Mississippi River, and with the Main Street Trolley at your door, this clean, comfy motel is an affordable gem. See p. 174.

4 THE MOST UNFORGETTABLE DINING EXPERIENCES

- **Tasting the Cuisine of a Rising Culinary Star:** Kelly English wasn't named one of *Food & Wine*'s Best Chefs of 2009 for nothing. At his new fine-dining

Restaurant Iris, 2146 Monroe Ave. (© **901/590-2828;** www.restaurantiris.com), French-Creole specialties are as inspired as they are delicious. See p. 193.

- **Savoring Soul Food:** Not far from the Stax Museum, **Four Way Restaurant,** 998 Mississippi Blvd. (© **901/507-1519**), churns out comforting Southern dishes such as fried catfish, green beans, black-eyed peas and sweet-potato pie. See p. 201.
- **Agonizing Over Who Has the Best Barbecue:** Some favor the dry, spice-rubbed ribs at the **Rendezvous,** 52 S. Second St. (© **901/523-2746;** www.hogsfly.com), while others drool over the sloppy-wet, pulled-pork sandwiches at **Corky's Ribs & BBQ,** 5259 Poplar Ave. (© **901/685-9744;** www.corkysmemphis.com). With dozens of dives, sit-down eateries, and drive-throughs devoted to 'cue, you could literally eat your way across Memphis to decide for yourself. See p. 199.

5 THE BEST THINGS TO DO FOR FREE (OR ALMOST)

- **Walkin' in Memphis:** The paved trails and grassy expanse of Tom Lee Park downtown provide breathtaking views of the Mississippi River and Memphis skyline. Take a brisk walk or loll on a bench and watch the barges glide by on their way to New Orleans. See p. 217.
- **Browsing for Bargains at A. Schwab Dry Goods Store:** Need Elvis aviator sunglasses? Voodoo candles? Sombreros or screwdrivers? Underpants or overalls? It's all here, and then some, at A. Schwab Dry Goods Store, 163 Beale St. (© **901/523-9782**). Opened in 1876 and little-changed since then, this beloved old-time dime store and antiques museum has creaky wooden floors, cheap prices, and a mind-boggling array of stuff you won't find anywhere else. See p. 239.
- **Shopping for the Tackiest Elvis Souvenir in the World:** The hip-swinging Elvis clock has become all too familiar, so why not try some stick-on Elvis sideburns, an Elvis temporary tattoo, an Elvis Christmas ornament, Elvis playing cards, an Elvis nightlight, or a little plastic tray displaying the infamous photo of Elvis arm-in-arm with President Richard Nixon. See "Shopping A to Z," in chapter 19.

13

Memphis in Depth

Memphis is just a few hours' drive from Nashville, but in many ways it seems worlds away. Though conservative and traditional, the city has spawned several of the most important musical forms of the 20th century—blues, rock 'n' roll, and soul. And although it has been unable to cash in on this musical heritage (at least to the profitable extent that Nashville has with country music), Memphis still seems like a scrappy underdog in its fight to proclaim musical superiority. Less progressive—or, some might say, polished—than Nashville, Memphis still proudly proclaims its significance as the *true* mecca of American music.

1 MEMPHIS TODAY

Memphis is primarily known for being the city where Graceland is located, but how long can the Elvis craze sustain itself? A city needs diversity and an identity of its own. To that end, in the past few years Memphis has made considerable progress. One of the greatest hurdles to overcome has been the legacy of racial tension that came to a head with the assassination here of Martin Luther King, Jr., and the rioting that ensued. Racial tensions are still frequently named as the city's foremost civic problem, even though the casual observer or visitor may not see any signs of these difficulties. Racial tensions combined with post–World War II white flight to the suburbs of East Memphis left downtown a mere shell of a city, but today, this is changing.

These days, downtown is the most vibrant area in metropolitan Memphis. A new baseball stadium, the renovation of Beale Street (known as the home of the blues), and a spate of newly constructed museums, hotels, restaurants, and shops are breathing fresh life into downtown Memphis. This has succeeded not only in keeping office workers here after hours to enjoy the live music in the street's many nightclubs but also in luring residents in the outlying suburban areas to flock downtown—a concept that was unheard of 10 years ago.

For the time being, though, Elvis is still King in Memphis. A quarter-century after the entertainer's death, Graceland remains the number-one tourist attraction in the city. Throughout the year, there are Elvis celebrations, which leave no doubt that this is still a city, and a nation, obsessed with Elvis Presley. Less popular, but equally worth visiting, are such attractions as Sun Studio, where Elvis made his first recording; the Rock 'n' Soul Museum; and the Memphis Music Hall of Fame, which has displays on Elvis and many other local musicians who made major contributions to rock, soul, and blues music.

2 LOOKING BACK AT MEMPHIS

Habitation of the bluffs of the Mississippi dates from nearly 15,000 years ago, but it was between A.D. 900 and A.D. 1600, during the Mississippian period, that the native peoples of this region reached a cultural zenith. During this 700-year period, people congregated in large, permanent villages. Sun worship, a distinctive style of artistic expression, and mound building were the main characteristics of this culture. The mounds, which today are the most readily evident reminders of this native heritage, were built as foundations for temples and can still be seen in places such as the Chucalissa Archaeological Museum. However, by the time the first Europeans arrived in the area, the mound builders had disappeared and been replaced by the Chickasaw Indians.

As early as 1541, Spanish explorer Hernando de Soto stood atop a 100-foot bluff and looked down on the mighty Mississippi River. More than 100 years later, in 1682, French explorer Sieur de La Salle claimed the entire Mississippi River valley for his country. However, it would be more than 50 years before the French would build a permanent outpost in this region.

In 1739, the French built Fort Assumption on the fourth Chickasaw bluff. From this spot, they hoped to control the Chickasaw tribes, who had befriended the English. By the end of the 18th century, the Louisiana Territory had passed into the hands of the Spanish, who erected Fort San Fernando, on the bluff over the Mississippi. Within 2 years the Spanish had decamped to the far side of the river and the U.S. flag flew above Fort Adams, which had been built on the ruins of Fort San Fernando.

A treaty negotiated with the Chickasaw Nation in 1818 ceded all of western Tennessee to the United States, and within the year, John Overton, General James Winchester, and Andrew Jackson (who would later become president of the United States) founded Memphis as a speculative land investment. The town was named for the capital of ancient Egypt, a reference to the Mississippi being the American Nile. However, it would take the better part of the century before the city began to live up to its grand name.

GROWTH OF A RIVER PORT The town of Memphis was officially incorporated in 1826, and for the next 2 decades grew slowly. In 1845, the establishment of a naval yard in Memphis gave the town a new importance. Twelve years later, the Memphis and Charleston Railroad linked Memphis to Charleston, South Carolina, on the Atlantic coast. With the Mississippi Delta region beginning just south of Memphis, the city played an important role as the main shipping port for cotton grown in the delta. This role as river port, during the heyday of river transportation in the mid–19th century, gave Memphis a link and kinship with other river cities to

DATELINE

- **1541** Hernando de Soto views Mississippi River from fourth Chickasaw bluff, site of today's Memphis.
- **1682** La Salle claims Mississippi Valley for France.
- **1739** French governor of Louisiana orders a fort built on fourth Chickasaw bluff.
- **1795** Manuel Gayoso, in order to expand Spanish lands in North America, erects Fort San Fernando on Mississippi River.
- **1797** Americans build Fort Adams on ruins of Fort San Fernando, and the Spanish flee to the far side of the river.
- **1818** Chickasaw Nation cedes western Tennessee to the United States.
- **1819** Town of Memphis founded.
- **1826** Memphis is incorporated.
- **1840s** Cheap land makes for boom times in Memphis.
- **1857** Memphis and Charleston Railroad completed, linking the Atlantic and the Mississippi.
- **1862** Memphis falls to Union troops but becomes an important smuggling center.
- **1870s** Several yellow-fever epidemics leave the city almost abandoned.

the north. With its importance to the cotton trade of the Deep South and its river connections to the Mississippi port cities of the Midwest, Memphis developed some of the characteristics of both regions, creating a city not wholly of the South or the Midwest, but rather, a city in between.

In the years before the Civil War began, the people of Memphis were very much in favor of secession, but it was only a few short months after the outbreak of the war that Memphis fell to Union troops. Both the Union and the Confederacy had seen the importance of Memphis as a supply base, and yet the Confederates had been unable to defend their city—on June 6, 1862, steel-nosed ram boats easily overcame the Confederate fleet guarding Memphis. The city quickly became a major smuggling center as merchants sold to both the North and the South.

Within 2 years of the war's end, tragedy struck Memphis. Cholera and yellow fever epidemics swept through the city, killing hundreds of residents. This was only the first, and the mildest, of such epidemics to plague Memphis over the next 11 years. In 1872 and 1878, yellow-fever epidemics killed thousands of people and caused nearly half the city's population to flee. In the wake of these devastating outbreaks of the mosquito-borne disease, the city was left bankrupt and nearly abandoned.

However, some people remained in Memphis and had faith that the city would one day regain its former importance. One of those individuals was Robert Church, a onetime slave, who bought real estate from people who were fleeing the yellow-fever plague. He later became the South's first African-American millionaire. In 1899, on a piece of land near the corner of Beale and Fourth streets, Church established a park and auditorium where African Americans could gather in public.

CIVIL RIGHTS MOVEMENT In the years following the Civil War, freed slaves from around the South flocked to Memphis in search of jobs. Other African-American professionals, educated in the North, also came to Memphis to establish new businesses. The center for this growing community was Beale Street. With all manner of businesses, from lawyers' and doctors' offices to bars and houses of prostitution, Beale Street was a lively community. The music that played in the juke joints and honky-tonks began to take on a new sound that derived from the spirituals, field calls, and work songs of the Mississippi Delta cotton fields. By the first decade of the 20th century, this music had acquired a name—the blues.

Blues music was the expression of more than a century of struggle and suffering by African Americans. By the middle of the

- **1879** Memphis declares bankruptcy, and its charter is revoked.
- **1880s** Memphis rebounds.
- **1890s** Memphis becomes largest hardwood market in the world, attracting African Americans seeking to share in city's boom times.
- **1892** First bridge across Mississippi south of St. Louis opens in Memphis.
- **1893** Memphis regains its city charter.
- **1899** Church Park and Auditorium, the city's first park and entertainment center for African Americans, are built.
- **1909** W. C. Handy, a Beale Street bandleader, becomes the father of the blues when he writes first blues song for mayoral candidate E. H. "Boss" Crump.
- **1916** Nation's first self-service grocery store opens in Memphis.
- **1925** Peabody hotel built. Tom Lee rescues 23 people from sinking steamboat.
- **1928** Orpheum Theatre opens.
- **1940** B. B. King plays for first time on Beale Street, at an amateur music contest.
- **1952** Jackie Brenston's "Rocket 88," considered the first rock-'n'-roll recording, is released by Memphis's Sun Studio.

continues

20th century, that long suffering had been given another voice—the civil rights movement. One by one, school segregation and other discriminatory laws and practices of the South were challenged. Equal treatment and equal rights with whites was the goal of the civil rights movement, and the movement's greatest champion and spokesman was Dr. Martin Luther King, Jr., whose assassination in Memphis threw the city into the national limelight in April 1968.

In the early months of 1968, the sanitation workers of Memphis, most of whom were African Americans, went on strike. In early April, Dr. King came to Memphis to lead a march by the striking workers; he stayed at the Lorraine Motel, just south of downtown. On April 4, the day the march was to be held, Dr. King stepped out onto the balcony of the motel and was gunned down by an assassin's bullet. Dr. King's murder did not, as perhaps had been hoped, end the civil rights movement. Today, the Lorraine Motel has become the National Civil Rights Museum. The museum preserves the room where Dr. King was staying the day he was assassinated and includes many evocative exhibits on the history of the civil rights movement. The museum recently received a major renovation and expansion.

By the time of Dr. King's murder, downtown Memphis was a classic example of urban decay. The city's more affluent citizens had moved to the suburbs in the post–World War II years, and the inner city had quickly become an area of abandoned buildings and empty storefronts. However, beginning in the 1970s, a growing desire to restore life to downtown Memphis saw renovation projects undertaken. By the 1980s, the renewal process was well under way, and the 1990s saw a continuation of this slow but steady revitalization of downtown.

The blues, rock 'n' roll, and soul are sounds that defined Memphis music, and together these styles have made a name for Memphis all over the world. Never mind that the blues is no longer as popular as it once was, that Memphis long ago had its title of rock-'n'-roll capital usurped (by Cleveland, home of the Rock and Roll Hall of Fame), and that soul music evolved into other styles. Memphis continues to be important to music lovers as the city from which these sounds first emanated.

The blues, the first truly American musical style, developed from work songs and spirituals common in the Mississippi Delta in the late 19th and early 20th centuries. But the roots of the blues go back even farther, to traditional musical styles of Africa. During the 19th century, these musical traditions (brought to America by slaves) went through an interpretation and translation in the cotton fields and

- **1955** Elvis Presley records his first hit record at Sun Studio.
- **1958** Stax Records, a leader in the soul-music industry of the 1960s, founded.
- **1968** Dr. Martin Luther King, Jr., assassinated at Lorraine Motel.
- **1977** Elvis Presley dies at Graceland, his home on the south side of Memphis.
- **1983** Renovated Beale Street reopens as tourist attraction and nightlife district.
- **1991** National Civil Rights Museum opens in former Lorraine Motel. Pyramid completed.
- **1992** Memphis elects its first African-American mayor.
- **1993** Two movies based on John Grisham novels, *The Firm* and *The Client*, are filmed in Memphis.
- **1998** Memphis booms with $1.4 billion in expansion and renovation projects.
- **2000** Memphis Redbirds baseball team play their first season in new, $68.5-million AutoZone Park downtown.
- **2001** Grizzlies move to Memphis, becoming city's first, long-awaited NBA team.
- **2002** Groundbreaking begins on FedExForum downtown.

churches—the only places where African Americans could gather at that time. By the 1890s, freed slaves had brought their music of hard work and hard times into the nightclubs of Memphis.

BEALE STREET It was here, on Beale Street, that black musicians began to fuse together the various aspects of the traditional music of the Mississippi Delta. In 1909, one of these musicians, a young bandleader named William Christopher Handy, was commissioned to write a campaign song for E. H. "Boss" Crump, who was running for mayor of Memphis. Crump won the election, and "Boss Crump's Blues" became a local hit. W. C. Handy later published his tune under the title "Memphis Blues." With the publication of this song, Handy started a musical revolution that continues to this day. The blues, which developed at about the same time that jazz was first being played down in New Orleans, would later give rise to both rock 'n' roll and soul music.

Beale Street became a center for musicians, who flocked to the area to learn the blues and showcase their own musical styles. Over the next 4 decades, Beale Street produced many of the country's most famous blues musicians. Among these was a young man named Riley King, who first won praise during an amateur music contest. In the 1940s, King became known as the Beale Street "Blues Boy," the initials of which he incorporated into his stage name when he began calling himself B. B. King. Today, B. B. King's Blues Club is Beale Street's most popular nightclub. A couple of times a year, King performs at the club, and the rest of the year blues bands keep up the Beale Street tradition. Other musicians who developed their style and their first followings on Beale Street include Furry Lewis, Muddy Waters, Albert King, Bobby "Blue" Bland, Alberta Hunter, and Memphis Minnie McCoy.

By the time B. B. King got his start on Beale Street, the area was beginning to lose its importance. The Great Depression shut down a lot of businesses on the street, and many never reopened. By the 1960s, there was talk of bulldozing the entire area to make way for an urban-renewal project. However, in the 1970s, an interest in restoring old Beale Street developed. Beginning in 1980, the city of Memphis, together with business investors, began renovating the old buildings between Second and Fourth streets. New clubs and restaurants opened, and Beale Street once again became Memphis's main entertainment district. Today true blues music is harder to find, however, as cover bands playing well-known Sun and Stax hits for tourists dominate the street.

- **2003** Sun Studio founder Sam Phillips dies.
- **2003** Soulsville USA: Stax Museum of American Soul Music opens in South Memphis.
- **2004** FedExForum basketball arena and concert venue opens at foot of Beale Street.
- **2005** Films including *Hustle & Flow, Forty Shades of Blue,* and *Walk the Line* are shot in Memphis.
- **2006** Craig Brewer's *Black Snake Moan* is shot in Memphis.
- **2007** Ground-breaking begins on Ground Zero Blues Club, a Clarksdale, Mississippi–based juke-joint and restaurant, partly owned by Oscar-winning actor Morgan Freeman.

HERE COMES THE KING From the earliest days of Beale Street's musical popularity, whites visited the street's primarily black clubs. However, it wasn't until the late 1940s and early 1950s that a few adventurous white musicians began incorporating into their own music the earthy sounds and lyrics they heard on Beale Street. One of these musicians was a young man named Elvis Presley.

In the early 1950s, Sun Studio owner Sam Phillips began to record such Beale Street blues legends as B. B. King, Howlin' Wolf, Muddy Waters, and Little Milton, but his consumer market was limited to the African-American population. Phillips was searching for a way to take the blues to a mainstream (read: white) audience, and a new sound was what he needed. That new sound showed up at his door in 1954 in the form of a young delivery-truck driver named Elvis Presley, who, according to legend, had dropped in at Sun Studio to record a song as a birthday present for his mother. Phillips had already produced what many music scholars regard as the first rock-'n'-roll record when, in 1952, he recorded Jackie Brenston's "Rocket 88."

Two years later, when Elvis showed up at Sun Studio, Phillips knew that he had found what he was looking for. Within a few months of Elvis's visit to Sun Studio, three other musicians—Carl Perkins, Jerry Lee Lewis, and Johnny Cash—showed up independently of one another. Each brought his own interpretation of the crossover sound between the blues and country (or "hillbilly") music. The sounds these four musicians crafted soon became known as rockabilly music, the foundation of rock 'n' roll. Roy Orbison would also get his start here at Sun Studio.

ROCK 'N' ROLL 'N' SOUL, TOO In the early 1960s, Memphis once again entered the popular-music limelight when Stax/Volt Records gave the country its first soul music. Otis Redding, Isaac Hayes, Booker T. and the MGs, and Carla Thomas were among the musicians who got their start at this Memphis recording studio.

Some 10 years after Sun Studio made musical history, British bands such as the Beatles and the Rolling Stones latched onto the blues and rockabilly music and began exporting their take on this American music back across the Atlantic. With the music usurped by the British invasion, the importance of Memphis was quickly forgotten. Today, Memphis is no longer the musical innovator it once was, though in late 2003 city planners began strategizing on a bold new initiative to promote Memphis as the independent-record-label capital of the industry. Notwithstanding that effort, there's still an abundance of good music to be heard in its clubs. Musicians both young and old are keeping alive the music that put the city on the map.

3 THE LAY OF THE LAND

Located at the far western end of Tennessee, Memphis sits on a bluff overlooking the Mississippi River. Directly across the river lies Arkansas, and only a few miles to the south is Mississippi. The area, which was long known as the "fourth Chickasaw bluff," was chosen as a strategic site by Native Americans as well as French, Spanish, and finally American explorers and soldiers. The most important reason for choosing this site for the city was that the top of the bluff was above the high-water mark of the Mississippi and thus was safe from floods. Although Memphis started out as an important Mississippi River port, urban sprawl has carried the city's business centers ever farther east—so much so that the Big Muddy has become less a reason for being than simply a way of distinguishing Tennessee from Arkansas.

4 MEMPHIS IN BOOKS & FILM

Authors most often associated with Memphis and the Mississippi Delta are an interesting assortment of people. There's Civil War historian Shelby Foote, of course, and literary heavyweight William Faulkner, whose stories of the people and characters of a segregated South are indelibly etched in American pop culture. The great playwright Tennessee Williams also spent formative years in Memphis, and he wrote and produced early works here. But let's face it: No other writer put Memphis on the pop-culture map in a bigger way than John Grisham did in the 1990s.

The former Memphis-area attorney wrote a string of best-selling legal thrillers, including *The Firm.* When Tom Cruise (and then-wife Nicole Kidman, who now calls Nashville home with country-singer hubby Keith Urban) came to Memphis to star in the book's film version, directed by Sydney Pollack, the city was completely star struck. Screaming fans waited on street corners for a glimpse of the famous actor. Locales featured in some of the movie's scenes became tourist hot spots, and a cottage industry sprang up to promote the city's association with the Memphis-area film shoots that followed.

Among the many Grisham films, some are more memorable than others. Susan Sarandon was terrific in *The Client.* Joel Schumacher directed that film, which co-starred Mary Louise Parker and Tommy Lee Jones. Matt Damon and Danny DeVito did star turns in *The Rainmaker,* and Matthew McConaughey became an overnight sensation after his first big starring role in *A Time to Kill.* Less commercially and critically successful was *The Chamber,* with Gene Hackman playing a death-row inmate.

In non-Grisham movies, there have been several significant offerings. European filmmaker Milos Forman chose to film *The People Vs. Larry Flynt* in Memphis. Needless to say, co-stars Woody Harrelson and Courtney Love provided loads of gossipy fodder during their days on location shooting this biopic about the porn pioneer's court cases.

More recently, filmmakers have continued to find inspiration in Memphis. Sean Penn and Naomi Watts came to town for the gritty drama *21 Grams.* And director Craig Brewer's *Hustle and Flow,* about an aspiring rapper played by Terrence Howard, drew rave reviews—and even nabbed an Academy Award for local rappers Three 6 Mafia, who were featured in the film's soundtrack. Brewer's follow-up, *Black Snake Moan,* didn't rise to the same level of acclaim as *Hustle and Flow,* however. The sultry drama is one for the collective Memphis scrapbook. It features Samuel L. Jackson, Christina Ricci, and another local musician-turned-superstar, Justin Timberlake, who is cultivating an acting career.

5 EATING & DRINKING IN MEMPHIS

Memphis's barbecue smoke is inescapable. It billows from chimneys all across the city, and though it is present all year long, it makes its biggest impact in those months when people have their car windows open. Drivers experience an inexplicable, almost Pavlovian response. They begin to salivate, their eyes glaze over, and they follow the smoke to its source—a down-home barbecue joint.

In a region obsessed with pork barbecue, Memphis lays claim to the title of being the pork-barbecue capital of the world. Non-Southerners may need a short barbecue primer. Southern pork barbecue is, for the most part, just exactly what its name says it is—pork that has been barbecued over a wood fire. There are several variations on barbecue, and most barbecue places offer the full gamut. My personal favorite is hand-pulled shoulder, which is a barbecued shoulder of pork from which meat is pulled by hand after it's cooked. What you end up with on your plate is a pile of shredded pork to which you can add your favorite hot sauces.

Barbecued ribs are a particular Memphis specialty; these come either dry-cooked or wet-cooked. If you order your ribs dry-cooked, they come coated with a powdered spice mix and it's up to you to apply the sauce, but if you order it wet-cooked, the ribs will have been cooked in a sauce. Barbecue is traditionally served with a side of coleslaw (or mustard slaw) and perhaps baked beans or potato salad. In a pulled-pork-shoulder sandwich, the coleslaw goes in the sandwich as a lettuce replacement. **Corky's Ribs & BBQ** (p. 199) is the undisputed king of Memphis barbecue, while the **Rendezvous** (p. 192) is famed for its dry-cooked ribs.

The city's other traditional fare is good old-fashioned American food—here, as in Nashville, known as "meat-and-three," which refers to the three side vegetables that you get with whatever type of meat you happen to order. While this is very simple food, in the best "meat-and-three" restaurants, your vegetables are likely to be fresh (and there's always a wide variety of choices). Perhaps because of the Southern affinity for traditions, Memphians, both young and old, flock to "meat-and-three" restaurants for meals just like Mom used to fix.

What if you don't like barbecue? Thankfully, there are plenty of other tasty indulgences. Memphis has a diverse dining scene that includes top-tier gourmet restaurants, moderately priced cafes, and scores of Asian, Mexican, and Italian eateries. Burgers, steaks, seafood, and vegetarian options are also available in nearly every area of the city.

But still, there's no escaping the pervasive aroma of sizzling pig meat.

14

Suggested Memphis Itineraries

Many of Memphis's must-see sites are located downtown and in nearby South Memphis. Therefore, it's feasible to tackle a good chunk of the city's best in a single, action-packed day. As with any destination, the seasons and your personal interests will dictate how you proceed. Besides musical attractions, Memphis has much to offer in terms of culture and history. In the spring, summer, and fall, take advantage of the longer days and get outdoors to enjoy some of the city's many parks and natural attractions. Of course, rainy or wintry days make museums, galleries, and antiques shops more practical diversions. Fortunately, most of the city's popular attractions may be enjoyed during any time of year.

THE NEIGHBORHOODS IN BRIEF

More important than neighborhoods in Memphis are the city's general divisions. These major divisions are how the city defines itself.

Downtown The oldest part of the city, downtown is constructed on the banks of the Mississippi River. After years of efforts toward revitalization, the area saw a boom in development about 10 years ago. However, the recent recession has been a setback, causing many of these new businesses to close. Still, there are scattered openings of new restaurants and shops, too. **Beale Street** remains the city's main entertainment district. Elsewhere downtown, interspersed with the vacant storefronts, are scores of great restaurants, night spots, and cultural attractions. Unchanged, however, are the breathtaking views of the Mississippi River.

Midtown This is primarily a residential area, though it's also known for its numerous hospitals, which are themselves collectively known as the Medical Center district. Though a far cry from bustling Beale Street, the **Overton Square** area—once the city's top entertainment district—isn't what it once was. Still, it's where the professional theater companies are located, and there are several excellent restaurants here, including Paulette's and the new Restaurant Iris. South of Overton Square, you'll find the proudly Bohemian **Cooper-Young neighborhood**—basically a single intersection with trendy eateries, coffeehouses, and interesting boutiques. Midtown is also where you will find **Overton Park,** which envelops the Memphis Zoo and Aquarium, the Memphis Brooks Museum of Art, and the prestigious Memphis College of Art.

East Memphis Heading still farther east from downtown brings you to East Memphis, which lies roughly on either side of I-240 on the east side of the city. From downtown, take Poplar Avenue to get there. It's a maddeningly busy, narrow, and traffic-choked multilane corridor, but it's still the shortest distance between the two points. In East Memphis you'll find scads of malls and shopping centers, restaurants, office complexes, and a few high-rise hotels.

1 THE BEST OF MEMPHIS IN 1 DAY

Today you will get a taste of the musical legends that put Memphis on the map at the city's best music museums before getting a chance to reflect on the sociopolitical context of the 1950s. Start your day where rock 'n' roll was born: at Sun Studio.

❶ Sun Studio ★★

Start your day where it all began: In the early 1950s, a shy, teenaged truck driver named Elvis Presley sauntered into Sam Phillips's tiny recording studio, asked to cut a birthday song for his mama, and ultimately launched the birth of rock 'n' roll. See p. 211.

❷ Soulsville USA: The Stax Museum of American Soul Music ★★★

Albert King; Al Green; Earth, Wind & Fire; Isaac Hayes; and the Staples Singers are just a handful of the musical greats whose inspiring stories unfold in this rousing, interactive museum. The funky music reverberating throughout will make you want to sing, dance, stomp, and shout. See p. 210.

3 FOUR WAY RESTAURANT ★★★

After getting funkdafied by the vibes at Stax, head down the block and hang with the locals at this family-oriented soul food restaurant. Crispy, piping-hot fried chicken, turnip greens, and candied yams with cornbread and butter are the perfect preludes to silky lemon meringue pie. But there's a lot of other comfort food, too. 998 Mississippi Blvd. ✆ **901/507-1519.** See p. 201.

❹ National Civil Rights Museum ★★★

After spending the morning rocking to the sounds of Memphis music, put some social and political context behind what you've seen and heard. The National Civil Rights Museum is an absorbing and deeply moving experience, as it traces the cruel history of oppression and discrimination in the American South. See p. 214.

❺ South Main Street Arts District

Walk north back toward Beale Street, window shopping at boutiques and stepping inside cozy art galleries that are beginning to emerge in this revitalized historic district.

❻ Beale Street ★★

This legendary strip, revered the world over as the birthplace of the blues, can be a rowdy, neon boozefest after dark. But during the day, it's a sea of curious tourists taking pictures, listening to live music at the outdoor W. C. Handy Park, and shopping for souvenirs. Join them. A. Schwab's, a 130-year-old dry-goods store, has the best bargains around. See p. 205.

7 BLUES CITY CAFÉ

Grab a bite at this juke joint and diner, which is my pick as the best of the Beale Street eats. Spicy tamales, lip-smackin' slabs of pork barbecue ribs, as well as cold beer, burgers, and rich gumbo are on the menu. With its weather-beaten booths and rural-Mississippi shack-inspired decor, the mojo here is laid-back. 138 Beale St. ✆ **901/526-3637.** See p. 202.

❽ Main Street Trolley

Take a ride on one of Memphis's antique restored trolley cars. They're old, they're creaky, their hard wooden seats are uncomfortable, and they're slow. But for a dollar or two you can sit back, relax, and ride the clanging, cumbersome streetcars from one end of downtown to the other, getting glimpses of the Pyramid, the Mississippi

River, and other local landmarks. See p. 30.

9 Center for Southern Folklore
Step inside the one-of-a-kind Center for Southern Folklore. Part coffeehouse, part outsider and folk-art gallery, and part intimate performance space, the center is a beloved, locally owned nonprofit that celebrates the region's rich diversity. See p. 203.

2 THE BEST OF MEMPHIS IN 2 DAYS

Okay, you're goin' to Graceland. If you're an Elvis Presley zealot, you probably couldn't wait until Day 2 to head to the home of the King, so you've already tried to squeeze it into Day 1. Fair enough. True fans should not miss seeing his homey (in a *Beverly Hillbillies* sort of way) mansion and taking the complete tour of all that's offered here. Tourists with no more than a mild interest in Elvis, though, might want to skip the full shebang and do a simple drive-by of the place instead. From here, you'll head back to Midtown and East Memphis for some fine art interspersed with flora and fauna. Cap off your day of critters and culture with a little rest and relaxation in the bohemian Cooper-Young neighborhood.

1 Graceland ★★
The blue-and-white living room where he and Priscilla entertained guests. The mirrored, yellow TV room where Elvis liked to unwind. His paisley pool room. You'll see it all and more on a tour of the mansion where Elvis lived—and where he died. Across the street from the house you can tour his Austin Powers–ish airplanes, watch Elvis movies, and even admire his car collection. See p. 208.

2 Overton Park
Back in Midtown, Overton Park is a beautiful setting that's home to the Memphis Zoo, the Memphis College of Art, and the Brooks Museum of Art. Visit the museum to get an overview of art through the ages. From Medieval and Impressionist to contemporary, a range of styles and media are represented. See p. 217.

3 BRUSHMARK RESTAURANT
Before or after browsing the masterpieces in the Brooks Museum of Art, take some refreshment in the Brushmark Restaurant. Sit outside on the terrace, order a light lunch, and enjoy the lush views of the wooded park surroundings. 1934 Poplar Ave. ✆ **901/544-6225.** See p. 203.

4 Memphis Zoo ★★
The two soulful, cuddly panda bears from China are the reigning stars of this world-class zoo. But there are plenty of other animals and exhibits to see. From snakes and lions to elephants and monkeys, this is where the wild things are. See p. 216.

5 Dixon Gallery and Gardens ★
In East Memphis, you'll find the next two stops on your itinerary: The Dixon Gallery and Gardens and the Memphis Botanic Garden are right across the street from each other. Impressionist works are a highlight of the Dixon, a posh residence-turned-museum. Shaded by towering trees, the meticulously landscaped grounds are perfect for strolling. It's especially gorgeous in the spring, when the dogwoods and azaleas are in bloom. See p. 213.

6 Memphis Botanic Garden ★
Nature enthusiasts will find much to love in this oasis of fragrant roses, iris beds,

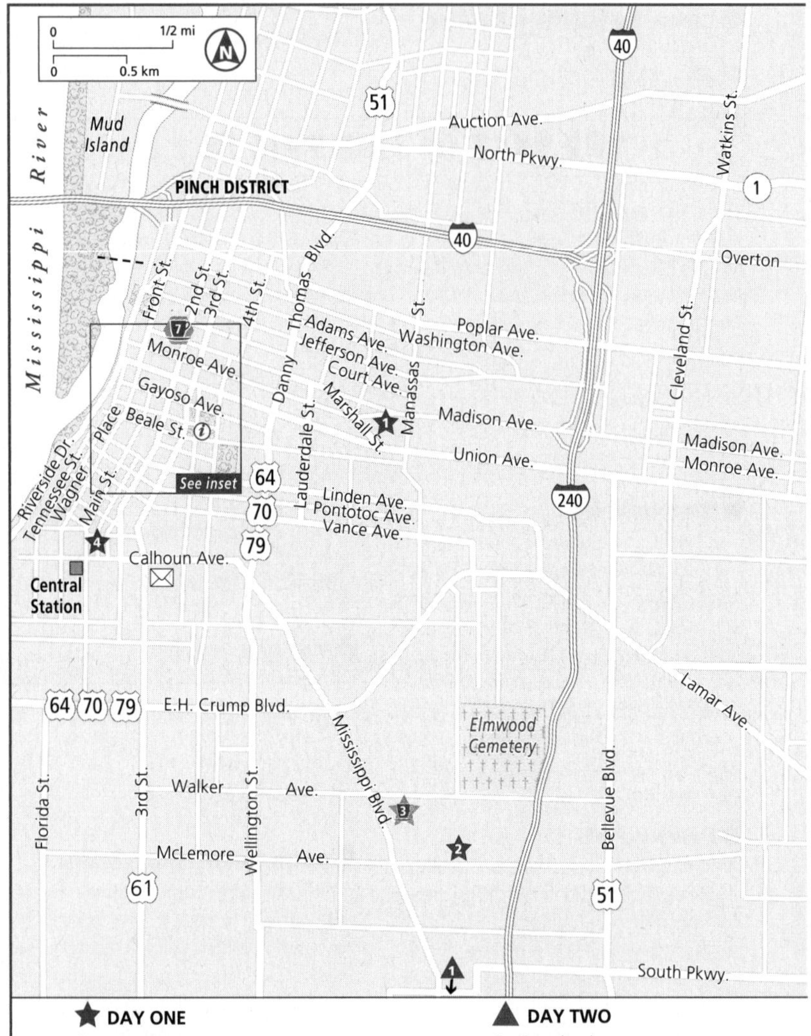

DAY ONE

1 Sun Studio
2 Soulsville USA: The Stax Museum of American Soul Music
3 Four Way Restaurant
4 National Civil Rights Museum
5 South Main Street Arts District
6 Beale Street
7 Blues City Café
8 Main Street Trolley
9 Center for Southern Folklore

DAY TWO

1 Graceland
2 Overton Park
3 The Brushmark Restaurant
4 Memphis Zoo
5 Dixon Gallery and Gardens
6 Memphis Botanic Garden
7 Cooper-Young Neighborhood
8 Young Avenue Deli
9 Hi-Tone Cafe

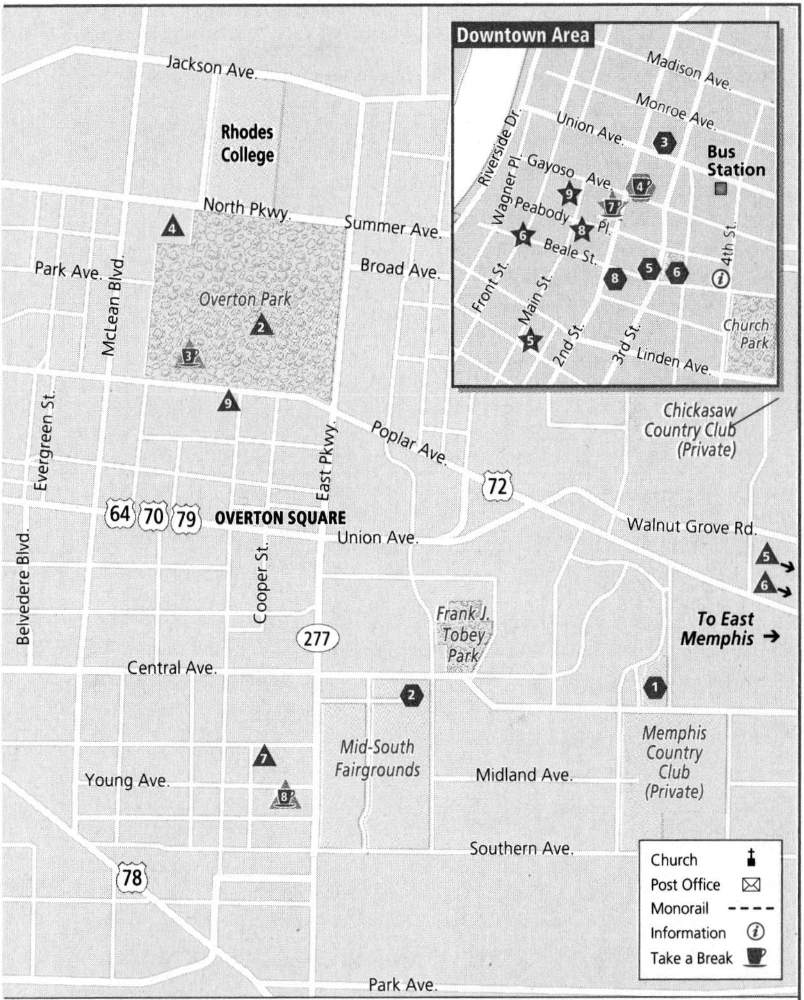
Downtown Area
Madison Ave.
Monroe Ave.
Union Ave.
Riverside Dr.
Gayoso Ave.
Bus Station
Wagner Pl.
Peabody Pl.
Beale St.
4th St.
Front St.
Main St.
2nd St.
3rd St.
Linden Ave.
Church Park
Jackson Ave.
Rhodes College
North Pkwy.
Summer Ave.
Park Ave.
Broad Ave.
McLean Blvd.
Overton Park
Evergreen St.
Poplar Ave.
East Pkwy.
Chickasaw Country Club (Private)
72
64
70
79
OVERTON SQUARE
Walnut Grove Rd.
Union Ave.
Belvedere Blvd.
Cooper St.
277
Frank J. Tobey Park
To East Memphis
Central Ave.
Mid-South Fairgrounds
Memphis Country Club (Private)
Young Ave.
Midland Ave.
Southern Ave.
78
Park Ave.
Church
Post Office
Monorail
Information
Take a Break

DAY THREE

1 Memphis Pink Palace Museum
2 Children's Museum of Memphis
3 Peabody Ducks
4 Automatic Slim's Tonga Club
5 Memphis Rock 'n' Soul Museum
6 W.C. Handy Park
7 The Rendezvous
8 B.B. King's Blues Club

Memphis
51
Wolf R.
40
Area shown
DOWN-TOWN
55
240
MIDTOWN
EAST MEMPHIS
72
78
Graceland
Memphis International Airport

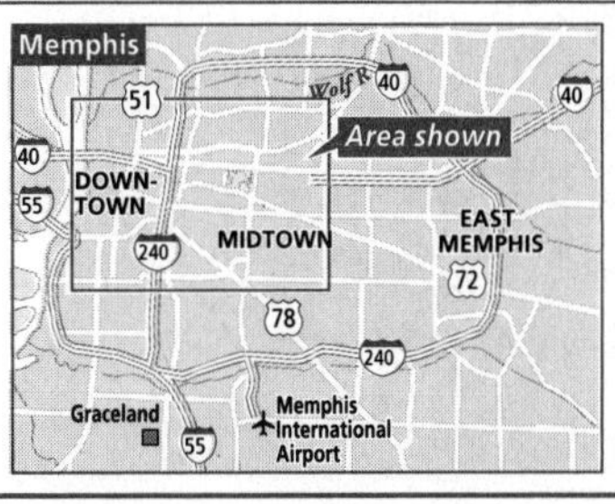

herb gardens, and acres of other flowering plants, majestic trees, and paved walking trails. The Japanese Garden of Tranquility, with its goldfish ponds, lanterns, and angular evergreens, is a favorite of romantics. See p. 218.

7 Cooper-Young Neighborhood

Drive back toward Midtown and explore the bohemian area known as Cooper-Young. If you like felines, peek inside the **House of Mews,** 933 S. Cooper St. (✆ **901/272-3777**), a storefront converted into a homelike sanctuary for stray cats awaiting adoption. Shop for gifts at specialty boutiques or step into one of the great restaurants and bars clustered around this intersection. See p. 155.

8 YOUNG AVENUE DELI

Flop a spell at this arty coffee shop (2119 Young Ave.; ✆ **901/278-0034;** p. 251) and enjoy the eccentric people-watching in this offbeat area of town. Or walk half a block to cull the bins at **Goner Records,** for vinyl rarities or other cheesy finds.

9 Hi-Tone Cafe

Tonight, head back over to the Overton Park area to see what's happening and who's playing at this hip nightclub. See p. 250.

3 THE BEST OF MEMPHIS IN 3 DAYS

Today begins with a bit of kids' stuff that will appeal to the child in all of us. You'll start at the Pink Palace Museum before heading over to the Children's Museum of Memphis. Then it's downtown to catch the ceremonious march of the Peabody ducks. The remainder of today you're downtown, taking in the Memphis Rock 'n' Soul Museum, W. C. Handy Park on Beale Street, and (I saved the best for last!) barbecued ribs at the Rendezvous. Tonight, say farewell to the city in style by taking in some smoldering live music at B. B. King's Blues Club.

1 Memphis Pink Palace Museum ★

Grocery store owner and entrepreneur Clarence Saunders, who pioneered the self-service grocery store with the Piggly Wiggly chain at the beginning of the 20th century, lived in this pink marble home. Today, it's a museum packed with educational exhibits, along with a planetarium and an IMAX Theatre. See p. 215.

2 Children's Museum of Memphis ★

A fire engine for climbing, a castle for dreaming, a kid-sized city with a bank for cashing play checks, and a grocery store for filling shopping carts are among the favorites at this Midtown museum, located next to the AutoZone Liberty Bowl Stadium. See p. 220.

3 Peabody Ducks

Sure, it's touristy, but you owe it to yourself to see what all the fuss is about. If you can make it by 11am, you'll get to see the ducks waddle out of the elevator and into the lobby fountain. But if not, they'll be here all afternoon. They make their return trip to the ducky penthouse at 5pm. See p. 169.

4 AUTOMATIC SLIM'S TONGA CLUB ★★

Head downtown for lunch at this funky restaurant. Great food and drinks, along with a vibrant clientele, always keep this hangout buzzing. 83 S. Second St. ✆ **901/525-7948.** See p. 190.

5 Memphis Rock 'n' Soul Museum ★

On the plaza outside the FedExForum you'll find the entrance to this museum that traces the importance of Memphis in the history of rock music, soul, and rhythm-and-blues. Browse the exhibits, jam to the classics, and learn something new about your favorite musical heroes. See p. 210.

6 W. C. Handy Park

Listen for the sounds of a bluesy rock band, or look for the statue of the early 20th century trumpeter, which dominates this open-air park and amphitheater. Take a load off at one of the benches, watch the crowds go by, and start tapping your feet to the beat. See p. 218.

7 THE RENDEZVOUS ★★

Make a beeline back down toward Union Avenue, find the alley across from The Peabody, and let your nose lead the way to the source of the sizzling pork barbecue aromas that pervade the area. Feast on the Rendezvous' famous spice-dusted ribs, or try a chopped-pork sandwich. 52 S. Second St. ✆ **901/523-2746.** See p. 192.

8 B. B. King's Blues Club ★★

Kick back and surrender to the blues tonight, taking in whatever act happens to be playing at B. B. King's namesake nightclub on Beale Street. See p. 245.

15

Getting to Know the Home of the Blues

When you hit town, you may be surprised, and even a bit baffled, by Memphis. The city is spread out, so getting around can be confusing and frustrating at first. Read this chapter, and your first hours in town should be less bewildering.

1 ORIENTATION

VISITOR INFORMATION

The city's main visitor information center, located downtown at the base of Jefferson Street, is the **Tennessee State Welcome Center,** 119 N. Riverside Dr. (✆ **901/543-6757**). It's open daily 24 hours but staffed only between 8am and 7pm (until 8pm in the summer months). Inside this large information center, you'll find soaring statues of both Elvis and B. B. King.

At the airport, you'll find information boards with telephone numbers for contacting hotels, as well as numbers for other helpful services. Other visitor centers are located off Interstate 40 just east of the Memphis city limits, and at Elvis Presley Boulevard just north of Graceland.

CITY LAYOUT

Memphis, built on the east bank of the **Mississippi River,** lies just above the Mississippi state line. Consequently, growth has proceeded primarily to the east and, to a lesser extent, to the north. The inexorable sprawl of the suburbs has pushed the limits of the metropolitan area far to the east, and today the area known as **East Memphis** is the city's business and cultural center. Despite the fact that the city has a fairly small and compact

Go, Cat, Go!

Elvis Presley finally has his own Tennessee license plate. Graceland unveiled the automotive honor in February 2008, placing the very first plate, hot off the assembly line, onto the King's purple 1956 Eldorado Cadillac. The white plates feature Elvis's signature in black cursive writing, along with a color caricature of the '50s-era Elvis playing a guitar. Profits from the plates will benefit the Elvis Presley Memorial Trauma Center at the Regional Medical Center. "The Med," as it's known, is a major Memphis hospital with the only Level-1 trauma center in a five-state region.

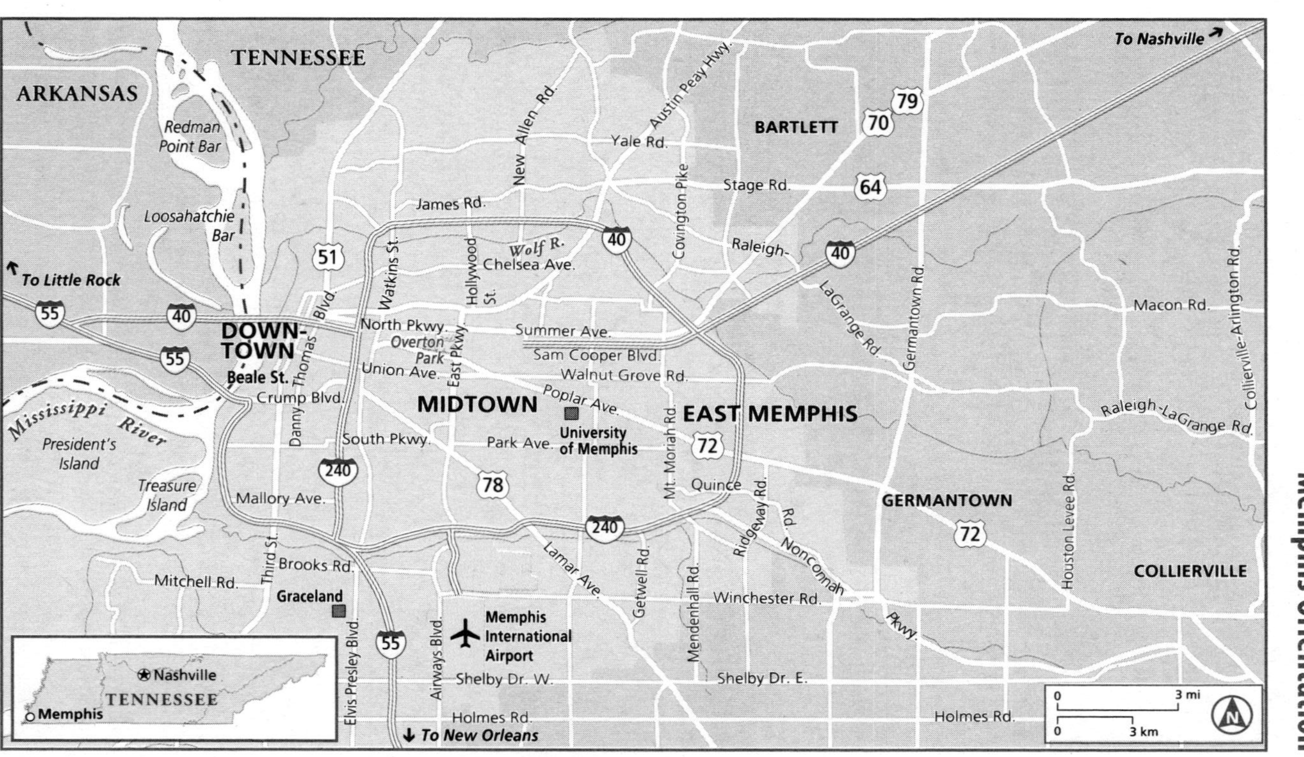
TENNESSEE
ARKANSAS
To Nashville
BARTLETT
Redman Point Bar
Loosahatchie Bar
To Little Rock
DOWN-TOWN
Beale St.
Mississippi River
President's Island
Treasure Island
MIDTOWN
EAST MEMPHIS
University of Memphis
GERMANTOWN
COLLIERVILLE
Graceland
Memphis International Airport
To New Orleans
New Allen Rd.
Austin Peay Hwy.
Yale Rd.
Stage Rd.
James Rd.
Covington Pike
Raleigh-LaGrange Rd.
Wolf R.
Chelsea Ave.
Hollywood St.
Watkins St.
Macon Rd.
Collierville-Arlington Rd.
Germantown Rd.
North Pkwy.
Overton Park
Summer Ave.
Sam Cooper Blvd.
Walnut Grove Rd.
Union Ave.
East Pkwy.
Poplar Ave.
Danny Thomas Blvd.
Crump Blvd.
South Pkwy.
Park Ave.
Mt. Moriah Rd.
Quince
Ridgeway Rd.
Nonconnah Pkwy.
Houston Levee Rd.
Mallory Ave.
Lamar Ave.
Getwell Rd.
Mendenhall Rd.
Winchester Rd.
Third St.
Brooks Rd.
Mitchell Rd.
Elvis Presley Blvd.
Airways Blvd.
Shelby Dr. W.
Shelby Dr. E.
Holmes Rd.
Holmes Rd.
Nashville
Memphis
TENNESSEE
0 3 mi
0 3 km

downtown area, the sprawl of recent years has made getting around difficult for residents and visitors alike. Traffic congestion on main east–west avenues is bad throughout the day, so you're usually better off taking the interstate around the outskirts of the city if you're trying to cross town.

In general, the city is laid out on a grid with a north–south axis. However, there are many exceptions, including downtown, which was laid out with "streets" parallel to the river and "avenues" running perpendicular to the river. Throughout the city you'll find that, for the most part, avenues run east–west and streets run north–south.

MAIN ARTERIES & STREETS Memphis is circled by **I-40,** which loops around the north side of the city, and **I-240,** which loops around the south side. **Poplar Avenue** and **Sam Cooper Boulevard/North Parkway** are the city's main east–west arteries. Poplar, heavily lined with businesses, is narrow, congested, and accident-prone. If you don't want to take the interstate, **Sam Cooper Boulevard** is an alternative route into downtown, as is **Central Avenue** between Goodlett Road in the east and Lamar Avenue in the west. **Union Avenue** is the dividing line between the north and south sides of the city. Other important **east–west roads** include Summer Avenue and Park Avenue. Major **north–south arteries** include (from downtown heading eastward) Third Street/U.S. 61, I-240, Elvis Presley Boulevard/U.S. 51, Airways Boulevard/East Parkway, and Mendenhall Road. Lamar Avenue is another important road.

Out in **East Memphis,** the main east–west arteries are Poplar Avenue and Winchester Road. The main north–south arteries are Perkins Road/Perkins Road Extended, Mendenhall Road, Hickory Hill Road, and Germantown Road.

FINDING AN ADDRESS Besides going online to find maps to your destination (or, better yet, using a GPS to indicate your route), your second-best bet for finding an address in Memphis is to call the place first and ask for directions or the name of the nearest main cross street. Though address numbers increase the farther you get from downtown, they do not increase along each block in an orderly fashion. It is nearly impossible to determine how many blocks out an address will be. However, there are some general guidelines to get you in the vicinity of where you're going. If an address is in the hundreds or lower, you should be downtown. If the address is an avenue or other east–west road in the 2000-to-4000 range, you'll likely find it in Midtown; if the number is in the 5000-to-7000 range, you should be out in East Memphis. If the address is on a

Fun Facts **Movie Mogul**

Tom Hanks played a dedicated overnight delivery pilot in the film *Castaway,* which included scenes filmed at the world headquarters for FedEx in Memphis. Fred Smith, the company's founder, has a film production company that has done movies including *My Dog Skip; The Sisterhood of the Traveling Pants; Racing Stripes; Insomnia; and Dude, Where's My Car?* His daughter, Molly Smith, was also a co-producer on Hillary Swank's 2007 romantic comedy *P.S. I Love You.* That film's supporting cast included Kathy Bates, a former Memphis resident and Academy Award–winning actress.

street, it will likely have a north or south prefix included. Union Avenue is the dividing line between north and south.

STREET MAPS Because the streets of Memphis can seem a bit baffling at times, you'll definitely need a good map. The **Tennessee State Welcome Center,** 119 N. Riverside Dr. (✆ **901/543-6757**), offers a simple map; you can also buy a more detailed one at any bookstore, pharmacy, or gas station. If you arrive at the airport and rent a car, the rental company will give you a basic map that will at least get you to your hotel or to the information center. Most hotels will also give you a free map at check-in, to help you navigate your way around the city.

If you happen to be a member of **AAA,** you can get free maps of Memphis and the rest of Tennessee either from your local AAA office or from the Memphis office at 5138 Park Ave., Memphis, TN 38117 (✆ **901/761-5371**); it's open Monday to Friday 9am to 6pm.

16

Where to Stay in Memphis

Where you stay in Memphis will depend on what brings you here. If you're in town for a convention, the place will probably be prearranged. And if you're an Elvis fan planning on spending the majority of your time at Graceland, there are several properties within spitting distance of the gated mansion in the southern suburbs. If you're coming to town as a tourist interested in the history of the blues, the birth of rock 'n' roll, and the civil rights movement, downtown is your best bet. Besides great views of the beautiful Mississippi River, it's here that you'll have the widest choice of properties, too, from the sleek Westin on Beale Street to the intimate Madison and posh River Inn of Harbor Town.

Then again, if you don't need to be downtown, consider booking a room in East Memphis, which is more than 20 miles by interstate highway from downtown. Comfortable chain hotels abound here, and these make sense for business travelers as well as for those with families wanting to avoid the drunken revelry that can sometimes consume the Beale Street area downtown.

More questionable is the Midtown area. Although convenient to the interstate and located midway between downtown and East Memphis, the few hotels here can feel rather isolated. Likewise, I don't recommend staying in the airport area if you can avoid it. It's not that there aren't adequate hotels here (I've listed a few of the better options in this chapter); it's just that the surrounding neighborhoods are rather dicey, and there is little of interest here except proximity to the terminals and car-rental agencies.

Keep in mind that there are many modern, reliable chain hotels located in the suburbs just outside the area covered in this book. If you want to stay in the suburbs of Germantown, Cordova, Collierville, or Southwind, or in Olive Branch or Southaven, Mississippi, there are hundreds of appealing chain hotels from which to choose. Just be aware that you'll have long driving times and traffic to contend with if you want to take in the city's main tourist attractions in the heart of Memphis.

Virtually all hotels now offer nonsmoking floors (or are completely smoke-free), and others are equipped for guests with disabilities. Many larger hotels are also adding special rooms for hearing-impaired travelers as well as rooms equipped with cardio exercise equipment, for fitness-minded guests. When making a reservation, be sure to request the type of room you need.

If you'll be traveling with children, always inquire about policies regarding children. Some hotels let children under 12 stay free, while others set the cutoff age at 18. Still others charge you for the kids, but let them eat for free in the hotel's restaurant.

In this chapter, I have listed the official published rates (also known as rack rates). Keep in mind that almost all hotels offer special corporate and government rates, so ask about discounts. Most of the more expensive hotels have lower weekend rates, while inexpensive hotels tend to raise their rates slightly on the weekend.

If you get quoted a price that seems exorbitantly high, you might have accidentally stumbled upon a special holiday or event rate. Such rates are usually in effect for major sports events or music festivals. If this is the case, try scheduling your visit for a different date if possible. Or try calling around to hotels farther out of town, where rates aren't as likely to be affected by special events. In fact, at any time, the farther you get from major business districts, the less you're likely to spend on a room.

For the purposes of this book, I have placed hotels in the following rate categories: **very expensive,** more than $200 for a double room; **expensive,** $150 to $200; **moderate,** $100 to $150; and **inexpensive,** less than $100. Please keep in mind, however, that the rates listed below do not include taxes, which in Memphis add up to a whopping 15.95% (9.25% sales tax and 6.7% room tax).

1 BEST HOTEL BETS

- **Most Romantic:** Discretely tucked off a quiet downtown side street, the intimate **Madison Hotel,** 79 Madison Ave. (✆ **866/44-MEMPHIS** [446-3674] or 901/333-1200; www.madisonhotelmemphis.com), is an upscale boutique property offering sumptuous furnishings, first-class service, and rooftop river views. See p. 168.
- **Best Historic Hotel:** Even if **The Peabody,** 149 Union Ave. (✆ **800/PEABODY** [732-2639] or 901/529-4000; www.peabodymemphis.com), weren't the *only* historic hotel in the city, it would likely still be the best. From the lobby, with its marble fountain full of live ducks, to the excellent restaurants and updated rooms, everything here spells tradition. See p. 168.
- **Best for Business Travelers:** Travelers with high expectations and pinched pocketbooks get the best of both worlds at the **Hampton Inn & Suites–Shady Grove,** 962 S. Shady Grove Rd. (✆ **800/HAMPTON** [426-7866] or 901/762-0056; www.hamptoninn.com), an exceptionally well-run, affordable hotel in a beautiful residential section of East Memphis. See p. 172.
- **Best Place to Unleash Your Inner Rock Star:** Guests at the new **Westin Memphis Beale Street,** 170 Lt. George W. Lee Ave. (✆ **800/WESTIN1** [937-8461] or 901/334-5900; www.westin.com/bealestreet), can call down to the front desk to have a classic 1956 Les Paul Goldtop VOS or one of several other Gibson guitars delivered to their rooms. With a virtual amp and headphones, you can pretend you're jamming next door at Ground Zero Blues Club—or headlining a tour across the street at the FedExForum. Available to VIPs and regular Joes alike, this free perk comes with no financial strings attached—except your credit card as security. See p. 169.
- **Best for Families:** Spacious suites with kitchens and comfy sectional-style sofas around 42-inch flatscreen TVs make **Hyatt Place,** 1220 Primacy Pkwy. (✆ **901/680-9700;** www.hyattplace.com), in East Memphis, my top pick for vacationing families. Close to restaurants and such kid-friendly attractions as the Lichterman Nature Center, it also offers a convenient, central location for exploring the city. See p. 179.
- **Best-Kept Secret:** Having opened just 2 years ago, the **River Inn of Harbor Town,** 50 Harbor Town Square (✆ **901/222-1531;** www.riverinnmemphis.com), is still somewhat of a hidden gem—a small, European-style hotel offering exquisite furnishings, gourmet food, impeccable service and breathtaking views of the Mississippi River. Need I say more? See p. 169.

2 DOWNTOWN

If you want to be where the tourist action is, your first choice ought to be downtown. Besides Beale Street, this area is also where the majority of the city's major sporting events, concerts, and cultural performances take place. If you want to feel as though you've been to Memphis, you need to experience the riverfront heart of it all.

VERY EXPENSIVE

Madison Hotel ★★ Moments A member of the prestigious Small Luxury Hotels of the World, this intimate hotel occupies the site of a former bank building. The graceful Beaux Arts architecture belies the bold, contemporary furnishings inside. From the chic lobby, with its grand piano and musical instrument motif, to the rich, solid colors in the guest rooms, the Madison is a contrast between classic and modern. Whirlpool baths or jet tubs are available in many rooms. Nightly turndown and twice-daily housekeeping service keep guests feeling pampered. Take the elevator to the outdoor rooftop for breathtaking views of the Mississippi River and surrounding downtown. Every Thursday evening from April through mid-October, the hotel hosts sunset parties here, featuring live jazz.

79 Madison Ave., Memphis, TN 38103. ✆ **866/44-MEMPHIS** (446-3674) or 901/333-1200. Fax 901/333-1297. www.madisonhotelmemphis.com. 110 units. $240–$280 double; $350 suite. AE, DC, DISC, MC, V. Valet parking $23; self-parking $6 (no in-and-out privileges). **Amenities:** Restaurant/lounge; concierge; health club; indoor pool; room service. *In room:* A/C, TV, hair dryer, minibar, Wi-Fi (free).

Memphis Marriott Downtown Located at the north end of downtown, on the Main Street trolley line, the 19-floor Marriott is connected to the convention center. Although the hotel is a bit off the beaten track, surrounded mostly by government buildings, it's accessible to the trolley that will take you up and down Main Street to where there's more action. The lobby is built on a grand scale with soaring ceilings, marble floors, and traditional furnishings. My favorite units here are the corner rooms, which have angled walls that provide a bit more character than others. The standard king rooms are also good bets. For views of the Mississippi, ask for a room on the 10th floor or higher.

250 N. Main St., Memphis, TN 38103. ✆ **800/557-8740** or 901/527-7300. Fax 901/526-1561. www.marriott.com. 600 units. $209 and up double; $349–$545 suite. AE, DC, DISC, MC, V. Valet parking $18; self-parking $12. **Amenities:** Restaurant; lounge; concierge; exercise room; hot tub; large indoor pool; room service; sauna; valet service. *In room:* A/C, TV, hair dryer, Wi-Fi ($5.95 per 24 hrs.).

The Peabody ★ Moments For years, The Peabody has enjoyed a reputation as one of the finest hotels in the South. While standard rooms aren't overly spacious or extraordinary, the public spaces dazzle. Marble columns, hand-carved and burnished woodwork, and ornate gilded plasterwork on the ceiling give the lobby the air of a palace. Its dominant feature is its Romanesque marble fountain. Here, the famous Peabody ducks, one of Memphis's biggest attractions, while away each day. **Chez Philippe** (p. 185), serving Asian- and French-inspired cuisine amid palatial surroundings, has long been among the best restaurants in Memphis. In-room Wi-Fi is included in the daily $9.95 hotel fee, which also includes morning coffee and tea, shoeshine, local telephone calls, and health club access.

149 Union Ave., Memphis, TN 38103. ✆ **800/PEABODY** (732-2639) or 901/529-4000. Fax 901/529-3677. www.peabodymemphis.com. 464 units. $230–$295 double; $670 and up suite. AE, DC, DISC, MC, V. Valet

The Peabody Ducks

It isn't often that you find live ducks in the lobby of a luxury hotel. However, ducks are a fixture at **The Peabody.** Each morning at 11am, the Peabody ducks, led by a duck-master, take the elevator down from their penthouse home, waddle down a red carpet, and hop into the hotel's Romanesque travertine-marble fountain. And each evening at 5pm they waddle back down the red carpet and take the elevator back up to the penthouse. During their entry and exit, the ducks waddle to John Philip Sousa tunes and attract large crowds of curious onlookers that press in on the fountain and red carpet from every side.

The Peabody ducks first took up residence in the lobby in the 1930s when Frank Schutt, the hotel's general manager, and friend Chip Barwick, after one too many swigs of Tennessee sippin' whiskey, put some of his live duck decoys in the hotel's fountain as a joke (such live decoys were legal at the time but have since been outlawed as unsportsmanlike). Guests at the time thought the ducks were a delightfully offbeat touch for such a staid and traditional establishment, and, since then, ducks have become a beloved fixture at The Peabody.

parking $21; self-parking $16. **Amenities:** 2 restaurants; 2 lounges; concierge; athletic facility; massage; small pool; room service; sauna; shoe-shine service; steam room; valet service. *In room:* A/C, TV, hair dryer, Wi-Fi ($9.95 per day).

River Inn of Harbor Town ★★★ As close to perfect as it gets, this posh, 28-room boutique hotel may be Memphis's best-kept secret. Opened in late 2007, the inn is ensconced in the upscale community of Harbor Town, on a small island a few blocks north of the Pyramid. With a west-facing, rooftop terrace offering breathtaking sunsets over the Mississippi River, the inn has a charming European flavor (the general manager is Austrian). The hotel brims with fresh roses and fine furnishings, and rooms are sumptuously furnished with four-poster beds, Frette linens, and Gilchrist & Soames bath products. A wood-burning fireplace in the cozy lobby, as well as free champagne or wine, welcomes guests at check-in. Nightly turn-down includes chocolate truffles and port. Popular with couples and female executives, it's also ideal for fitness-minded folks who relish early-morning or sunset workouts. Manicured walking trails and picnic areas on the Mississippi River bank are just steps away. Service is exceedingly gracious and intuitive, with staff ready to anticipate guests' every request.

50 Harbor Town Square, Memphis, TN 38103. ✆ **877/222-1531** or 901/260-3333. Fax 901/260-3291. www.riverinnmemphis.com. 28 units. $189–$340 double; $375–$595 suite. Rates include gourmet breakfast. AE, DISC, MC, V. Free parking. **Amenities:** 2 restaurants; concierge; exercise room. *In room:* A/C, TV, hair dryer, MP3 docking stations, Wi-Fi (free).

The Westin Memphis Beale Street ★★ Downtown's newest full-service luxury hotel is a stunner: The city's first Westin has a plum perch at the foot of famed Beale Street. Exquisitely appointed two-room corner suites overlook the NBA Grizzlies' FedEx-Forum and the Gibson Guitar plant. Hotel guests can call down to the front desk to have a classic 1956 Les Paul Goldtop VOS or one of several other Gibson guitars delivered to

Memphis Accommodations: Downtown & Midtown

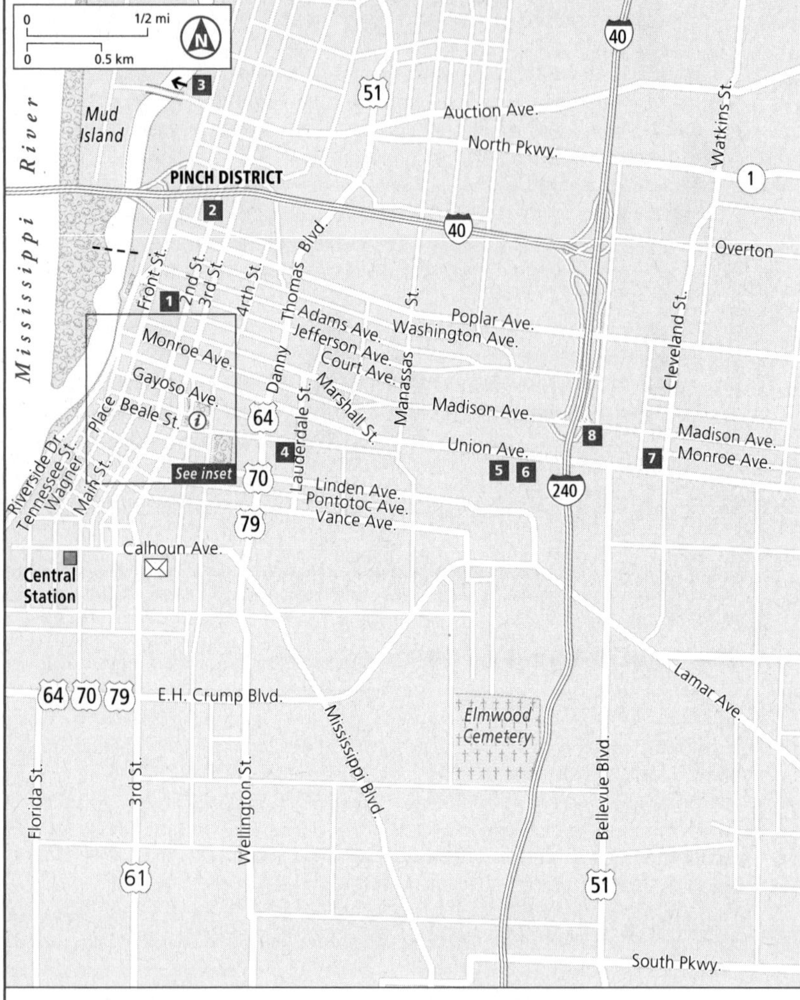

Comfort Inn Downtown **13**
Crowne Plaza Memphis **10**
Doubletree Hotel Memphis **19**
Gen X Inn **8**
Hampton Inn & Suites–Beale Street **11**
Holiday Inn Select Downtown **17**
Inn at Hunt-Phelan **4**
Madison Hotel **15**
Memphis Marriott Downtown **2**
Motel 6 **5**
Red Roof Inn **6**
Residence Inn by Marriott Memphis Downtown **16**
River Inn of Harbor Town **3**
Sleep Inn–Downtown at Court Square **1**
SpringHill Suites by Marriott **14**

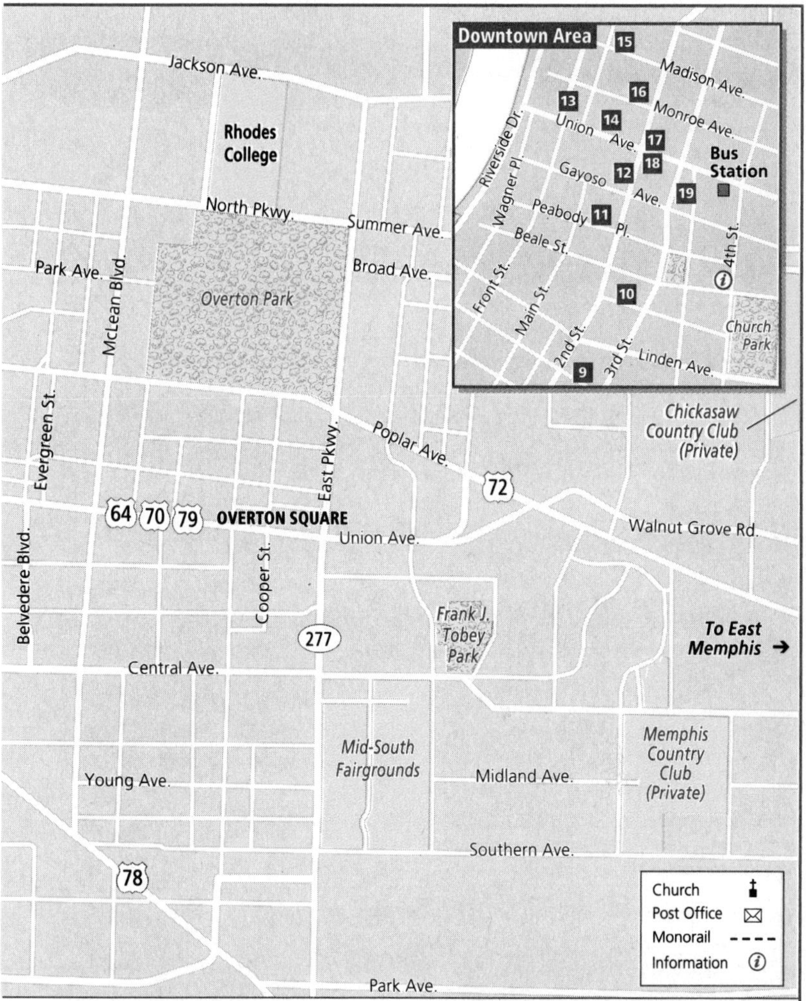

Downtown Area
Madison Ave.
Monroe Ave.
Union Ave.
Gayoso Ave.
Peabody Pl.
Beale St.
Linden Ave.
Riverside Dr.
Wagner Pl.
Front St.
Main St.
2nd St.
3rd St.
4th St.
Bus Station
Church Park
15
16
13
14
17
18
12
19
11
10
9
Jackson Ave.
Rhodes College
North Pkwy.
Summer Ave.
Broad Ave.
Park Ave.
McLean Blvd.
Overton Park
Evergreen St.
East Pkwy.
Poplar Ave.
72
Chickasaw Country Club (Private)
64
70
79
OVERTON SQUARE
Union Ave.
Walnut Grove Rd.
Belvedere Blvd.
Cooper St.
277
Frank J. Tobey Park
To East Memphis →
Central Ave.
Mid-South Fairgrounds
Midland Ave.
Memphis Country Club (Private)
Young Ave.
Southern Ave.
78
Park Ave.
Church
Post Office
Monorail
Information

Talbot Heirs Guesthouse **12**

The Peabody **18**

The Westin Memphis Beale Street **9**

Memphis
Wolf R.
40
51
Area shown
40
55
DOWN-TOWN
240
MIDTOWN
EAST MEMPHIS
72
78
240
Graceland
55
Memphis International Airport

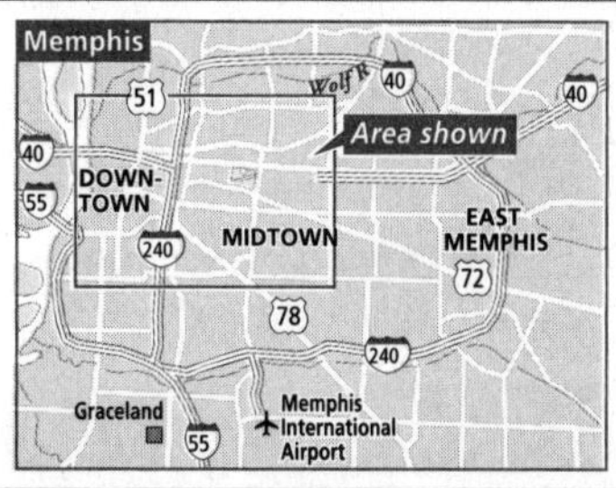

their rooms, along with a virtual amp and headphones. The perk is free, and not just for VIPs. Other hotel features include a 24-hour business center with computers and free Internet access. Westin's signature "Heavenly Beds," with plush, pillowtop mattresses and 250-thread-count sheets, as well as thick bath robes and oversized showers with dual massaging shower heads, nurture relaxation.

170 Lt. George W. Lee Ave., Memphis, TN 38103 ✆ **800/WESTIN1** (937-8461) or 901/334-5900. www.westin.com/bealestreet. Fax 901/334-5901. 203 units. $170–$269 double; $649–$1,299 suite. AE, DISC, MC, V. Valet parking $24; self-parking $18. **Amenities:** Restaurant; lounge; concierge; health club; room service; shoe-shine stand. *In room:* A/C, TV w/pay movies and videogames, hair dryer, minibar, MP3 docking station, Wi-Fi ($6.95–$13).

EXPENSIVE

Doubletree Memphis Across the street from AutoZone Park baseball stadium, the all-wireless Doubletree is housed in a former Radisson property that features a T.G.I. Friday's restaurant off the ground-floor lobby. This hotel, which stays packed with tour groups and conventions, has a very busy and rather impersonal feel. However, the location is ideal if you're arriving by bus (the station is across the street) or if Beale Street and/or baseball are on your agenda. Regular rooms are large and have modern furnishings and standard-size bathrooms.

185 Union Ave., Memphis, TN 38103. ✆ **800/222-8733** or 901/528-1800. Fax 901/524-0759. www.doubletree.com. 280 units. $119–$299 double; $219–$309 suite. AE, DC, DISC, MC, V. Valet parking $20; no self-parking. **Amenities:** Restaurant; lounge; small exercise room; outdoor pool. *In room:* A/C, TV w/pay movies, hair dryer, Wi-Fi (free).

Hampton Inn & Suites–Beale Street You can't get closer to spending the night on Beale Street unless you pass out on the pavement after a blues-soaked binge of bar-hopping. This award-winning property is not your typical chain hotel; in fact, it's touted by Hampton as their top hotel in the world. This stylish, curved building sits on a corner lot, jutting out into the heart of the action along Beale and Peabody Place. (Try to get a corner room with an iron balcony and watch the revelry like it's Mardi Gras.) You'll want to keep your ear phones (or ear plugs) at the ready if you plan to do any sleeping while you're here. It stays pretty rowdy all night long and into the wee hours.

175 Peabody Place, Memphis, TN 38103. ✆ **901/260-4000.** Fax 901/260-4050. www.hampton-inn.com. 144 units. $185 double; $265 suite. Rates include continental breakfast. AE, DC, DISC, MC, V. Parking $20. **Amenities:** Exercise room; indoor pool. *In room:* A/C, TV w/pay movies, Wi-Fi (free).

Holiday Inn Select Downtown ★ Across the street from The Peabody, this Holiday Inn is in the heart of the downtown action. The guest rooms, though not large, have comfortable chairs and big windows. But be advised that some of those windows butt up against other concrete buildings. Rooms facing south afford the best views of the bustle along Union Avenue below. The entire property is wireless. Foodies may appreciate that the hotel is mere footsteps away from the city's best barbecue rib joint—the **Rendezvous** (p. 192)—not to mention across the corner from Huey's, Memphis's beloved burger-and-beer joint. The hotel also houses one of the freshest sushi bars in town (**Sekisui;** p. 190).

160 Union Ave., Memphis, TN 38103. ✆ **888/HOLIDAY** (465-4329) or 901/525-5491. Fax 901/529-8950. www.hiselect.com. 192 units. $199–$209 double. AE, DC, DISC, MC, V. Parking $12. **Amenities:** Restaurant; lounge; off-site health club ($7 per day); modest outdoor pool on rooftop terrace; room service. *In room:* A/C, TV w/pay movies, hair dryer, Wi-Fi (free).

The Inn at Hunt-Phelan If you want to get a taste of being a wealthy plantation owner in the Old South, head a few blocks east of Beale Street's neon to this antebellum mansion that's now a bed-and-breakfast. Built in the 1820s, the estate is said to have served as General Ulysses S. Grant's temporary headquarters during the Civil War. Now restored and furnished with period antiques, the security-gated inn looks out of place amid its gritty, urban surroundings. Inside, however, you'll find 10 elegant guest rooms and suites, all with private bathrooms. The upscale restaurant specializes in French Creole dishes. Call well in advance if you want to make a weekend reservation here, as the entire inn gets booked for weddings and private parties.

533 Beale St., Memphis, TN 38103. ✆ **901/525-8225** or 901-523-2509. www.huntphelan.com. 10 units. $240–$295 double. AE, DC, DISC, MC, V. Free parking. **Amenities:** Restaurant; lounge. *In room:* A/C, TV, Wi-Fi (free).

Residence Inn by Marriott Memphis Downtown ★★ One of the newer hotels in downtown Memphis is located in a 13-story Art Deco building that dates back to the 1930s. The fully renovated high-rise features 90 suites, ranging from studio rooms with queen and sofa beds, to 2-bedroom units with fully stocked kitchens and sitting rooms with pull-out sofas and fireplaces. Close to attractions, great restaurants, and the Main Street Trolley line, its location is ideal. Other perks include a complimentary social hour each weekday evening, and a complimentary breakfast with freshly made waffles.

110 Monroe Ave., Memphis, TN 38103. ✆ **901/578-3700.** Fax: 901/578-3999. www.marriott.com. 90 units (all suites). $179–$259 suite. Rates include cooked-to-order breakfast. AE, DISC, MC, V. Valet parking $16; off-site self-parking $8. Pets accepted (nonrefundable $100 cleaning fee). **Amenities:** exercise room; room service; complimentary social hour; valet service; Wi-Fi (free, in lobby and breakfast area). *In room:* A/C, TV, hair dryer; Internet (free), fully furnished kitchens.

SpringHill Suites by Marriott ★ A good value for tourists who want a clean, comfortable suite at a reasonable price in a great location, this property is just a block from the Mississippi River. Step out the back door and hop on the trolley to reach Beale Street and other attractions. A cheerful lobby and adjacent breakfast room provide guests with a welcome greeting. Suites are spacious, tastefully decorated, and include well-lighted work spaces with multiline speaker phones, kitchenettes, and soft couches. Rooms with south-facing windows have nice views of Court Square, a leafy park that dates back to the late 1800s. On the ground floor in front of the hotel, the small outdoor pool is gated and landscaped, though not very private.

21 N. Main St., Memphis, TN 38103. ✆ **901/522-2100.** Fax 901/522-2110. www.marriott.com. 102 units. $169 double. AE, DC, DISC, MC, V. Parking $12. **Amenities:** Outdoor pool; valet service. *In room:* A/C, TV w/pay movies, hair dryer, fridge, Wi-Fi (free).

Talbot Heirs Guesthouse ★★ (Finds) Trendy, contemporary styling is not something one often associates with the tradition-oriented South, which is what makes this downtown B&B so unique. Each of the rooms is boldly decorated, in solid colors ranging from fire-engine red to peaceful periwinkle. Other rooms are done in rich, subtle earth tones and traditional furnishings. Most rooms have interesting modern lamps, and many have kilim rugs. The rooms vary in size from large to huge. Call ahead with your grocery list, and they'll have the fridge stocked for your arrival (for an added fee). Lots of interesting contemporary art further adds to the hip feel of this inn. Talbot Heirs is located right across the street from The Peabody hotel and steps away from Beale Street.

99 S. Second St., Memphis, TN 38103. ✆ **800/955-3956** or 901/527-9772. Fax 901/527-3700. www.talbothouse.com. 8 units. $130–$250 double. Rates include continental breakfast. AE, DC, DISC, MC, V. Parking $10. **Amenities:** Concierge; massage. *In room:* A/C, TV, CD player, hair dryer, Wi-Fi (free).

MODERATE

Comfort Inn Downtown (Value) Memphis's only rooftop swimming pool is the best boast of this otherwise basic hotel that has a prime location on Front Street overlooking the Mississippi River. Despite updated exterior work and new signage, the hotel's rooms are a bit more outdated than others in its price range. Quite often, you'll see busloads of school and tour groups staying at the hotel. So if you're after a more intimate setting, you might want to look elsewhere first. Rooms are bigger than expected, though, making it a good value for the money.

100 N. Front St., Memphis, TN 38103. ✆ **901/526-0583.** Fax 901/525-7512. www.choicehotels.com. 71 units. $110–$140 doubles and suites. AE, DC, DISC, MC, V. Parking $6. **Amenities:** Outdoor pool; Wi-Fi (free, in lobby and pool area). *In room:* A/C, TV, hair dryer, Internet (free).

Crowne Plaza Memphis The 11-story Crowne Plaza (formerly a Wyndham) offers an excellent location if your trip will take you to the nearby convention center or to St. Jude Children's Research Hospital. However, if you're a tourist who wants to be closer to the action of Beale Street and good restaurants, I don't recommend this property in downtown's dull north end. Perhaps because of the transition in ownership, the hotel feels a bit isolated and out of the loop, like a place that is used mainly for overflow from other hotels. When I visited recently, service was indifferent at best. All units have standard amenities, including work desks and 32-inch flatscreen TVs.

300 N. Second St., Memphis, TN 38103. ✆ **901/525-1800.** Fax 901/524-1859. www.cpmemphishotel.com. 230 units. $149 single or double. AE, DC, DISC, MC, V. Parking $15. **Amenities:** Exercise room; outdoor pool. *In room:* A/C, TV w/pay movies, hair dryer, Wi-Fi (free).

Sleep Inn–Downtown at Court Square ★ You can't beat the location of this upscale motel, which fills up quickly during weekends when there is a lot happening downtown. Wedged between nostalgic Court Square and the banks of the Mississippi River, it's also on the Main Street trolley line. At only six stories, this motel is dwarfed by surrounding buildings. The modern design and economical rates, along with wireless access throughout, ensure its appeal. Most rooms are large and comfortable, and business-class rooms come with fax machines, work desks, VCRs, and dual phone lines. The motel shares a parking lot with the adjacent SpringHill Suites.

40 N. Front St., Memphis, TN 38103. ✆ **877/424-6423** or 901/522-9700. Fax 901/522-9710. www.choicehotels.com. 124 units. $95–$170 double. Rates include continental breakfast. AE, DC, DISC, MC, V. Parking $12. **Amenities:** Small exercise room. *In room:* A/C, TV, hair dryer, Wi-Fi (free).

3 MIDTOWN

Midtown probably isn't the best area of town to stay as a tourist, but there are some moderate to inexpensive choices here. One of the newest places is a small boutique hotel that took over a rather ugly office building near the Southern College of Optometry in the medical center area. **Gen X Inn,** 1177 Madison (✆ **901/692-9136**), is a smoke-free Best Western property with a spare, modern look, clean rooms, free Wi-Fi throughout, and plenty of free parking. It appeals primarily to students and other budget-conscious travelers who don't mind its location, a short cab ride from downtown. Rates average around $99 per night.

Other reasonably priced options include the **Holiday Inn Select Medical Center/Midtown,** 1180 Union Ave. (✆ **901/276-1175**), charging as low as $89 for a double;

Red Roof Inn, 42 S. Camilla St. (© **901/526-1050**), charging $79 for a double; and **Motel 6,** 210 S. Pauline St. (© **901/528-0650**), charging $54 for a double.

4 EAST MEMPHIS

If your visit to Memphis brings you to any of the suburban business parks in the perimeter of the city, East Memphis is a smart choice. It's centrally located between downtown hot spots and outlying suburbs, where top employers such as FedEx and International Paper have their corporate headquarters.

EXPENSIVE

Doubletree Hotel Memphis This East Memphis Hilton-owned hotel is a bit closer to Midtown museums than other hotels in this area. However, the hotel's real appeal is that it is within walking distance of a couple of excellent restaurants, and it has a large indoor/outdoor pool. It's also only a very short drive to Corky's Ribs & BBQ, one of the best barbecue joints in town. Built around a glass-walled atrium throughout the hotel, the eight-floor hotel has glass elevators so you can enjoy the views. Most rooms here are designed with the business traveler in mind and have two phones, radio/television speakers in the bathrooms, and large desks. Angled windows make the rooms seem a bit larger than standard hotel rooms.

5069 Sanderlin Ave., Memphis, TN 38117. © **800/445-8667** or 901/767-6666. Fax 901/683-8563. www.doubletree.com. 276 units. $179–$279 double; $219–$259 suite. AE, DC, DISC, MC, V. Free parking. **Amenities:** Restaurant; lounge; exercise room; indoor/outdoor pool; room service. *In room:* A/C, TV w/pay movies, fridge, hair dryer, Wi-Fi (free).

Embassy Suites ★ (Kids) The courtyard-style lobby is rather dark and a bit outdated, despite pretty landscaping with tropical plants. Yet the spacious surroundings and open-air ambience are clean and welcoming. All the guest rooms here are fairly large two-room suites that have kitchenettes, dining tables, two televisions, two phones, and sofa beds. Accommodations here are a safe bets for families and business travelers alike. The complete, cooked-to-order breakfast is served in the atrium, where, in the evening, there's also a complimentary manager's reception with free drinks. The moderately priced **Frank Grisanti's Italian Restaurant** (p. 198), just off the atrium, serves lunch and dinner and is one of the best Italian restaurants in the city.

1022 S. Shady Grove Rd., Memphis, TN 38120. © **800/EMBASSY** (362-2779) or 901/684-1777. Fax 901/685-8185. www.embassysuites.com. 220 units (all suites). $139–$219 suite. Rates include full breakfast and nightly manager's reception. AE, DC, DISC, MC, V. Free parking. **Amenities:** Restaurant; lounge; free airport transfers; exercise room; hot tub; indoor pool; room service; sauna; valet service; Wi-Fi (free, in business center). *In room:* A/C, TV w/pay movies and video games, fridge, hair dryer, Wi-Fi ($9.95 per day; free for Hilton HHonors members).

Hilton Memphis ★★ This gleaming, round high-rise dominates the skyline in an upscale East Memphis area that's also convenient to Germantown and Collierville as well as to downtown and Midtown. The open, airy lobby has an arty, modern ambience. In addition to featuring all the latest amenities, including digital climate control, rooms were expanded and redecorated in cream and pastel colors. However, the property's popularity as a convention hotel can sometimes make the Hilton feel crowded. This is a nice, contemporary hotel, but common areas can become very crowded with all the banquets, breakfasts, and special events that take place here.

 Family-Friendly Hotels

Embassy Suites (p. 175) The indoor pool and gardenlike atrium lobby provide a place for the kids to play even on rainy or cold days, and the two-room suites give parents a private room of their own. In addition, there's a small video game room that gets a workout from kids and adults alike.

Homewood Suites (below) With a pool and basketball court and grounds that resemble an upscale apartment complex, this East Memphis hotel is a good bet for families. Plus, the evening social hour includes enough food to serve as dinner (and thus save you quite a bit on your meal budget).

Hyatt Place (p. 179) Larger-than-expected suites have comfy, sectional-style furniture and ottomans, ideal for spreading out to nap or to watch sports or play video games on the massive, flatscreen TV. With spacious kitchenettes and plush beds, this affordably priced hotel offers all the comforts of home in a safe, convenient location.

La Quinta Inn & Suites (p. 179) Many rooms here have refrigerators and microwaves—ideal for extended family stays. And there's an outdoor pool.

939 Ridge Lake Blvd., Memphis, TN 38120. ✆ **800/774-1500** or 901/684-6664. Fax 901/762-7496. www.hilton.com. 405 units. $149–$219 double; $279–$679 suite. AE, DC, DISC, MC, V. Free parking. Located off Ridgeway Center Pkwy., at I-240 and Poplar Ave., exit 15 east. **Amenities:** Restaurant; lounge; free airport shuttle; health club; hot tub; outdoor pool; room service; valet service; Wi-Fi (free, in lobby). *In room:* A/C, TV w/pay movies, hair dryer, Wi-Fi ($10 per day).

Homewood Suites (Kids) If you don't mind the location on a wedge of property surrounded by interstate traffic, the Homewood Suites offers clean, casual accommodations. The suites, which are arranged around a landscaped central courtyard with a swimming pool and basketball court, resemble an apartment complex rather than a hotel. The lobby features pine furnishings and artwork. Early American styling sets the tone in the suites, many of which have wrought-iron beds. There are two televisions in every suite, as well as a full kitchen and big bathroom with plenty of counter space. Though there's no restaurant on the premises, you can pick up microwave meals in the hotel's convenience shop. There is also a complimentary social hour on weeknights that includes enough food to pass for dinner.

5811 Poplar Ave. (just off I-240), Memphis, TN 38119. ✆ **800/CALL-HOME** (225-5466) or 901/763-0500. Fax 901/763-0132. www.homewood-suites.com. 140 units (all suites). $169–$209 suite. Rates include cooked breakfast. AE, DC, DISC, MC, V. Free parking. **Amenities:** Free airport transfers; basketball court; exercise room; hot tub; outdoor pool; valet service; complimentary social hour. *In room:* A/C, TV, kitchen, hair dryer, Internet (free).

Residence Inn by Marriott ★ Though it's not as attractively designed as the nearby Homewood Suites, this extended-stay property offers many of the same conveniences and amenities. The hotel also benefits from being within walking distance of several excellent restaurants. Some suites have rooms that open onto the lobby, while others have windows to the outside and tiny triangular balconies. You can choose a one-bedroom or

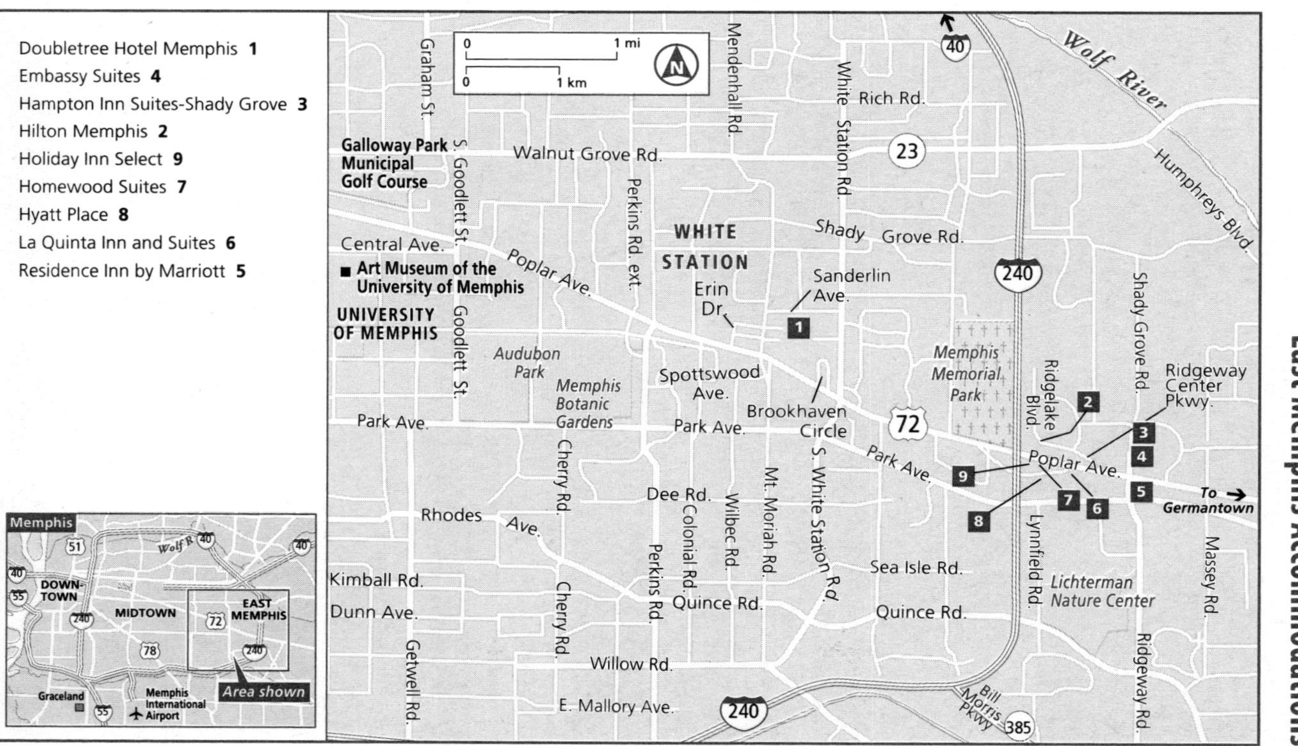
Doubletree Hotel Memphis 1
Embassy Suites 4
Hampton Inn Suites-Shady Grove 3
Hilton Memphis 2
Holiday Inn Select 9
Homewood Suites 7
Hyatt Place 8
La Quinta Inn and Suites 6
Residence Inn by Marriott 5
0 1 mi
0 1 km
Graham St.
Mendenhall Rd.
White Station Rd.
Rich Rd.
Wolf River
Humphreys Blvd.
Galloway Park Municipal Golf Course
S. Goodlett St.
Walnut Grove Rd.
Perkins Rd. ext.
WHITE STATION
Shady Grove Rd.
Central Ave.
Poplar Ave.
Art Museum of the University of Memphis
UNIVERSITY OF MEMPHIS
Goodlett St.
Erin Dr.
Sanderlin Ave.
Audubon Park
Memphis Botanic Gardens
Spottswood Ave.
Brookhaven Circle
Memphis Memorial Park
Ridgelake Blvd.
Shady Grove Rd.
Ridgeway Center Pkwy.
Park Ave.
Poplar Ave.
To Germantown
Cherry Rd.
Dee Rd.
Colonial Rd.
Wilbec Rd.
Mt. Moriah Rd.
S. White Station Rd.
Rhodes Ave.
Kimball Rd.
Dunn Ave.
Perkins Rd.
Quince Rd.
Sea Isle Rd.
Lynnfield Rd.
Lichterman Nature Center
Massey Rd.
Ridgeway Rd.
Getwell Rd.
Willow Rd.
E. Mallory Ave.
Bill Morris Pkwy
Memphis
DOWN-TOWN
MIDTOWN
EAST MEMPHIS
Wolf R.
Graceland
Memphis International Airport
Area shown

two-bedroom suite, but whichever size suite you choose, you'll have plenty of space, including a full kitchen and perhaps a fireplace. The two-bedroom suites have loft sleeping areas. Be sure to ask for a room on the side away from the railroad tracks.

6141 Old Poplar Pike, Memphis, TN 38119. ✆ **800/331-3131** or 901/685-9595. Fax 901/685-1636. www.marriott.com. 105 units (all suites). $149–$209 suite. Rates include continental breakfast as well as light dinner (Mon–Thurs 5:30–7pm). AE, DC, DISC, MC, V. Free parking. **Amenities:** Outdoor pool; complimentary social hour; sports court; valet service; Wi-Fi (free, in lobby). *In room:* A/C, TV w/pay movies, hair dryer, Internet (free).

MODERATE

Hampton Inn Suites–Shady Grove ★★ Finds Located next door to the Embassy Suites off Poplar Avenue in East Memphis, this 10-year-old property (that looks brand new) is an overlooked gem. Tucked into a tree-shaded, affluent neighborhood surrounded by great restaurants, it appeals to travelers with high expectations and stretched budgets. This is a lot of hotel for the money, with a large lobby that has the look and feel of a coffee shop and Internet cafe. There's also a cozy fireplace, oversized leather chairs, and a separate kitchen area with granite countertop island, white cabinets, and stashes of fresh fruits and beverages. Rooms are immaculate, furnished with crisp linens and "lap" desks stocked with snacks and the TV remote, as well as standard work desks and comfortable seating.

962 S. Shady Grove Rd., Memphis, TN 38119. ✆ **800/HAMPTON** (426-7866) or 901/762-0056. Fax 901/962-0033. www.hamptoninn.com. 124 units. $99–$149 double. AE, DC, DISC, MC, V. Free parking. **Amenities:** Outdoor pool. *In room:* A/C, TV w/pay movies, hair dryer, Wi-Fi (free).

Holiday Inn Select Often congested with harried tour groups and well-dressed banquet-goers, this 10-story hotel just off the interstate in East Memphis caters primarily to corporate travelers. They also do a big business with local, special events. Otherwise, this Holiday Inn is just an average hotel that offers all the basics, including a sunny indoor pool area and nice-sized rooms. Suites include a microwave and fridge.

Starting the Chain: The Story of the Holiday Inn

Wherever in the world your travels take you, the next time you're looking to book a clean, comfortable hotel room, you might want to thank Kemmons Wilson. The Memphis entrepreneur founded the first Holiday Inn back in 1952, before there was such a concept as chain hotels that aimed for consistency and reliability across many locations. The Holiday Inn franchise went international in 1960; today the brand is owned by the Intercontinental Hotel Group (IHG), which operates properties worldwide.

Wilson, who was known in Memphis as somewhat of a character, died in 2003. His autobiography, *Half Luck and Half Brains,* tells the interesting story of the Holiday Inn. His legacy lives on at the University of Memphis, where the Kemmons Wilson School at the Fogelman College of Business and Economics, trains new generations of hoteliers and tourism professionals.

The university's Holiday Inn is at 3700 Central Ave., Memphis, TN 38111 (✆ **901/678-8200;** www.holidayinn.com).

5795 Poplar Ave., Memphis, TN 38119. ✆ **800/HOLIDAY** (465-4329) or 901/682-7881. Fax 901/685-2407. www.hiselect.com/mem-epoplar. 243 units. $109–$159 double; $250–$350 suite. AE, DC, DISC, MC, V. Free parking. **Amenities:** Free airport shuttle; exercise room; indoor pool; room service; whirlpool; valet service. *In room:* A/C, TV, hair dryer, Wi-Fi (free).

Hyatt Place ★ (Kids) This place is ideal for families. Larger-than-expected suites have comfy, oversized sofa sleepers and large ottomans, making them ideal for stretching out to nap or to watch sports or movies on the 42-inch, high-definition plasma TVs. With spacious kitchenettes and plush beds, this affordably priced, contemporary hotel is a great choice for travelers looking for above-average accommodations in a safe, convenient location close to restaurants and shopping.

1220 Primacy Pkwy., Memphis, TN 38119. ✆ **901/680-9700.** Fax 901-681-0102. www.hyattplace.com. AE, DC, DISC, MC, V. 126 units. $109–$149 double. Rates include breakfast. Free parking. **Amenities:** Exercise room; outdoor pool. *In room:* A/C, TV, hair dryer; Wi-Fi (free).

INEXPENSIVE

La Quinta Inn & Suites (Value) (Kids) Adjacent to the Hyatt Place is this familiar chain hotel with the Spanish-style architecture and pet-friendly policies. Also an excellent choice for families, this clean, well-maintained hotel offers rates as low as $69 per night. With an array of amenities throughout the large property, you almost certainly won't find a better deal on a comparable hotel anywhere in town. Some rooms have microwaves and refrigerators, making them ideal for frugal extended stays.

1236 Primacy Pkwy., Memphis, TN 38119. ✆ **901/680-9700.** Fax 901-374-0330. www.laquinta.com. 131 units. $69–$99 double. Rates include breakfast. Free parking. **Amenities:** Exercise room; outdoor pool. *In room:* A/C, TV, hair dryer, Wi-Fi (free).

5 THE AIRPORT & GRACELAND AREAS

Obviously, if you need to be near the airport, any of these properties will suit your needs. But truthfully, the airport area encompasses neighborhoods most locals do not feel safe driving in. To get a sense of what Memphis is all about, you really should try to stay in or near downtown. Besides, with the plethora of tour buses and shuttle services available, access to Graceland is as easy from downtown as it is from the airport area. Still, if you want to go it alone, be aware that there is not much besides Elvis's former home to offer tourists in this area. Along Elvis Presley Boulevard there are many cheap motels scattered among the fast-food restaurants, gas stations, cash-advance stores and other businesses, but book these at your own risk.

EXPENSIVE

Courtyard Memphis Airport ★ This clean, well-maintained property, located a few miles from the main airport terminal, has earned a reputation as the airport area's top choice among corporate road warriors. Located in a pleasant, secure office park, the hotel offers rooms (including 14 suites) well equipped for business travelers. There are large work desks, daily newspaper delivery, and dinner delivery service from local restaurants. The property underwent a complete renovation in 2006.

1780 Nonconnah Blvd., Memphis, TN 38132. ✆ **901/396-3600.** Fax 901/332-0706. www.marriott.com. 145 units. $149–$169 double; $179 suite. AE, DC, DISC, MC, V. Free parking. **Amenities:** Exercise room; outdoor pool; whirlpool. *In room:* A/C, TV w/pay movies, hair dryer, Wi-Fi (free).

MODERATE

Elvis Presley's Heartbreak Hotel–Graceland ★ Moments If your visit to Memphis is a pilgrimage to Graceland, there should be no question as to where to stay. This Graceland-operated hotel has a gate right into the Graceland parking lot, with Elvis's home right across Elvis Presley Boulevard. In the lobby, you'll find two big portraits of the King and decor that would fit right in at the mansion. In the back courtyard, there's a smallish, heart-shaped outdoor pool. Indoors, four themed suites include the irresistibly named "*Burning Love* Suite." (Feel your temperature rising?) If you don't want to shell out big bucks for the entire suite, ask to split it and just rent a portion (or one room) of the suite. Many guests do this, I'm told.

3677 Elvis Presley Blvd., Memphis, TN 38116. ✆ **877/777-0606** or 901/332-1000. Fax 901/332-1636. www.elvis.com/epheartbreakhotel. 128 units. $112–$160 regular suite; $549–$595 themed suites. Rates include continental breakfast. AE, DC, DISC, MC, V. Free parking. **Amenities:** Heart-shaped outdoor pool. *In room:* A/C, TV w/24-hr. Elvis movies, fridge, hair dryer, microwave.

Holiday Inn Select Memphis Airport This basic chain hotel in the airport area offers security guards both inside the property and on patrol in the parking lot—reassuring, given the rough part of town in which it's located. In a pinch, this hotel would be okay for an overnight stay. Suites include refrigerators and microwaves.

2240 Democrat Rd., Memphis, TN 38132. ✆ **901/332-1130.** Fax 901/398-5206. www.hiselect.com. 374 units. $99–$119 double; $369 suite. AE, DC, DISC, MC, V. Free parking. **Amenities:** Restaurant; free airport shuttle; exercise room; outdoor pool; room service; tennis court. *In room:* A/C, TV w/pay movies, hair dryer, Wi-Fi (free).

Radisson Hotel Memphis Airport If you're in town for an airport-area business meeting or you plan to arrive in Memphis very late at night, this hotel right on the grounds of the airport fits the bill. All the rooms are well soundproofed so you don't have to worry about losing sleep because of overhead jets. The rooms themselves are rather

Elvis Slept Here

You might not mistake this former housing project for an upscale hotel, but, then again, this is Memphis—where offbeat surprises seem to lurk around every corner.

Elvis Presley lived here at Lauderdale Courts with his parents, Vernon and Gladys, when he was still a wide-eyed teenager (1949–53). Spared from demolition, in recent years the site has been transformed into **Uptown Square,** 252 N. Lauderdale, a trendy apartment complex that has preserved its sole historic unit as **"The Elvis Suite."**

For $250 a night, tourists may rent this first-floor apartment that includes a 1950s-style kitchen and sleeping room for four people. Before you book, be aware that this is a smoke-free property without wheelchair access, and that there's a 2-night minimum and 6-night maximum stay. Black-out dates apply during Elvis week (Aug) and other tourist-heavy times, when the property is in demand for guided tours but not for overnight lodging. For reservations, call ✆ **901/523-8662** (www.lauderdalecourts.com).

dark and not very memorable, but many are set up for business travelers with a desk and comfortable chair. The outdoor pool is set in a pleasant (though sometimes noisy) sunken garden area between two wings of the hotel.

2411 Winchester Rd., Memphis, TN 38116. ✆ **800/333-3333** or 901/332-2370. Fax 901/398-4085. www.radisson.com. 211 units. $119 double; $159 suite. AE, DC, DISC, MC, V. Free parking. **Amenities:** Restaurant; lounge; free airport shuttle; exercise room; outdoor pool; room service; 2 tennis courts. *In room:* A/C, TV, hair dryer, Wi-Fi (free).

INEXPENSIVE

Days Inn at Graceland With Graceland right across the street, it's no surprise that Elvis is king at this budget motel. Just look for the Elvis mural on the side of the building and the neon guitar sign out front, and you'll have found this unusual Days Inn. In the lobby, and on the room TVs, are round-the-clock Elvis videos. Service here is usually very friendly, too.

3839 Elvis Presley Blvd., Memphis, TN 38116. ✆ **800/329-7466** or 901/346-5500. Fax 901/345-7452. www.daysinn.com. 61 units. $79–$89 double. Rates include continental breakfast. AE, DC, DISC, MC, V. Free parking. **Amenities:** Guitar-shaped outdoor pool. *In room:* A/C, TV, Wi-Fi (free).

17

Where to Dine in Memphis

For a city most often associated with pork barbecue and Elvis's famous fried peanut-butter-and-banana sandwiches, Memphis has a surprisingly diverse restaurant scene. From escargot to étouffée and fajitas to focaccia, there's all manner of ethnic and gourmet fare around town. You'll also find plenty of barbecued ribs, fried pickles, purple-hull peas, butter beans, meatloaf, and mashed potatoes. And you might be surprised by the wealth of trendy restaurants you'd expect to encounter in any major metropolitan area. Drawing on influences from around the country and around the world, these New American and New Southern restaurants serve dishes so complex and creative that they often take a paragraph to describe on a menu.

Gourmet and ethnic foods aside, what Memphis can claim as its very own is slow-smoked, hand-pulled pork shoulder barbecue, to which you can add the spicy sauces of your choosing—chili vinegar, hot sauce, whatever. If this doesn't appeal to you, then maybe Memphis's famous ribs will. These are cooked much the same way as the pork shoulder and come dry or wet—that is, with the sauce added by you (dry) or cooked in (wet). See the "Barbecue" section later in this chapter.

Among the better chain restaurants to be found in Memphis are **Bonefish Grill,** 1250 N. Germantown Pkwy. (© **901/753-2220;** www.bonefishgrill.com); **Carrabba's,** 5110 Poplar Ave. (© **901/685-9900;** www.carrabbas.com); **P.F. Chang's,** 1181 Ridgeway Rd. (© **901/818-3889;** www.pfchangs.com); **Ruth's Chris Steakhouse,** 6120 Poplar at Shady Grove (© **901/761-0055;** www.ruthschris.com); and **Texas de Brazil Churrascaria,** 150 Peabody Place (© **901/526-7600;** www.texasdebrazil.com), featuring tableside, hand-carved meats.

For these listings, I have classified restaurants in the following categories (estimates do not include beer, wine, or tip): **very expensive** for meals costing more than $50; **expensive** if a complete dinner would cost $30 or more; **moderate,** where you can expect to pay between $15 and $30 for a complete dinner; and **inexpensive,** where a complete dinner can be had for less than $15.

1 BEST DINING BETS

- **Best Spot for a Romantic Dinner: Currents,** 50 Harbor Town Square (© **901/260-3333;** www.riverinnmemphis.com), the fine-dining restaurant at the intimate, European-style River Inn of Harbor Town, is the perfect place to pop the question or to enjoy a superb meal with someone special. The posh decor, gracious service, and gourmet cuisine will help ensure an evening to remember. See p. 188.
- **Best for Kids:** Like Nashville, downtown Memphis has a cavernous **Spaghetti Warehouse,** 40 W. Huling. (© **901/521-0907;** www.meatballs.com), that's been a long-time favorite for children. They can dine in an old trolley car while deciding whether to order the burger or a plate of pasta and meatballs. See p. 192.

- **Best Nostalgic Diner:** If you want to feel as if you've gone back in time, grab a booth at **The Arcade Restaurant,** 540 S. Main St. (© **901/526-5757;** www.arcade restaurant.com), a last-of-its-kind downtown institution. Home-style breakfasts, burgers, and pizzas are best bets at this old-school eatery that's anchored this corner since 1919. See p. 191.
- **Best Soul Food:** What Swett's is to Nashville, the **Four Way Restaurant,** 998 Mississippi Blvd. (© **901/507-1519**), is to Memphis—a historic, minority-owned restaurant that makes the best sweet-potato pie, fried catfish, and black-eyed peas you're ever likely to encounter. Always busy, it's a spacious, family-friendly restaurant offering full service (as opposed to the cafeteria format of Swett's). See p. 201.
- **Best New Restaurant:** Up-and-coming culinary star Kelly English wasn't named one of *Food & Wine* magazine's Best Chefs of 2009 for nothing. At his French-Creole **Restaurant Iris,** 2146 Monroe Ave. (© **901/590-2828;** www.restaurantiris.com), located in a Victorian house in Midtown, he presides over unforgettably delectable multicourse meals. Even the leftovers are special, gift-wrapped in pretty boxes tied with gold ribbon. See p. 193.

2 RESTAURANTS BY CUISINE

American

The Arcade Restaurant ★ (Downtown, $, p. 191)
brontë: A Novel Bistro (East Memphis, $, p. 203)
Café 1912 (Midtown, $$, p. 194)
Currents ★★★ (Downtown, $$$, p. 188)
D'Bo's Wings n' More ★ (South Memphis, $, p. 201)
Grill 83 ★★ (Downtown, $$$, p. 188)
Huey's ★ (Downtown, $, p. 192)
Just for Lunch (Midtown, $, p. 203)
The Majestic Grille ★ (Downtown, $$, p. 190)
Piccadilly (South Memphis, $ p. 202)
Spaghetti Warehouse ★ (Downtown, $, p. 192)

Barbecue

A&R Bar-B-Q (South Memphis, $, p. 202)
Blues City Café (Downtown, $$, p. 202)
The Rendezvous ★★ (Downtown, $, p. 192)
Corky's Ribs & BBQ ★ (East Memphis, $$, p. 199)
Cozy Corner (Midtown, $, p. 202)
Interstate Bar-B-Que ★ (South Memphis, $, p. 201)
Leonard's Pit Barbecue (Downtown, $, p. 202)
Neely's B-B-Q (Downtown, $, p. 202)
Payne's (South Memphis, $, p. 202)

Breakfast/Brunch

Beignet Café ★★ (Downtown, $, p. 191)
Brother Juniper's ★★ (East Memphis, $, p. 200)
Café Eclectic (Midtown, $, p. 195)
Krispy Kreme Doughnuts (South Memphis, $, p. 201)
Miss Polly's Soul City Cafe (Downtown, $, p. 203)
Owen Brennan's ★ (East Memphis, $$, p. 199)

Burgers

Dyer's Burgers (Downtown, $, p. 191)

Key to Abbreviations: $$$$ = Very Expensive $$$ = Expensive $$ = Moderate $ = Inexpensive

Cajun/Creole

Beignet Café ★★ (Downtown, $, p. 191)
The Inn at Hunt Phelan (Downtown, $$$, p. 188)
Owen Brennan's ★ (East Memphis, $$, p. 199)
Pearl's Oyster House ★ (Downtown, $, p. 192)
Restaurant Iris ★★★ (Midtown, $$$, p. 193)

Californian

Napa Café (East Memphis, $$$, p. 198)

Continental

Chez Philippe ★ (Downtown, $$$$, p. 185)
Currents ★★★ (Downtown, $$$, p. 188)
Grill 83 ★★ (Downtown, $$$, p. 188)
The Inn at Hunt Phelan (Downtown, $$$, p. 188)
Paulette's ★ (Midtown, $$, p. 194)

Deli

Kwik-Chek Deli (Midtown, $, p. 195)

French

Chez Philippe ★ (Downtown, $$$$, p. 185)
La Baguette (East Memphis, $$, p. 203)
Grace Restaurant ★ (Midtown, $$$, p. 193)
Restaurant Iris ★★★ (Midtown, $$$, p. 193)

Italian

Andrew Michael Italian Kitchen (East Memphis, $$$, p. 196)
Café Toscana (East Memphis, $$, p. 198)
Frank Grisanti ★ (East Memphis, $$$, p. 198)
Spaghetti Warehouse (Downtown, $, p. 192)
Spindini ★★ (Downtown, $$$, p. 189)

Japanese/Sushi

Noodle Doodle Do (Midtown, $, p. 195)
Sekisui of Japan ★★ (Downtown, Midtown, $$, p. 190)

Mediterranean

Casa Grill ★★ (Midtown, $$, p. 194)

Mexican/Southwestern

Salsa Cocina Mexicana ★★ (East Memphis, $, p. 200)

New American

Automatic Slim's Tonga Club (Downtown, $$, p. 190)
Beauty Shop ★★ (Midtown, $$$, p. 193)
Café Society ★ (Midtown, $$, p. 194)
Circa ★★ (Downtown, $$$, p. 185)
Grace Restaurant ★ (Midtown, $$$, p. 193)
Erling Jensen ★★★ (East Memphis, $$$, p. 196)
Napa Café (East Memphis, $$$, p. 198)

New Southern

Brushmark Restaurant (Midtown, $$, p. 203)
Chez Philippe ★ (Downtown, $$$$, p. 185)
Circa ★★ (Downtown, $$$, p. 185)
The Grove Grill ★ (East Memphis, $$, p.199)
McEwen's on Monroe ★ (Downtown, $$$, p. 189)

Pacific Rim

Tsunami ★★ (Midtown, $$$, p. 193)

Sandwiches

Café Eclectic (Midtown, $, p. 195)

Seafood

Noodle Doodle Do (Midtown, $, p. 195)

Sole Restaurant & Raw Bar ★ (Downtown, $$$, p. 189)
Soul Fish Cafe ★★ (Midtown, $, p. 196)
Tsunami ★★ (Midtown, $$$, p. 193)

Southern

Alcenia's (Downtown, $, p. 191)
Blue Plate Cafe (East Memphis, $, p. 199)
Four Way Restaurant ★★★ (South Memphis, $, p. 201)
Gus's World Famous Fried Chicken ★★ (Downtown, $, p. 191)
Little Tea Shop (Downtown, $, p. 203)
Patrick's Steaks & Spirits ★ (East Memphis, $, p. 200)
Piccadilly (South Memphis, $ p. 202)
Soul Fish Cafe ★★ (Midtown, $, p. 196)

Steak

Blues City Café (Downtown, $$, p. 202)
Folk's Folly Prime Steak House ★★ (East Memphis, $$$, p. 198)
The Majestic Grille ★ (Downtown, $$, p. 190)

Vietnamese

Pho Saigon (Midtown, $, p. 195)
Saigon Le ★ (Midtown, $, p. 195)

Thai

Mosa Asian Bistro (East Memphis, $, p. 200)

3 DOWNTOWN

VERY EXPENSIVE

Chez Philippe ★ CONTINENTAL/FRENCH/NEW SOUTHERN Still the most opulent dining room in Memphis (though The Peabody's palatial flagship restaurant has lost a bit of its cache in recent years), Chez Philippe still enthralls affluent gourmands who relish its Old South splendor. On the menu, Cuban-born, French-trained Chef Reinaldo Alfonso exploits Asian influences in dishes such as seaweed salad with soba noodles, cucumbers, and daikon radishes in a sugar-cane-sesame vinaigrette; and wild salmon slathered in citrus-soy barbecue sauce with a crispy, sushi-rice cake and carrot-ginger puree. Other options include the unusual veal osso buco dumplings as well as the comforting warm apple fritters with walnut-maple ice cream. Prices are the steepest in town, but expect to be pampered.

In The Peabody hotel, 149 Union Ave. ✆ **901/529-4188.** www.peabodymemphis.com. Reservations recommended. *Prix-fixe* menus $70 for 3 courses, or $78 for 5 courses (without wine, tax, or tip). AE, DC, DISC, MC, V. Tues–Sat 6–10pm.

EXPENSIVE

Circa ★★ NEW AMERICAN/NEW SOUTHERN One of the newest fine-dining restaurants and upscale bars downtown, Circa has been a place to see and be seen since it opened in mid 2007. Young local restaurateur and French-trained chef-owner John Bragg has pulled out all the stops to create a sleek, cosmopolitan space dominated by wall-to-ceiling wine racks dividing rows of candle-lit tables. Polished service, including expert wine recommendations made from an extensive list, make meals here feel special. I enjoyed the crisp spinach salad with crab meat; seared five-spice-encrusted tuna with wasabi mashed potatoes; and a generous surf-and-turf combo that paired succulent lobster with juicy, lean steak. Braised lamb shanks, crispy duck breast, and pan-roasted grouper are among the menu's other entrees. Plan ahead if you want to order the bananas Foster soufflé, which takes 30 minutes to prepare.

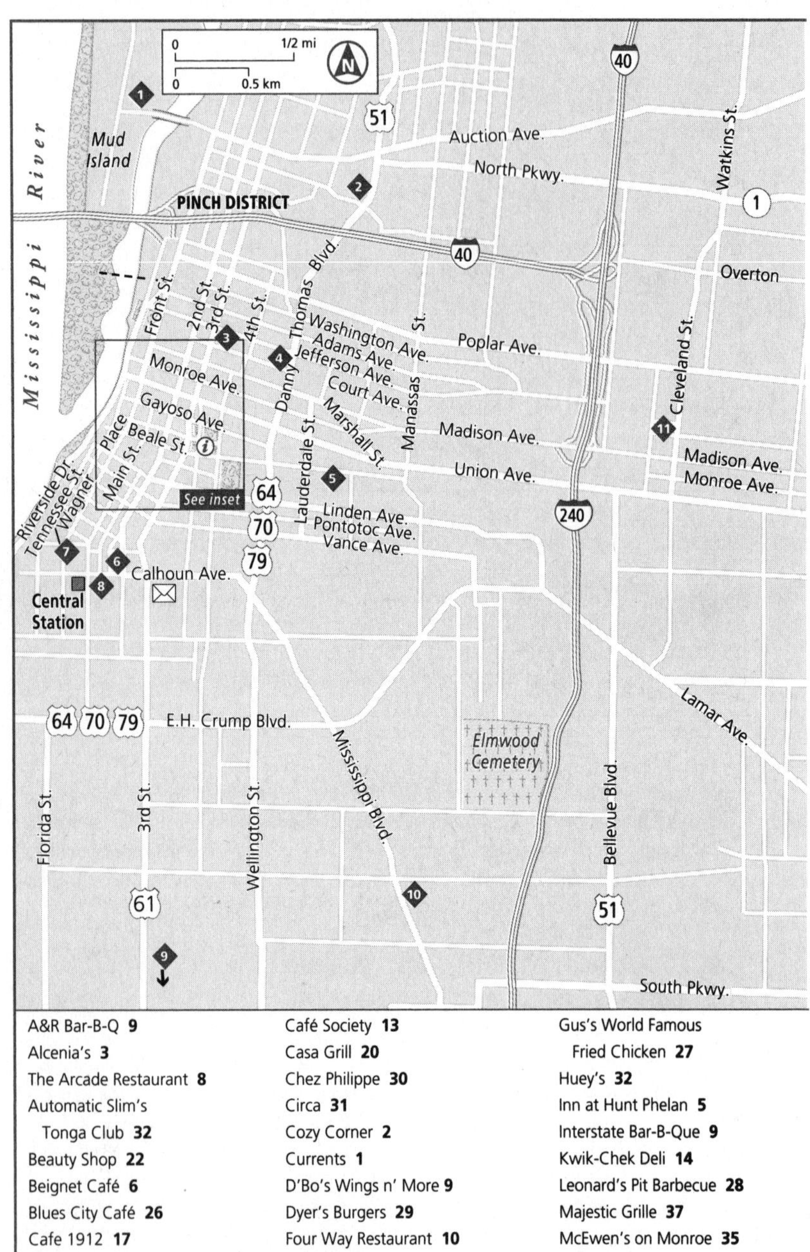

A&R Bar-B-Q **9**
Alcenia's **3**
The Arcade Restaurant **8**
Automatic Slim's Tonga Club **32**
Beauty Shop **22**
Beignet Café **6**
Blues City Café **26**
Cafe 1912 **17**
Café Eclectic **12**
Café Society **13**
Casa Grill **20**
Chez Philippe **30**
Circa **31**
Cozy Corner **2**
Currents **1**
D'Bo's Wings n' More **9**
Dyer's Burgers **29**
Four Way Restaurant **10**
Grill 83 **36**
Gus's World Famous Fried Chicken **27**
Huey's **32**
Inn at Hunt Phelan **5**
Interstate Bar-B-Que **9**
Kwik-Chek Deli **14**
Leonard's Pit Barbecue **28**
Majestic Grille **37**
McEwen's on Monroe **35**
Neely's B-B-Q **4**

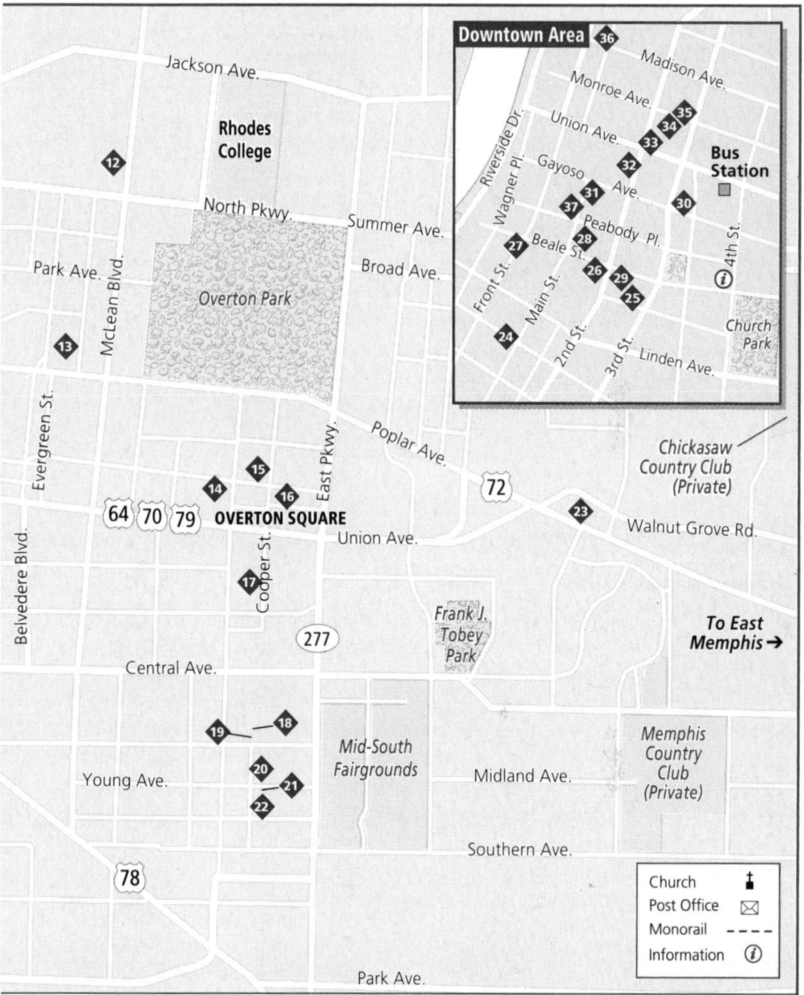

Downtown Area
Madison Ave.
Monroe Ave.
Union Ave.
Gayoso Ave.
Peabody Pl.
Beale St.
Linden Ave.
Riverside Dr.
Wagner Pl.
Front St.
Main St.
2nd St.
3rd St.
4th St.
Bus Station
Church Park
36 35 34 33 32 31 30 37 28 27 26 29 25 24

Jackson Ave.
Rhodes College
North Pkwy.
Summer Ave.
Broad Ave.
Park Ave.
McLean Blvd.
Overton Park
Evergreen St.
Poplar Ave.
East Pkwy.
Chickasaw Country Club (Private)
72
Walnut Grove Rd.
64 70 79
OVERTON SQUARE
Union Ave.
Belvedere Blvd.
Cooper St.
277
Frank J. Tobey Park
To East Memphis →
Central Ave.
Mid-South Fairgrounds
Midland Ave.
Memphis Country Club (Private)
Young Ave.
Southern Ave.
78
Park Ave.
12 13 14 15 16 17 18 19 20 21 22 23

Church
Post Office
Monorail
Information

Noodle Doodle Do **21**
Paulette's **15**
Payne's **9**
Pearl's Oyster House **24**
Pho Saigon **23**
Piccadilly **9**
Rendezvous **34**
Restaurant Iris **16**
Saigon Le **11**
Sekisui of Japan **33**
Sole Restaurant and Raw Bar **25**
Soul Fish Cafe **18**
Spaghetti Warehouse **7**
Tsunami **19**

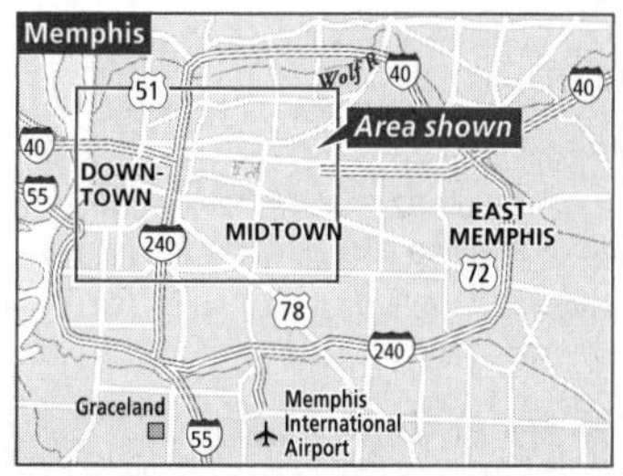

 Family-Friendly Restaurants

Corky's Ribs & BBQ (p. 199) Kids and grandparents alike love Corky's boisterous atmosphere, rollicking rock oldies music, and big pork platters paired with sky-high stacks of onion rings.

Four Way Restaurant (p. 201) Good, old-fashioned home cooking means kids might be asked to eat their vegetables along with fried chicken and pork chops. But when the green beans are seasoned with pork and the mashed potatoes are drenched in butter, who but the fussiest little eaters would object?

The Majestic Grille (p. 190 Vintage Popeye cartoons and silent movies play on a large video screen at one end of this upscale-ish but affordable family restaurant with enough menu choices for all tastes).

Spaghetti Warehouse (p. 192) Antique trolley cars and hearty Italian comfort food, including thick slabs of lasagna and kid-friendly spaghetti-and-meatballs, make this inexpensive restaurant a family favorite.

119 S. Main, Ste. 100. ✆ **901/522-1488.** www.circamemphis.com. Main courses $26–$37. AE, DISC, DC, MC, V. Sun–Thurs 5–9:30pm; Fri–Sat 5–10pm.

Currents ★★★ AMERICAN/CONTINENTAL Critics have raved that this new restaurant is "reminiscent of an old New Orleans fine-dining establishment." That sums it up perfectly. White tablecloths, fine china, fresh roses, and impeccable service enhance Chef David Schrier's excellent American cuisine. Currents recently launched a three-course $29 *prix-fixe* menu that offers incredible value with such entree choices as pan-roasted wild salmon, braised Niman Ranch pork osso buco, or oven-roasted Cornish game hen with sides of savory bread pudding and butternut squash. For $5 more you can opt for the thick, perfectly cooked filet of beef with Dijon-leek potato hash, haricots verts, and a Creole mustard demi-glace. For dessert, treat yourself to the decadent warm pecan tart with caramel ice cream. There's an extensive wine list and a full bar, as well. The restaurant is located inside the River Inn of Harbor Town.

50 Harbor Town Sq. ✆ **901/260-3333.** www.riverinnmemphis.com. Reservations recommended. Main courses $15–$36. AE, DC, DISC, MC, V. Daily 5–9pm.

Grill 83 ★★ AMERICAN/CONTINENTAL Tucked inside the intimate boutique Madison Hotel is this chic, dimly lit, fine-dining restaurant and lounge. It is a dark, narrow room with vintage black-and-white photographs on the walls and well-dressed diners enjoying brandies and ports after multicourse gourmet meals. Open for breakfast and lunch, Grill 83 shines at dinner. Exquisitely prepared steaks (the signature is a 16-oz. Kansas City bone-in filet) and succulent seared sea bass are served with artful garnishes and such sides as grilled asparagus with lemon butter. Service is polished and professional.

The Madison Hotel, 83 Madison Ave. ✆ **901/333-1224.** www.gril183.com. Reservations recommended. Main courses $24–$48. AE, DC, DISC, MC, V. Sun–Thurs 6:30am–10pm; Fri–Sat 6:30am–11pm.

The Inn at Hunt Phelan CAJUN/CREOLE/CONTINENTAL What's so much fun about dining at the Inn at Hunt Phelan is how cozy and welcome you can feel in such a grand, storied place. The restaurant—made up of a collection of small dining rooms on the first floor of a restored 1828 antebellum mansion—is a welcome retreat just outside the hustle of downtown Memphis. Inside the mansion, now a lovely B&B, the restaurant caters to inn guests and to outside visitors. On a recent visit here, the salad of artichokes, wild boar pancetta, and olive vinaigrette were a delightful beginning. The morel mushrooms with a grit cake, fava beans, and okra were rich and a nice tip of the hat to Southern-food tradition, but the lamb with couscous entree proved that the chef is definitely not living in the past. An impressive dessert and wine list round out the menu—your waiter will be happy to make recommendations, should you not know where to begin.

533 Beale St. ✆ **901/525-8225.** www.huntphelan.com. Reservations recommended. Main courses $27–$34 dinner; Sun brunch $11–$24. AE, DC, MC, V. Wed–Sat 5–11pm; Sun brunch 10am–2:30pm.

McEwen's on Monroe ★ NEW SOUTHERN The exposed-brick walls, white tablecloths, and well-spaced tables are your first clue that McEwen's is a classy, comfortable kind of place. It offers a relaxed yet sophisticated atmosphere with food to match. Located downtown on Monroe Avenue, McEwen's is a lunchtime favorite with the business crowd, but at night it caters to a wide swath of folks looking for delicious food in a genial setting. "Southern fusion" appetizers include sweet potato empanadas, barbeque duck confit enchiladas, and buttermilk fried oysters, and entrees such as pan-seared scallops with stone-ground cheddar grits or peppered seared beef tenderloin served with a lobster potato cake. Though this is no place to stick to your diet, they do have a few options on the lighter side. At lunchtime, go for the soup-and-salad combo. After dark, try the watercress salad, with mandarin oranges, roasted red and yellow bell peppers, with a cotija cheese blood-orange vinaigrette. Ask to see their sizeable wine list. For dessert, nothing will make you happier than McEwen's famous banana cream pie. The award-winning confection will make you swoon, Southern style.

122 Monroe Ave. ✆ **901/527-7085.** www.mcewensonmonroe.com. Main courses $7–$12 lunch; $20–$29 dinner. AE, DC, MC, V. Mon–Fri 11am–2pm; Mon–Thurs 5:30–10pm; Fri–Sat 5:30–11pm. Bar open later.

Sole Restaurant & Raw Bar ★ SEAFOOD Generally speaking, hotel restaurants can be rather ho-hum, which is why I was so pleasantly surprised by Sole. It's the newly minted eatery inside the Westin Memphis Beale Street. Serving three meals daily, this place offers an impressive Southern breakfast spread (including biscuits and sausage gravy). But it's at dinner when Sole really shines. Set against the backdrop of soft lighting and warm, wood-paneled booths and tables set with ocean-blue napkins, the restaurant offers delicious seafood dishes such as oysters on the half shell, and fresh-market-catch specials on such selections as Hawaiian sunfish, Maine lobster, and blue prawns. Steaks, sandwiches, and salads are also on the menu, along with poultry. The juicy, free-range baked chicken breast that is served with a crisp-fried, creamy polenta cake and a side of collard greens is absolutely delicious. Service is helpful and very friendly.

Located inside the Westin Beale St., 221 S. Third. ✆ **901/334-5950.** www.solememphis.com. Reservations accepted. Main courses $21–$30. AE, DC, DISC, MC, V. Daily for breakfast, lunch, and dinner.

Spindini ★★ ITALIAN Judd Grisanti comes from a long line of Italian chef/restaurateurs who have earned well-deserved success and recognition in Memphis. Spindini is the newest venture from the Grisanti clan, and it is a sophisticated showstopper. Opened in 2007 in downtown's South Main arts district, the long, narrow restaurant is flanked by a banquette with tightly spaced tables and a classy bar adorned with decorative glass sculptures. A wood-burning oven at the back of the restaurant emits a warm glow, as the kitchen churns out appetizers and entrees that have been cooked, or rather "kissed by the fire" there. Wood-fired steaks, seared fish, and fresh pasta dishes are excellent. The Tuscan Butter may be one of the best appetizers in town—an ice-cream-sized scoop of spreadable mascarpone and goat cheese drenched in a tangy tomato sauce and served with soft, slender slices of warm garlic bread. The only thing that keeps me from giving this restaurant three stars is its service, which can be indifferent as the busy waitstaff rushes to turn over tables to people wait-listed in the cramped lounge seating area near the front door.

383 S. Main St. ✆ **901/578-2767.** www.spindinimemphis.com. Reservations recommended. Pizzas and main courses $13–$32. AE, DISC, DC, MC, V. Sun–Wed 5–10pm; Thurs–Sat 5–11pm.

MODERATE

Automatic Slim's Tonga Club NEW AMERICAN Recent ownership changes have affected consistency at this once-hot restaurant, but it's still a fun place to hang for a late-night bite of fried fish, jerk chicken, or tobacco fries. The name "Automatic Slim" comes from an old blues song, and the Tonga Club was a local teen hangout popular in the early 1960s. Artists from New York and Memphis created the decor (they're credited on the menu), including zebra-print upholstered banquettes, slag-glass wall sconces, and colorfully upholstered bar stools. Be sure to try a cocktail with some of the fruit-soaked vodka.

83 S. Second St. ✆ **901/525-7948.** www.automaticslimsmemphis.com. Reservations accepted. Main courses at dinner $17–$26; late-night plates $10–$15. AE, DC, MC, V. Mon–Sat 11am–3am; Sun 10am–4pm.

The Majestic Grille ★ Kids AMERICAN/STEAK Silent movies, old Popeye cartoons, and such black-and-white classics as Marx Brothers comedies are shown on a big screen at one end of this stylish bistro that's new to downtown. It's appropriate, given the building's history as an early 1900s movie theater. Polished and sophisticated, it's also a comfortable dining room, with tables and booths set on two levels. The large and widely varied menu includes something for everyone, from aged steaks including filet mignon and a 16-ounce, bone-in rib eye. Signature flatbreads (thin-crust pizzas) come with a choice of toppings, while sandwiches and burgers are served with tendrils of crispy Parmesan fries. Pasta, grilled fish, beef ribs, and a pork tenderloin round out the dinner options. Desserts are a revelation: Shot-glasses of key lime pie, cheesecake, and other treats provide just a few bites to satisfy the sweet tooth, and they're only $2 each.

145 S Main St. ✆ **901/522-8555.** www.majesticgrille.com. Main courses $12–$29. AE, DISC, MC, V. Mon–Thurs 11am–11pm; Fri–Sat 11am–midnight; Sun 11am–9pm.

Sekisui of Japan ★★ JAPANESE/SUSHI Unlike Japanese restaurants that almost go overboard on tranquillity, Sekisui is a noisy and active place, especially on weekends. The sushi bar prepares platters of assorted fish, from appetizer tidbits to a huge sushi boat that includes octopus, conch, snapper, and flying-fish-roe sushi. Fiery wasabi, a splash of soy, and shredded ginger add zing. Tempura, teriyaki, and *yakizakana* dinners come with rice, a wonderful miso soup, and salad. Some locations offer a separate *robata* grill menu. Among the other Sekisui locations are those at 25 S. Belvedere St. (✆ **901/725-0005**) in Midtown, and under the name **Sekisui Pacific Rim,** at 4724 Poplar Ave. (✆ **901/767-7770**), in East Memphis.

Inside the Holiday Inn Select downtown, 160 Union Ave. ✆ **901/523-0001.** www.sekisuiusa.com. Reservations recommended Sat–Sun. Main courses $9–$26. AE, DC, DISC, MC, V. Mon–Fri 11:30am–2pm; Sun–Thurs 5–9pm; Fri–Sat 5–10pm.

INEXPENSIVE

Alcenia's SOUTHERN This down-to-earth breakfast/lunch hangout looks like the kind of place where Stella got her groove back. The decor is shabby chic, where orange walls and purple beaded curtains blend right in with the potted plants, African artwork, and tulle draped from the ceiling. Best known for its homemade preserves, Alcenia's serves up salmon croquettes, pancakes, and biscuits for breakfast. Sandwiches and Southern-style munchies are available at other hours. Call ahead to see if Alcenia's famous bread pudding is on the menu that day.

317 N. Main St. ✆ **901/523-0200.** Main courses $7–$9. AE, DC, MC, V. Tues–Fri 11am–5pm; Sat 9am–1pm. (Occasionally open evenings for special events; call ahead.)

The Arcade Restaurant ★ **Value** AMERICAN Established in 1919, the Arcade stands as a reminder of the early part of the century when this was a busy neighborhood, bustling with people and commerce. Although this corner is not nearly as lively as it once was, the restaurant attracts loyal Memphians and out-of-towners who stop by for the home-style cooking and pizzas. Because the proprietors have an annoying habit of closing down when business is slow, you might want to call ahead if you're making the Arcade your destination.

540 S. Main St. ✆ **901/526-5757.** www.arcaderestaurant.com. Breakfast $6–$8; lunch $6–$8; pizza $7–$20. DC, DISC, MC, V. Daily 7am–3pm.

Beignet Café ★★ **Finds** BREAKFAST/BRUNCH/CAJUN/CREOLE With hot, crisp, sugar-dusted beignets every bit as mouth-watering as the famed Café Du Monde's in New Orleans—and some of the best jambalaya in town—this newly opened cafe is a hidden gem. Run by an enterprising foodie from Louisiana, this eatery is tucked off a side street behind the National Civil Rights Museum. On one of my visits (during the River Arts Fest in the South Main Historic District), succulent ribs were being grilled on an outdoor smoker at the corner. Full of unpretentious charm and friendly people enjoying such comfort food as po' boys, bread pudding, and fried macaroni-and-cheese balls, this place is one of my new favorites.

124 G. E. Patterson Blvd. ✆ **901/527-1551.** Under $10. MC, V. Tue–Thurs 8am–8pm; Fri–Sat 8am–9pm; Sun 9am–3pm.

Dyer's Burgers **Overrated** BURGERS I feel obliged to include this retro diner only because it's garnered so much attention on Food Network, the Travel Channel, and in several national and international magazines. Why? Sure, it's got an appealing, old-timey look, but the greasy spoon's notoriety is their claim that they've been deep-frying their hamburgers and French fries in the same vat of cooking oil—for nearly a century. Let me set you straight: With food that's average at best, this place is just another novelty for easy-to-please bar-hoppers on Beale Street. But if you're dying for a deep-fried Twinkie, it's your funeral.

205 Beale St. ✆ **901/527-3937.** Under $10. AE, DC, MC, V. Sun–Thurs 11am–1am; Fri–Sat 11am–5am.

Gus's World Famous Fried Chicken ★★ SOUTHERN In a decidedly dingy juke-joint setting off the beaten path downtown sits this franchise of the legendary Gus's in Mason, Tennessee. Black and white, young and old, hip and square—they and every other demographic all converge here for spicy-battered chicken, beans, slaw, and pies. Service is friendly but slow, so don't go here if you're in a hurry. (If you'd like to take a road trip to the Real McCoy, the original Gus's is at 505 Hwy. 70 W., Mason; ✆ **901/ 294-2028.** Call ahead for hours.)

310 S. Front St. ✆ **901/527-4877.** Main courses $6–$9. AE, MC, V. Daily 11am–9pm (Sat–Sun until 10pm).

Huey's ★ AMERICAN Ask Memphians where to get the best burger in town, and you'll invariably be directed to Huey's. This good-times tavern also has one of the most extensive beer selections in town. The original Huey's, at 1927 Madison Ave. (✆ **901/ 726-4372**), in the Overton Square area, is still in business. In recent years, suburban locations have also sprouted up in East Memphis and beyond.

77 S. Second St. ✆ **901/527-2700.** www.hueyburger.com. Reservations not accepted. Main courses $5–$10. AE, DISC, MC, V. Daily 11am–3am.

Pearl's Oyster House ★ CAJUN/CREOLE An old warehouse in downtown's South Main Street district has found renewed energy as a spacious, laid-back Gulf Coast–style seafood joint. Platters of plump oysters can be ordered raw or fried, or try the juicy pan-roasted mussels. Cajun gumbos and étouffée are rich, roux-based soups studded with chunks of andouille sausage and fish. Fried-shrimp po' boys are encased in shredded lettuce inside chewy French baguettes. More substantial fare includes fresh catfish fried in butter, and the seasonal crawfish boil—a spicy-hot favorite with corn-on-the-cob and new potatoes.

299 S. Main St. ✆ **901/522-9070.** www.pearlsoysterhouse.com. Main courses $10–$19. AE, DISC, DC, MC, V. Mon–Sat from 11am; closing times vary.

The Rendezvous ★★ Moments BARBECUE The Rendezvous has been a downtown Memphis institution since 1948, and it has a well-deserved reputation for serving the best ribs in town. You can see the food being prepared in an old open kitchen as you walk in, but more important, your sense of smell will immediately perk up as the fragrance of hickory-smoked pork wafts past. You'll also likely be intrigued by all manner of strange objects displayed in this huge but cozy cellar. And when the waiter comes to take your order, there's no messin' around; when you come in, you're expected to know what you want—an order of ribs. Also be sure to ask if they still have any of the red beans and rice that are served nightly, until the pot is empty. This Memphis landmark is tucked along General Washburn Alley, across from The Peabody. Upstairs, you'll find a large bar.

52 S. Second St. ✆ **901/523-2746.** www.hogsfly.com. Main plates $6.50–$18. AE, DC, DISC, MC, V. Tues–Thurs 4:30–10:30pm; Fri 11am–11pm; Sat 11:30am–11pm.

Spaghetti Warehouse ★ Kids AMERICAN/ITALIAN Families and tourists on budgets seek out this sprawling, noisy old warehouse brimming with antiques and amusing collectibles. Food is middle-of-the-road. Simple American burgers are served alongside Italian staples such as lasagna and spaghetti. Though this longtime Memphis eatery may lack the buzz of newer restaurants, it certainly has staying power.

40 W. Huling. ✆ **901/521-0907.** www.meatballs.com. Main plates $6–$16. AE, MC, V. Sun–Thurs 11am–10pm; Fri–Sat 11am–11pm.

4 MIDTOWN

For locations of restaurants in this section, see the "Memphis Dining: Downtown & Midtown" map, on p. 186.

EXPENSIVE

Beauty Shop ★★ NEW AMERICAN The first and most important thing you need to know is *not* that this hip eatery sits inside an old 1960s-style beauty shop, but that it's the brainchild of Karen Blockman Carrier, the creative force behind Memphis's coolest restaurant (Automatic Slim's). Yes, the atmosphere is kitschy and fun. You can indeed dine in refurbished hair-dryer chairs. But what keeps the place packed with all the beautiful people is the fantastic food: globally inspired salads (I loved the Thai Cobb), entrees such as the whole striped bass, or the best BLTA (bacon, lettuce, tomato, and avocado sandwich) you've ever tasted.

966 S. Cooper St. ✆ **901/272-7111.** Reservations highly recommended. Main courses $19–$26. AE, MC, V. Mon–Sat 11am–2pm; brunch Sun 10am–3pm; dinner Mon–Sat Thurs 5–10pm.

Grace Restaurant ★ FRENCH/NEW AMERICAN One of the newest upscale bistros to open in the Cooper-Young area is Grace, a small but cozy dining room that has a clean, contemporary look. Freshness and simplicity extend to young Chef Ben Vaughn's menu as well, which features a daily vegetable plate and entrees, salads, desserts, and appetizers that showcase foods from local farmers and growers. On a recent visit, I sampled savory grilled fish dishes and flavorful salads. Quail, chicken, and duck dishes were also on the menu that night. The dessert, a strawberry crumble, wasn't overly sweet, with sliced red berries sprinkled with buttery shortbread crumbs and a delicate mound of ice cream. Service was a little shaky, but I will chalk that up to opening-month jitters.

938 S. Cooper St. ✆ **901/274-8511.** www.gracememphis.com. Reservations recommended. Main courses $20–$28. AE, DC, DISC, MC, V. Mon–Sat 5–11pm.

Restaurant Iris ★★★ CAJUN/CREOLE/FRENCH Chef/owner Kelly English, named one of *Food & Wine*'s Best Chefs of 2009, has been garnering rave reviews—and fully booked tables—at his Midtown fine-dining restaurant. Opened in 2008, it occupies a charming bungalow that once housed the city's esteemed La Tourelle restaurant. Raised in Louisiana and trained at the famed Culinary Institute of America, English excels in combining French and Creole influences in creative and inspired dishes that are never over the top. Already a menu staple is the lobster-knuckle sandwich, along with other generously portioned appetizers including bacon-braised Brussels sprouts salad. Entrees vary but might include slow-cooked Kobe rib "pot roast" with root vegetables; shrimp and grits; New York strip steak stuffed with crabmeat and blue cheese; and pan-seared fish. Desserts are a delight. I particularly like the pecan-studded bread pudding, topped with house-made vanilla or cinnamon ice cream. Friendly servers are extremely knowledgeable about food and wine, and their professionalism greatly enhances the dining experience here.

2146 Monroe Ave. ✆ **901/590-2828.** www.restaurantiris.com. Reservations recommended. Main courses $21–$32. AE, MC, V. Tue–Sat 5–10pm; Sun 11am–3pm.

Tsunami ★★ PACIFIC RIM/SEAFOOD Consistently ranked by locals as one of their favorite restaurants in Memphis, Tsunami serves creative Pacific Rim cuisine. Tropical colors over cement floors and walls enliven the otherwise uninspired setting. But the food's the thing. Appetizers run the gamut from pot sticker dumplings with chili-soy dipping sauce, to shrimp satay with Thai peanut sauce. Among chef/owner Ben Smith's other specialties are roasted sea bass with black Thai rice and soy beurre blanc, wasabi-crusted tuna, and duck breast with miso-shiitake risotto. Crème brûlée fans should not miss Smith's sublime Tahitian-vanilla version of this classic. A judicious list of Australian and French wines includes champagne and a handful of ports.

928 S. Cooper St. ✆ **901/274-2556.** www.tsunamimemphis.com. Reservations recommended. Main courses $20–$30; small plates $12–$15. AE, MC, V. Mon–Fri 11am–2pm; Mon–Sat 5:30–10pm.

MODERATE

Cafe 1912 AMERICAN At the edge of the Cooper-Young district in Midtown, this casual bistro and bar is especially popular with neighborhood residents. Rickety wooden tables and straw-seat chairs line the painted cement floor in the main dining room, behind which is a separate bar area. (Ask for a table away from the front door, where it can become cold and drafty in chilly weather.) Daily specials include fresh fish and soups, or try the perennially popular beef tenderloin encrusted with smoked olive tapenade, potato puree, and red-wine sauce. The best dessert here is the ample fruit-and-cheese plate, featuring generous wedges of soft, semisoft, and hard cheeses.

243 S. Cooper ✆ **901/722-2700.** Main courses $16–$25. www.cafe1912.com. AE, DISC, DC, MC, V. Mon–Thurs 5:30–9:30pm; Fri–Sat 5:30–10:30pm; Sun 5:30–9pm.

Café Society ★ NEW AMERICAN Named after a Parisian cafe, this lively bistro has a vague country-inn feel about it and is a popular ladies' lunch spot and pre-theater restaurant. As in a French cafe, you'll find convivial conversations at the small bar and outdoor seating on the street where you can sit and people-watch. Start out with some French onion soup or honey-baked brie, followed up with the likes of salmon with a sesame- and poppy seed crust or braised lamb shank with a pear brandy and walnut glaze. Lunches are reasonably priced and offer a chance to sample some of the same fine food that is served at dinner. There are also monthly four-course wine and food tastings, for which reservations are required.

212 N. Evergreen St. ✆ **901/722-2177.** Reservations recommended. Main courses $13–$27. AE, DC, MC, V. Mon–Fri 11:30am–2pm; Mon–Sun 5–10:30pm.

Casa Grill ★★ MEDITERRANEAN Craving a "Big Mac of the Middle East"? You can get the so-called falafel pita sandwich at this comfortably exotic eatery in the Cooper-Young neighborhood. The chef/owner imports all his spices and ingredients, such as olive oil, from his native Middle East. A hard-working, congenial host, he mingles with customers and offers helpful suggestions for appetizers such as baba ghanouj, pureed lentil soup, and silky hummus served with a basket of soft, warm pita bread. You can also indulge in generously stuffed gyros or Greek salads, including tabbouleh or crisp lettuce with olives and feta cheese. Entrees include grilled rack of lamb with mango sauce, and Holy Land shish kebob. Exotic Moroccan tagine dishes—seafood or lamb baked in clay pots—serve two people.

2156 Young Ave. ✆ **901/722-2700.** www.casablancamemphis.com. Main courses $10–$16; sandwiches $6–$8. AE, DISC, DC, MC, V. Daily 10am–10pm.

Paulette's ★ CONTINENTAL Paulette's has long been one of Memphis's most beloved restaurants. Cozy as a French country inn, the space is filled with antiques and traditional European paintings. Specialties here include the Hungarian *gulyas* and *uborka salata* (cucumber salad in a sweet vinegar dressing). Not to be missed are the popovers with strawberry butter that accompany most entrees. Among the main courses, the beef filet is delicious, as are the chicken livers bourguignon, and Louisiana crab cakes. Though the dessert list is quite extensive, you should be sure that someone at your table orders the Kahlúa-mocha pie, made with a pecan-coconut crust.

2110 Madison Ave. ✆ **901/726-5128.** www.paulettes.net. Reservations recommended. Main courses $9–$25. AE, DC, DISC, MC, V. Sun–Thurs 11am–9pm; Fri–Sat 11am–10:30pm.

INEXPENSIVE

Café Eclectic SANDWICHES/BREAKFAST/BRUNCH Near Rhodes College and the Memphis Zoo, in the pretty residential neighborhood known as Vollintine-Evergreen, this new cafe has quickly attracted a devoted following. A laid-back bakery and coffee shop that's usually full of students on their laptops and families heading here from the elementary school across the street, this has become a gathering place. Although it doesn't sell alcohol (you can bring your own wine, for corkage fee), there's a comfy bar countertop and stools, quirky artwork on the walls, a small sofa strewn with pillows, and a picket fence sectioning off one corner of the dining room. Sandwiches, such as the bacon, avocado, and tomato, come with sides such as roasted sweet and russet potatoes. Soups, salads, and breakfast eats round out the simple menu. There's a long list of coffee and tea drinks, as well, and baguettes and other loaves of fresh-baked bread are sold from a glass case near the cash register.

603 N. McLean Blvd. ✆ **901/725-1718.** www.cafeeclectic.net. Main dishes under $10. DC, DISC, MC, V Mon–Wed 6:30am–10pm; Thurs–Sat 6:30am–10pm (coffees, pastries, and ice cream until 1am); Sun 9am–3pm (coffees, pastries, and desserts until 10pm).

Noodle Doodle Do JAPANESE/SUSHI/SEAFOOD Spare furnishings in this brick storefront overlooking the intersection of Cooper and Young streets in Midtown keep the focus on people-watching and tasting. Celebrated local restaurateur and caterer Karen Blockman Carrier is the force behind this sushi restaurant, called Do (pronounced "dough"), where the menu includes everything from sashimi rolls and seaweed salad to noodle dishes and soups. Clean, vibrant flavors and friendly, knowledgeable service are hallmarks here.

964 Cooper St. ✆ **901/272-0830.** Main courses under $10. AE, DC, DISC, MC, V. Tues–Sat 11:30am–4pm; Mon–Sat 5–11pm.

Kwik-Chek Deli (Finds) DELI A slab of meat roasting on a spit is the most out-of-place thing you'll immediately notice about this nondescript convenience store in Midtown. Order the Hey Zeus, a tortilla wrap with turkey, roast beef and a tangy blast of marinated veggies. Gyros and other sandwiches, made (while you wait) from freshly sliced meats and cheeses, have kept loyal folks coming back here for years.

2013 Madison Ave. ✆ **901/274-9293.** Under $10. MC, V. Mon–Sat 10am–9pm; Sun 10am–7pm.

Pho Saigon (Value) VIETNAMESE Noodle dishes, spring and egg rolls, and piquant soups are served in plentiful portions at this clean, family-run restaurant off Poplar Avenue near Midtown. There's nothing fancy about Pho Saigon's interior, but basic chairs and tables and a few knickknacks are all that's necessary. Although service can be inconsistent, the menu is extensive and the food is fresh.

2946 Poplar Ave. ✆ **901/458-1644.** Main courses $5–$8. MC, V. Daily 10am–9pm.

Saigon Le ★ (Finds) VIETNAMESE A popular lunch spot, Saigon Le is in an urban neighborhood close to the medical-center district and is popular with hospital workers. Friendly service and generous portions of Chinese and Vietnamese dishes are the standards here. The kung pao beef is spicy, and the vegetable egg foo yong is plump with vegetables. Saigon Le's Vietnamese specialties include flavorful noodle, meat, fish, and vegetable dishes such as charbroiled pork, spring rolls with vermicelli, and clear noodle soup with barbecued pork, shrimp, and crabmeat. At just under $6, the lunch special may be the best bargain in town.

51 N. Cleveland St. ✆ **901/276-5326.** www.saigon-le.com. Main courses $6–$15. DC, DISC, MC, V. Mon–Sat 11am–9pm.

Soul Fish Cafe ★★ SOUTHERN/SEAFOOD The crispiest, most mouth-watering fried catfish in town is served at this wildly popular new haunt at the edge of the Cooper-Young area. A narrow old house has been filled with tables and a short bar against the far end of the room. Sit here at one of the barstools to admire the fishing lures embedded in the countertop, while sipping a cold beer or iced tea. Baskets of fried catfish come with lettuce, tomatoes, and creamy remolded sauce. Abundant sides include home-style macaroni and cheese, green beans, and Cajun cooked cabbage (it's great, packing a tomato-ey, sweet-and-sour zip). The hush puppies alone are worth the trip. Eat in or order for take-out. And try to avoid going on Friday nights, when there's a line outside the door.

862 S. Cooper St. ✆ **901/725-0722.** www.marksmenus.com. Main courses under $12. AE, MC, V. Mon–Sat 11am–10pm; Sun 11am–9pm.

5 EAST MEMPHIS

EXPENSIVE

Andrew Michael Italian Kitchen ITALIAN Fresh produce, meats, and cheeses from local farms and food purveyors are hallmarks of this new rustic Italian eatery located in a converted East Memphis house. Known for handmade potato gnocchi, ravioli, and other pastas, the young chefs—Andrew Ticer and Michael Hudman—are childhood friends who recently fulfilled their dream to open a restaurant. Besides pasta, menu standouts are seafood dishes like calamari, halibut, and swordfish boosted by leeks, fennel, tarragon, and other piquant flavors. At dinner, black-olive tapenade comes with warm, crusty loaves of bread. In season, the Caprese salad of heirloom tomatoes, freshly shredded buffalo mozzarella, and pesto is divine. The lovely restaurant, with dark hardwood floors and elegant furnishings, has a nice patio out back. There's also a full bar.

712 W. Brookhaven Circle. ✆ **901/347-3569.** www.andrewmichaelitaliankitchen.com. Reservations recommended. Main courses $18–$32. AE, MC, V. Mon–Sat 5–10pm.

Erling Jensen ★★★ NEW AMERICAN Chef Erling Jensen made a name for himself at the popular La Tourelle and has now ventured out on his own at this eponymous restaurant located in a converted home just off Poplar Avenue at I-240. Understated elegance and contemporary art set the tone for Jensen's innovative cuisine. The Danish-born chef offers a "deconstructed" lobster Bolognese ravioli and other appetizers, including crispy oysters over mixed greens with roasted corn relish and Pernod-scented buttermilk dressing. A diverse entree assortment makes decision-making difficult. Options might range from seared ahi tuna with ratatouille and truffled basil coulis, to more than a dozen meat and game dishes, including lamb, bison, beef, and veal. Sorbets

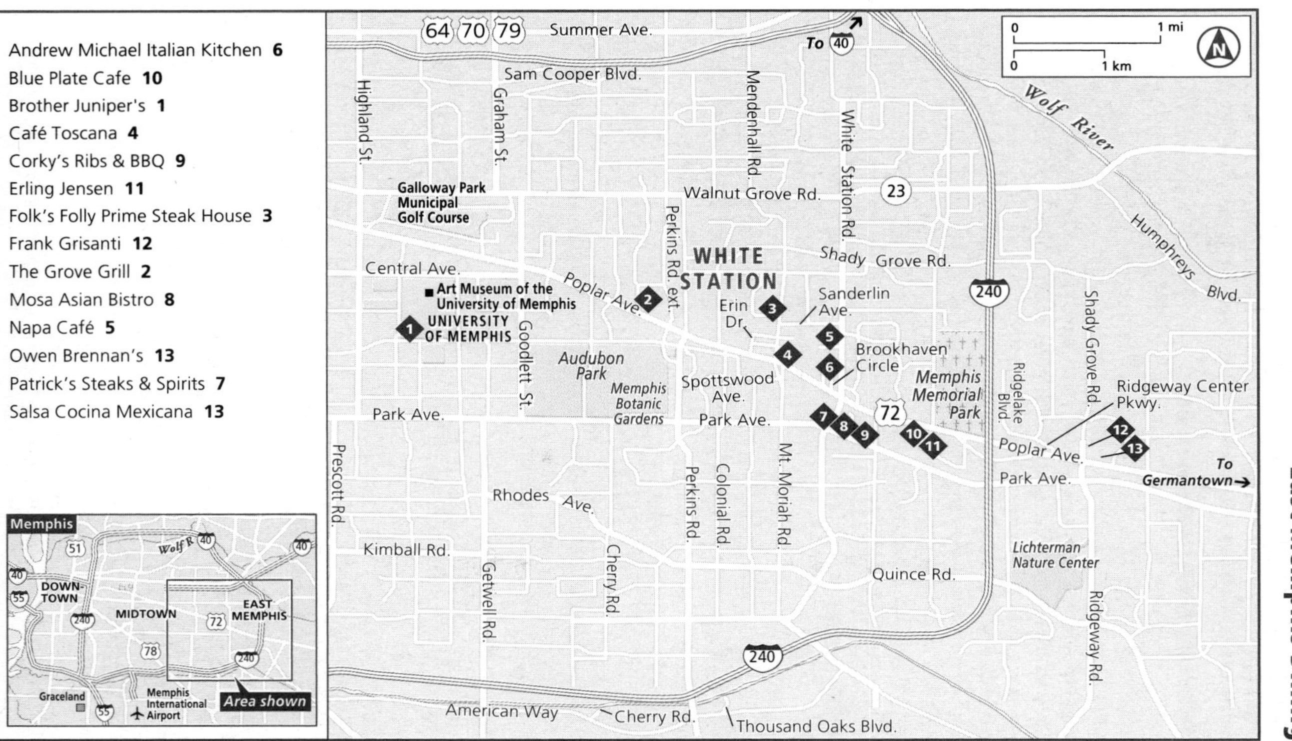
Andrew Michael Italian Kitchen 6
Blue Plate Cafe 10
Brother Juniper's 1
Café Toscana 4
Corky's Ribs & BBQ 9
Erling Jensen 11
Folk's Folly Prime Steak House 3
Frank Grisanti 12
The Grove Grill 2
Mosa Asian Bistro 8
Napa Café 5
Owen Brennan's 13
Patrick's Steaks & Spirits 7
Salsa Cocina Mexicana 13
Summer Ave.
Sam Cooper Blvd.
Highland St.
Graham St.
Mendenhall Rd.
White Station Rd.
Walnut Grove Rd.
Galloway Park Municipal Golf Course
Perkins Rd. ext.
WHITE STATION
Shady Grove Rd.
Central Ave.
Poplar Ave.
Art Museum of the University of Memphis
UNIVERSITY OF MEMPHIS
Goodlett St.
Audubon Park
Memphis Botanic Gardens
Spottswood Ave.
Park Ave.
Erin Dr.
Sanderlin Ave.
Brookhaven Circle
Memphis Memorial Park
Ridgelake Blvd.
Ridgeway Center Pkwy.
To Germantown
Humphreys Blvd.
Wolf River
To 40
Prescott Rd.
Rhodes Ave.
Kimball Rd.
Getwell Rd.
Cherry Rd.
Perkins Rd.
Colonial Rd.
Mt. Moriah Rd.
Quince Rd.
Lichterman Nature Center
Ridgeway Rd.
American Way
Thousand Oaks Blvd.
1 mi
1 km
Memphis
DOWNTOWN
MIDTOWN
EAST MEMPHIS
Wolf R.
Graceland
Memphis International Airport
Area shown

 and soufflés anchor a constantly updated dessert menu. Staff is well trained to provide exemplary service.

1044 S. Yates St. ✆ **901/763-3700.** www.ejensen.com. Reservations highly recommended. Main courses $31–$46. AE, DC, MC, V. Daily 5–10pm.

Folk's Folly Prime Steak House ★★ STEAK There are better-known chain steakhouses in Memphis, but none is more beloved than this local institution. You'll find Folk's Folly just off Poplar Avenue—it's the corner building with the royal-blue awning. Just off the parking lot is a tiny butcher shop that's part of the restaurant; in the meat cases inside, you'll see the sort of top-quality meats they serve here (the likes of which you'll probably never see at your neighborhood market). Steaks are the specialty of the house, and steaks are what they do best. However, you can start your meal with anything from blackened catfish to seafood gumbo or even fried pickles. Among the prime cuts of beef are aged sirloins, filet mignons, and T-bones. Seafood offerings include Alaskan king crab legs, salmon filets, and jumbo Maine lobsters.

551 S. Mendenhall Rd. ✆ **901/762-8200.** www.folksfolly.com. Reservations recommended. Main courses $20–$45. AE, DC, MC, V. Mon–Thurs 5:30–10pm; Fri–Sat 5:30–11pm; Sun 5:30–9pm.

Frank Grisanti ★ ITALIAN Tucked into a corner of the lobby of the Embassy Suites Hotel, this classy little restaurant serves some of the most authentic Italian food in Memphis. The atmosphere evokes the Old South far more than it does the trattorias of Rome, and the clublike setting attracts a well-heeled clientele. If you prefer a more casual setting, ask for a table on the atrium patio. The seafood and veal dishes are among the strong points here, and there are plenty of these to choose from. The *bistecca toscano* and *scampi portofino* are two of the most popular dishes here. If pasta is what you're after, the Elfo Special is worth considering—plenty of big shrimp and lots of garlic. There is also an elegant little bar in case you happen to arrive early.

In the Embassy Suites Hotel, 1022 S. Shady Grove Rd. ✆ **901/761-9462.** www.frankgrisanti.com. Reservations recommended Sat–Sun. Main courses $18–$29. AE, DC, DISC, MC, V. Mon–Thurs 11am–10pm; Fri–Sat 11am–10:30pm; Sun 5–10pm.

Napa Café CALIFORNIAN/NEW AMERICAN In an upscale East Memphis shopping center near the Doubletree Hotel is this comfortable restaurant specializing in California cuisine. Favored entrees are the potato-encrusted halibut and the rack of lamb. As its name implies, Napa Café has an award-winning wine list. What's more, private dinners for parties of two or more are available in the restaurant's cozy wine cellar if you book them in advance.

5101 Sanderlin Dr., Ste. 122. ✆ **901/683-0441.** www.napacafe.com. Reservations recommended. Main courses $16–$29. AE, DC, DISC, MC, V. Mon–Fri 11am–2pm; Mon–Thurs 5–9pm; Fri–Sat 5–10pm.

MODERATE

Café Toscana ITALIAN Dark-red walls and colorful still life paintings provide aesthetic oomph to this intimate Italian cafe in East Memphis. Grilled steaks, seafood entrees, meaty pasta dishes, and fresh green salads make this a pleasant after-work dinner-date spot. Its out-of-the-way location (off the main Poplar Avenue thoroughfare) gives it a quainter appeal than it might otherwise have. Enjoy another glass of wine, but skip the desserts, which are uninspired.

5007 Black Rd. ✆ **901/761-9522.** www.cafetoscanausa.com. Reservations recommended. Main courses $12–$22. AE, DISC, MC, V. Mon–Thurs 5–10pm; Fri–Sat 5–10:30pm.

Corky's Ribs & BBQ ★ Kids BARBECUE Corky's is good-natured and boisterous, with rock-'n'-roll tunes piped both indoors and out. Aromatic barbecue permeates the air. An argument over which is the best barbecue restaurant in Memphis persists, but this one pretty much leads the pack when it comes to pulled-pork-shoulder barbecue topped with tangy coleslaw. Photographs and letters from satisfied customers line the rough-paneled lobby, where you always have to wait for a table. Corky's even has a toll-free number (✆ **800/9-CORKYS** [926-7597]) to get their delicious ribs shipped "anywhere." There's also a drive-up window for immediate barbecue gratification. A downtown location, at 175 Peabody Place (✆ **901/529-9191**), is right around the corner from Beale Street. The suburbs have a Corky's at Dexter Road in Cordova (✆ **901/737-1988**).

5259 Poplar Ave. ✆ **901/685-9744.** www.corkysbbq.com. Reservations not accepted. Main courses $4–$20. AE, DC, DISC, MC, V. Sun–Thurs 10:45am–9:30pm; Fri–Sat 10:45am–10pm.

The Grove Grill ★ NEW SOUTHERN Located in one of East Memphis's upscale shopping plazas, this big restaurant and oyster bar is a merger of contemporary and traditional decor and cuisine. The menu focuses primarily on seafood (and so does the art on the walls), with contemporary renditions of Southern favorites predominating. Three varieties of fresh oysters on the half shell are available. If you don't opt for the oysters, consider the crab and crawfish cakes with lemon-fennel remoulade or the oyster and artichoke soup. For an entree, the low-country shrimp and grits is a natural, or, for a richer and less traditional dish, try the grilled pompano with crawfish beurre blanc. Entrees are served a la carte, so you'll need to pick a few dishes from the side-orders list, which reads like the veggie list in a traditional meat-and-three restaurant—warm blue-cheese slaw, grilled asparagus, and fried grit soufflé. The lunch menu is light on entrees other than sandwiches but does have plenty of interesting appetizers, soups, and salads.

Laurelwood Shopping Center, 4550 Poplar Ave. ✆ **901/818-9951.** www.thegrovegrill.com. Reservations recommended. Main courses $9–$30. AE, DC, DISC, MC, V. Daily 11am–2:30pm and 5:30–10pm.

Owen Brennan's ★ BREAKFAST/BRUNCH/CAJUN/CREOLE Located in one of East Memphis's most upscale shopping plazas and used as a set in the movie *The Firm,* Owen Brennan's has long been an East Memphis tradition, particularly for power lunches. The interior manages to conjure up the Big Easy with its Mardi Gras jesters and float decorations. Cuisine is flamboyant Cajun and Creole, from fluffy crab beignets to silky turtle soup. House specialties include the requisite blackened dishes, as well as hearty gumbos bursting with seafood. Desserts are so heavy they might make you woozy: The dense bread pudding is moistened with rum, and the caramelized bananas Foster is drenched in it as well.

Regalia Shopping Center, 6150 Poplar Ave. ✆ **901/761-0990.** www.brennansmemphis.com. Reservations recommended. Main courses $11–$23. AE, DC, DISC, MC, V. Mon–Thurs 11am–9pm; Fri 11am–10pm; Sat 9:30am–10:30pm; Sun 10am–2pm.

INEXPENSIVE

Blue Plate Cafe SOUTHERN Hearty breakfasts brimming with fried sausage, bacon, ham, and eggs at this cottage help Memphis retain its ranking as one of the most overweight populations in the United States. Southern-style grits and buttermilk biscuits with gravy also do their part. Lunch and dinner are also served, featuring home-style meat-and-three choices in plentiful portions. The food is better than the service, which can be blunt.

5469 Poplar Ave. ✆ **901/761-9696.** Main courses $5–$9. AE, DISC, DC, MC, V. Mon–Sat 6am–8pm; Sun 7am–2pm.

Brother Juniper's ★★ BREAKFAST/BRUNCH In the University of Memphis area, one of the best breakfast spots in town occupies a plain little house behind a white picket fence. Inside, it's cheerful but nothing fancy, and there's limited seating. As a result, a steady of stream of diners are perpetually at the door, beginning at the crack of dawn, waiting for a table at which to sample scrumptious eggs, buttermilk biscuits, blintzes, sausages, and gyros. The family-run eatery is vegetarian-friendly, too, with such offerings as the feta-rich spanakopita omelet and a breakfast tofu stir-fry.

3519 Walker Ave. ✆ **901/324-0144.** www.brotherjunipers.com. Breakfasts under $10. AE, DISC, DC, MC, V. Tue–Fri 6:30am–1pm; Sat 7am–12:30pm; Sun 8am–1pm.

Mosa Asian Bistro ★ THAI Rice plates, red and green curries, and noodle dishes fill the extensive menu at this busy Asian bistro that recently opened in the White Station area of East Memphis. Eat inside the pleasant dining room, or call ahead for take-out orders, which are meticulously packaged, sacked, and securely taped shut—and include chopsticks. Crab-cheese wontons and pot stickers are more traditional appetizers, but my favorite is the basil rolls—glass noodles, cucumbers, carrots, bean sprouts, and a fresh basil leaf wrapped in rice paper. An order of two comes with peanut and sweet-chili dipping sauces. An ice cooler by the cash register is stocked with bottles of beer and other cold drinks. Everything I've sampled here is delicious, giving me high hopes that this place will stay in business for years to come.

850 S. White Station Rd. ✆ **901/683-8889.** www.mosaasianbistro.com. Main courses under $10. AE, DISC, DC, MC, V. Mon–Thurs 11am–9pm; Fri–Sat 11am–10pm; Sun 11am–8:30pm.

Patrick's Steaks & Spirits ★ SOUTHERN The daily plate lunches are what keep the loyal clientele coming back to this popular diner. Homemade yeast rolls and fat cornbread muffins are served warm from the oven. Whether you order the calf's liver smothered in onions, the Tuesdays-only fried chicken, or the hefty homemade meatloaf, you can be sure the portions will be large. Entrees come with your choice of two vegetables from a long list that includes fried okra, turnip greens, purple-hull peas, and cheesy baked-macaroni shells.

Park Ave., at Mt. Moriah. ✆ **901/682-2852.** www.patricksmemphis.net. Main courses $8–$18. AE, DISC, MC, V. Daily 11am–10pm.

Salsa Cocina Mexicana ★★ MEXICAN/SOUTHWESTERN For more than 15 years now, my favorite Mexican restaurant has remained a stalwart. Salsa is a locally owned gem tucked into an upscale shopping center behind Ruth's Chris Steakhouse. Mexican standards are scrumptious, as are the flavorful chicken in citrus-chipotle sauce, and a sirloin steak topped with grilled poblano peppers. You can even relish the side dishes, including creamy refried beans and a robust salsa picante. Wash it all down with an icy margarita. Service is attentive—they really care that you enjoy your meal. Mexican music plays softly in the background. When vast platters of enchiladas, guacamole, and rice show up at your table, you'll know that you've come to the right place.

Regalia Shopping Center, 6150 Poplar Ave. ✆ **901/683-6325.** Reservations accepted only for parties of 6 or more. Main courses $5–$14. AE, DC, DISC, MC, V. Mon–Sat 11am–10pm.

6 SOUTH MEMPHIS & GRACELAND AREA

INEXPENSIVE

D'Bo's Wings n' More ★ AMERICAN Order a beer and a basket of wings and watch the game on TV, or call ahead and take home a couple hundred of these succulent chicken drummies and tips that are deep-fried and then slathered in mild, hot, or "suicidal" red sauces. Entrepreneur David Boyd and his wife started D'Bo's more than a decade ago, selling wings out of a food trailer at area festivals. Their lip-smacking wings caught on like wildfire. Now there are D'Bo's locations throughout the city and beyond. If wings aren't your thing, the restaurant also serves great hamburgers and fries. D'Bo's has a nice location (there are others throughout the area), near the Reverend Al Green's church, Full Gospel Tabernacle, but unfortunately, this particular location isn't open on Sundays.

4407 Elvis Presley Blvd. ✆ **901/345-9464.** www.dboswings.com. Main courses $5–$9. AE, DC, DISC, MC, V. Mon–Thurs 11am–10pm; Fri–Sat 11am–midnight.

Four Way Restaurant ★★★ Value Kids SOUTHERN If you're looking for the legendary Fourway Grill, this is it. The cherished South Memphis family restaurant serves the tastiest soul food in town. Eat dessert first. Try the velvety sweet-potato pie or strawberry cake. Then dig into some juicy fried green tomatoes, pork chops, catfish, or chicken and round it out with black-eyed peas and crumbly cornbread. If he's not too busy, ask the proprietor to reminisce about the old days of this historic black neighborhood, which locals hope is poised for a comeback. The restaurant doesn't serve soft drinks or alcohol, so plan on ordering lemonade or iced tea with your meal.

998 Mississippi Blvd. ✆ **901/507-1519.** Reservations recommended for large groups. Main courses $6–$9. MC, V. Tues–Sat 11am–7pm; Sun 11am–5pm.

Interstate Bar-B-Que ★ BARBECUE Corky's Ribs & BBQ may be a bit flashier, but Interstate Bar-B-Que has the kind of grit and street cred that no suburban East Memphis eatery could muster. Located off I-55 on South Third Street (a great stop-off if you're driving south from downtown to Graceland), Interstate is a former grocery-store-turned-barbecue-joint. Insurance agent Jim Neely launched the biz in the 1970s in a then-dicey part of town. Though urban renewal efforts seem to have eluded the still-blighted neighborhood, Interstate Bar-B-Que is a bright, welcoming spot. Long before *USA Today* proclaimed it the best place in America for a pork barbecue sandwich, locals and tourists already knew it. Along with pork and beef ribs and shredded barbecue, Interstate smokes a mean, spice-rubbed turkey breast. Chicken halves are slow-roasted in hickory-wood pits, to achieve a tender, moist flavor. Sides include sugary baked beans, coleslaw, potato salad, and barbecued spaghetti. For worldwide delivery, call ✆ **888/227-2793.**

2265 S. Third St. ✆ **901/775-2304.** www.interstatebarbecue.com. Sandwiches $4.85–$5.30; dinner platters $6.25–$8.75. MC, V. Mon–Thurs 11am–10pm; Fri–Sat 11am–11pm; Sun 11am–5pm.

Krispy Kreme Doughnuts BREAKFAST/BRUNCH Perhaps you've experienced one of these heavenly grease bombs—deep-fried pillows of dough that have been drenched in a tooth-achingly sugary glaze. You may catch a drift of that unmistakable, yeasty aroma before you spot the big red-and-green sign along Elvis Presley Boulevard. If you're lucky, you'll get to place your order when the doughnuts are still warm, and at their most mouth-wateringly decadent.

4244 Elvis Presley Blvd. ✆ **901/332-0620.** www.krispykreme.com. Dozen donuts $6.54. AE, MC, V. Drive-through 24 hours; inside daily 5am–10pm.

Piccadilly ★ AMERICAN/SOUTHERN Elvis would've left the building (nearby Graceland, that is) for a meal at this down-home cafeteria, had it been around when he was still living in the neighborhood. One of the better restaurant suggestions in this otherwise fast-food-rampant part of town, Piccadilly is a refreshing change of pace. A clean, well-run chain restaurant, it packs people in for old-fashioned fried chicken, roast beef, baked fish, and hefty portions of sides and desserts. This is one of Piccadilly's several Memphis locations. So if you're in town to see the King's quarters, skip the mediocre, overpriced food courts within the Graceland compound, and come here instead.

3968 Elvis Presley Blvd. ✆ **901/398-5186.** www.piccadilly.com. Most entrees under $10. AE, DC, V. Daily 11am–8:30pm.

7 BARBECUE

Memphis claims to be the barbecue capital of the world, and with more than 100 barbecue restaurants and the annual Memphis in May World Championship Barbecue Cooking Contest, it's hard to argue the point. The standard barbecue here comes in two basic types—hand-pulled pork shoulder (pulled off the bone rather than cut off) and pork ribs. The latter can be served wet or dry (that is, with or without sauce). The best pulled pork shoulder in town is at **Corky's Ribs & BBQ** (p. 199), and the best ribs are served at **the Rendezvous** (p. 192).

However, it isn't just pork shoulder and ribs that get barbecued here in Memphis. You can get barbecued spaghetti, barbecued pizza, and even barbecued bologna! Everyone in town seems to have his or her own favorite barbecue joint. My personal preference is **Blues City Café,** 138 Beale St. (✆ **901/526-3637**), far and away the best and most authentic restaurant on Beale Street. Thick steaks, shrimp and grits, and delicious tamales are also on the menu, along with their signature barbecued ribs.

If you're unsure about all the fuss, or if you're new to 'que, graze the chaffing dishes at **Leonard's Pit Barbecue,** downtown at 103 N. Main St. (✆ **901/528-0882**). At their daily buffet, you can have an absolute pork pig-out while sampling soul foods including pulled pork shoulder, fried catfish, barbecued beans, hush puppies, and coleslaw. They have an East Memphis location too, at 5465 Fox Plaza Dr. (✆ **901/360-1963**).

Looks can be deceiving, as in this case of the foreboding hole-in-the-wall known as **Cozy Corner,** 745 N. Parkway (✆ **901/527-9158**). Step inside, and make yourself at home. The friendly little barbecue spot is a Midtown landmark. Even before the Food Network brought fame and fortune to its "down-home," lovey-dovey husband-and-wife owners, **Neely's B-B-Q,** 670 Jefferson Ave. in downtown (✆ **901/521-9798**), and at 5700 Mt. Moriah Rd. in East Memphis (✆ **901/795-4177**), was a local favorite. They do it all, including barbecued spaghetti and barbecued bologna. Down near Graceland, there is an abundance of time-worn, no-frills barbecue joints and bona fide dives. Try **Payne's,** 1393 Elvis Presley Blvd. (✆ **901/942-7433**), **Interstate Bar-B-Que** (p. 201), and **A&R Bar-B-Q,** 1802 Elvis Presley Blvd. (✆ **901/774-7444**), all of which draw universal raves for barbecue authenticity.

8 DELIS, CAFES & BAKERIES

Sure, there's a Starbucks at practically every other intersection, but wouldn't you really rather patronize a coffee shop where you can soak up some local atmosphere? If so, your first stop should be downtown, to the **Center for Southern Folklore,** Pembroke Square (✆ **901/525-3655**). It's a one-of-a-kind cafe of culture where you can belt back a cappuccino while admiring local crafts, outsider art, and hear great music almost any time of day. Another downtown lunch spot I highly recommend is **The Little Tea Shop,** 69 Monroe Ave. (✆ **901/525-6000**), which has been doling out excellent Southern cooking for decades. Although the menu changes daily, you can expect fried chicken, catfish, mashed potatoes and (vegetarians, rejoice) meatless turnip greens—a real rarity in the pork-simmered South. Iced sweet tea is a must.

If you're down on Beale Street, there are tons of bars, restaurants, and places to grab a cup of coffee. One of the homiest is **Miss Polly's Soul City Cafe,** 154 Beale St. (✆ **901/527-9060;** www.misspollysmemphis.com), where you can get a cheap morning-after breakfast of waffles, eggs, and fried potatoes.

At the edge of the gay-friendly Cooper-Young neighborhood, you can quaff a cup o' joe and listen to live music or poetry at **Otherlands,** 641 S. Cooper St. (✆ **901/278-4994**). Farther down the street, you'll find **Java Cabana,** 2170 Young Ave. (✆ **901/272-7210;** www.javacabanacoffeehouse.com), a grungy dive with a cement floor and flea-market furnishings. Good coffee, muffins, and brownies are just right over a game of chess or during one of the frequent open-mic nights.

The most bucolic cafe view in town can be found inside the Memphis Brooks Museum of Art, where the classy **Brushmark Restaurant,** 1934 Poplar Ave. (✆ **901/544-6225;** www.brooksmuseum.org), overlooks the lush greenery of Overton Park. Beloved local chef Wally Joe oversees the kitchen. This is an elegant lunch spot (and on Thurs nights you can have dinner here too).

Quiche Lorraine, zesty tomato bisque, and chicken salad sandwiches on chewy loaves of French bread are delectable choices at **La Baguette** (✆ **901/458-0900**). Well-to-do "ladies who lunch" frequent this patisserie, as well as **Just for Lunch** (✆ **901/323-3287**), a nearby cafe. Both are located inside the Chickasaw Oaks shopping center, 3088 Poplar Ave., in Midtown.

Farther east, be on the lookout for Davis-Kidd Booksellers. Part coffee shop, part wine bar and cafe with indoor/outdoor seating, **brontë: A Novel Bistro,** 387 Perkins Rd. Extended (✆ **901/374-0881;** www.daviskidd.com), located inside the bookstore, is where the intelligentsia gather for delectable salads and sandwiches, conversation, and liquid refreshment.

A stone's throw away, in the Sanderlin Center plaza, is the city's newest bakery. Riding the nationwide cupcake-craze, locally owned **Muddy's Bake Shop,** 5101 Sanderlin Ave. (✆ **901/683-8844**), touts its use of organic ingredients. Small, plainly decorated cupcakes come in a slew of flavors. To be honest, I'm not bowled over by this place, but the locals seem to love it. The selection of sweets varies each day, so before you get your heart set on snickerdoodles, call ahead to see what kinds of fresh-baked pies, cakes, and cookies are available.

18 Exploring Memphis

Just as in Nashville, music is the heart of Memphis, and many of the city's main attractions are related to its musical heritage. The blues first gained widespread recognition here on Beale Street, and rock 'n' roll was born at Sun Studio. W. C. Handy, the father of the blues, lived here for many years, and Elvis Presley made his Memphis home—Graceland—a household word. The history of the Memphis sound comes alive in multiple museums around the city, and each one offers its own unique spin.

Downtown Memphis has weathered its share of hardships over the years. About 10 years ago, the city started to see a long-awaited renaissance, with a flurry of new construction projects taking place. However, the recent U.S. economic recession has hit hard, leaving such visible scars as vacant mixed-use developments, unleased condos, and closed restaurants.

However, this shouldn't deter you from visiting downtown. There are still many worthwhile tourist spots (the National Civil Rights Museum is tops on the list), clubs, and eateries that are holding their own or doing well, despite the tough times. And regardless of the prosperity levels at any given point in time, downtown Memphis remains the heart and soul of the city. To get a sense of what it's all about, you need to stand on the bluff overlooking the Mississippi River, stroll Beale Street to hear live blues being played in the bars, and "duck" into the city's most beloved historic hotel, The Peabody, to witness its most time-honored tradition. (See p. 168.)

A few blocks south of downtown is Soulsville, USA: the Stax Museum of American Soul Music is a must-see site. It gets my pick as the best of the city's music attractions, and I never tire of visiting it year in, year out. Stax is located in a grittier neighborhood than downtown, but seeing it may help give you a sense of what Memphis was like a generation or two ago. (Besides, it's where Aretha Franklin and scads of other legends grew up.) Farther south, you'll want to head on down the highway to Graceland. There are several old-school barbecue joints along the way. Savor all of these things, because they're collectively part of the definitive Memphis tourist experience.

1 GRACELAND, BEALE STREET & MORE

If you're going to Memphis, you're most likely going to **Graceland,** but there are also several other museums and sites here tied to the history of rock and blues music.

Impressions

The seven wonders of the world I have seen, and many are the places I have been. Take my advice, folks, and see Beale Street first.

—W. C. Handy

Ernest C. Withers

African-American Ernest C. Withers was a respected photojournalist who documented Beale Street in the 1950s, and most of the important events of the Civil Rights movement. He died in 2007, at age 85. Known throughout the world for his black-and-white photographs of such martyrs as the Reverend Martin Luther King, Jr., Withers was one of Memphis's most beloved local figures. At his funeral, the Reverend Samuel Kyles emphasized Withers's significance in helping transform 20th-century attitudes: "It is said that a drop of water can knock holes in stone, not by violence but by oft-falling . . . (Withers' camera) knocked holes in the stones of ignorance—one click at a time." Today, there's talk of a gallery for his work to be opened on Beale Street.

Although the blues was born down in the Mississippi Delta, south of Memphis, it was on Beale Street that this soulful music first reached an urban audience. Today, after a period of abandonment, **Beale Street** is once again Memphis's busiest entertainment district. Visitors can hear blues, rock, jazz, country, and even Irish music on Beale Street. To learn more about the various musical styles that originated along the Mississippi River, visit the **Mississippi River Museum,** on Mud Island (p. 214), where there are several rooms full of exhibits on New Orleans jazz, Memphis blues, rockabilly, and Elvis. All of these places are more fully described below.

In addition to being the birthplace of the blues and the city that launched Elvis and rock 'n' roll, Memphis played an important role in soul music during the 1960s. Isaac Hayes and Booker T and the MGs recorded here at **Stax Studio.** Other musicians who launched their careers from Memphis include Muddy Waters, Albert King, Al Green, Otis Redding, Sam and Dave, Sam the Sham and the Pharaohs, and the Box Tops.

Below are the sites that music fans won't want to miss while in Memphis.

Beale Street ★★ **Moments** To blues fans, Beale Street is the most important street in America. The musical form known as the blues—with roots that stretch back to the African musical heritage of slaves brought to the United States—was born here. W. C. Handy was performing on Beale Street when he penned "Memphis Blues," the first published blues song. Shortly after the Civil War, Beale Street became one of the most important streets in the South for African Americans. Many of the most famous musicians in the blues world got their starts here; besides Handy, other greats include B. B. King, Furry Lewis, Alberta Hunter, Rufus Thomas, and Isaac Hayes.

And the blues continues to thrive here. Today, though parts of downtown Memphis has been abandoned in favor of suburban sprawl, Beale Street continues to draw fans of blues and popular music, and nightclubs line the blocks between Second and Fourth streets. The Orpheum Theatre, once a vaudeville palace, is now the performance hall for Broadway road shows, and the New Daisy Theatre features performances by up-and-coming bands and once-famous performers. Historic markers up and down the street relate the area's colorful past, and two statues commemorate the city's two most important musicians: W. C. Handy and Elvis Presley. In addition to the many clubs featuring nightly live music (including B. B. King's Blues Club and the Hard Rock Cafe), there's also a small often-overlooked museum, the W. C. Handy House—and the museumlike

Memphis Attractions: Downtown & Midtown

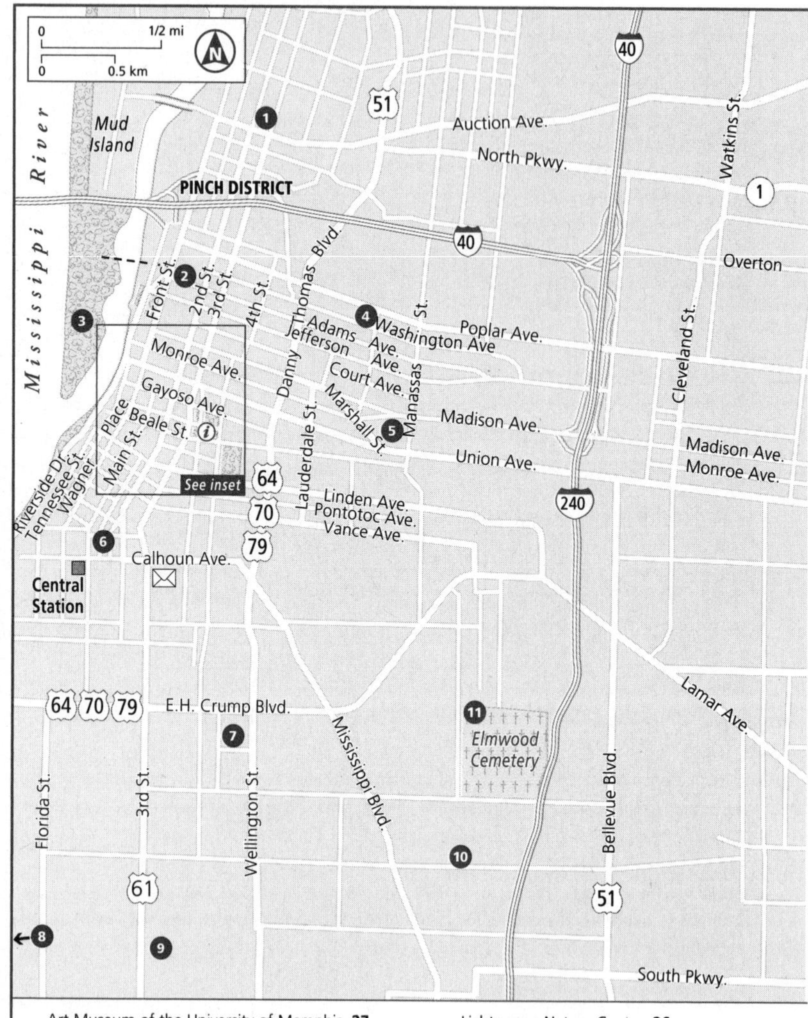

Art Museum of the University of Memphis **27**
Beale Street **17**
Belz Museum of Asian & Judaic Art **18**
Children's Museum of Memphis **23**
Church Park **22**
The Cotton Museum at the Memphis Cotton Exchange **16**
Elmwood Cemetery **11**
Fire Museum of Memphis **2**
Graceland **9**
Lichterman Nature Center **26**
Mason Temple **7**
Memphis Botanic Garden **24**
Memphis Brooks Museum of Art **12**
Memphis River Boats **15**
Memphis Rock 'n' Soul Museum **20**
Memphis Zoo and Aquarium **14**
Mud Island River Park **3**
National Civil Rights Museum **6**
National Ornamental Metal Museum **8**

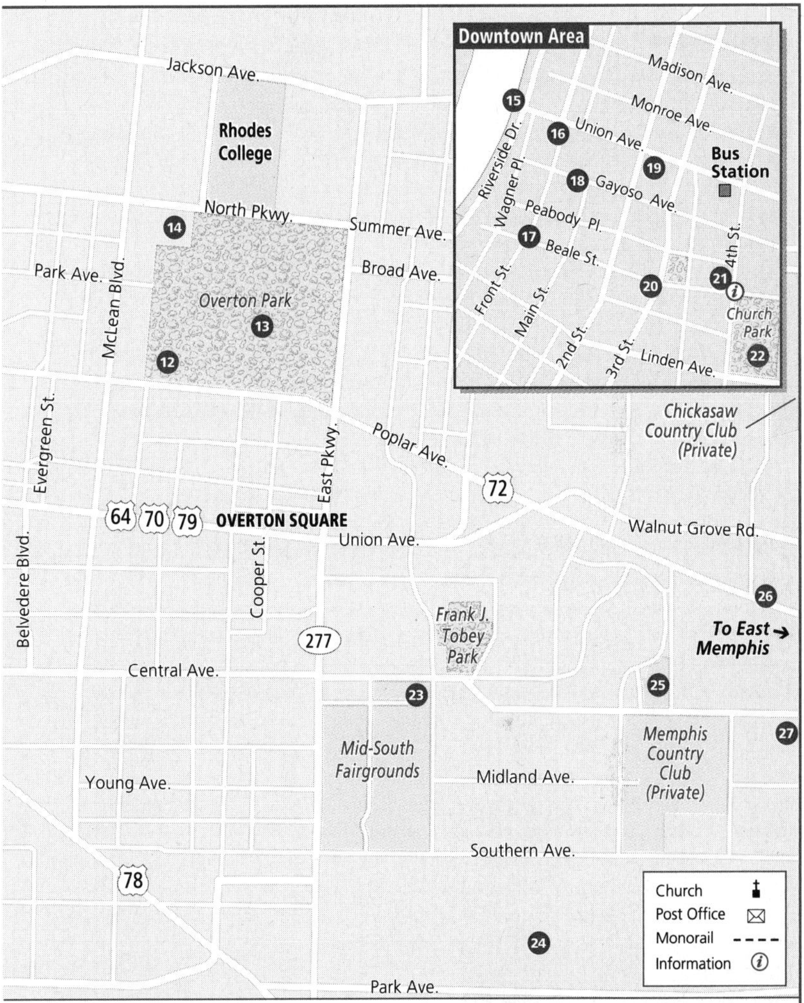

Downtown Area
Madison Ave.
Monroe Ave.
Union Ave.
Bus Station
Gayoso Ave.
Peabody Pl.
Beale St.
Riverside Dr.
Wagner Pl.
Front St.
Main St.
2nd St.
3rd St.
4th St.
Linden Ave.
Church Park
15
16
17
18
19
20
21
22
Jackson Ave.
Rhodes College
North Pkwy.
Summer Ave.
Broad Ave.
Park Ave.
McLean Blvd.
Overton Park
14
13
12
Evergreen St.
East Pkwy.
Poplar Ave.
72
Chickasaw Country Club (Private)
64
70
79
OVERTON SQUARE
Union Ave.
Walnut Grove Rd.
Belvedere Blvd.
Cooper St.
277
Frank J. Tobey Park
26
To East Memphis
Central Ave.
23
25
27
Mid-South Fairgrounds
Young Ave.
Midland Ave.
Memphis Country Club (Private)
Southern Ave.
78
24
Church
Post Office
Monorail
Information
Park Ave.

Overton Park **13**
Peabody Ducks **19**
Pink Palace Museum and Planetarium **25**
Slavehaven/Burkle Estate Museum **1**
Soulsville USA: Stax Museum of
American Soul **10**
Sun Studio **5**
W.C. Handy House Museum **21**
Woodruff Fontaine House **4**

Memphis
Wolf R.
40
51
40
Area shown
40
55
DOWN-TOWN
240
MIDTOWN
EAST MEMPHIS
72
78
240
Graceland
55
Memphis International Airport

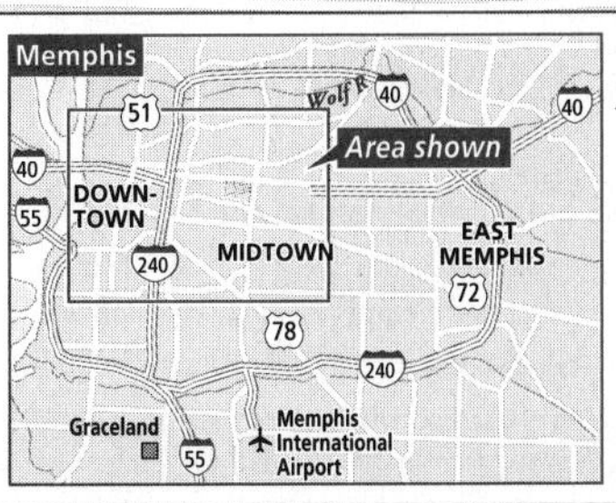

A. Schwab Dry Goods Store. For an update of events, check out www.bealestreet.com. Allow a full afternoon to browse the shops and restaurants, or make a night of it if you're into bar-hopping and live music.

Graceland ★★ It seems hard to believe, but Graceland, the former home of rock-'n'-roll-legend Elvis Presley and annually the destination of tens of thousands of love-struck pilgrims searching for the ghost of Elvis, is the second most visited home in America. Only the White House receives more visitors each year. A look around at the crowds waiting in various lines at this sprawling complex makes it clear that Elvis, through his many recordings, numerous movie roles, and countless concerts, appealed to a wide spectrum of people. Today, more than 3 decades after Elvis's death, Graceland draws visitors of all ages from all over the world.

Purchased in the late 1950s for $100,000, Graceland today is Memphis's biggest attraction and resembles a small theme park or shopping mall in scope and design. There are his two personal jets, the Elvis Presley Automobile Museum, the "Sincerely Elvis" collection of Elvis's personal belongings, the *Walk a Mile in My Shoes* video, and, of course, guided tours of the Graceland mansion. If your time here is limited to only one thing, by all means, go for the mansion tour. It's the essence of the Big E. All the rest is just icing on Elvis's buttercream-frosted cake.

The Elvis Presley Automobile Museum includes not only his famous 1955 pink Cadillac, a 1956 purple Cadillac convertible, and two Stutz Blackhawks from the early 1970s, but also motorcycles and other vehicles. Accompanying this collection are videos of Elvis's home movies and a fast-paced compilation of car-scene clips from dozens of Elvis movies, which are shown in a sort of drive-in-theater setting.

A re-creation of an airport terminal serves as the entrance to the *Lisa Marie* and *Hound Dog II* private jets. The former was once a regular Delta Air Lines passenger jet that was customized (at a cost of $800,000) after Elvis purchased it in 1975 for $250,000. The *Hound Dog II* is much smaller and was purchased after the *Lisa Marie* was acquired.

"Sincerely Elvis" is Graceland's most revealing exhibit. This is a collection of many of Elvis's personal belongings. Here you'll see everything from some of Elvis's personal record collection (including albums by Tom Jones and Ray Charles) to a pair of his sneakers. One exhibit displays gifts sent to Elvis by fans. Included are quilts, needlepoint, and even a plaque made from woven chewing gum wrappers.

The Graceland exhibits strive to reveal Elvis the man and Elvis the star. Some of the surprising facts passed on to visitors include these: Elvis was an avid reader and always traveled with lots of books; Elvis didn't like the taste of alcohol; among his favorite movies were *Blazing Saddles* and the films of Monty Python.

The Memphis Music Experience

Want to save $20 on admission to the city's Top 5 music attractions—Graceland, Sun Studio, Stax Museum, Rock 'N' Soul Museum, and the Gibson Guitar Factory? Then purchase your tickets at one of two Memphis visitor centers. The exclusive offer is available only at the Arlington Road visitor center, off Intestate 40, at exit 25, east of the Memphis city limits. The other location is near Graceland in the south Memphis suburb of Whitehaven, at 3205 Elvis Presley Blvd. For more information, call ✆ **888/633-9099.**

Elvis Trivia

- Elvis's first hit single was "Mystery Train." Recorded at Sun Studio, it made it to number one on the country charts in 1955.
- In 1956, Elvis became the second white person to have a number-one single on *Billboard*'s rhythm-and-blues chart. The song was "Don't Be Cruel." The B-side was "Hound Dog."
- Elvis's first million-selling single and gold record came in 1956, when he recorded "Heartbreak Hotel" as his first release for RCA.
- During his career, Elvis won three Grammy Awards, all of which were for gospel recordings. Two of these awards were for the same song—a studio version and a live version of "How Great Thou Art."
- Elvis made 31 films and sang in all but one of these. *Charro!,* a Western released in 1969, was the only movie in which he didn't break into song at some point.
- The soundtrack to Elvis's movie *G.I. Blues* was on the album chart for a total of 111 weeks, 10 of which were at number one. This was his first movie after returning from service in the army.
- Highway 51 South, which runs past the gates of Graceland, was renamed Elvis Presley Boulevard in 1971, while Elvis was still alive.
- Elvis's first network-television appearance came in January 1956 when he appeared on *Stage Show,* which was hosted by Tommy and Jimmy Dorsey.
- On a night in 1975, Bruce Springsteen, hoping to meet Elvis, jumped the fence at Graceland and ran up to the house. Unfortunately, Elvis wasn't at home, and the guards escorted Springsteen off the property.
- The King holds the record for sold-out shows in Vegas: 837 performances at the Las Vegas Hilton over a 10-year period.
- In 2003, an Elvis CD featuring his 30 number-one hits was released and became an international success. To date, sales have reached triple platinum.
- Elvis has sold more than a billion records worldwide, according to some industry estimates. That's more than any other act in recorded history.

Throughout the year there are several special events at Graceland. Elvis's birthday (Jan 8, 1935) is celebrated each year with several days of festivities. However, mid-August's Elvis Week, commemorating his death, on August 16, 1977, boasts the greatest Elvis celebrations both here at Graceland and throughout Memphis. Each year from Thanksgiving until January 8, Graceland is decorated with Elvis's original Christmas lights and lawn decorations.

Early risers should be aware that most mornings it is possible to visit Elvis's grave before Graceland officially opens. This special free walk-up period is daily from 7:30 to 8:30am. If you're buying a ticket for the whole shebang, allow at least 2 to 3 hours or more (depending upon your devotion to the King).

3734 Elvis Presley Blvd. ✆ **800/238-2000** or 901/332-3322. www.elvis.com. Graceland Mansion Tour $28 adults; $25 seniors and students; $12 children 7–12. The Platinum Tour (includes admission to all Graceland attractions, including Elvis's Automobile Museum, tours of Elvis's custom jets [the *Lisa Marie* and *Hound Dog II*], and Sincerely Elvis film presentation) $32 adults; $29 seniors; $15 children 7–12. Graceland Elvis Entourage VIP Tour (includes the "Elvis After Dark" exhibit) $69 for all ages. Tour reservations can be made 24 hrs. in advance and are recommended if you have a tight schedule. Mar–Oct Mon–Sat 9am–5pm, Sun 10am–4pm; Nov–Feb 10am–4pm daily. (Dec–Feb mansion tour does not operate Tues.) Closed Thanksgiving, Dec 25, and Jan 1. Take Bellevue South (which turns into Elvis Presley Blvd.) a few miles south of downtown, past Winchester Ave. Graceland is on the left.

Memphis Rock 'N' Soul Museum ★ With rare recordings and videos, archival photographs and interactive multimedia displays, the past century of American popular music is presented in "Social Crossroads," the first exhibition ever presented by the Smithsonian Institution outside of Washington, D.C. From field hollers and gospel hymns to the turn-of-the-century blues of W. C. Handy, it's all here. Narrated tours on portable audio players allow visitors to customize their tours and musical selections. And with each new artist, from Otis Redding and Al Green to Earth, Wind & Fire, Memphis shines. Allow an hour. ***Note:*** Call ahead if you're planning a visit, as the museum often closes early to host private parties.

191 Beale St. ✆ **901/205-2533.** www.memphisrocknsoul.org. Admission $10 adults, $7 children 5–17. Daily 10am–7pm (last tour starts at 6:15pm). Downtown at the new FedExForum arena, a half-block south of Beale and Third sts.

Soulsville USA: Stax Museum of American Soul Music ★★★ **Moments** Groove on down to Soulsville USA, one of the city's best attractions, which celebrates Memphis soul music. Opened in spring 2003, the museum sits near the site of the original (sadly, long-ago demolished) Stax recording studio, which during the 1960s and 1970s cranked out world-famous hits by Otis Redding; Booker T and the MGs; The Bar-Kays; Al Green; Aretha Franklin; Earth, Wind & Fire; and others. Don't miss Isaac Hayes's (of *Shaft* and *South Park* fame) gold-plated, shag-carpeted *Superfly* Cadillac, which is on display. First-rate multimedia exhibitions, beginning with a thrilling video introduction in a darkened theater, take visitors back to a place and time when racism deeply divided the South. Stax, however, was an anomaly, a virtually colorblind collaborative where black and white musicians, staff, and studio executives worked together in a shared musical passion. At interactive kiosks, you'll get a chance to hear hundreds of songs and watch archival video. Stax ties to Elvis, the Beatles, and Elton John are mentioned. Elsewhere, Bono, Elvis Costello, and scores of other rock stars offer heartfelt tributes to the lasting legacy of Stax (and Memphis's Sun) recording studios. Allow at least 90 minutes—or an entire afternoon, if you're a true soul sister—to tour the museum. And if the spirit moves, you can also cut loose on its psychedelic dance floor.

Fun Facts Chef's Salad Days

One of Memphis's best-loved soul legends died in 2008. Long before he garnered fame at Stax recording studio in Memphis, before the *Theme from Shaft* won him an Academy Award, and way before his gig as the voice of *South Park*'s beloved character Chef made him a household name for a whole new generation of fans . . . Isaac Hayes worked as a shoeshine boy on Beale Street.

Elvis Beyond the Gates of Graceland

You've come to Memphis on a pilgrimage and spent the entire day at Graceland. You've cried, you've laughed, you've bought a whole suitcase full of Elvis souvenirs, but still you want more of Elvis. No problem. Elvis is everywhere in Memphis.

If you're a hard-core Elvis fan and plan to visit his grave during the early-morning free visitation period at Graceland, you'll want to find a hotel as close to the mansion as possible. Directly across the street from Graceland are two properties that cater specifically to Elvis fans. Both the **Heartbreak Hotel–Graceland** (p. 108) and the **Days Inn at Graceland** (p. 181) offer round-the-clock, free, in-room Elvis videos. The former hotel actually has a pathway into the Graceland parking lot, while the latter motel has a guitar-shaped swimming pool.

Also, if you can, plan your visit for dates around Elvis's January 8 birthday festivities or during **Elvis Week,** which commemorates his death on August 16. During these festivities, you might catch an all-Elvis concert by the Memphis Symphony Orchestra, the *Taking Care of Business* Elvis-tribute ballet by Ballet Memphis, or the Elvis laser-light show at the Sharpe Planetarium in the **Pink Palace Museum.**

Any time of year, you can visit **Sun Studio** (p. 211) the recording studio that discovered Elvis and where he made his first recordings. Though the studio isn't very large, its musical history is enough to give people goose bumps and bring tears to their eyes. A highlight of a visit here is a chance to actually touch the microphone that Elvis used to make his first recordings. The late Sam Phillips (who died in 2003), once brought his new musicians here to sign contracts, and this is where Elvis most certainly whiled away many hours. For a tongue-in-cheek tribute to Elvis, check out the coin-operated shrine to the King at the **Center for Southern Folklore** (p. 203) in Pembroke Square downtown. In Midtown, take a 20-minute tour that details Elvis Presley's connection with the historic Memphian Theater. Find out which movies Elvis used to watch here with his entourage, and hear stories about his visits. Tickets are $5; for reservations, call Playhouse on the Square at ✆ **901/725-0776.**

To visit the spots around town where Elvis once walked, book a tour with **American Dream Safari** (✆ **901/527-8870**), which tools guests around town in a 1955 Cadillac to see such Elvis haunts as Humes High School, Sun Studio, and the housing project where he lived as a teenager.

926 E. McLemore Ave. ✆ **901/946-2535.** www.staxmuseum.com. Admission $12 adults, $11 seniors, $9 children 9–12, free for children 8 and under with paid adult or senior admission. Mar–Oct Mon–Sat 9am–4pm, Sun 1–4pm; Nov–Feb Mon–Sat 10am–4pm, Sun 1–4pm. Closed major holidays. Take Danny Thomas Blvd. south to Mississippi Blvd. Turn left onto Mississippi Blvd., then left on E. McLemore Ave.

Sun Studio ★★ If Elvis Aaron Presley hadn't come to Sun Studio in the early 1950s to record a song as a birthday present for his mother (so the story goes), musical history

Impressions

Before Elvis, there was nothing.

—John Lennon

today might be very different. Owner and recording engineer Sam Phillips first recorded, in the early 1950s, such local artists as Elvis Presley, Jerry Lee Lewis, Roy Orbison, and Carl Perkins, who together created a sound that would shortly become known as rock 'n' roll. Over the years Phillips also helped start the recording careers of the blues greats B. B. King and Howlin' Wolf, and country giant Johnny Cash. By night, Sun Studio is still an active recording studio and has been used by such artists as U2, Spin Doctors, the Tractors, and Bonnie Raitt. The place has great vibes, and for those who know their music history, touching Elvis's microphone will be a thrill beyond measure. However, if you aren't wellversed in this particular area of pop culture, a visit to this one-themed Sun Studio may leave you wondering what all the fuss is about. Allow an hour.

706 Union Ave. (at Marshall Ave.) ✆ **800/441-6249** or 901/521-0664. www.sunstudio.com. Admission $12 adults, free for children 11 and under accompanied by parent. Daily 10am–6pm (studio tours conducted at the bottom of the hour, 10:30am–5:30pm). Closed some holidays.

W. C. Handy House Museum *Finds* A far cry from the opulence of Graceland, this tiny clapboard shotgun shack was once the Memphis home of the bluesman W. C. Handy—"the father of the blues"—and was where he was living when he wrote "Beale Street Blues" and "Memphis Blues." Although the house has only a small collection of Handy memorabilia and artifacts, there are numerous evocative old photos displayed, and the commentary provided by the museum guide is always highly informative. The tour lasts about 20 minutes.

352 Beale St. (at Fourth Ave.). ✆ **901/527-3427.** Admission $3 adults, $2 children 4–17, free for children 3 and under. Summer Tues–Sat 10am–5pm; winter Tues–Sat 11am–4pm.

2 NONMUSICAL MEMPHIS ATTRACTIONS

MUSEUMS

Art Museum of the University of Memphis Memphis takes its name from the ancient capital of Egypt, and here in the Art Museum of the University of Memphis you can view artifacts from ancient Memphis. An outstanding collection of Egyptian art and artifacts makes this one of the most interesting museums in Memphis. Among the items on display is a loaf of bread dating from between 2134 B.C. and 1786 B.C. A hieroglyph-covered sarcophagus contains the mummy of Iret-iruw, who died around 2,200 years ago. Numerous works of art and funerary objects show the high level of skill achieved by ancient Egyptian artists. In addition to the Egyptian exhibit, there is a small collection of West African masks and woodcarvings, and changing exhibitions in the main gallery. Allow 30 minutes to an hour. ***Tip:*** Your best bet for parking on campus is the Fogelman Executive Center garage, which costs about $1 an hour.

3750 Norriswood St., CFA Building, Rm. 142. ✆ **800/669-2678** or 901/678-2224. www.amum.org. Free admission. Mon–Sat 9am–5pm. Closed university holidays and for changing exhibitions. Turn south off Central Ave. onto Deloach St. (btw. Patterson and Zach Curlin sts.) to Norriswood St.

Belz Museum of Asian & Judaic Art Founded in 1998 by world travelers and art lovers Jack and Marilyn Belz (he's the owner of The Peabody hotel empire), this unexpected downtown museum features pieces culled from the couple's extensive collection. Chinese art from the Qing and Tang dynasties include stunning silver boxes, imperial tomb figurines, ink-on-paper portraits, and intricate jade and ivory carvings. Alongside these treasures are European art objects, Russian lacquer boxes, as well as contemporary modern Jewish art. Give yourself about an hour here.

119 S. Main St. ✆ **901/523-ARTS** (2787). www.belzmuseum.org. $6 adults, $5 seniors, $4 students. Tues–Fri 10:30am–5pm; Sat–Sun noon–5pm.

The Cotton Museum at the Memphis Cotton Exchange "Glorious and notorious." Both adjectives apply to the history of cotton, one of the most significant agricultural crops in the history of the Deep South. African slaves did the back-breaking labor of picking the cotton, while in downtown Memphis, wealthy merchants and brokers bought and sold the lucrative commodity that was loaded onto Mississippi River barges for shipment to the entire world. This interesting museum, on the site of the 1939 Memphis Cotton Exchange building, features exhibits that explore cotton's legacy and its importance to Memphis's growth. Allot a half hour to visit the museum.

65 Union Ave. ✆ **901/531-7826.** www.memphiscottonmuseum.org. Admission $8 adults, $7.50 seniors, $7 students, $3 children 6–12. Mon–Sat 10am–5pm; Sun noon–5pm.

Dixon Gallery & Gardens ★ The South's finest collection of French and American Impressionist and post-Impressionist artworks is the highlight of this exquisite museum, set on 17 wooded acres. The museum, art collection, and surrounding 17 acres of formal and informal gardens once belonged to Margaret and Hugo Dixon, who were avid art collectors. After the deaths of the Dixons, their estate opened to the public as an art museum and has since become one of Memphis's most important museums. The permanent collection includes works by Henri Matisse, Pierre Auguste Renoir, Edgar Degas, Paul Gauguin, Mary Cassatt, J. M. W. Turner, and John Constable. With strong local support, the museum frequently hosts temporary exhibits of international caliber. Twice a year, the Memphis Symphony Orchestra performs outdoor concerts in the Dixon's formal gardens. Allow an hour for the museum, and more time for the gardens. ***Tip:*** Admission is free from 10am to noon on Saturdays.

4339 Park Ave. ✆ **901/761-5250.** www.dixon.org. Admission $7 adults, $5 seniors and students, $3 children 7–17. Tues–Fri 10am–4pm; Sat 10am–5pm; Sun 1–5pm. Located adjacent to Audubon Park, off Park Ave. at Cherry Rd. (btw. Getwell Rd. and Perkins Rd.).

Memphis Brooks Museum of Art First opened in 1916 as the Brooks Memorial Art Gallery, this is the oldest art museum in Tennessee; it contains one of the largest art

Fun Facts Elvis-in-Chief

You probably already knew that former president Bill Clinton's U.S. Secret Service code name was "Elvis." Now the King and the Commander-in-Chief are further linked in history. Clinton's presidential library, in Little Rock, Arkansas, features his personal collection of Elvis memorabilia. Most of the items are gifts given to the president during his two terms in the White House.

Fun Facts The Men Who Would be King

In 2007, Graceland sanctioned an impersonators' competition, dubbed the Ultimate Elvis Tribute Artist Contest. Stakes were high as competitors tried to hip-shake and out-snarl each other: The winner received $5,000 cash, a $5,000 Graceland shopping spree, and both a recording session at Memphis's Sun Records (where Elvis got his big break in the 1950s) as well as a contract to perform on a cruise ship. It's now an annual event. See www.elvis.com.

collections of any museum in the mid-South. With more than 7,000 pieces in the permanent collection, the Brooks frequently rotates works on display. The museum's emphasis is on European and American art of the 18th through the 20th centuries, with a very respectable collection of Italian Renaissance and baroque paintings and sculptures as well. Some of the museum's more important works include pieces by Auguste Rodin, Pierre Auguste Renoir, Thomas Hart Benton, and Frank Lloyd Wright. Take a break from strolling through the museum with a stop in the Brushmark Restaurant. Allow an hour to 90 minutes. ***Tip:*** On Wednesdays, admission is "pay-what-you-can" from 10am to 4pm.

Overton Park, 1934 Poplar Ave. (btw. N. McLean Blvd. and E. Parkway N.). ✆ **901/544-6200.** www.brooksmuseum.org. Admission $9 adults, $8 seniors, $5 students, free for children 5 and under. Wed and Fri 10am–4pm; Thurs 10am–8pm; Sat 10am–5pm; Sun 11am–5pm.

Mud Island River Park Kids Mud Island is more than just a museum. The 52-acre park on Mud Island is home to several attractions, including the **River Walk** and the **Mississippi River Museum.** If you have seen any pre-1900 photos of the Memphis waterfront, you may have noticed that Mud Island is missing from the photos. This island first appeared in 1900 and became permanent in 1913. In 1916, the island joined with the mainland just north of the mouth of the Wolf River, but a diversion canal was dug through the island to maintain a free channel in the Wolf River.

To learn all about the river, you can follow a 5-block-long scale model of 900 miles of the Mississippi River. Called the **River Walk,** the model is complete with flowing water, street plans of cities and towns along the river, and informative panels that include information on the river and its history.

On Mud Island you can rent bicycles, kayaks, and paddleboats (the latter two are not for use on the Mississippi River itself, of course) by the hour or half day, allowing plenty of time for a leisurely exploration of the area. Evenings during the summer, the **Mud Island Amphitheater** hosts such touring acts as Jimmy Buffett, Norah Jones, and Rob Thomas. Allow an hour, or make a day of it.

125 N. Front St. (at Adams Ave.). ✆ **800/507-6507** or 901/576-7241. www.mudisland.com. Mississippi River Museum $8 adults, $6 seniors, $5 children 5–12; grounds only free. Summer Tues–Sun 10am–8pm; spring and fall Tues–Sun 10am–5pm. Closed Nov–Mar. To reach Mud Island, take the monorail from Front St. at Adams Ave.

National Civil Rights Museum ★★★ Moments Dr. Martin Luther King, Jr., came to Memphis in early April of 1968 in support of the city's striking garbage collectors. He checked into the Lorraine Motel, as he always did when visiting Memphis. On April 4, he stepped out onto the balcony outside his room and was shot dead by James Earl Ray. The assassination of King struck a horrible blow to the American civil rights movement and incited riots in cities across the country. However, despite the murder of the movement's most important leader, African Americans continued to struggle for the equal rights that were guaranteed to them under the U.S. Constitution.

Saved from demolition, the Lorraine Motel was remodeled and today serves as the nation's memorial to the civil rights movement. In evocative displays, the museum chronicles the struggle of African Americans from the time of slavery to the present. Multimedia presentations and life-size, walk-through tableaux include historic exhibits: a Montgomery, Alabama, public bus like the one on which Rosa Parks was riding when she refused to move to the back of the bus; a Greensboro, North Carolina, lunch counter; and the burned shell of a Freedom-Ride Greyhound bus. Allow 2 to 3 hours.

450 Mulberry St. (at Huling Ave.). ✆ **901/521-9699.** www.civilrightsmuseum.org. Admission $13 adults, $11 seniors and students, $9.50 children 4–17, free for children 3 and under. Wed–Sat and Mon 9am–5pm, Sun 1–5pm; closed major holidays. Admission is free Mon after 3pm for Tennessee residents.

National Ornamental Metal Museum ★ Finds Set on parklike grounds on a bluff overlooking the Mississippi, this small museum is dedicated to ornamental metalworking in all its forms. There are sculptures displayed around the museum's gardens, a working blacksmith shop, and examples of ornamental wrought-iron grillwork such as that seen on balconies in New Orleans. Sculptural metal pieces and jewelry are also prominently featured both in the museum's permanent collection and in temporary exhibits. Be sure to take a look at the ornate museum gates; they were created by 160 metalsmiths from 17 countries and feature a fascinating array of imaginative rosettes. Just across the street is a community park that includes an ancient Native American mound. Allow 1 hour or more.

374 Metal Museum Dr. ✆ **877/881-2326** or 901/774-6380. www.metalmuseum.org. Admission $5 adults, $4 seniors, $3 students and children 5–18, free for children 4 and under. Tues–Sat 10am–5pm; Sun noon–5pm. Closed 1 week btw. exhibit changes and the week btw. Christmas and New Year's. Take Crump Blvd. or I-55 toward the Memphis-Arkansas Bridge and get off at exit 12-C (Metal Museum Dr.), which is the last exit in Tennessee; the museum is 2 blocks south.

Pink Palace Museum ★ Kids "The Pink Palace" was the name locals gave to the ostentatious pink-marble mansion that grocery store magnate Clarence Saunders built shortly after World War I. It was Saunders who had revolutionized grocery shopping with the opening of the first Piggly Wiggly self-service market in 1916. Unfortunately, Saunders went bankrupt before he ever finished his "Pink Palace," and the building was acquired by the city of Memphis for use as a museum of cultural and natural history.

Among the exhibits here is a full-scale reproduction of the maze of aisles that constituted an original Piggly Wiggly. Other walk-through exhibits include a pre–Piggly Wiggly general store and an old-fashioned pharmacy with a soda fountain. Memphis is a major medical center; accordingly, this museum has an extensive medical-history exhibit. On the lighter side, kids enjoy such exhibits as a life-size mechanical triceratops, a real mastodon skeleton, and a hand-carved miniature circus that goes into animated action. In the planetarium, there are frequently changing astronomy programs as well as rock-'n'-roll laser shows (the annual Aug Elvis laser show is the most popular). There is also an IMAX movie theater here. Allow 1 to 2 hours.

3050 Central Ave. (btw. Hollywood and Highland). ✆ **901/320-6320** or 901/763-IMAX (4629) for IMAX schedule. www.memphismuseums.org. Museum $8.75 adults, $6.25 seniors, $5.75 children 3–12, free for children 2 and under. IMAX $14 adults, $9.50 seniors, $6.25 children 3–12. Combination tickets available. Call for IMAX show times. Museum hours Mon–Sat 9am–5pm; Sun noon–5pm.

Slavehaven Underground Railroad Museum/Burkle Estate *Finds* Secret tunnels and trap doors evoke a period before the Civil War, when this house was a stop on the underground railroad used by runaway slaves in their quest for freedom. The house is filled with 19th-century furnishings and has displays of artifacts from slavery days. It takes about an hour to get through the house.

826 N. Second Ave. (btw. Chelsea and Bicknell aves.). ✆ **901/527-3427.** Admission $6 adults, $4 students. Summer Mon–Sat 10am–4pm; winter Wed–Sat 10am–4pm.

Woodruff-Fontaine House Located in a downtown neighborhood known as Victorian Village, the Woodruff-Fontaine House displays an elaborate Victorian aesthetic, in this case influenced by French architectural styles. Built in 1870, the fully restored 16-room home contains period furnishings. Mannequins throughout the house display the fashions of the late 19th century. Allow 30 minutes.

Victorian Village, 680 Adams Ave. ✆ **901/526-1469.** Admission $10 adults, $8 seniors, $6 students. Wed–Sun noon–3:30pm. Guided tours every 30 min. Btw. Neely and New Orleans sts., next to Mallory-Neely House.

OTHER MEMPHIS ATTRACTIONS

Chucalissa Archaeological Museum *Kids* The main drawback of this site is its rather isolated, hard-to-find location, several miles south of nearly everything else in Memphis. (That is, unless you do this on your way to or from Tunica, Mississippi.) Chucalissa Archaeological Museum is built on the site of a Mississippian-period (A.D. 900–1600) Native American village. Dioramas and displays of artifacts discovered in the area provide a cultural history of Mississippi River Valley Native Americans. The reconstructed village includes several family dwellings, a shaman's hut, and a chief's temple atop a mound in the center of the village compound. The chance to walk through a real archaeologist's trench and to explore a Native American village thrills most children. Allow 1 to 2 hours.

1987 Indian Village Dr. ✆ **901/785-3160.** www.memphis.edu/chucalissa. Admission $5 adults, $3 seniors and children 4–11, free for children 3 and under. Tues–Sat 9am–5pm; Sun 1–5pm. South of Memphis off U.S. 61 and adjacent to the T. O. Fuller State Park.

Memphis Zoo & Aquarium ★★ *Kids* Teton Trek, opened in 2009, is an exhibit that showcases the wildlife of the Greater Yellowstone ecosystem. Grizzly bears, elk, grey wolves, sandhill cranes, and trumpeter swans are featured in this addition, located in the zoo's Northwest Passage area. Polar bears, seals, and sea lions also inhabit this particular nook. Elsewhere, a pair of adorable panda bears from China are top draws at this great

White Elephant?

On North Riverside Drive at the base of the Hernando-Desoto Bridge to Arkansas you'll see this 32-story, stainless-steel landmark. Built in the early 1990s in honor of Memphis's Egyptian namesake, the long-vacant former concert arena and sports venue is reportedly being eyed as a potential new location for retail giant Bass Pro Shops. However, that's been the story for years now, with no definitive action having been taken. So stay tuned.

zoo. Built to resemble an ancient Egyptian temple, the zoo's entry is covered with traditional and contemporary hieroglyphics. The attraction also includes a 5-acre primate habitat, an exhibit of nocturnal animals, and an extensive big-cat area with habitats that are among the best zoo exhibits in the country. Allow 3 hours or more.

Overton Park, 2000 Prentiss Place. ✆ **901/276-WILD** (9453). www.memphiszoo.org. Admission $13 adults, $12 seniors, $8 children 2–11. Admission free to Tennessee residents Tues after 2pm. Parking $3 during summer season. Mar–late Oct daily 9am–6pm; late Oct–Feb daily 9am–5pm. Located inside Overton Park off of Poplar Ave. (2000 block), btw. N. McLean Blvd. and E. Parkway N.

PARKS & GARDENS

In downtown Memphis, between Main Street and Second Avenue and between Madison and Jefferson avenues, you'll find **Court Square,** the oldest park in Memphis. With its classically designed central fountain, restored gazebo, and stately old shade trees, this park was long a favored gathering spot of Memphians. Numerous historic plaques around the park relate the many important events that have taken place in Court Square. (***Tip:*** Don't sit here and expect to enjoy a snack or picnic lunch—you'll be accosted by dive-bombing pigeons and aggressive, overweight squirrels.)

A block to the west, you'll find **Jefferson Davis Park,** which overlooks Mud Island and Riverside Drive. Several Civil War cannons face out toward the river from this small park. Below Jefferson Davis Park, along Riverside Drive, you'll find **Tom Lee Park,** which stretches for 1½ miles south along the bank of the Mississippi and is named after a local African-American hero who died saving 32 people when a steamer sank in the Mississippi in 1925—even though Lee, himself, could not swim. This park is a favorite of joggers and is the site of various festivals, including the big Memphis in May celebration. A parallel park called **Riverbluff Walkway** is the newest development atop the bluff on the east side of Riverside Drive. And just north of the Pyramid in Harbor Town, an exclusive, 950-home planned community neighborhood (similar to Seaside, Florida), lies **Greenbelt Park.** Its tree-shaded trails and pristine picnic area offers the city's most picturesque, unspoiled views of the Mississippi River.

Located in Midtown and bounded by Poplar Avenue, East Parkway North, North Parkway, and North McLean Boulevard, **Overton Park** is one of Memphis's largest parks and includes not only the Memphis Zoo and Aquarium but also the Memphis Brooks Museum of Art, the Memphis College of Art, and the Overton Park Municipal Golf Course, as well as tennis courts, hiking and biking trails, and an open-air theater. The park's large, old shade trees make this a cool place to spend an afternoon in the summer, and the surrounding residential neighborhoods are some of the wealthiest in the city.

Elmwood Cemetery Victims of war, disease, and natural causes are buried in this historic garden cemetery on the outskirts of downtown Memphis. Dating back to 1852, the majestic, 80-acre sanctuary is brimming with elaborate marble sculptures, simple headstones, and towering shade trees. Take a guided tour or stroll the grounds alone to get a sense of the city's rich history. Descendants such as 1920s bandleader Jimmie Lunceford, Civil War historian and author Shelby Foote, and African-American Civil Rights photographer Ernest Withers are laid to rest here. Most haunting, however, is "No Man's Land," public lots marking the gravesites of 1,500 victims of the 1878 yellow fever epidemic. Maps are available in the Victorian Garden Cottage that serves as the Visitors Center. Allot 1 to 2 hours for a visit here.

824 South Dudley St. ✆ **901/774-3212.** www.elmwoodcemetery.org. Free admission (donations accepted). Grounds open daily 8am–4:30pm; office closed Saturday at noon and Sunday.

Lichterman Nature Center Often overlooked by tourists, this well-maintained, wooded nature preserve in the heart of East Memphis is one of the city's most family-friendly attractions. Open year-round, the center offers hiking trails, scientific demonstrations, and other hands-on activities on 65 acres and within its museumlike Backyard Wildlife Center. With a grassy meadow and lake as well as woods, there are plenty of educational opportunities for learning about various wildlife habitats. Lichterman is part of the Memphis Museum System, which also includes the Pink Palace and other sites. Give yourself 2 to 3 hours here.

5992 Quince Rd. ✆ **901/767-7322.** www.memphismuseums.org. $6 adults, $5.50 seniors, $4.50 children 3–12. Tues–Thurs 9am–4pm; Fri–Sat 9am–5pm.

Memphis Botanic Garden ★ With 20 formal gardens covering 96 acres, this rather large botanical garden requires a bit of time to visit properly. You'll find something in bloom at almost any time of year, and even in winter, the Japanese garden offers a tranquil setting for a quiet stroll. In April and May, the Ketchum Memorial Iris Garden, one of the largest in the country, is in bloom, and during May, June, and September the Municipal Rose Garden is alive with color. A special Sensory Garden is designed for people with disabilities and has plantings that stimulate all five senses. In 2009, a new 2.5-acre Children's Garden opened, offering a "tree top adventure" that ascend into the tree line, and a tunneling excursion that offers kids a worm's-eye point of view. Allow at least 2 hours.

Audubon Park, 750 Cherry Rd. ✆ **901/576-4100.** www.memphisbotanicgarden.com. Admission $5 adults, $4 seniors and students, $3 children 3–12. Mar–Oct Mon–Sat 9am–6pm, Sun 11am–6pm; Nov–Feb Mon–Sat 9am–4:30pm, Sun 11am–4:30pm. Located across from Audubon Park Golf Course on Cherry Rd., btw. Southern and Park aves.

3 AFRICAN-AMERICAN HERITAGE IN MEMPHIS

For many people, the city of Memphis is synonymous with one of the most significant, and saddest, events in recent American history—the assassination of Dr. Martin Luther King, Jr. The Lorraine Motel, where King was staying when he was shot, has in the years since the assassination become the **National Civil Rights Museum** (p. 214).

Long before the civil rights movement brought King to Memphis, the city had already become one of the most important cities in the South for blacks. After the Civil War and the abolition of slavery, Memphis became a magnet for African Americans, who came here seeking economic opportunities. **Beale Street** (p. 205) was where they headed to start their search. Beale Street's most famous citizen was W. C. Handy, the father of the blues, who first put down on paper the blues born in the cotton fields of the Mississippi Delta. **W. C. Handy Park,** with its statue of the famous blues musician, is about halfway down Beale Street, and Handy's small house, now the **W. C. Handy House Museum** (p. 212), is also now on Beale Street. At the **Memphis Rock 'N' Soul Museum** (p. 210), just a block off Beale Street, you can learn more about Handy and other famous African-American blues musicians who found a place for their music. Best of all is the **Soulsville USA: Stax Museum of American Soul Music** (p. 210), which has been drawing rave reviews since it opened a few years ago in a resurgent South Memphis neighborhood. Another museum with exhibits on famous black musicians is the **Pink Palace Museum** (p. 215).

Church Park, on the corner of Beale and Fourth streets (and once the site of a large auditorium), was established by Robert R. Church, a former slave and Memphis

Fun Facts Sexy Swing

Grammy-winning pop star and avid golfer **Justin Timberlake** bought and renovated an old country club near the northern suburb of Millington, where he's from. The new **Mirimichi Golf Club,** a par-72 course that opened in July 2009, features more than 7,400 yards, 80 bunkers, four waterfalls, six lakes and two creeks that run between holes. It is also the first eco-friendly course certified by the Audubon Classic Sanctuary Program. To reserve a tee time, or get directions to the course, contact Mirimichi Golf Club, 6195 Woodstock Cuba Rd., Millington, TN (✆ **901/295-3800;** www.mirimichi.com). Meanwhile, construction on a new clubhouse is expected to be completed in 2011.

businessman who became the city's first black millionaire. The park was a gathering place for African Americans in the early 1900s, when restrictive Jim Crow laws segregated city parks.

Gospel music was part of the inspiration for the blues that W. C. Handy wrote, and that music came from the churches of the black community. The tradition of rousing musical accompaniment in church continues at many of the city's churches, but none is more famous than the **Full Gospel Tabernacle,** 787 Hale Rd. (✆ **901/396-9192**), which is where one-time soul-music star Al Green now takes to the pulpit as a minister. Sunday service is at 11am. **Mason Temple Church of God in Christ,** 930 Mason St. (✆ **901/947-9300**), is the international headquarters of the Church of God in Christ and was where Dr. Martin Luther King, Jr., gave his "I've been to the mountaintop" speech shortly before his death. Tourists are welcome to visit and step inside. Donations are accepted. Sunday services are no longer held here, however.

If you'd like a guide to lead you through the most important sites in Memphis's African-American heritage, contact **Heritage Tours** (✆ **901/527-3427**), which offers both a 1-hour Beale Street Walking Tour ($5) and 3- to 4-hour Memphis Black Heritage Tour ($25 adults, $15–$20 children). Heritage Tours also operates both the W. C. Handy House Museum and the Slavehaven/Burkle Estate Museum.

Heritage Tours also visits another worthwhile out-of-town attraction, the **Alex Haley House Museum** (✆ **731/738-2240**). If you prefer to go on your own, it's a pleasant day trip by car to reach the small town of Henning, about 45 miles north of downtown Memphis on U.S. 51. The home is now a museum containing memorabilia and old portraits of the Haley family. Nearby is the family burial site, where Haley (author of *Roots: The Saga of an American Family*) and many of his ancestors, including Chicken George, are buried. The museum is open Tuesday to Saturday 10am to 5pm and Sunday 1 to 5pm. Admission is $5 for adults and $3 for students.

4 ESPECIALLY FOR KIDS

Many of Memphis's main attractions will appeal to children as well as to adults, but there are also places that are specifically geared toward kids. In addition to the attractions listed below, see also the Pink Palace Museum (p. 215), the Memphis Zoo and Aquarium (p. 216), the Chucalissa Archaeological Museum (p. 216), the Mud Island/Mississippi River Museum (p. 214), and the Peabody Ducks (p.169).

Children's Museum of Memphis ★ Located adjacent to the Liberty Bowl Memorial Stadium, the children's museum offers fun, hands-on activities that can be enjoyed by children and adults alike. A real fire engine invites climbing, while the museum's kid-sized city lets little ones act like grown-ups: They can go shopping for groceries, stop by the bank to cash a check, or climb up through a 22-foot-tall skyscraper. Special traveling exhibitions are often booked at the museum, so call ahead to find out what special programs are being offered during your stay. Allow 2 to 3 hours.

2525 Central Ave. ✆ **901/458-2678.** www.cmom.com. Admission $10 adults, $6 seniors and children 1–12. Mon–Sat 9am–5pm; Sun noon–5pm. Closed some holidays. Btw. Airways and Hollywood.

Fire Museum of Memphis Billed as the only fire museum in the country that combines history along with an interactive fire-safety educational program, this often-overlooked kids' attraction has lots to offer, and safety lessons to teach. Highlights include a talking horse and a simulation that allows visitors to feel as if they are standing inside a burning house. Though far from being a "thrill-ride" experience, parents should keep in mind that the scene, which includes a sofa bursting into flames and a rise in temperature as the fire engulfs the house, may be too intense for easily frightened youngsters. Allow an hour and a half for a visit.

118 Adams St. ✆ **901/320-5650.** www.firemuseum.com. $6 adults, $5 children 3–12. Mon–Sat 9am–5pm.

Golf & Games Family Park Located on the east side of town just off I-40 at exit 12A, this miniature golf and games complex claims to be the largest of its kind in the world; whether or not that claim is true, your kids will find plenty to do. There are more than 50 holes of miniature golf, a driving range, baseball batting cages, a go-kart track, swimming pool, video game room, and picnic tables. A laser-tag arena is also an option. Allow 2 to 3 hours.

5484 Summer Ave. (at Pleasant View Rd.). ✆ **901/386-2992.** www.golfandgamesmemphis.com. All-day wristband $25. Sun–Thurs 8am–11pm; Fri–Sat 8am–midnight. (Closes 1 hr. earlier during school year).

5 STROLLING AROUND MEMPHIS

If you like to walk, consider doing the tour outlined below, which takes in some of the city's best attractions, including Beale Street and the National Civil Rights Museum.

WALKING TOUR DOWNTOWN MEMPHIS

START:	**The Peabody hotel, on the corner of Union Avenue and Second Street.**
FINISH:	**Cotton Row and The Cotton Museum at the Memphis Cotton Exchange, corner of Front Street and Union Avenue.**
TIME:	**Approximately 2 hours, not including time spent at museums, shopping, meals, and other stops. It's best to plan on spending the whole day doing this walking tour.**
BEST TIMES:	**Spring and fall, when the weather isn't so muggy, and Friday and Saturday, when the Rendezvous is open for lunch.**
WORST TIMES:	**Summer days, when the weather is just too muggy for doing this much walking. Be mindful of safety, and don't attempt this walking tour after dark.**

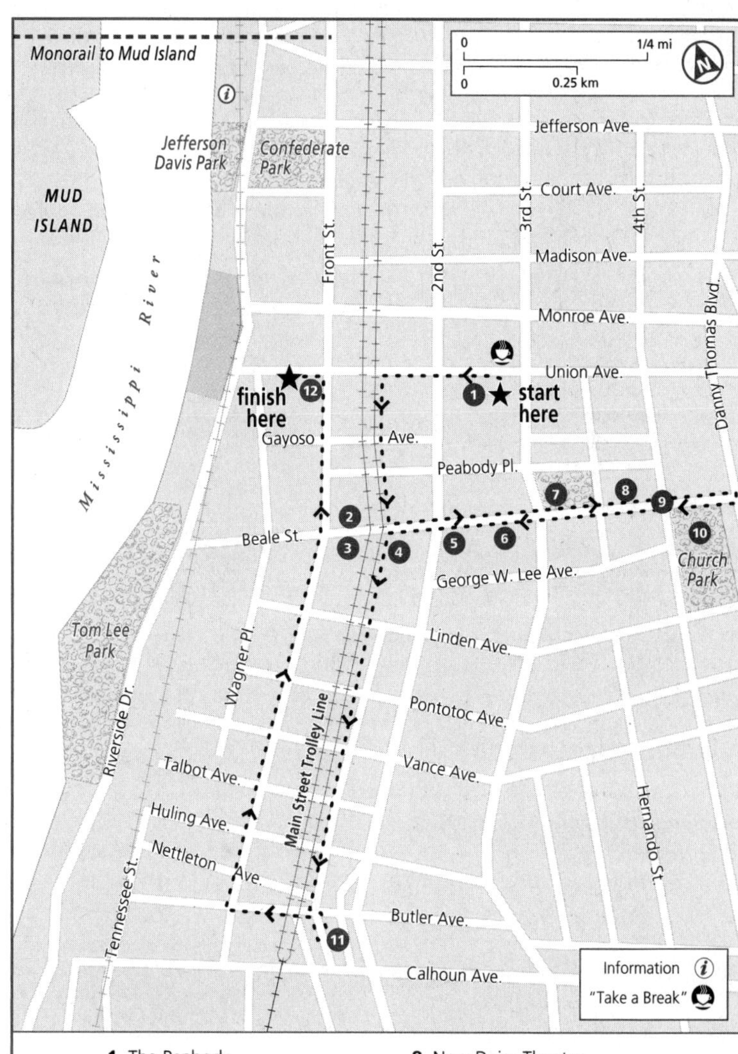

1 The Peabody
2 Beale Street
3 Orpheum Theatre
4 Statue of Elvis Presley
5 B.B. King's Blues Club
6 A. Schwab Dry Goods Store
7 W.C. Handy Park
8 New Daisy Theatre
9 W.C. Handy House
10 Church Park
11 National Civil Rights Museum
12 Cotton Row and Cotton Museum

Start your tour of Memphis's main historic districts at:

❶ The Peabody hotel

This is the home of the famous Peabody ducks, which spend their days contentedly floating on the water of a marble fountain in the hotel's lobby. The ducks make their grand, red-carpet entrance each morning at 11am (and the crowds of onlookers begin assembling before 10:30am).

TAKE A BREAK

By the time the crowds thin out and you've had a chance to ogle The Peabody's elegant lobby, you may already be thinking about lunch. If it's a Friday or Saturday, you can fortify yourself at the **Rendezvous,** 52 S. Second St., one of Memphis's favorite barbecue spots.

From The Peabody, walk 1 block west to Main Street, which is a pedestrian mall down which runs an old-fashioned trolley. Turn left, and in 2 blocks you'll come to:

❷ Beale Street

This is where W. C. Handy made the blues the first original American music when he committed "Memphis Blues" to paper. Today, this street of restored buildings is Memphis's main evening-entertainment district.

On the corner of Main and Beale, you can't miss the:

❸ Orpheum Theatre

Originally built as a vaudeville theater in 1928, the Orpheum features a classic theater marquee and beautiful interior decor. Today, it's Memphis's main performing-arts center.

Across Main Street from the theater stands a:

❹ Statue of Elvis Presley

A visit to this statue is a must for Elvis fans. Bring your camera.

Continuing east on Beale Street to the corner of Second Street will bring you to:

❺ B. B. King's Blues Club

Named for the Beale Street Blues Boy himself, this is the most popular club on the street, and though B. B. King only plays here twice a year, there is still great live blues here almost every night.

A few doors down the street, you'll come to the:

❻ A. Schwab Dry Goods Store

This store has been in business at this location since 1876, and once inside, you may think that nothing has changed since the day the store opened. You'll find an amazing array of the odd and the unusual.

At Beale and Third streets, you can take a breather in:

❼ W. C. Handy Park

There always seems to be some live music in this park, also the site of a statue of Handy.

A block south along Beale Street from this park you'll find the:

❽ New Daisy Theatre

This is a popular venue for contemporary music, including rock, blues, and folk.

A few doors down from the New Daisy, you'll find the restored:

❾ W. C. Handy House

Though it wasn't always on this site, this house was where Handy lived when making a name for himself on Beale Street.

Diagonally across the intersection is:

❿ Church Park

Robert Church, a former slave who became the city's first African-American millionaire, gave the African-American citizens of Memphis this park in 1899.

Now head back up Beale Street and take a left on Main. This is the street down which the trolley runs, so if you're feeling tired, you can hop on the trolley and take it south a few blocks. If you walk, turn left on Butler Street, and if you ride, walk east on Calhoun Street. In a very short block, you'll come to the:

⓫ National Civil Rights Museum

Once the Lorraine Motel, it was here that Dr. Martin Luther King, Jr., was assassinated on April 4, 1968. The motel has been converted into a museum documenting the struggle for civil rights.

After visiting this museum, head west on Butler Street and turn right on Front Street. You will now be walking through:

⓬ Cotton Row and The Cotton Museum

In the days before and after the Civil War, and continuing into the early part of the 20th century, this area was the heart of the Southern cotton industry. Most of America's cotton was once shipped through the docks 2 blocks away. This area of warehouses and old storefronts is now a designated historic district, and many of the buildings have been renovated.

6 ORGANIZED TOURS

RIVER TOURS

Although the economic heart of Memphis has moved to the eastern suburbs, this is still a Mississippi River town; no visit to Memphis would be complete without spending a bit of time on Ole Man River. **Memphis Riverboats,** 45 S. Riverside Dr. (✆ **800/221-6197** or 901/527-5694; www.memphisriverboats.net), operates several paddle-wheelers, all of which leave from a dock on "the cobblestones" at the foot of Monroe Avenue in downtown Memphis. From March through November, there are 1½-hour sightseeing cruises, and in the summer, there are sunset dinner cruises and party cruises. The barbecue-buffet dinner cruises include live music. The 1½-hour sightseeing cruise costs $20 for adults; $17 for seniors, military, and students; $10 for children 4 to 17 (free for children 3 and under). The evening dinner cruise costs $45 for adults, $43 for seniors and military, and $30 for children.

CITY TOURS

You'll find half a dozen or more horse-drawn carriages lined up in front of The Peabody most evenings, operated by **Carriage Tours of Memphis** (✆ **888/267-9100** or 901/527-7542; www.carriagetoursofmemphis.com). Gentle equine giants with such names as Chester, Marley, Doc, and Jane proudly clop along city streets while human tour guides—accompanied by big, friendly dogs, sometimes wearing funny hats—regale passengers with Memphis trivia. Tours are offered year-round (see-through plastic canopies keep you relatively dry during rainy weather); and rates vary.

Backbeat Tours, 140 Beale Street (✆ **866/392-BEAT** [2328] or 901/272-2328; www.backbeattours.com), does a booming business from its convenient Beale Street ticket

Fun Facts **Funny Faithful?**

First Congregational Church (1000 S. Cooper; ✆ **901/278-6786;** www.firstcongo.com) is widely regarded as an all-inclusive, welcoming church with a progressive view on social issues—and a sense of humor. Better known to locals as "First Congo," it attracts new worshippers with irreverent ads, including one that mentions its unicyclists and art-house theater connections among its Top 10 Reasons to Visit. In traffic-choked Memphis, where road-rage is rampant, no. 8 on that list holds special appeal: "So much parking you won't even *care* if the person next to you takes two spaces."

office. For these guys, "Rockin' Rides through Memphis Music History" is more than just a tag line. In this case, these fun-loving tour operators actually strum guitars and perform Sun-era songs while showing off the local sites. Best of all is the actual bus, "Miss Claudy." She's a 1959 cream-and-crimson colored, city-transit beauty. Fully restored, the comfy bus still has those cheesy Naugahyde seat covers. Tour-package pricing starts at $25 for adults for the 90-minute Memphis Mojo Tour ($23 for seniors, $14 children 7–12) and goes on up to $44 per adult for the gig to Graceland ($44 for seniors, $32 for children 7–12.) They also offer a Historic Memphis Walking Tour, which lasts about 90 minutes. Prices are $15 for adults and seniors and $10 for children.

Blues City Tours of Memphis, 325 Union Ave. (✆ **901/522-9229;** www.bluescitytours.com), offers tours similar to the Gray Line tours. There is a half-day city tour that takes you past all the city's most important attractions, and there are also Graceland tours, Beale Street night-on-the-town tours, and casino tours to Mississippi. Before taxes, the city tour costs $24 for adults and $16 for children; the Elvis Graceland Tour, $30 for adults and $19 for children; after-dark dinner tour, $60 for adults and $50 for children (includes an evening on Beale Street with two clubs, two shows, two drinks, two meals with a choice of barbecue, chicken, or catfish and any cover charges, at specified places). They also offer tours to the Tunica, Mississippi, casinos—a smart bet if you plan to drink alcohol while you're there.

For a thoroughly unique tour of Memphis, book a tour with **American Dream Safari** (✆ **901/527-8870;** www.americandreamsafari.com). This is your chance to be chauffeured around town in a '55 Cadillac, with stops at such key Elvis sites as Humes High School (where he went to school) and the now-closed but still-standing Poplar Tunes (where he used to buy records). Other popular itineraries include a Sunday morning gospel tour and brunch, or the irreverently named (given Memphis's high crime rate) "Drive-By-Shooting" photographers' tour. Really, though, what American Dream Safari offers would be better described as authentic experiences than mere tours. Prices vary, from the Jukejoint Full of Blues for $75 per person (which includes admission to three Delta-area clubs), to $225 per person for an 8-hour pilgrimage along historic Highway 61. It includes blues-museum admission and lunch in Clarksdale, Mississippi.

7 OUTDOOR ACTIVITIES

GOLF Memphis's public golf courses include the **Stoneridge Golf Course,** 3049 Davies Plantation Rd. (✆ **901/382-1886**), as well as those operated by the Memphis Parks Commission: **Audubon Park,** 4160 Park Ave. (✆ **901/683-6941**); the **Davy Crockett Park Municipal Golf Course,** 4380 Range Line Rd. (✆ **901/368-3374**); **Fox Meadows Park,** 3064 Clark Rd. (✆ **901/362-0232**); **The Links at Galloway,** 3815 Walnut Grove Rd. (✆ **901/685-7805**); and **Overton Park,** 2080 Poplar Ave. (✆ **901/725-9905**).

TENNIS The Memphis Parks Commission operates seven public tennis courts all over the city. The most convenient to downtown and Midtown is **Leftwich,** 4145 Southern Ave. (✆ **901/685-7907**).

8 SPECTATOR SPORTS

BASEBALL The **Memphis Redbirds Baseball Club,** 175 Toyota Plaza, Ste. 300 (✆ **901/721-6050;** www.memphisredbirds.com), a Triple-A affiliate of the St. Louis Cardinals, plays at AutoZone Park, located 2 blocks east of The Peabody hotel on Union Avenue.

BASKETBALL The **Memphis Grizzlies** (✆ **901/205-1234;** www.nba.com/grizzlies) are the city's first NBA team, having relocated from Vancouver, British Columbia, in 2001. Since 2004, they have played at their new downtown arena, the FedExForum.

The **University of Memphis Tigers** (✆ **888/867-UOFM** [8636] or 901/678-2331; www.gotigersgo.com) regularly pack in crowds of 20,000 or more people when they play the FedExForum. The Tigers often put up a good showing against nationally ranked NCAA teams, which makes for some exciting basketball. Call for ticket and schedule information.

FOOTBALL The **AutoZone Liberty Bowl Classic** (✆ **901/729-4344;** www.libertybowl.org) is the biggest football event of the year in Memphis and pits two of the country's top college teams in a December postseason game. As with other postseason college bowl games, the Liberty Bowl is extremely popular and tickets go fast. This game is held at the **Liberty Bowl Memorial Stadium** (www.libertybowl.org), on the Mid-South Fairgrounds at the corner of East Parkway South and Central Avenue.

GOLF TOURNAMENTS The **St. Jude Classic** (✆ **901/748-0534;** www.stanfordstjude.com), a PGA charity tournament, is held each year in late spring at the Tournament Players Club at Southwind.

GREYHOUND RACING Across the river in Arkansas, greyhounds race at the **Southland Greyhound Park,** 1550 N. Ingram Blvd., West Memphis, Arkansas (✆ **800/467-6182** or 870/735-3670). Matinee post time is at 1pm; evening races start at 7:30pm.

HORSE SHOWS Horse shows are popular in Memphis, and the biggest of the year is the **Germantown Charity Horse Show** (✆ **901/754-0009;** www.gchs.org), held each June at the Germantown Horse Show Arena, which is just off Poplar Pike at Melanie Smith Lane in Germantown.

TENNIS The **Regions Morgan Keegan Championships** and **Cellular South Cup** (✆ **901/765-4401** or 901/685-ACES; www.memphistennis.com), part of the ATP Tour, are held each year in February at the Racquet Club of Memphis. Call for ticket and schedule information.

9 SIDE TRIPS FROM MEMPHIS

Because of its location in the far southwestern corner of Tennessee, Memphis doesn't have the wealth of convenient day-trip options that Nashville has. For example, you could head west into Arkansas if you're interested in seeing Bill Clinton's presidential library in Little Rock, or drive north if the flat expanse of rural Missouri's boot heel holds any appeal (probably not). Look east, and you're at least a 3-hour drive to Nashville. Due to the distances involved, all of these options are perhaps better suited to overnight trips than simple daylong escapes. But here's the good news: Head south from downtown Memphis, and you're only a few miles from the Mississippi Delta—the mother lode for blues-loving pilgrims who travel here from all over the world.

CLARKSDALE

An unmistakable vibe pervades the languid Mississippi Delta town of Clarksdale, about an hour's drive south of Memphis, Tennessee. It's by turns eerie and endearing, a flat landscape where fertile fields, endless railroad tracks, and run-down shacks are giving way to pockets of progress—an upscale restaurant, a strip mall full of dollar stores and fast-food drive-throughs, a museum celebrating the blues music that took root here in the early 20th century and changed the course of popular music.

Clarksdale also happens to be Tennessee Williams country. The cherished American playwright, author of such masterworks as *A Streetcar Named Desire* and *The Glass Menagerie,* grew up here. Young Tom, who later adopted the name "Tennessee," lived in the parsonage of St. George's Episcopal Church, where his grandfather was pastor. Self-guided walking tours of the historic neighborhood are available.

If you don't plan to return to Memphis the same day, this is a good place to begin a driving tour of legendary **Highway 61 (U.S. 61),** the two-lane road that took blues legends such as Muddy Waters, Robert Johnson, and B. B. King north from the impoverished cotton plantations of the south to the cities of Memphis and Chicago to the north. The long drive south will take you through the proverbial dusty Delta towns, and cities such as Greenville, Vicksburg, and finally, where Mississippi meets Louisiana in the southwest part of the state, historic Natchez.

Essentials

GETTING THERE **By Car** The major route into Clarksdale is **Highway 61** from Memphis to the north.

VISITOR INFORMATION Contact the **Clarksdale/Coahoma County Chamber of Commerce,** 1540 Desoto Ave., Clarksdale, MS 39614 (✆ **800/626-3764** or 662/627-7337; www.clarksdaletourism.com).

What to See & Do

As you ease into town, your first stop should be at **The Crossroads,** at the intersection of highways 49 and 61. The site is legendary as the place where bluesman Robert Johnson is said to have sold his soul to the devil in exchange for the guitar prowess that has made him one of the most revered musicians of the past century. A guitar statue marks the spot.

From here, your next stop should be the **Delta Blues Museum,** 1 Blues Alley (✆ **662/627-6820;** www.deltabluesmuseum.org). Housed in a renovated train depot built in 1918, it includes a treasure-trove of old blues memorabilia, including the log cabin where Muddy Waters grew up, on a cotton plantation not far from here. There are displays, musical instruments, and costumes of some of the Mississippi-born greats, such as Albert King, James Cotton, and Son House. Admission is $7 adults, $5 children 6 to 12; it is open daily except Sunday. Bessie Smith fans can do a drive-by tour of the **Riverside Hotel,** 615 Sunflower Ave. (✆ **662/624-9163**), the former blacks-only hospital where the great blues singer died after a car crash in 1937. Blues legends Sonny Boy Williamson II, Ike Turner, Robert Nighthawk, and even politician Robert F. Kennedy once stayed here. Today it still operates as a motel, but most visitors see it only from their windshields.

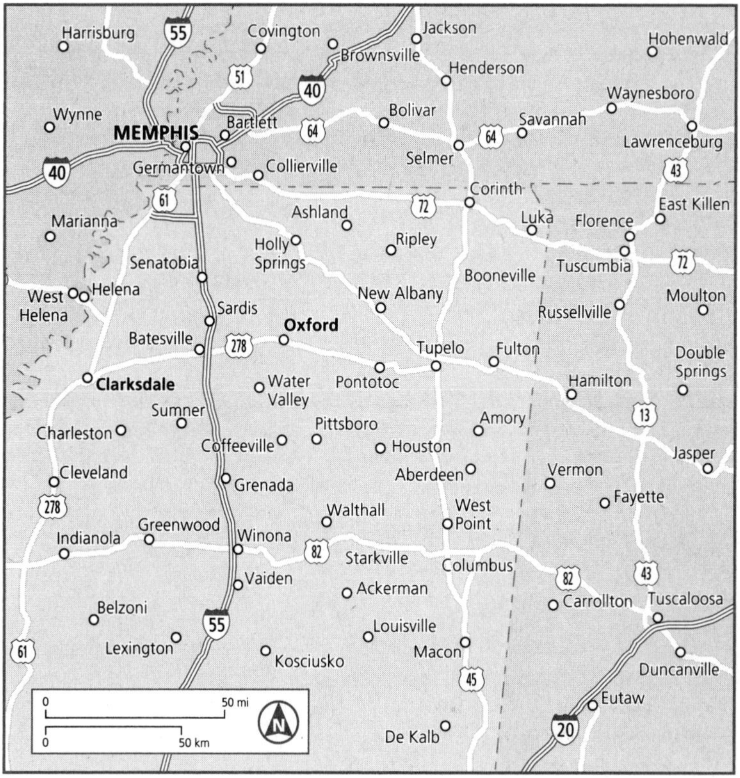

While downtown, don't miss **Cathead Delta Blues & Folk Art,** 252 Delta Ave. (✆ **662/624-5992;** www.cathead.biz). The store sells new blues CDs, DVDs, and books as well as eye-catching—and affordable—folk and outsider art. The hepcat-cool hot spot also serves as a clearinghouse for what's going on around town. Check Cathead's chalkboard that tells of weekly music events and updates. The store also occasionally has book signings and special events. You'll likely find the owner chatting up tourists who've made the pilgrimage here for some serious blues sightseeing.

Where to Stay & Dine

There's a pitiful lack of decent hotels in Clarksdale. Your best bet is to grab one of the inexpensive to moderately priced chain properties along State Street. Clean and modern with comfortable rooms and discounted rates is the **Executive Inn,** 710 S. State St. (✆ **662/627-9292**).

Hands-down the best restaurant in town is **Madidi Fine Dining,** 164 Delta Ave. (✆ **662/627-7770;** www.madidires.com), the upscale eatery and bar opened in 2001 by actor Morgan Freeman, who grew up in the area and is still seen around town from time

Shacking Up

In the lodging category of too-creepy for anyone but the most die-hard blues fan, there's the one-of-a-kind **Shack Up Inn,** 001 Commissary Circle (✆ **662/624-8329;** www.shackupinn.com), on old Highway 49 south of Clarksdale. Billed as Mississippi's oldest B&B (and that stands for Bed and Beer), the property is on the site of a weedy rural cotton gin littered with rusting antique farming implements, old road signs, and crumbling sharecropper shacks that have been modernized enough to accommodate easy-to-please travelers in search of a good time and a place to crash—and great music at the on-premises Commissary club. In 2004, the inn opened up 10 new "gin bins," private rooms within the gin warehouse that's now a makeshift "inn." Rates, which range from $65 to $95 per room, include a Moon Pie on your pillow. Sweet dreams . . .

to time. (He is also a partner in **Ground Zero Blues Club,** reminiscent of an old juke-joint, in downtown.) Other popular venues are **Abe's Bar-B-Que,** 616 State St. (✆ **662/624-9947**); and **Sarah's Kitchen,** 203 Sunflower Ave. (✆ **662/627-3239**), which serves Southern cooking 3 days a week—lunch and dinner Thursdays through Saturdays only.

OXFORD

Home to the University of Mississippi, "Ole Miss," Oxford is a quaint small town where daily life revolves around its 150-year-old Court Square. A popular weekend destination for out-of-towners and visiting alumni, Oxford offers an enticing array of great art galleries, bookstores, restaurants, and historic homes. Although its proximity to Memphis (about 70 miles away) makes it a doable day-trip, Oxford's offbeat charms might entice you to stay a day or two.

Essentials

GETTING THERE **By Car** The major route into Oxford is **I-55** from both the north (Memphis) and south (Jackson). It's about a 90-minute drive.

VISITOR INFORMATION Contact the **Oxford Convention & Visitors Bureau,** 107 Courthouse Sq., Ste. 1, Oxford, MS 38655 (✆ **800/758-9177** or 662/234-4680; www.touroxfordms.com).

Exploring the Area

Oxford's favorite son is Nobel Prize–winning author William Faulkner, whose residence from 1930 until his death in 1963 was his beloved home, **Rowan Oak,** Old Taylor Road (✆ **662/234-3284**). A tour of the grounds, with its graceful magnolias and old farm buildings, is a trip back in time. Inside, literary enthusiasts can still marvel at the author's old manual typewriter, and read his handwritten outline for *A Fable,* which is scrawled on the wall of his study. It's closed Mondays and major holidays. Admission is free on Wednesdays but costs $5 other days.

The most popular pastime in Oxford is simply strolling **The Square,** where travelers might spot former local residents such as John Grisham. **Square Books,** 160 Courthouse

Sq. (© **662/236-2262;** www.squarebooks.com), in business since 1870, is regarded as one of the best independent bookstores in the country. Down the street is its bargain-priced annex, **Off Square Books,** 129 Courthouse Sq. (© **662/236-2828**). Thousands of discounted and remaindered books cram shelves and bins. It's also the site of Square Books' author signings and readings, as well as *Thacker Mountain Radio,* Oxford's original music and literature radio show. Best-selling authors such as Robert Olen Butler, Elmore Leonard, and Ray Blount, Jr., have read their works on the live show. Musical guests have run the gamut from Elvis Costello and Marty Stuart to the Del McCoury band and the North Mississippi Allstars. The show is recorded live on Thursdays from 6 to 7pm.

Next door, **Southside Gallery,** 150 Courthouse Sq. (© **662/234-9090**), is an always-interesting place that showcases everything from photography, painting, and sculpture to outsider art by the likes of Howard Finster.

Southern Foodways Alliance: It's Gravy

Even if you're not a foodie, you've got to love an organization whose newsletter is called *Gravy.* That's the fun and informative missive of the **Southern Foodways Alliance** (SFA), an institute of the Center for the Study of Southern Culture at the University of Mississippi.

Led by noted food writer and author John T. Edge (*Southern Food: At Home, on the Road, in History; Cornbread Nation: The Best of Southern Food Writing;* and *Southern Belly: The Ultimate Food Lover's Companion to the South*), the nonprofit SFA is based on the Ole Miss campus in Oxford. However, its reach extends across several states, from Louisiana and Alabama to the Carolina Low Country and the Appalachians. With about 800 members, the SFA celebrates and documents Southern cooking traditions through its publications, oral history projects, and events such as the Potlikker Film Festival.

An annual symposium includes an array of lectures, discussions, and social outings focused on such topics as turnip greens, vine-ripened tomatoes, hoecakes, cornbread, and fried chicken. Chefs, farmers, barbecue champs, academics, and people who simply love to eat and to learn about food are participants in this eclectic group. At its 2009 event, guest speakers included humorist Roy Blount, Jr., as well as New Orleans's Nick Spitzer, host of National Public Radio's *American Routes.*

Only about 10 years old, the SFA also bestows lifetime achievement awards to people who uphold high culinary and cultural standards. The awards are named for Craig Claiborne, *New York Times* food editor, who was raised in the small Mississippi Delta town of Sunflower, not far from Oxford.

To get helpful travel advice on where to go and what to eat, go online to download the SFA's "Mississippi Delta Hot Tamale Trail," "Southern BBQ Trail," "Southern Boudin Trail," and "Southern Gumbo Trail." You can also sign up for field trips and special events, in 2010 and beyond, by contacting the SFA (© **662/915-5993;** www.southernfoodways.org).

The Blind Side: A Memphis Movie

Despite being filmed in Georgia rather than in Tennessee, the blockbuster 2009 movie *The Blind Side,* starring Sandra Bullock (who won an Academy Award for Best Actress) and Nashville country singer Tim McGraw, is based on a heartwarming, real-life story from Memphis. Movie fans, of course, know the plot: Sean and Leigh Anne Tuohy, a well-to-do suburban white couple, adopted Michael Oher, a 300-pound, homeless, black teenager from the projects.

Against all odds, Oher became a football star at Memphis's elite Briarcrest Christian School, before going on to play at Ole Miss (the University of Mississippi). In 2009, he was a first-round draft pick of the NFL's Baltimore Ravens, signing a contract worth more than $13 million. He started every game of his rookie season on the Ravens' offensive line.

The Blind Side, now available on DVD, also stars Academy Award–winning actress (and former Memphis resident) Kathy Bates as Oher's tutor, Miss Sue. The movie was produced by FedEx founder Fred Smith's Alcon Entertainment company, with daughter Molly Smith as an executive producer. Their company also produced the 2010 Denzel Washington hit, *The Book of Eli.* For more about the Smiths and the films they have worked on, see "Movie Mogul" box, in chapter 15.

Where to Stay & Dine

Because of its proximity to Memphis, Oxford is a popular day-trip destination for many travelers. Perhaps as a result, there are only a handful of hotels and motels, most of them chains on the outskirts of town that cater to the parents of college kids and other travelers to the university.

Among the cleanest and most modern choices are the **Comfort Inn,** 1808 Jackson Ave. S. (✆ **662/234-6000**), which has a small outdoor pool ($225); the larger **Days Inn,** 1101 Frontage Rd. (✆ **662/234-9500;** $70); and **Holiday Inn Express Hotel & Suites,** 112 Heritage Rd. (✆ **800/465-4329** or 662/236-2500; $75–$85).

Call ahead and book early if you want to reserve a room at one of the city's bed-and-breakfast properties, which are often booked during weekends when Ole Miss has home football games or other major events. You won't see it advertised much because the place is always full, but try to book a stay at **Puddin' Place,** 1008 University Ave. (✆ **662/234-1250**), a spotless, cheerfully decorated 1892 house that has two large suites with private bathrooms. The owner is in the process of adding a private cottage in the tree-shaded back yard. Gourmet breakfasts are included in the room rates, which usually run $145 for a double (during Ole Miss football season it's $350 for the 2-night minimum weekend stay, and the hotel sells out these weekends months in advance).

For guests who don't mind rather simple furnishings and a lack of pizzazz, try the **512 Inn,** 512 Van Buren Ave. (✆ **662/234-8043**). The white-columned, redbrick structure has a welcoming front porch packed with potted plants and flowers. There are six guest rooms, all with private bathroom but no phone. Rates run $105 to $175 for a double; continental breakfast is available weekdays, and a full breakfast is served on weekends.

City Grocery, 152 Courthouse Sq. (✆ **662/232-8080;** www.bigbadbreakfast.com), is one of the best restaurants in Mississippi. New Orleans–born chef John Currence finesses spicy cheese grits topped with plump shrimp, mushrooms, and smoked bacon, while offering an array of tempting gourmet salads, soups, and Cajun delicacies. Main courses cost $20 to $32. Reservations are recommended.

Bottletree Bakery, 923 Van Buren Ave. (✆ **662/236-5000**), is a must if you crave caffeine and the aroma of warm muffins being pulled from the oven. The cheery nook serves pastries and freshly baked breads as well as fine coffees, sandwiches, and salads.

Oxford's favorite dive bar is **Proud Larry's,** 211 S. Lamar Blvd. (✆ **662/236-0050**), where live music and drink specials augment a simple menu of burgers, pasta, salads, and hand-tossed pizzas.

19 Shopping in Memphis

Tacky Elvis souvenirs and made-in-China trinkets can be found all over town, especially on Beale Street and in the shops surrounding Graceland. For more discriminating tastes, The Peabody hotel downtown has some high-priced boutiques offering designer clothes, fine art, jewelry, and collectibles. Otherwise, your best shopping bets are going to be in East Memphis and the affluent suburbs. Although downtown had attracted a good array of new retail tenants as recently as 5 years ago, with the recent economic recession, most have closed up shop, leaving vacant storefronts in their wake. Hopes are high that the scene will eventually rebound, however. Meanwhile, there are plenty of good retail therapy options in other parts of the metro area.

1 THE SHOPPING SCENE

As in Nashville and other cities of the New South, the shopping scene in Memphis is spread out. If you want to go shopping in this city, you'll need to arm yourself with a good map, get in the car, and start driving. Most people head to the shopping malls and plazas (there are dozens) in East Memphis to find quality merchandise. However, in recent years, a few funky shops and worthwhile boutiques have started to pop up in the South Main Historic District of downtown.

Shopping malls and department stores are generally open Monday to Saturday 10am to 9pm and Sunday noon to 6pm. Many smaller mom-and-pop stores located outside malls and shopping centers are closed on Sundays. Call ahead to check store hours.

2 SHOPPING A TO Z

ANTIQUES

Memphis's main antiques district isn't what it once was. There used to be loads of good stores clustered at the intersection of Central Avenue and South Cooper Street. The two listed below are still going strong. However, you can find shops selling antique jewelry, furniture, and collectibles in shopping districts throughout the greater Memphis area. In addition to these stores, most businesses are open Monday to Saturday, with the exception of large shopping malls, which are open 7 days a week.

Flashback With 1950s furniture becoming more collectible with each passing year, it should come as no surprise that Memphis, the birthplace of rock 'n' roll in the early 1950s, has a great vintage furniture store. In addition to 1950s furnishings and vintage clothing, this store sells stuff from the '20s, '30s, and '40s, including a large selection of European Art Deco furniture. 2304 Central Ave. ✆ **901/272-2304.** www.flashbackmemphis.com.

Toad Hall Antiques Furniture, primitives, lamps, and mirrors make up the eclectic merchandise selection at this Cooper-Young landmark. Look for the frog in checked tights, painted on the outside of the brick building. Inside, browse for French and English as well as American decorative objects, jewelry, and other affordably priced gifts. 2129 Central Ave. ✆ **901/726-0755.** www.toadhallmemphis.com.

ART

Center for Southern Folklore Folk-art finds and other interesting Delta-inspired gifts and souvenirs are affordably priced at this beloved Memphis nonprofit, known as the Center for Southern Folklore. It's a one-stop shop for soaking up the region's culture, from art, history, and food to live music. 119 S. Main. ✆ **901/544-9965.** www.southernfolklore.com.

David Lusk Gallery In the most sophisticated, upscale art gallery in town, owner David Lusk showcases the South's finest contemporary artists. A wide variety of media are represented, including glass and photography. Lively receptions, educational events, and charitable efforts make this one of the most active galleries in the city. Laurelwood Center, 4540 Poplar Ave. ✆ **901/767-3800.** www.davidluskgallery.com.

Jay Etkin Gallery Artist and gallery owner Jay Etkin, a native New Yorker who also works out of Santa Fe, New Mexico, has for 2 decades been one of Memphis's most outspoken and active advocates for local contemporary artists. His spacious gallery and studio on Union Avenue (just down the street from Sun Studio in the emerging "Edge" district), is a must for anyone in search of affordable, often delightfully offbeat works of art. 484 Union Ave. ✆ **901/550-0064.** www.jayetkingallery.com.

Joysmith Gallery ★ **Finds** Brenda Joysmith, a longtime San Francisco–area artist who trained at the Art Institute of Chicago, had earned an international reputation before she returned to her native Memphis a few years ago. Best known for her pastel portraits of African-American women and children, Joysmith's works are featured in many national museums, in corporate collections, in books, and on the sets of popular television shows. Maya Angelou and Oprah Winfrey are among her celebrity fans. There's a retail shop in her studio selling affordable prints and other merchandise. 46 Huling Ave. ✆ **901/543-0505.** www.joysmith.com.

BIKES

Midtown Bike Co. Full-service bicycle sales, repair, and rentals are offered at this great little shop in the historic South Main historic downtown. Check out the choice selection of two-wheelers, helmets, and other essentials. Then chat up the knowledgeable store clerks to get the low-down on the best bike trails, including the Mississippi River Trail that passes through Memphis on its way from northern Minnesota to New Orleans. 509 S. Main St. ✆ **901/522-9757.** www.midtownbikeco.com.

BOOKS

Bookstar Housed in the converted Plaza Theatre, a big shopping plaza movie theater, this is the city's biggest discount bookstore. Many selections are marked down 20% to 30%, including the latest *New York Times* hardcover and paperback bestsellers. The store also sells gift items and has a coffee shop. 3402 Poplar Ave. ✆ **901/323-9332.**

Memphis Shopping: Downtown & Midtown

Amro Music Stores **14**
A. Schwab Dry Goods Store **19**
Burke's Book Store **12**
Casino Factory Shoppes **6**
Center for Southern Folklore **20**
Champion's Pharmacy and Herb Store **7**
Chickasaw Oaks Village **15**
Delphinium **3**
Flashback **10**
Gibson Beale Street Showcase **2**
Goner Records **13**
Jay Etkin Gallery **17**
Joysmith Gallery **4**
Kittie Kyle Kollection **15**
Lansky 126 **22**
Memphis Drum Shop **9**
Memphis Farmer's Market **5**
Memphis Flea Market **13**

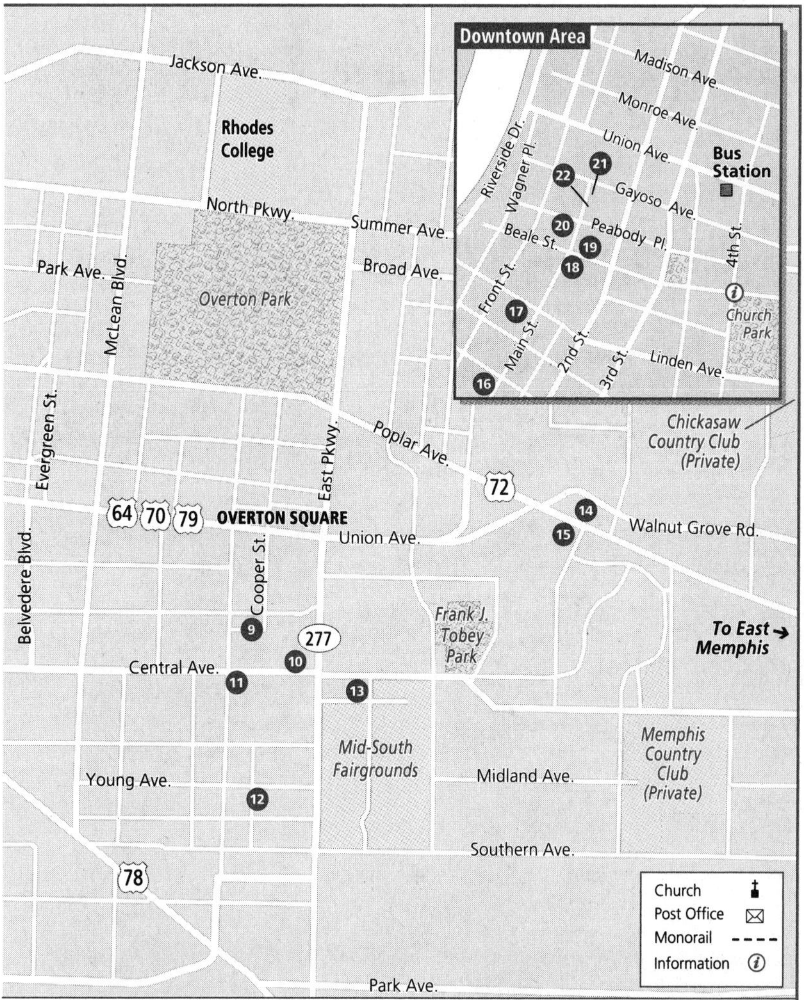

Downtown Area
Madison Ave.
Monroe Ave.
Union Ave.
Bus Station
Riverside Dr.
Wagner Pl.
Gayoso Ave.
Beale St.
Peabody Pl.
4th St.
Front St.
Church Park
Main St.
2nd St.
3rd St.
Linden Ave.
Jackson Ave.
Rhodes College
North Pkwy.
Summer Ave.
Park Ave.
Broad Ave.
McLean Blvd.
Overton Park
Evergreen St.
East Pkwy.
Poplar Ave.
Chickasaw Country Club (Private)
64
70
79
OVERTON SQUARE
72
Walnut Grove Rd.
Belvedere Blvd.
Union Ave.
Cooper St.
Frank J. Tobey Park
277
To East Memphis
Central Ave.
Mid-South Fairgrounds
Memphis Country Club (Private)
Young Ave.
Midland Ave.
Southern Ave.
78
Church
Post Office
Monorail
Information
Park Ave.

Memphis Music **18**
Midtown Bike Co. **16**
Miss Cordelia's Grocery **1**
Peabody Place **22**
The Peanut Shoppe **21**
Shangri-La Records **8**
Toad Hall Antiques **11**

Memphis
Wolf R.
51
40
Area shown
DOWN-TOWN
55
240
MIDTOWN
EAST MEMPHIS
72
78
Graceland
Memphis International Airport

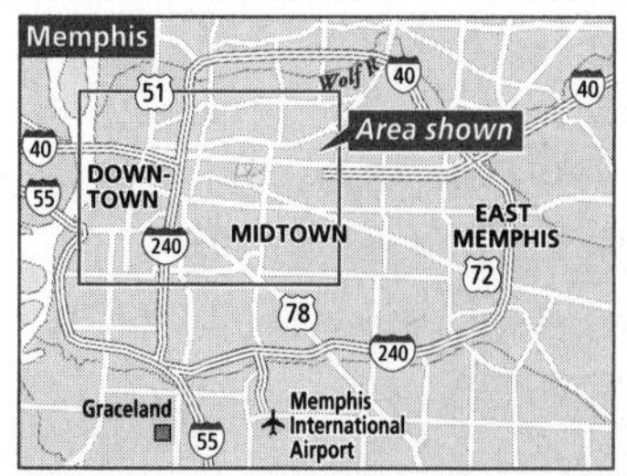

Burke's Book Store ★ Finds After decades in the same location, the region's best and most beloved independent bookstore relocated to new digs in the flourishing Cooper-Young neighborhood nearby. Burke's specializes in used, old, and collectible books. However, they have a good selection of new books as well. When favorite Memphis son John Grisham pens a new bestseller, this is usually where he holds his first book signing before embarking on national tours. 936 S. Cooper ✆ **901/278-7484.** www.burkesbooks.com.

Davis-Kidd Booksellers ★★ Kids Located in the prestigious Laurelwood Center shopping plaza, this large bookstore is a perennial favorite of Memphis readers. Books, periodicals, a cozy cafe, and a delightful assortment of unique gift items make for some of the most pleasurable browsing in the East Memphis area. A children's play area will keep the little ones occupied with fun and educational pursuits. Laurelwood Center, 387 Perkins Rd. Extended. ✆ **901/683-9801.** www.daviskidd.com.

DEPARTMENT STORES

Dillard's Dillard's is a Little Rock, Arkansas–based department store that has expanded across the country. Good prices and plenty of choices make this store a favorite of Memphis shoppers. You'll find Dillard's department stores in the Oak Court Mall (✆ **901/685-0382**), Wolfchase Galleria (✆ **901/383-1029**), and The Avenue Carriage Crossings (✆ **901/850-2229**).

Macy's Macy's department stores are the most upscale in Memphis. The **Oak Court Mall** location, at 4545 Poplar Ave. (✆ **901/766-4199**), is probably the most convenient for visitors to the city. Other stores can be in the Wolfchase Galleria, 2760 N. Germantown Pkwy. (✆ **901/937-2600**), and The Avenue Carriage Crossings (✆ **901/850-2229**).

DISCOUNT SHOPPING

Casino Factory Shoppes If you're willing to make the drive south to Mississippi—or if you're planning a day trip there anyway, to take in some Tunica casino action—you'll want to hunt for some bargains at the Mid-South's best outlet mall. Casino Factory Shoppes is a 40-store center boasting such brand names as Bass, Izod, Lane Bryant, GNC, Hibbet Sports, Nautica, Old Navy, rue21, and Zales. 13118 U.S. Hwy. 61 North, Robinsonville, MS. ✆ **662/363-1940.** www.casinofactoryshoppes.com.

Williams-Sonoma Clearance Outlet Williams-Sonoma, one of the country's largest mail-order companies, has a big distribution center here in the Memphis area, and this store is where they sell their discontinued lines and overstocks. If you're lucky, you just might find something that you wanted but couldn't afford when you saw it in the catalog. 4708 Spottswood Ave. ✆ **901/763-1500.** www.williams-sonoma.com.

FASHION

Men's

James Davis You'll find Giorgio Armani here for both men and women. In addition to tailored and casual clothing, sportswear, outerwear, and shoe brands such as Bruno Magli and Cole Haan, they carry women's apparel, accessories, and lingerie, as well as glamorous evening gowns. Laurelwood Center, 400 Grove Park Rd. ✆ **901/767-4640.** www.jamesdavisstore.com.

East Memphis Shopping

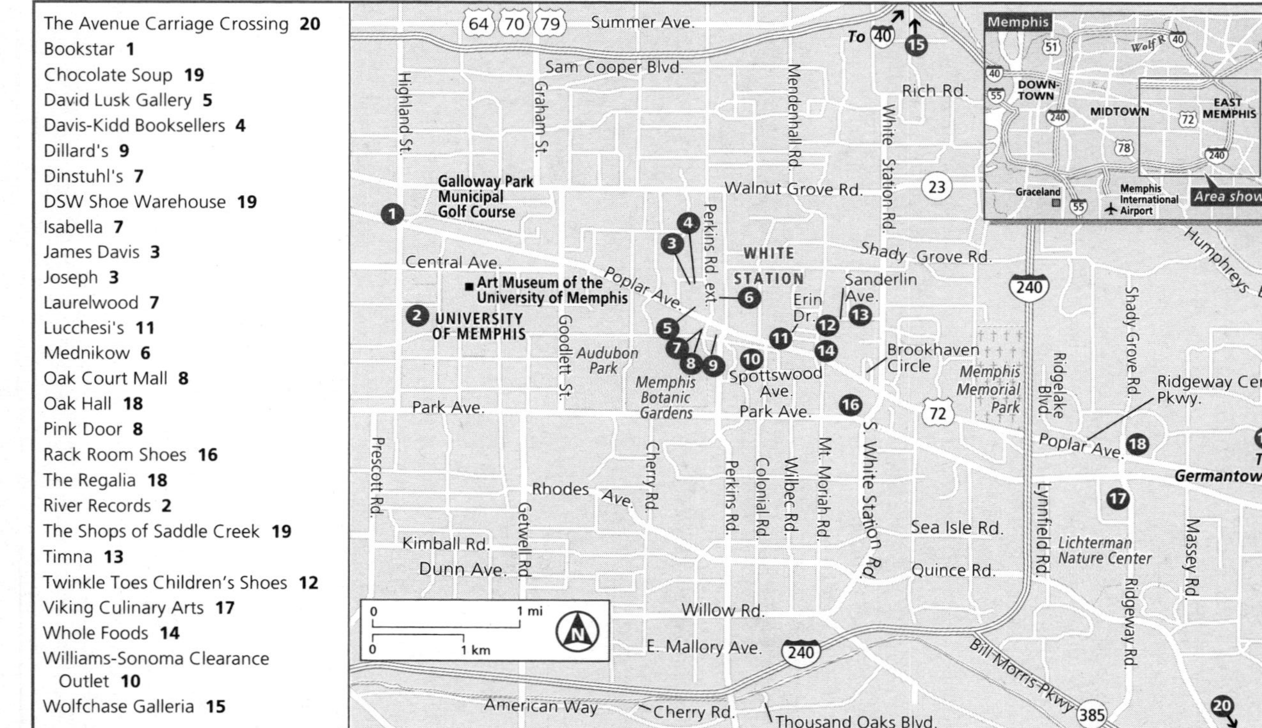

Lansky 126 ★ For the most stylish selection of jeans and clothing for young men, look to Lansky's—best known as "Clothier to The King." The Lansky Brothers have a long history dating back to the 1950s, when they dressed a young Elvis Presley in flashy threads. This shop, as well as other Lansky-brand clothing and gifts stores, is located in the lobby of the Peabody hotel in downtown Memphis. 149 Union Ave. ✆ **901/529-9070.** www.lanskybros.com.

Women's

Delphinium ★ Finds Hand-cut, scented soaps and a wide array of cosmetics, including Bare Escentuals, Mario Badescu, and Smashbox, are among the trendy brands offered in this vibrant new boutique. Reasonably priced jewelry and gifts are arranged in creative displays. Hot buys include hand-woven neck scarves and embroidered coin purses, as well as supple black satchels made of recycled bicycle tires. 107 G. E. Patterson Ave. ✆ **901/522-8600.** www.delphiniumboutique.com.

Isabella This chic women's boutique carries designers not usually found in other Memphis stores, such as Anlo, Rachel Pally, Trina Turk, and Ella Moss. If you're craving a stylish new pair of jeans, this is the place to scour. You might even find a belt or other invaluable accessory. Laurelwood Collection, 4615 Poplar Ave. ✆ **901/683-3538.**

Joseph ★ *Harper's Bazaar* named this high-fashion, East Memphis favorite as one of the top 95 specialty stores in America. With everything from cosmetics and shoes to coats by such noted designers as Zac Posen and Norma Kamali, it's easy to see why. 418 S. Grove Park. ✆ **901/767-1609.** www.josephstores.com.

Kittie Kyle Kollection You'll find this tony little shop in the Chickasaw Oaks Plaza. The boutique represents small designers from around the country, with an emphasis not on current fashion trends but on personal and functional style. There's also a wide selection of jewelry and accessories. 3092 Poplar Ave. ✆ **901/452-2323.**

The Pink Door If you're looking for classic, preppy clothing and accessories, check out this Lilly Pulitzer signature store in East Memphis. In addition to Lilly Pulitzer, the boutique carries such brands as Vineyard Vines, Elegant Baby, Molly B, and Lacoste. 4615 Poplar Ave. ✆ **901/682-2107.** www.thepinkdoormemphis.com.

Children's

Chocolate Soup This store is practically crammed with clothes that are colorful and easy to care for. Designs that grow with the child and hand-sewn appliqués make the clothing here unique. There are also plenty of brightly colored toys and assorted things to keep kids entertained. Germantown Village Square, Poplar Ave. and Germantown Pkwy. ✆ **901/754-7157.**

Twinkle Toes Children's Shoes Why shop department or discount stores when you can indulge your little tykes with customized service at this East Memphis boutique? From ECCO, Lacoste, and Oilily to New Balance, this kid-friendly retailer carries merchandise for infants through children's size 7. 5040 Sanderlin Ave. ✆ **901/766-2900.**

FOOD

Dinstuhl's Fine Candies Southern favorites, such as buttered-nut brittles, divinity, and chocolate-covered marshmallow "hash," are specialties at this local proprietor. The Dinstuhl family has been making fudge, chocolates, and other candies in Memphis for 5 generations. You'll find these sweets sold in venues around town, including many hotel gift shops. Laurelwood Shopping Center, 436 Grove Park. ✆ **901/682-3373.** www.dinstuhls.com.

Lucchesi's Fettuccine, tortellini, and other fresh-made pastas, along with homemade sauces, hearty breads, and take-and-bake pizzas, are prepared daily at this East Memphis market. Green garden salads as well as creamy prepared salads (potato, pasta, chicken, and the like) are available by the pound, along with Gorgonzola, balsamic, and other dressings. Sandwiches, panini, and ready-to-heat entrees such as eggplant lasagna and ravioli with meat sauce also tempt hungry shoppers. 540 S. Mendenhall (at Sanderlin). ✆ **901/766-9922.** www.lucchesis.com.

Miss Cordelia's ★★ Picnic goodies such as deli sandwiches, bakery-style cookies and cakes, and fresh fruits are available at this small local grocery store and market in Harbor Town, just north of the Pyramid. Bottled juices, teas, and even prepackaged sushi kits (chopsticks and wasabi included) from local restaurant Sekisui make it easy to grab a meal to enjoy at nearby Greenbelt Park on the Mississippi River. 737 Harbor Bend Rd. ✆ **901/526-4772.** www.misscordelias.com.

Whole Foods Market ★ Hands down the city's best grocery store, Whole Foods acquired this former Wild Oats Market in 2008. Along with the national chain's usual mix of organic produce, bins of bulk beans, rice and grains, and health-conscious frozen and packaged foods, there are deli-style counters offering fresh salads, meats, cheeses, sandwiches, pastries, breads, and other baked goods. 5022 Poplar Ave. ✆ **901/685-2293.** www.wholefoods.com.

GIFTS & SOUVENIRS

A. Schwab Dry Goods Store ★★★ Kids Moments This store is as much a Memphis institution and attraction as it is a place to shop. With its battered wood floors and tables covered with everything from plumbing supplies to religious paraphernalia, A. Schwab is a step back in time to the days of general stores. The offerings here are fascinating, even if you aren't in the market for a pair of size-74 men's overalls. You can still check out the 44 kinds of suspenders, the wall of voodoo love potions and powders, and the kiosk full of Elvis souvenirs. What else will you find at Schwab's? Bongo drums and crystal balls; shoeshine kits and corncob pipes; long thermal underwear and cotton petticoats; voodoo potions and praying hands; and plastic back-scratchers. Don't miss this place! 163 Beale St. ✆ **901/523-9782.**

Champion's Pharmacy and Herb Store Finds Offbeat doesn't begin to describe this one-of-a-kind medicine-wagon museum and old-school drugstore. Champion's sells an eye-popping array of herbal remedies and nostalgic patent medicines with such names as Packer's Pine Tar Soap, Lydia E. Pinkham Tonic, Red Clover Salve, Old Red Barn Ointment. 2369 Elvis Presley Blvd. (2¼ miles north of Graceland). ✆ **901/948-6622.** www.theherbalman.com.

The Peanut Shoppe Kids In business since 1951, this tiny but mightily aromatic shop is easily spotted: Look for the larger-than-life Mr. Peanut character tapping with his cane on the front window of the shop. Inside, you'll inhale the warm, toasty scent of all kinds of nuts—freshly roasted on the premises and still displayed in nostalgic glass counters and then weighed on old-fashioned scales. For fans of the monacled big guy, there's also lots of Mr. Peanut memorabilia on display. 24 S. Main St. ✆ **901/525-1115.** www.memphispeanutshoppe.com.

Viking Culinary Arts ★ Everything and the kitchen sink await inside this spacious retail store and demonstration area for Greenwood, Mississippi–based Viking ranges and appliances. Recently relocated from downtown to this East Memphis shopping center, the store offers top-of-the-line cookware and gadgets galore, making it a great place to shop for the cooking enthusiast on your gift list. 1215 Ridgeway Blvd. ✆ **901/763-3747.** www.vikinghomechef.com.

JEWELRY

Mednikow Open since 1891, this is one of the largest and most highly respected jewelry stores in Memphis, offering exquisite diamond jewelry, Rolex and Cartier timepieces, Mikimoto pearls, David Yurman designs, and other beautiful baubles. 474 Perkins Rd. Extended. ✆ **901/767-2100.** http://mednikow.com.

Timna Adjacent to the East Memphis Doubletree, Timna features hand-woven fashions and hand-painted silks by nationally acclaimed artists. A broad selection of contemporary jewelry includes fanciful pieces made of metals and stones as well as harder-edged industrial designs, with prices ranging from $40 to several hundred dollars. 5101 Sanderlin Centre. ✆ **901/683-9369.**

MALLS/SHOPPING CENTERS

The Avenue Carriage Crossing The metropolitan area's newest mall is an open-air shopping plaza in the far southeastern reaches of Shelby County, near the FedEx World Headquarters in Collierville, Tennessee, and close to the Mississippi state line. Dillard's and Macy's department stores anchor the center, which also includes scores of men's and women's apparel stores such as Aeropostale, Hollister, Talbots, and Jos. A. Bank. Specialty stores include Yankee Candle, Build-A-Bear Workshop, Bed Bath & Beyond, and Barnes & Noble. Among the dozens of eateries are upscale chains Carrabba's Italian Grill and Bonefish Grill, along with a Starbucks and Ben & Jerry's. From downtown Memphis, take I-40 west to I-240 south, to the Bill Morris Parkway (Hwy. 385), and exit at Houston Levee Road. ✆ **901/854-8240.** www.shoptheavenue.com.

Chickasaw Oaks Village ★ La Baguette bakery and Just for Lunch, a cafe popular with well-to-do "ladies-who-lunch," are top dining draws at this indoor shopping center in Midtown. Interior designers, salons, and galleries such as Perry Nicole Fine Art, and upscale ladies' clothing boutiques Ella and the Kittie Kyle Kollection, have beautifully appointed shops here, where you can spend a delightful afternoon of retail therapy. 3092 Poplar Ave. ✆ **901/794-6022.** www.chickasawoaksvillage.com.

Laurelwood ★★ Conveniently located in East Memphis, about halfway between downtown and the suburbs of Germantown and Cordova, this upscale shopping plaza has an enviable variety of thriving retail options, including popular restaurants such as Grove Grill and the wonderful Davis-Kidd Booksellers. The immaculate stores here specialize in top-quality antiques, home furnishings, stationery, and apparel, featuring well-known chains such as Chico's. Poplar Ave. and Perkins Rd. Extended. ✆ **901/682-8436.** www.laurelwoodmemphis.com.

Oak Court Mall ★ With both a Macy's and a Dillard's and dozens of specialty shops, this mall has parklike landscaping with mature shade trees in the heart of the city. It's also the shopping mall that's most conveniently located to downtown and East Memphis. 4465 Poplar Ave., at Perkins Rd. ✆ **901/682-8928.** www.oakcourtmall.com.

Peabody Place Sadly, this massive new downtown development bustled with clothing boutiques, gift shops, a 22-screen movie theater, and great clubs and restaurants a few years ago. No more. A victim of the recession, the mall is mostly vacant, with only a few tenants still standing. 150 Peabody Place. No phone. www.peabodyplace.com.

The Regalia Several vacant storefronts also haunt this once-swank shopping plaza next door to the Embassy Suites Hotel and just off I-240; yet, it's worth a look. Cokesbury still has a nice Christian bookstore here, while Oak Hall does steady business selling upscale men's and women's apparel. In addition to a Ruth's Chris Steakhouse, the center has three of Memphis's best locally owned restaurants—Salsa, Owen Brennan's, and (inside Embassy Suites) Grisanti's. Poplar Ave. and Ridgeway Rd. ✆ **901/767-0100.**

The Shops of Saddle Creek Technically located in the city of Germantown, Saddle Creek is considered part of the greater Memphis area. The affluent bedroom community's retail scene is viewed as more elite than anywhere else's. Saddle Creek includes familiar national chain stores such as Chico's, Banana Republic, Crabtree & Evelyn, Ann Taylor, and GapKids, as well as restaurants and small shops. 5855 River Bend Rd. ✆ **901/761-2571.** www.shopsofsaddlecreek.com.

Wolfchase Galleria The Cordova suburb's biggest mall is this mammoth (more than 1-million-sq.-ft.) retail center out near the interstate. It includes Dillard's and Macy's department stores, plus scores of restaurants and specialty shops. From Pottery Barn finds and Godiva chocolates to Looney Tunes toys at the Warner Brothers store, this always-crowded mall also has a children's carousel and a multiplex cinema with stadium-style seating. 2760 N. Germantown Pkwy. ✆ **901/381-2769.** www.wolfchasegalleria.com.

MARKETS

Memphis Farmers' Market (Kids) Each Saturday morning at the train station downtown, farmers from throughout the region bring their produce to sell at this open-air market. Look for red-ripe Tennessee tomatoes; turnip, mustard, and collard greens; and other Southern crops. Children's activities and a great community camaraderie pervade this market, which operates seasonally from May through the end of October. 545 S. Main St. ✆ **901/575-0580.** www.memphisfarmersmarket.com.

Memphis Flea Market A bargain-browser's paradise or a junk collector's dream, this flea market, known locally as "The Big One," is held on the third weekend of every month. Hundreds of vendors hawk all manner of goods, from discount jeans and perfumes to antiques and other collectibles. 955 Early Maxwell Blvd., Mid-South Fairgrounds. ✆ **901/276-3532.** www.memphisfleamarket.com.

MUSIC

Goner Records ★ Take a stroll in the Cooper-Young neighborhood, and you'll stumble across this home-grown late-'70s-style record shop. Punk, funk, rock, rhythm-and-blues, and everything in between, coexist here. Flip through bins of vinyl LPs, old 45s, and CDs for affordably priced finds like late Delta-blues great Junior Kimbrough's releases on the Fat Possum label. Sun, Stax, Volt, Loverly, and Goner are among the other better-known Memphis-label rarities here. Goner also sells turntables and doubles as a fledgling indie record company. While you're here, ask for details about Gonerfest, one the region's most buzzed-about, up-and-coming annual music events. 2152 Young Ave. ✆ **901/722-0095.** www.goner-records.com.

Memphis Music Recordings by legendary blues men such as Leadbelly and Memphis Minnie are a specialty of this otherwise touristy music shop that also sells Memphis souvenirs and T-shirts with images of iconic blues, rock, and jazz musicians. Watch your wallet, and you may want to consider doing your shopping *before* imbibing in the Beale Street bars. 149 Beale St. ✆ **901/526-5047.**

River Records The weathered little storefront on the scabby outskirts of the University of Memphis campus may look abandoned, but it's not. Once the city's premier record shop for serious collectors, River Records is still in business after 4 decades, selling comic books, posters, and vinyl records. 822 S. Highland St. ✆ **901/324-1757.**

Shangri-La Records ★★ Finds With Memphis's best selection of new and used rockabilly, as well as soul, R&B, reggae, and rock, Shangri-La is a bona fide gold mine for bargain browsers with offbeat musical appetites. It's all stuffed inside this nondescript old house in Midtown. Hang here to get the latest on what's happening in the local music scene. 1916 Madison Ave. ✆ **901/274-1916.** www.shangri.com.

MUSICAL INSTRUMENTS

Amro Music Stores A family-owned and -operated store that's been in business since 1921, Amro is a name that has become synonymous with music. The small business sells a large array of musical instruments, as well as sheet music and accessories. There are several locations around town, but this large showroom in Midtown is the flashiest. 2918 Poplar Ave. ✆ **901/323-8888.** www.amromusic.com.

Gibson Beale Street Showcase Not only can you watch Gibson guitars being manufactured, and hear them performed, you may also purchase a variety of Gibson and Epiphone stringed instruments and other merchandise. Public tour times vary, so call ahead and make a reservation before you head out. 145 Lt. George W. Lee Ave. ✆ **800/444-2766** or 901/544-7998. www.gibsonmemphis.com.

Memphis Drum Shop ★ At the edge of the Cooper-Young district is this Midtown retailer that's been selling drums for 3 decades. The knowledgeable staff will help you find new, used, vintage, and custom drums, cymbals, parts, and accessories. Percussion instruments are also repaired, and can even be rented, at this fun shop. 878 S. Cooper St. ✆ **901/276-2328.** www.memphisdrumshop.com.

SHOES & BOOTS

In addition to the following shoe and boot stores, you'll find an excellent selection of shoes at the **Dillard's** department store in the Mall of Memphis shopping mall.

DSW Shoe Warehouse With savings of 20% to 50% off standard retail prices and an excellent selection of major-label shoes, this store is open 7 days a week. Germantown Village Square, Germantown Pkwy., at Poplar Ave. ✆ **901/755-2204.** www.dswshoe.com.

Oak Hall Men with exquisite taste and deep pockets have turned to this exclusive clothier for nearly 150 years. The store sells men's and women's clothing as well as top-of-the-line shoes by Mark Mason, Gravati, Ermenegildo Zegna, and Canali. 6150 Poplar. ✆ **901/761-3580.** www.oakhall.com.

Rack Room Shoes In East Memphis, 1 block west of Poplar Avenue, this large store offers good discounts on Timberland, Rockport, Nike, Reebok, and Bass shoes, among other lines. Eastgate Shopping Center, 5110 Park Ave. ✆ **901/682-1584.** www.rackroomshoes.com.

20 Memphis After Dark

For a century, Memphis has nurtured one of the liveliest club scenes in the South, and the heart and soul of that nightlife has always been Beale Street. Whether your interest is blues, rock, opera, ballet, or Broadway musicals, you'll probably find entertainment to your liking on this lively street. However, there is more to Memphis nightlife than just Beale Street. In downtown Memphis, historic South Main Street has emerged as a fledgling arts community, with galleries, boutiques, and a growing number of buzz-worthy restaurants. You'll also find several theater companies performing in Midtown near Overton Square, which has several popular bars, restaurants, and a few clubs. Nightlife is livelier in the gay-friendly Cooper-Young neighborhood, at the intersection of Cooper Street and Young Avenue. Delis, boutiques, and a handful of excellent restaurants keep the young crowds coming.

Other places to check for live music are downtown alleys and the respective rooftops of The Peabody hotel and the Madison Hotel. Each summer, the hotels sponsor sunset cocktail parties that are extremely popular. Sometimes, after-work parties are held in alleyways closed off from traffic.

To find out about what's happening in the entertainment scene while you're in town, check with the ***Memphis Flyer*** (www.memphisflyer.com), Memphis's free arts-and-entertainment weekly, which comes out on Thursday. You'll find it in convenience, grocery, and music stores; some restaurants; and nightclubs. You could also check the website of the ***Commercial Appeal,*** Memphis's morning daily newspaper. The Friday edition has thorough events listings.

For tickets to sporting events and performances at the FedExForum and other venues, your best bet is to contact **Ticketmaster** (✆ **800/745-3000;** www.ticketmaster.com).

1 BEALE STREET & DOWNTOWN

Beale Street is the epicenter of Memphis's nightclub scene. This street, where the blues gained widespread recognition, is now the site of scores of nightclubs, bars, restaurants, and souvenir shops. Relatively tame and family-friendly by day, the neon district gets quite rowdy after dark, when barricades allow for pedestrians only. While blues purists looking for authenticity may be disappointed at the predominance of local cover bands that reign here, others, including curious conventioneers and hard-drinking partiers, seem eager enough to accept the commercialism that has homogenized much of Beale Street. For links to various clubs and other businesses along Beale, click on **www.bealestreet.com**.

Clustered around Beale Street are many other notable restaurants and bars with after-hours activity. Some, such as Earnestine and Hazel's, are tired-looking, time-worn stalwarts that boast more bar credibility than some of the swank new, citified "juke joints," such as Ground Zero Blues Club. Nevertheless, there's something for just about all entertainment appetites within the span of a few short blocks.

Alfred's ★ This spacious club on the corner of Third and Beale has rock 'n' roll most weekends, with a variety of bands currently packing the house. With its corner location and upstairs, outdoor patio, Alfred's also makes a great vantage point for people-watching and late-night drinking and eating. The kitchen's open until 3am. 197 Beale St. ✆ **901/525-3711.** www.alfredsonbeale.com. Cover $5–$10.

B. B. King's Blues Club ★★ Moments Yes, the club's 80-something namesake "King of the Blues" does play here occasionally, though not on a regular basis. However, any night of the week you can catch blazing blues played by one of the best house bands in town. Because of the name, this club attracts famous musicians who have been known to get up and jam with whoever is on stage that night. Upstairs, a new third-floor restaurant, called Itta Bena, is named for B. B.'s Mississippi hometown. 147 Beale St. ✆ **800/443-0972** or 901/524-5464; www.bbkingsclub.com. Cover $7–$10 (usually $50–$170 for B. B.'s increasingly infrequent, but always sold-out, concerts).

Impressions

Beale Street is the life to me. We that play the blues, we're proud of it. It's somethin' religious.

—B. B. King

Blues City Cafe ★★ This club across the street from B. B. King's Blues Club takes up two old storefronts, with live blues wailing in one room (called the Band Box) and an excellent, casual restaurant serving steaks, tamales, and barbecue in the other. If you're looking to tank up on good food before a night of crawling the clubs along Beale Street, this is the best place to do it. 138–140 Beale St. ✆ **901/526-3637.** www.bluescitycafe.com. Cover $4–$5.

Center for Southern Folklore ★ Finds After bouncing between various locations on or around Beale Street, this offbeat treasure that's part coffeehouse/part folk-art flea market has landed in Pembroke Square. Warm and welcoming, it's a laid-back space where you can get a meal or some munchies, sip a latte or a beer, surf the Internet, or buy anything from books, CDs, and postcards to handmade quilts and cornhusk dolls. Best of all, you can hear the Delta's most authentic roots musicians performing at almost any time of day. 119 S. Main St. ✆ **901/525-3655.** www.southernfolklore.com. No cover.

Earnestine & Hazel's ★ Finds Although it's actually 4 blocks south of Beale Street, this downtown dive, which was once a sundry store that fronted for an upstairs brothel, has become one of Memphis's hottest nightspots. In 2004, it was the greasy backdrop for the Jack White/Loretta Lynn video *Portland, Oregon.* On Friday and Saturday nights, there's a piano bar early; and then later in the night, the best jukebox in Memphis keeps things on a slow simmer. Things don't really get cookin' here until after midnight. 531 S. Main St. ✆ **901/523-9754.** No cover.

Ground Zero Blues Club Oscar-winning actor Morgan Freeman co-owns this new nightclub that's an exact replica of the one he has operated for years in nearby Clarksdale, Mississippi. Blues music 4 nights a week with no cover charge and Southern-style eats are plusses at this venue. On the down side, with its perfectly graffitied walls and faux juke-joint decor, you might not be able to shake the notion that this club that feels so right in the gritty Mississippi Delta seems out of place next door to a luxury hotel (the Westin Beale Street). 158 Lt. George W. Lee St. ✆ **901/522-0130.** www.groundzerobluesclub.com. No cover.

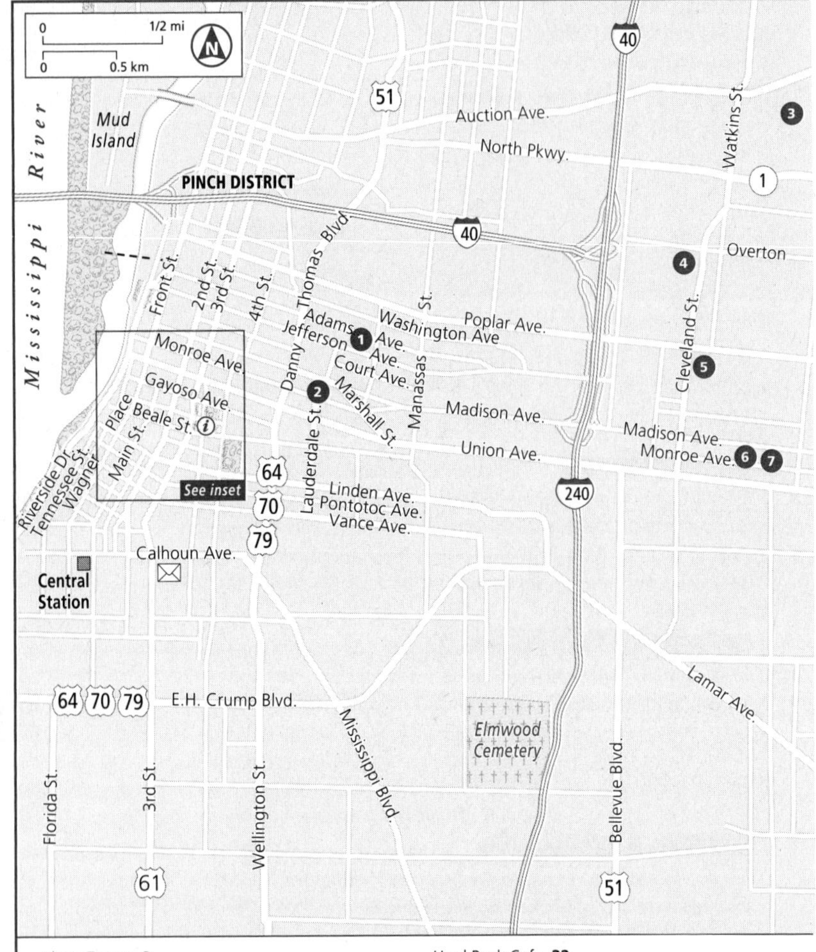

- Alex's Tavern **8**
- Alfred's **33**
- Automatic Slim's Tonga Club **27**
- Automatic Slim's Tonga Club **9**
- B.B. King's Blues Club **20**
- Bluefin **22**
- Blues City Cafe **23**
- Boscos Squared **13**
- Center for Southern Folklore **24**
- Club 152 **21**
- Earnestine & Hazel's **19**
- Flying Saucer Draught Emporium **22**
- Ground Zero Blues Club **35**
- Hard Rock Cafe **32**
- Hi-Tone Cafe **10**
- Huey's **12**
- Itta Bena **30**
- Java Cabana **15**
- King's Palace Café **29**
- Kudzu's **2**
- Le Chardonnay Wine Bar **14**
- Levitt Shell **11**
- Minglewood Hall **7**
- Metro Memphis **4**
- Mollie Fontaine Lounge **1**
- Newby's **25**

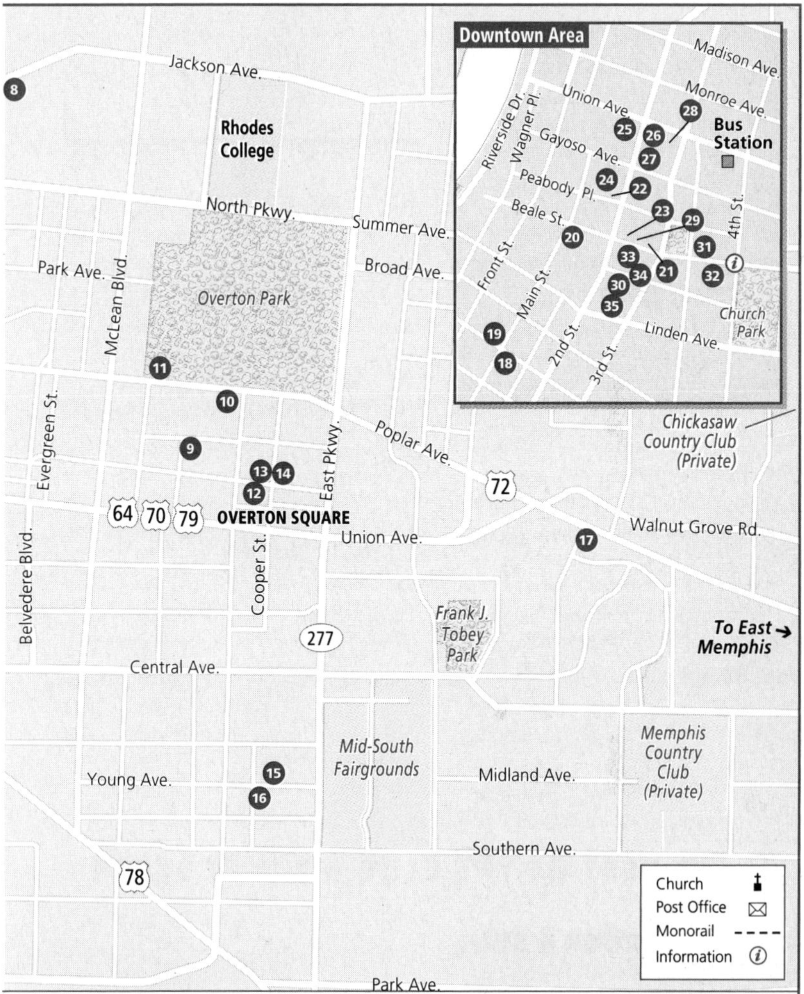

The New Daisy Theatre **31**
P and H Cafe **6**
The Peabody Lobby Bar **28**
Pumping Station **5**
Raiford's **18**
The Rendezvous **26**
Rum Boogie Cafe **21**
Senses **17**
Sole Restaurant and Raw Bar **34**
Wild Bill's **3**
Young Avenue Deli **16**

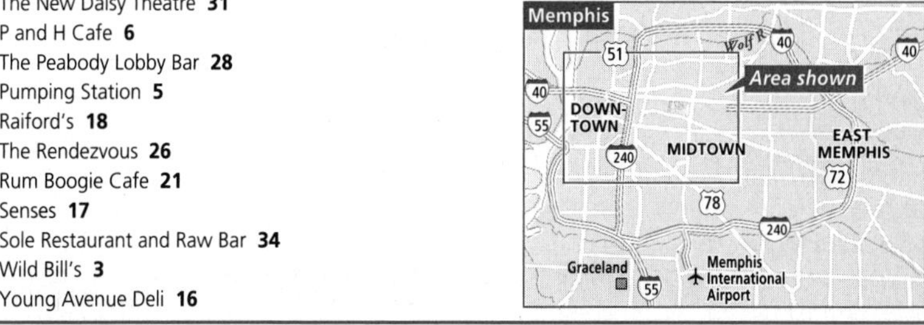

Hard Rock Cafe If you want the obligatory T-shirt, you'll want to check out this Hard Rock location that's, as expected, packed with rock and blues memorabilia. Look for gold musical notes on the brick sidewalk out front that celebrate famous Memphis musicians through the years. Live music is offered only occasionally, and it's usually staged in conjunction with local charity benefits. Impress your friends with this bit of trivia: The global Hard Rock Cafe chain was founded by Isaac Tigrett, a philanthropist-entrepreneur and former Memphis resident. 315 Beale St. ✆ **901/529-0007.** www.hardrock.com. Cover usually around $5 after 9pm.

Impressions

I'd rather be here than any place I know.

—W. C. Handy, referring to Beale Street

King's Palace Café ★ With its battered wood floor, this bar has the most authentic, old-time feel of any club on Beale Street. Though primarily a restaurant serving decent Cajun food, including a knockout gumbo, there's frequent live jazz and blues on tap here. Popular with tour groups and locals alike, King's Palace has been a consistently good Beale Street venue for many years now. 162 Beale St. ✆ **901/521-1851.** www.kingspalacecafe.com. No cover.

New Daisy Theatre The stage at the New Daisy has long been the place to see regional and national rock bands, but these days the theater books a surprisingly wide variety of entertainment, from boxing matches to touring alternative-rock bands. Bob Dylan filmed a video here from his Grammy-winning *Time Out of Mind* CD (fitting, because Memphis musicians were featured on that work). More recent acts to have played the venue include hometown heroes Justin Timberlake and the North Mississippi Allstars. 330 Beale St. ✆ **901/525-8981.** www.newdaisy.com. Ticket prices vary according to event.

Rum Boogie Cafe Dozens of autographed guitars, including ones signed by Carl Perkins, Stevie Ray Vaughan, Joe Walsh, George Thorogood, and other rock and blues guitar wizards, hang from the ceiling at the Rum Boogie. There's live music nightly, with guest artists alternating with the house band, which plays everything from blues to country. 182 Beale St. ✆ **901/528-0150.** www.rumboogie.com. Cover $3–$5 after 9pm.

2 THE REST OF THE CLUB & MUSIC SCENE

ACOUSTIC, ROCK & SOUL

Levitt Shell In lovely Overton Park, this Hollywood Bowl–like amphitheater has a fascinating history. Built during the Depression by the WPA, it initially hosted musical theater and orchestral concerts. But on July 30, 1954, a relatively unknown Elvis Presley opened for Slim Whitman, in what some musicologists call the first-ever rock-'n'-roll show. Over the years, musicians ranging from Johnny Cash to the Grateful Dead took to the stage, before it fell into disrepair. Preservationists rallied to revitalize the hall, which recently saw the launch of a major, national tour by local rock band Lucero. 1930 Poplar Ave. ✆ **901/272-5159.** www.levittshell.org. Ticket prices vary.

Minglewood Hall ★ Currently the most popular live-music venue in town, it's also one of the newest. A year ago, Minglewood opened in a vacant Midtown building that was formerly a bread factory and then a music store. The midsize hall has an elevated stage and can hold up to 1,500 dance-happy concertgoers. Neko Case, Old Crow Medicine Show, and Lyle Lovett are among the entertainers who've played here so far. 1555 Madison Ave. ✆ **901/312-6058.** www.minglewoodhall.com. Ticket prices vary.

Newby's Located close to the University of Memphis, this cavernous club is a popular college hangout with two stages—one large, one small. There's live rock, mostly by local and regional acts, most nights of the week. Funk and alternative rock have been pretty popular here of late. While you're there, try their new energy cocktail: the Rock Star. 539 S. Highland St. ✆ **901/452-8408.** www.newbysmemphis.com. Cover $5–$10.

Wild Bill's ★★★ Beer sells by the quart, but you'll have to bring your own hard liquor to this gritty urban juke joint that's also as many light-years away from the glitz of Beale Street as you can get. Locals and rhythm-and-blues-loving tourists pack the nondescript room and sit in hard-back chairs at long tables before the band stars cranking out soul and blues classics. The music is hypnotizing, and sweaty patrons—young and old, black and white—drink and dance with abandon. If you want an authentic Memphis music experience, check it out. 1580 Vollintine Ave. ✆ **901/726-5473.** Cover $5–$10.

Impressions

People ask me what I miss about Memphis. And I said, "Everything."

—Elvis Presley

FOLK

Java Cabana Located just down from the corner of Cooper and Young streets, this 1950s retro coffeehouse has occasional poetry readings and live acoustic music, singer-songwriters, and open-mic nights. Although you can't get alcohol here, you can indulge in all manner of coffees—and enjoy a smoke-free environment. 2170 Young St. ✆ **901/272-7210.** No cover.

3 BARS, PUBS & LOUNGES

BARS

Downtown

Automatic Slim's Tonga Club ★★ With funky decor, a cool menu, and live music on weekends, Automatic Slim's Tonga Club attracts the arty and upscale 20-, 30- and 40-something crowd. Yummy Popsicle-flavored cocktails are a bar specialty, and the mimosas are popular for Sunday brunch. 83 S. Second St. ✆ **901/525-7948.** www.automaticslimsmemphis.com.

Itta Bena ★★ Named for the tiny Mississippi town where B. B. King was born, this restaurant on the third floor of the blues legend's namesake nightclub seems more like a sophisticated speakeasy or a cabaret lounge than just another eatery. It's got dark lighting from blue chandeliers and windows that look down onto Beale Street, and a cozy bar that's perfect for enjoying a meal and drinks. Having a glass of wine or a cocktail here, above the rowdy blues club below, feels like a secret indulgence. Be aware that you must climb two flights of stairs to reach this bar, which is inaccessible to people in wheelchairs or for those with limited mobility. 143 Beale Street. ✆ **901/578-3031.**

Mollie Fontaine Lounge ★ Beloved local restaurateur Karen Blockman Carrier opened up this suave martini bar and lounge a few years ago in a restored Victorian house that dates back to 1886. Located on a quiet residential street near the Medical Center in Midtown, Mollie's is a classy yet comfortable place to enjoy mellow piano music while sipping cocktails in fashionable surroundings. Tapas and other small-plate items are on the menu. Music starts at 9pm, and there's no cover. 679 Adams Ave. ✆ **901/524-1886.**

The Peabody Lobby Bar ★ There's no more elegant place in Memphis for a drink, but be sure you drop in well after the crowds—who gather to watch the Peabody ducks do their daily march—have dispersed, usually shortly after 5pm. Piano music is featured in the evenings. If you're a middle-aged or older traveler with refined tastes and an appreciation of historic, Old South charm, you'll feel right at home relaxing here with a glass of bourbon or merlot. The Peabody, 149 Union Ave. ✆ **901/529-4000.** www.peabodymemphis.com.

The Rendezvous Although best known for its barbecued ribs and waiters with attitude, the Rendezvous also has a big beer hall upstairs from the restaurant. It's a noisy, convivial spot, and a convenient place to start a night on the town or kill some time while you wait for a table in the restaurant. 52 S. Second St. ✆ **901/523-2746.** www.hogsfly.com.

Midtown

Alex's Tavern Bikers, working professionals, barflies, and nearby Rhodes College students all feel at home at this laid-back bar. You won't find many tourists here, but if you want to hang with the locals, play a little shuffleboard, and groove to the jukebox, stop in for a cheeseburger and an ice-cold beer. 1445 Jackson Ave. ✆ **901/278-9086.**

Hi-Tone Cafe ★★ Cutting-edge acts along the lines of the Disco Biscuits and Michelle Shocked headline frequent late-night gigs at this ultrahip hangout, located across the street from the Memphis College of Art in Overton Park. Elvis Costello liked it so much he and the Imposters filmed a live concert here for their DVD release *Club Date: Live in Memphis.* 1913 Poplar Ave. ✆ **901/278-8663.** www.hitonememphis.com.

Huey's This funky old dive is a Midtown Memphis institution, known as the home of the best burgers in town. However, it's also a great place to sip a beer. But be warned: Spitting cocktail toothpicks at the ceiling is a favorite pastime of patrons. Sounds silly, but it's fun. Graffiti on the walls is also encouraged. 1927 Madison Ave. ✆ **901/726-4372.** www.hueyburger.com.

Kudzu's Named for the creeping wild vines that smother Southern landscapes in Chia Pet–like green shag carpeting, Kudzu's is a longtime local bar favorite with an unmistakable, deep-green paint job. Wildly popular for its trivia quiz nights, the place has a friendly Irish-pub sort of vibe. Pints of Guinness, along with other beers, are available, as is wine. The grub is pretty good, too; Kudzu's has excellent burgers, along with salads, sandwiches, and tamales. 603 Monroe Ave. ✆ **901/525-4924.**

Le Chardonnay Wine Bar Near the ragged-looking former entertainment district known as Overton Square sits Memphis's original wine bar. With a dark, wine-cellar feel, Le Chardonnay tends to attract casual young executive types, as well as people heading to or from nearby Playhouse on the Square. Consistently lauded for having the best wine list in town, Le Chardonnay is a time-honored institution and a great place to have a drink, if you want to feel like one of the locals. 2094 Madison. ✆ **901/725-1375.**

P and H Cafe A dilapidated-looking hole in the wall as well as a beloved neighborhood landmark, the P & H ("Poor and Hungry") is a smoke-choked bar that has been a favored hangout for drinking, smoking, and shooting pool since 1961. Beer flows freely, washing down such cheap eats as spaghetti and meat sauce, stuffed burgers, and chicken-fried steak (about $7 each). Unthinkable a generation ago, the P & H now hosts karaoke on some nights. 1532 Madison Ave. ✆ **901/726-0906.** www.pandhcafe.com.

Sole Restaurant & Raw Bar Inside the Westin Beale Street is this casual, new night spot where patrons can sip wine, suck down some oysters, or watch the game on TV over some beers. Located in a corner nook just steps from the FedExForum and the Gibson Guitar factory, this is a perfect place to kick back with friends and just chill. Westin Hotel, 221 S. Third. ✆ **901/334-5950.** www.westinmemphis.com.

Young Avenue Deli ★ Buzzing with activity at all times of the afternoon and evening, this hangout is not so much a delicatessen as a trendy gathering place for young adults who like to drink coffee and/or alcohol. Way laid-back, the deli and sidewalk patio out front are at the epicenter of coolness in the Cooper-Young neighborhood. There's an impressive list of beers by the bottle and draft, and munchies such as Greek salads, chili-cheese fries, and a build-your-own quesadilla station. 2119 Young Ave. ✆ **901/278-0034.** www.youngavenuedeli.com. Cover $5–$20, depending on bands playing.

East Memphis

Belmont Grill A great neighborhood bar, Belmont is a popular watering hole for locals who like to stop by after work to unwind. As plain as a rundown roadhouse, it's unpretentious and casual. The eatery, which some might call a "greasy spoon," also happens to serve terrific pub grub. Try the cheeseburgers or go for the catfish po' boys. 4970 Poplar Ave. ✆ **901/767-0305.**

Fox and Hound Perhaps the most gregarious sports bar in town, this preppie watering hole is within walking distance of the East Memphis Doubletree Hotel. It's a favorite choice for fans who want to catch a game on a big-screen while kicking back with buddies over beer and billiards. Corporate road-warrior business travelers will also feel at home here. 5101 Sanderlin Ave. ✆ **901/763-2013.** www.fhrg.com.

BREWPUBS

Boscos Squared Live jazz sizzles on Sundays at this popular Overton Square brew pub, known for its Famous Flaming Stone Beer. Locally owned, Boscos also boasts a terrific restaurant menu with great wood-fired-oven pizzas. An outdoor patio is perfect for large parties. If you're a cheap date (or you just like saving money), you'll appreciate that parking is free and much less hassle than at the downtown and Beale Street brewpubs. Plus, the food is better. 2120 Madison Ave. ✆ **901/432-2222.** www.boscosbeer.com.

Flying Saucer Draught Emporium When Beale Street becomes too crowded, the locals make tracks to this beer lovers' paradise right around the corner. Frequent music and a lively pub atmosphere, with diversions such as trivia contests, keep the blues at bay and patrons satisfied—and coming back for more. 130 Peabody Place. ✆ **901/523-8536.** www.beerknurd.com.

DANCE CLUBS

Club 152 ★ Beale Street's best dance club is a favorite with energetic young straight adults who bump and grind the night away on three floors. DJs crank up techno, house, and alternative dance music for revelers who don't usually stop until the early-morning hours. 152 Beale St. ✆ **901/544-7011.** www.club152memphis.com. Cover varies.

Raiford's With a notorious history of opening, closing, then reopening, you'll want to call ahead before you disco on down to this pimped-out dive a few blocks from Beale Street. Its proprietor, Robert "Hollywood" Raiford, retired in 2007, after 32 years at the helm of the dance floor. Now he's reportedly back, DJ-ing at the wildly popular disco club on Fridays and Saturdays, the only 2 nights Raiford's is open. Seventies music, mirror balls, 40-ounce beers, and a strict "no-discrimination" policy (signs are posted to that effect) have made this place worth the hassle. Keep your fingers crossed that it's open when you're in Memphis and feel the urge to do the Hustle. 115 Vance Ave. ✆ **901/525-9210.** www.hollywooddisco.com. Cover varies.

Senses A nondescript warehouse in a dreary part of Midtown by day, this sizzling dance club comes alive late at night. A strict dress code (no jeans) helps maintain the upscale vibe, as gorgeous male and female 20-somethings weave between Senses' six different clubs, sipping fancy cocktails and grinding into the wee hours. 2866 Poplar Ave. ✆ **901/454-4081.** www.sensesmemphis.com. Cover $5–$10.

GAY BARS

Backstreet Memphis Like at Memphis's other few gay bars, karaoke and cabaret drag shows keep things lively here, but it's dancing that draw many young, energetic party-goers to this Midtown nightspot. 2018 Court Ave. ✆ **901/276-5522.** www.backstreetmemphis.com.

Metro Memphis A hot dance club that also offers weekly karaoke and drag shows, this popular gay bar is one where lesbians and straight party-goers can feel at home. 1349 Autumn St. ✆ **901/274-8010.** www.metromemphisclub.com.

The Pumping Station Darts, billiards, and explicit videos are after-hours pursuits at this discrete Midtown haunt. There's also a crudely constructed treehouse on the patio out back. A strictly gay-male bar, it's known for catering to a slightly more mature crowd. 1382 Poplar Ave. ✆ **901/272-7600.** www.pumpingstationmemphis.com.

4 THE PERFORMING ARTS

With Beale Street forming the heart of the city's nightclub scene, it seems appropriate that Memphis's main performance hall, the Orpheum Theatre, is located here as well. A night out at the theater can also include a visit to a blues club after the show.

CLASSICAL MUSIC, OPERA & BALLET

Although blues and rock 'n' roll dominate the Memphis music scene, the city also manages to support a symphony, an opera, and a ballet. The symphony performs, and big-name performers and lecturers often appear, at the 2,100-seat **Cannon Center for the Performing Arts,** 255 N. Main St. (✆ **800/726-0915;** www.thecannoncenter.com), adjacent to the downtown center. Another of the city's premier performing-arts venues is the **Orpheum Theatre,** 203 S. Main St. (✆ **901/525-3000;** www.orpheum-memphis.com), which was built in 1928 as a vaudeville hall. The ornate, gilded plasterwork on the walls and ceiling gives this theater the elegance of a classic opera house and makes this the most spectacular performance hall in the city.

In addition to performing at the Cannon Center, the orchestra also occasionally performs at other venues, including the suburban Germantown Performing Arts Center and outdoor concerts at the lovely Dixon Gallery and Gardens. The extremely popular **Sunset Symphony,** an outdoor extravaganza held on the banks of Tom Lee Park overlooking the Mississippi River each year as part of the Memphis in May International Festival, is always a highlight of the symphony season and one of the city's definitive Memphis experiences. The **Memphis Symphony Orchestra** (© **901/324-3627;** www.memphissymphony.org) box office is at 3100 Walnut Grove Rd. (tickets $12–$76).

Opera Memphis (© **901/257-3100;** www.operamemphis.org) also performs at both the Orpheum and Cannon Center, annually staging three or four operas (tickets $20–$70). The company, which for more than 50 years has been staging the best of classical opera and innovative new works for appreciative Memphis audiences, also has built a reputation for its extensive educational outreach program.

Ballet Memphis (© **901/737-7322;** www.balletmemphis.org), widely regarded as the city's crown jewel of performing-arts groups, performs at both the Orpheum and Cannon Center (tickets $20–$70). For sentimentalists, the highlight of each season is the annual holiday performance of *The Nutcracker,* but exciting world premieres and contemporary dance works also rate high priority on the company's mission.

THEATER

Memphis has a relatively well-developed theater scene with numerous opportunities to attend live stage productions around the city. **Theatre Memphis,** 630 Perkins Rd. Extended (© **901/682-8323;** www.theatrememphis.org), is a commendable community theater that's been around for more than 75 years. Located on the edge of Audubon Park, it has garnered regional and national awards for excellence. There are two stages here—a 435-seat main theater that does standards, and a 100-seat, black-box theater, known as Next Stage, where less mainstream productions are staged.

Staging productions of a higher artistic caliber are two sister theaters in Midtown: **Circuit Playhouse,** 1705 Poplar Ave. (© **901/726-4656**), and **Playhouse on the Square,** 51 S. Cooper St. (© **901/726-4656;** www.playhouseonthesquare.org), are the only professional theaters in Memphis, and between them they stage about 25 productions each year. Off-Broadway plays are the rule at the Circuit Playhouse (with the occasional premiere), while at Playhouse on the Square, Broadway-worthy dramas, comedies, and musicals dominate.

Another good option is the **Hattiloo Theatre,** 656 Marshall (© **901/502-3486;** www.hattilootheatre.org), Memphis's Black repertory theater. Recent productions included *For Colored Girls Who Have Considered Suicide When the Rainbow is Enuf,* and former Memphis resident Tennessee Williams's classic *A Streetcar Named Desire.*

OTHER VENUES

Since its opening in 2004, the 18,400-seat **FedExForum,** 191 Beale St. (© **901/205-1234;** www.fedexforum.com), though primarily the venue for the NBA Memphis Grizzlies team, has booked big-name concert acts such as Justin Timberlake, Elton John, Miley Cyrus, and the Rolling Stones.

From late spring through early fall, Memphians frequently head outdoors for their concerts, and the **Mud Island River Park Amphitheatre,** 125 N. Front St. (© **800/507-6507** or 901/576-7241; www.mudisland.com), is where they head most often. With the downtown Memphis skyline for a backdrop, the 5,000-seat Mud Island Amphitheatre is

Gambling on the Mississippi

Move over Las Vegas and Atlantic City. Gamblers craving glitzy surroundings to go with their games of chance have a new option at the north end of the Mississippi Delta. Just south of Memphis, across the Mississippi state line, casinos are sprouting like cotton plants in the spring. In fact, these casinos are being built in the middle of the Delta's cotton fields, rapidly replacing the region's white gold as the biggest business this neck of the Delta has seen since cotton was king.

Back in the heyday of paddle-wheelers on the Mississippi, showboats and gamblers cruised the river, entertaining the masses and providing games of chance for those who felt lucky. Those days have recently returned to the Mississippi River as riverboats, and floating casinos have opened in states bordering Tennessee. You still won't find any blackjack tables in God-fearing Tennessee, but you don't have to drive very far for a bit of Vegas-style action.

The nearest casinos are about 20 miles from downtown Memphis, near the town of Robinsonville, Mississippi, while others are about 35 miles south of Memphis, near Tunica, Mississippi. From Memphis, take either Tenn. 61 or I-55 south. If you take the interstate, get off at either the Miss. 304 exit or the Miss. 4 exit, and head west to the river, watching for signs as you drive.

Twelve miles south of the Mississippi state line, off U.S. 61 near the town of Robinsonville, you'll find **Goldstrike,** 1010 Casino Center Dr. (✆ 888/24K-PLAY [245-7529] or 866/245-7511), and **Sheraton,** 1107 Casino Center Dr. (✆ 800/391-3777 or 662/363-4900). Continuing south on U.S. 61 and then west on Miss. 304, you come to **Sam's Town,** 1477 Casino Strip Blvd. (✆ 800/456-0711 or 662/363-0711); **Fitz,** 711 Lucky Lane (✆ 800/766-LUCK [5825] or 662/363-5825); **Hollywood,** 1150 Commerce Landing (✆ 800/871-0711 or 662/357-7700); and **Harrah's,** 1100 Casino Strip Blvd. (✆ 800/HARRAHS [427-7247] or 662/363-7777). Continuing south on U.S. 61 to Tunica and then heading west on either Mhoon Landing Road or Miss. 4, you'll come to **Bally's,** 1450 Bally's Blvd. (✆ 800/38-BALLY [382-2559). Besides the casinos, the area also offers outlet-mall shopping, golf, spas, riverboat rides, and other activities. For more information, go to www.tunicamiss.com.

the city's main outdoor stage. The concert season includes many national acts with the emphasis on rock and country music concerts; recent headliners included Norah Jones and Willie Nelson. Though the monorail usually runs only during the summer months, it runs here year-round on concert evenings.

Fast Facts

1 FAST FACTS: NASHVILLE

AREA CODES The telephone area code in Nashville is **615.**

AUTOMOBILE ORGANIZATIONS Motor clubs will supply maps, suggested routes, guidebooks, accident and bail-bond insurance, and emergency road service. The **American Automobile Association (AAA)** is the major auto club in the United States. If you belong to a motor club in your home country, inquire about AAA reciprocity before you leave. You may be able to join AAA even if you're not a member of a reciprocal club; to inquire, call AAA at ✆ **800/222-4357** (www.aaa.com), which is also their nationwide emergency road service number.

BUSINESS HOURS Banks are generally open Monday to Thursday 9am to 4pm, Friday 9am to 5 or 6pm, and Saturday morning. Office hours in Nashville are usually Monday to Friday 8:30am to 5pm. In general, stores in downtown Nashville are open Monday to Saturday 10am to 6pm. Shops in suburban Nashville malls are generally open Monday to Saturday 10am to 9pm and Sunday 1 to 6pm. Bars in Nashville are frequently open all day and are allowed to stay open daily until 3am, but might close between 1 and 3am.

DRINKING LAWS The legal age for purchase and consumption of alcoholic beverages is 21; proof of age is required and often requested at bars, nightclubs, and restaurants, so it's always a good idea to bring ID when you go out.

Bars are allowed to stay open until 3am every day. Beer can be purchased at convenience, grocery, or package stores, but wine and liquor are sold through package stores only.

Do not carry open containers of alcohol in your car or any public area that isn't zoned for alcohol consumption. The police can fine you on the spot. Don't even think about driving while intoxicated.

DRIVING RULES See "Getting There & Getting Around," p. 23.

ELECTRICITY Like Canada, the United States uses 110 to 120 volts AC (60 cycles), compared to 220 to 240 volts AC (50 cycles) in most of Europe, Australia, and New Zealand. Downward converters that change 220 to 240 volts to 110 to 120 volts are difficult to find in the United States, so bring one with you.

EMBASSIES & CONSULATES All embassies are located in the nation's capital, Washington, D.C. Some consulates are located in major U.S. cities, and most nations have a mission to the United Nations in New York City. If your country isn't listed below, call for directory information in Washington, D.C. (✆ **202/555-1212**) or check **www.embassy.org/embassies.**

The embassy of **Australia** is at 1601 Massachusetts Ave. NW, Washington, DC 20036 (✆ **202/797-3000;** www.usa.embassy.gov.au).

The embassy of **Canada** is at 501 Pennsylvania Ave. NW, Washington, DC 20001 (✆ **202/682-1740;** www.canadianembassy.org). Other Canadian consulates are in Buffalo (New York), Detroit, Los Angeles, New York, and Seattle.

The embassy of **Ireland** is at 2234 Massachusetts Ave. NW, Washington, DC 20008 (✆ **202/462-3939;** www.embassyofireland.org). Irish consulates are in Boston, Chicago, New York, San Francisco, and other cities. See website for complete listing.

The embassy of **New Zealand** is at 37 Observatory Circle NW, Washington, DC 20008 (✆ **202/328-4800;** www.nzembassy.com). New Zealand consulates are in Los Angeles, Salt Lake City, San Francisco, and Seattle.

The embassy of the **United Kingdom** is at 3100 Massachusetts Ave. NW, Washington, DC 20008 (✆ **202/588-7800;** ukinusa.fco.gov.uk). Other British consulates are in Atlanta, Boston, Chicago, Cleveland, Houston, Los Angeles, New York, San Francisco, and Seattle.

EMERGENCIES Dial ✆ **911** for fire, police, emergency, or ambulance. If you get into desperate straits, call **Travelers' Aid** of the Nashville Union Mission, 639 Lafayette St. (✆ **615/255-2475** or 615/780-9471). It's primarily a mission that helps destitute people, but if you need help in making phone calls or getting home, they might be able to help.

GASOLINE (PETROL) At press time, the average price for a gallon of gasoline in Nashville was about $2.50. Taxes are already included in the printed price. One U.S. gallon equals 3.8 liters or .85 imperial gallons.

HOLIDAYS Banks, government offices, post offices, and many stores, restaurants, and museums are closed on the following legal national holidays: January 1 (New Year's Day), the third Monday in January (Martin Luther King, Jr., Day), the third Monday in February (Presidents' Day), the last Monday in May (Memorial Day), July 4 (Independence Day), the first Monday in September (Labor Day), the second Monday in October (Columbus Day), November 11 (Veterans' Day/Armistice Day), the fourth Thursday in November (Thanksgiving Day), and December 25 (Christmas). The Tuesday after the first Monday in November is Election Day, a federal government holiday in presidential-election years (held every 4 years, and next in 2012).

For more information on holidays see "Calendar of Events," p. 16.

HOSPITALS The following hospitals offer emergency medical treatment: **St. Thomas Hospital,** 4220 Harding Rd. (✆ **615/222-2111**), and **Vanderbilt University Medical Center,** 1211 Medical Center Dr., in the Vanderbilt area (✆ **615/322-5000**).

INSURANCE For information on traveler's insurance, trip-cancellation insurance, and medical insurance while traveling, please visit www.frommers.com/planning.

INTERNET ACCESS Free Wi-Fi is available in most coffee shops and many restaurants and public places, including Centennial Park. Internet access is also available (along with computers) at public-library branches and FedEx Office.

LAUNDROMATS One good option for your laundry needs is Coin Laundry Express, 2130 21st Ave. S. (✆ **615/297-6871**).

LEGAL AID If you are "pulled over" for a minor infraction (such as speeding), never attempt to pay the fine directly to a police officer; this could be construed as attempted bribery, a much more serious crime. Pay fines by mail, or directly into the hands of the clerk of the court. If accused of a more serious offense, say and do nothing before consulting a lawyer. Here the burden is on the state to prove a person's guilt beyond a reasonable doubt, and everyone has the right to remain silent, whether he or she is suspected of a crime or actually arrested. Once arrested, a person can make one telephone call to a party of his or her choice. International visitors should call your embassy or consulate.

MAIL At press time, domestic postage rates were 28¢ for a postcard and 44¢ for a letter. For international mail, a first-class letter of up to 1 ounce costs 98¢ (75¢ to Canada and 79¢ to Mexico); a first-class postcard costs the same as a letter. For more information go to **www.usps.com**.

If you aren't sure what your address will be in the United States, mail can be sent to you, in your name, c/o General Delivery at the main post office of the city or region where you expect to be. (Call ✆ **800/275-8777** for information on the nearest post office.) The addressee must pick up mail in person and must produce proof of identity (driver's license, passport, and so forth). Most post offices will hold your mail for up to 1 month, and are open Monday to Friday from 8am to 6pm, and Saturday from 9am to 3pm.

Always include zip codes when mailing items in the U.S. If you don't know your zip code, visit www.usps.com/zip4.

NEWSPAPERS & MAGAZINES The ***Tennessean*** is Nashville's morning daily and Sunday newspaper. The alternative weekly is the ***Nashville Scene.***

PASSPORTS See www.frommers.com/planning for information on how to obtain a passport. See "Embassies & Consulates," above, for whom to contact if you lose yours while traveling in the U.S. For other information, please contact the following agencies:

For Residents of Australia Contact the **Australian Passport Information Service** at ✆ **131-232,** or visit the government website at www.passports.gov.au.

For Residents of Canada Contact the **Passport Canada,** Department of Foreign Affairs and International Trade, Ottawa, ON K1A 0G3 (✆ **800/567-6868;** www.ppt.gc.ca).

For Residents of Ireland Contact the **Passport Office,** Setanta Centre, Molesworth Street, Dublin 2 (✆ **01/671-1633;** www.irlgov.ie/iveagh).

For Residents of New Zealand Contact the **Passports Office** at ✆ **0800/225-050** in New Zealand or 04/474-8100, or log on to www.passports.govt.nz.

For Residents of the United Kingdom Visit your nearest passport office, major post office, or travel agency or contact the United Kingdom's **Identity & Passport Service** at ✆ **0870/521-0410,** or search its website at www.ukpa.gov.uk.

For Residents of the United States To find your regional passport office, either check the U.S. Department of State website or call the **National Passport Information Center** toll-free number (✆ **877/487-2778**) for automated information.

POLICE For police emergencies, phone ✆ **911.**

SMOKING Smoking is banned from most workplaces and restaurants (outdoor patios are an exception), but smoking is allowed in over-21 venues including bars, and in certain hotel and motel rooms.

TAXES In Davidson County, the combined state and local sales tax is 9.25%. This tax applies to goods as well as all recreation, entertainment, and amusements. However, in the case of services, the tax is often already included in the admission price or cost of a ticket. The Nashville hotel and motel room tax is 5%, which when added to the 9.25% makes for a total hotel room tax of 15.25% plus $2 city tax, per night. Car-rental taxes total 13.25%.

The United States has no value-added tax (VAT) or other indirect tax at the national level. Every state, county, and city may levy its own local tax on all purchases, including hotel and restaurant checks and airline tickets. These taxes will not appear on price tags.

TELEPHONES Many convenience groceries and packaging services sell **prepaid calling cards** in denominations up to $50; for international visitors these can be the least expensive way to call home. Many public pay phones at airports now accept American Express, MasterCard, and Visa credit cards. **Local calls** made from pay phones in most locales cost either 25¢ or 35¢. Most long-distance and international calls can be dialed directly from any phone. **For calls within the United States and to Canada,** dial 1 followed by the area code and the seven-digit number. **For other international calls,** dial 011 followed by the country code, city code, and the number you are calling.

Calls to area codes **800, 888, 877,** and **866** are toll-free. However, calls to area codes **700** and **900** (chat lines, bulletin boards, "dating" services, and so on) can be very expensive—usually a charge of 95¢ to $3 or more per minute, and they sometimes have minimum charges that can run as high as $15 or more.

For **reversed-charge or collect calls,** and for person-to-person calls, dial the number 0 then the area code and number; an operator will come on the line, and you should specify whether you are calling collect, person-to-person, or both. If your operator-assisted call is international, ask for the overseas operator.

For **local directory assistance** ("information"), dial 411; for long-distance information, dial 1, then the appropriate area code and 555-1212.

TIME Nashville is in the Central Time Zone—and observes Central Standard Time (CST) or Central Daylight Time (CDT), depending on the time of year—making it 2 hours ahead of the West Coast and 1 hour behind the East Coast.

The continental United States is divided into **four time zones:** Eastern Standard Time (EST), Central Standard Time (CST), Mountain Standard Time (MST), and Pacific Standard Time (PST). Alaska and Hawaii have their own zones. For example, when it's 9am in Los Angeles (PST), it's 7am in Honolulu (HST), 10am in Denver (MST), 11am in Chicago (CST), noon in New York City (EST), 5pm in London (GMT), and 2am the next day in Sydney.

Daylight saving time is in effect from 1am on the second Sunday in March to 1am on the first Sunday in November, except in Arizona, Hawaii, the U.S. Virgin Islands, and Puerto Rico. Daylight saving time moves the clock 1 hour ahead of standard time.

TIPPING In hotels, tip **bellhops** at least $1 per bag ($2–$3 if you have a lot of luggage) and tip the **chamber staff** $1 to $2 per day (more if you've left a disaster area for him or her to clean up). Tip the **doorman** or **concierge** only if he or she has provided you with some specific service (for example, calling a cab for you or obtaining difficult-to-get theater tickets). Tip the **valet-parking attendant** $1 every time you get your car.

In restaurants, bars, and nightclubs, tip **service staff** and **bartenders** 15% to 20% of the check, tip **checkroom attendants** $1 per garment, and tip **valet-parking attendants** $1 per vehicle.

As for other service personnel, tip **cab drivers** 15% of the fare; tip **skycaps** at airports at least $1 per bag ($2–$3 if you have a lot of luggage); and tip **hairdressers** and **barbers** 15% to 20%.

TOILETS You won't find public toilets or "restrooms" on the streets in most U.S. cities but they can be found in hotel lobbies, bars, restaurants, museums, department stores, railway and bus stations, and service stations. Large hotels and fast-food restaurants are often the best bet for clean facilities. Restaurants and bars in resorts or heavily visited areas may reserve their restrooms for patrons.

VISAS For information about U.S. Visas go to **http://travel.state.gov** and click on "Visas." Or go to one of the following websites:

Australian citizens can obtain up-to-date visa information from the **U.S. Embassy Canberra,** Moonah Place, Yarralumla, ACT 2600 (✆ **02/6214-5600**) or by checking the U.S. Diplomatic Mission's website at **http://canberra.usembassy.gov/consular**.

British subjects can obtain up-to-date visa information by calling the **U.S. Embassy Visa Information Line** (✆ **0891/200-290**) or by visiting the "Visas to the U.S." section of the American Embassy London's website at **www.usembassy.org.uk**.

Irish citizens can obtain up-to-date visa information through the **Embassy of the USA Dublin,** 42 Elgin Rd., Dublin 4, Ireland (✆ **353/1-668-8777;** or by checking the "Visas to the U.S." section of the website at **http://dublin.usembassy.gov**.

Citizens of **New Zealand** can obtain up-to-date visa information by contacting the **U.S. Embassy New Zealand,** 29 Fitzherbert Terrace, Thorndon, Wellington (✆ **644/472-2068**), or get the information directly from the website at **http://wellington.usembassy.gov**.

VISITOR INFORMATION On the baggage-claim level of Nashville International Airport, you'll find the **Airport Welcome Center** (✆ **615/275-1675**), where you can pick up brochures, maps, and bus information, and get answers to any questions you may have about touring the city. This center is open daily from 6:30am to midnight. In downtown Nashville, you'll find the **Nashville Convention & Visitors Bureau Visitors Center,** Fifth Avenue and Broadway (✆ **800/657-6910** or 615/780-9401), the main source of information on the city and surrounding areas. The information center (open daily during daylight hours) offers free Wi-Fi service and is located at the base of the radio tower of the Sommet Center. Signs on interstate highways around the downtown area will direct you to the arena. Information is also available from the main office of the **Chamber of Commerce/Nashville Convention & Visitors Bureau,** in the lower level of the US Bank building at the corner of Fourth Avenue North and Commerce (✆ **615/259-4730**). The office is open Monday to Friday 8am to 5pm.

For information on the state of Tennessee, contact the **Tennessee Department of Tourism Development,** P.O. Box 23170, Nashville, TN 37202 (✆ **615/741-2158**).

2 FAST FACTS: MEMPHIS

AREA CODES The telephone area code in Memphis is **901.**

AUTOMOBILE ORGANIZATIONS See above, under "Fast Facts: Nashville."

BUSINESS HOURS Banks are generally open Monday to Thursday 8:30am to 4pm, with later hours on Friday. Office hours in Memphis are usually Monday to Friday 8:30am to 5pm. In general, stores located in downtown Memphis are open Monday to Saturday 10am to 5:30pm. Shops in suburban Memphis malls are generally open Monday to Saturday 10am to 9pm and on Sunday 1 to 5 or 6pm. Bars are allowed to stay open until 3am, but may close between 1 and 3am.

DRINKING LAWS See above, under "Fast Facts: Nashville."

DRIVING RULES See "Getting There & Getting Around," p. 23.

ELECTRICITY See above, under "Fast Facts: Nashville."

EMBASSIES & CONSULATES See above, under "Fast Facts: Nashville."

EMERGENCIES For police, fire, or medical emergencies, phone ✆ **911.**

GASOLINE (PETROL) At press time, the average price for a gallon of gasoline in Memphis was $2.45. Taxes are already included in the printed price. One U.S. gallon equals 3.8 liters or .85 imperial gallons.

HOLIDAYS See above, under "Fast Facts: Nashville."

HOSPITALS Major hospitals in the downtown/Midtown areas are **Methodist Healthcare,** at 1211 Union Ave. (✆ **901/516-7000**), and the **Regional Medical Center/Elvis Presley Trauma Center,** at 877 Jefferson Ave. (✆ **901/545-7100**).

INSURANCE For information on traveler's insurance, trip cancellation insurance, and medical insurance while traveling, please visit www.frommers.com/planning.

INTERNET ACCESS Free Internet access is available in most coffee shops and many restaurants around town. Computers with Internet access are also available at public libraries and FedEx Office.

LEGAL AID See above, under "Fast Facts: Nashville."

MAIL See above, under "Fast Facts: Nashville."

NEWSPAPERS & MAGAZINES The ***Commercial Appeal*** is Memphis's daily newspaper. The arts-and-entertainment weekly is the ***Memphis Flyer.*** Out-of-town newspapers are available at Davis-Kidd Booksellers and Borders.

PASSPORTS See above, under "Fast Facts: Nashville."

POLICE For police emergencies, phone ✆ **911.**

SMOKING Smoking is banned in most workplaces and inside restaurants (patios are an exception), but is allowed in bars and establishments exclusively for people over 21.

TAXES The state sales tax is 9.25%. An additional room tax of 6.7% on top of the state sales tax brings the total hotel-room tax to a whopping 15.95%.

The United States has no value-added tax (VAT) or other indirect tax at the national level. Every state, county, and city may levy its own local tax on all purchases, including hotel and restaurant checks and airline tickets. These taxes will not appear on price tags.

TELEPHONES See above, under "Fast Facts: Nashville."

TIME See above, under "Fast Facts: Nashville."

TIPPING See above, under "Fast Facts: Nashville."

TOILETS See above, under "Fast Facts: Nashville."

VISAS See above, under "Fast Facts: Nashville."

VISITOR INFORMATION The city's main visitor information center, located downtown at the base of Jefferson Street, is the **Tennessee State Welcome Center,** 119 N. Riverside Dr. (✆ **901/543-6757**). It's open daily 24 hours but staffed only between 8am and 7pm (until 8pm in the summer months). Inside this large information center, you'll find soaring statues of both Elvis and B. B. King.

At the airport, you'll find information boards with telephone numbers for contacting hotels and numbers for other helpful services. Other visitor centers are located off I-40, just east of the Memphis city limits, and at Elvis Presley Boulevard just north of Graceland.

3 AIRLINE, HOTEL & CAR-RENTAL WEBSITES

MAJOR AIRLINES

American Airlines
www.aa.com

Continental Airlines
www.continental.com

Delta Air Lines
www.delta.com

Northwest Airlines
www.nwa.com

United Airlines
www.united.com

US Airways
www.usairways.com

BUDGET AIRLINES

AirTran Airways
www.airtran.com

JetBlue Airways
www.jetblue.com

Southwest Airlines
www.southwest.com

MAJOR HOTEL & MOTEL CHAINS

Best Western International
www.bestwestern.com

Clarion Hotels
www.choicehotels.com

Comfort Inn
www.ComfortInn.com

Courtyard by Marriott
www.marriott.com/courtyard

Crowne Plaza Hotels
www.ichotelsgroup.com/crowneplaza

Days Inn
www.daysinn.com

Doubletree Hotels
www.doubletree.com

EconoLodge
www.choicehotels.com

Embassy Suites
www.embassysuites.com

Fairfield Inn by Marriott
www.fairfieldinn.com

Four Seasons
www.fourseasons.com

Hampton Inn
http://hamptoninn1.hilton.com

Hilton Hotels
www.hilton.com

Holiday Inn
www.holidayinn.com

Howard Johnson
www.hojo.com

Hyatt
www.hyatt.com

InterContinental Hotels & Resorts
www.ichotelsgroup.com

La Quinta Inns & Suites
www.lq.com

Loews Hotels
www.loewshotels.com

Marriott
www.marriott.com

Motel 6
www.motel6.com

Omni Hotels
www.omnihotels.com

Quality
www.QualityInn.com

Radisson Hotels & Resorts
www.radisson.com

Ramada Worldwide
www.ramada.com

Red Carpet Inns
www.bookroomsnow.com

Red Lion Hotels
www.redlion.rdln.com

Red Roof Inns
www.redroof.com

Renaissance
www.renaissancehotels.com

Residence Inn by Marriott
www.marriott.com/residenceinn

Rodeway Inn Hotels
www.RodewayInn.com

Sheraton Hotels & Resorts
www.starwoodhotels.com/sheraton

Super 8 Motels
www.super8.com

Travelodge
www.travelodge.com

Vagabond Inns
www.vagabondinn.com

Westin Hotels & Resorts
www.starwoodhotels.com/westin

Wyndham Hotels & Resorts
www.wyndham.com

CAR-RENTAL AGENCIES

Alamo
www.alamo.com

Auto Europe
www.autoeurope.com

Avis
www.avis.com

Budget
www.budget.com

Dollar
www.dollar.com

Enterprise
www.enterprise.com

Hertz
www.hertz.com

Kemwel (KHA)
www.kemwel.com

National
www.nationalcar.com

Payless
www.paylesscarrental.com

Rent-A-Wreck
www.rentawreck.com

Thrifty
www.thrifty.com

INDEX

See also Accommodations and Restaurant indexes, below.

General Index

A

AAA (American Automobile Association), 26, 255
- Memphis, 165
- Nashville, 48
  - 48, 5

Access Ride, 32

Accommodations. ***See also*** **Accommodations Index**
- Clarksdale, 227–228
- Memphis, 166–181
  - airport and Graceland areas, 179–181
  - best, 2, 167
  - downtown, 168–174
  - East Memphis, 175–179
  - family-friendly, 176
  - Midtown, 174–175
  - price categories, 167
- Nashville, 49–64
  - best, 2, 50
  - downtown area, Music Row & The West End, 50–59
  - family-friendly, 56
  - Music Valley and the airport area, 59–64
- Oxford (Mississippi), 230

A Country Christmas (Nashville), 20

A Cowboy Town (Whites Creek), 111

Addresses, finding
- Memphis, 164–165
- Nashville, 46

Adventure Science Center (Nashville), 99

Africa in April Cultural Awareness Festival (Memphis), 20

African-Americans, 10–11
- in Memphis
  - history of, 149–151
  - National Civil Rights Museum, 214–215
  - sights and attractions, 218–219
  - Slavehaven Underground Railroad Museum/Burkle Estate (Memphis), 216
- in Nashville
  - art gallery, 116
  - sights and attractions, 101
  - special events, 19–21
  - tours, 110

African Street Festival (Nashville), 19

Airports, getting into town from, 24–25

Airport Welcome Center (Nashville), 45

Air travel, 23–25

AITO (Association of Independent Tour Operators), 34

Alamo Rent-A-Car, Nashville, 27

Alex Haley House Museum (Memphis), 219

Alex's Tavern (Memphis), 250

Alfred's (Memphis), 245

American Airlines, 23, 24

American Artisan Festival (Nashville), 18

American Automobile Association (AAA), 26, 255
- Memphis, 165
- Nashville, 48

American Dream Safari (Memphis), 211, 224

Amro Music Stores (Memphis), 242

Amtrak, 27

Antiques
- Memphis, 232–233
- Nashville, 113

The Apple Barn Cider Mill & General Store (Nashville), 119

Architecture, Nashville, 12–13

Area codes
- Memphis, 259
- Nashville, 255

Art Deco architecture, best, 3

Art galleries
- Memphis, 233
- Nashville, 113, 116
- Oxford (Mississippi), 229

Art Museum of the University of Memphis, 212

Art museums
- Memphis
  - Art Museum of the University of Memphis, 212
  - Belz Museum of Asian & Judaic Art, 213
  - Dixon Gallery & Gardens, 213
  - Memphis Brooks Museum of Art, 213–214
  - National Ornamental Metal Museum (Memphis), 215
- Nashville
  - Cheekwood Botanical Garden & Museum of Art, 99, 100, 137
  - Frist Center for the Visual Arts, 99, 108, 136–137

The Arts Company (Nashville), 113

A. Schwab Dry Goods Store (Memphis), 222, 239

Association of Independent Tour Operators (AITO), 34

A Thousand Faces (Nashville), 118

ATMs (automated-teller machines), 31

Attractions. ***See*** **Sights and attractions**

Audubon Park (Memphis), 224

Australia
customs regulations, 23
embassy, 255
passports, 257
visas, 259
Authentic Tours of Historic Black Nashville and Beyond, 33
Automatic Slim's Tonga Club (Memphis), 249
Auto racing, Nashville, 112
AutoZone Bowl Classic (Memphis), 225
AutoZone Liberty Bowl Football Classic (Memphis), 22
The Avenue Carriage Crossing (Memphis), 240
Avis Rent-A-Car
Memphis, 29
Nashville, 27

Backbeat Tours (Memphis), 223–224
Backstreet Memphis, 252
Bakeries
Memphis, 203
Nashville, 86–87
Ballet Memphis, 253
Barbecue
Memphis, 153–154
restaurants, 202
Nashville restaurants, 85–86
Bars
Memphis, 249–252
Nashville, 133–134
Baseball
Memphis, 225
Nashville, 112
The Basement (Nashville), 130
Basketball, Memphis, 225
B. B. King's Blues Club (Memphis), 151, 222, 245
B. B. King's Blues Club (Nashville), 106, 131
Beale Street Labor Day Music Festival (Memphis), 21
Beale Street (Memphis), 151, 155, 218, 222
nightlife, 244–248
sights and attractions, 204–212
Beale Street Zydeco Music Festival (Memphis), 20
Beer Sellar (Nashville), 133
Belcourt Theatre (Nashville), 137
Belle Meade (Nashville), 39
Belle Meade Plantation Fall Fest (Nashville), 19
Belle Meade Plantation (Nashville), 96
Belmont Grill (Memphis), 251
Belmont Mansion (Nashville), 96–97
Belmont University (Nashville), 33
Belz Museum of Asian & Judaic Art (Memphis), 213
Berry Hill (Nashville), 39
Betty Boots (Nashville), 122
Bicentennial Capitol Mall State Park (Nashville), 101
Bicycle store, Memphis, 233
Big River Grille & Brewing Works (Nashville), 134
Black Business Association, 33
Blackstone Restaurant & Brewery (Nashville), 134
***The Blind Side* (movie), 230**
The Bluebird Cafe (Nashville), 130
Bluegrass Nights at the Ryman (Nashville), 18
Blues City Cafe (Memphis), 245
Blues City Tours of Memphis, 224
Blues on the Bluff (Memphis), 21
Boat rentals, Nashville, 111
Boat tours
Memphis, 223
Nashville, 111
Bonnaroo Music & Arts Festival (Manchester), 142
BookMan/BookWoman (Nashville), 116
Books, Memphis in, 153
Bookstar (Memphis), 233
Bookstores
Memphis, 233, 236
Nashville, 116
Oxford, 228–229
Boone, Daniel, 8
Boot Country (Nashville), 122
Borders (Nashville), 116
Boscos (Nashville), 134
Boscos Squared (Memphis), 251
Bourbon Street Blues and Boogie Bar (Nashville), 132
Breezenet.com, 26
Brewpubs
Memphis, 251
Nashville, 134
BR549, 125
Briley Parkway (Nashville), 46
Budget Rent-A-Car
Memphis, 29
Nashville, 27
Buffalo Billiards (Nashville), 133
Burke's Book Store (Memphis), 236
Burkle Estate (Memphis), 216
Bury Your Blues Blowout on Beale (Memphis), 22
Business hours
Memphis, 259
Nashville, 255
Bus travel, 26
Memphis, 29–30
Nashville, 28

Cafes
Memphis, 203
Nashville, 86–87
Calendar of events, 16–22
Canada
customs regulations, 23
embassy, 256
passports, 257
Cannon Center for the Performing Arts (Memphis), 252
Carbonfund, 34
Carbon Neutral, 34
Carl Van Vechten Gallery (Nashville), 101
Carnival Memphis, 20–21
Carnton Plantation & Battlefield (Franklin), 139
Car rentals
Memphis, 29
Nashville, 27
Carriage Tours of Memphis, 223
The Carter House (Franklin), 140
Car travel
Clarksdale, 226
Memphis, 29
Nashville, 27
to Nashville and Memphis, 25–26
Casino Factory Shoppes (Memphis), 236
Casinos, on the Mississippi, 254
Cathead Delta Blues & Folk Art (Clarksdale), 227
Cellular South Cup (Memphis), 225
Centennial Park (Nashville), 102

Center for Southern Folklore (Memphis), 203, 211, 233, 245
Central Avenue (Memphis), 164
Central Station (Nashville), 27
Chaffin's Barn Dinner Theatre (Nashville), 137
Chamber of Commerce/Nashville Convention & Visitors Bureau, 45
Champion's Pharmacy and Herb Store (Memphis), 239
Checker Cab (Nashville), 28
Checker/Yellow Cab (Memphis), 30
Cheekwood Botanical Garden & Museum of Art (Nashville), 99, 100, 137
Chickasaw Oaks Village (Memphis), 240
Children, families with
- Memphis
  - accommodations, 176
  - restaurants, 188
  - shopping, 238
  - sights and attractions, 219–220
- Nashville
  - accommodations, 56
  - sights and attractions, 104–105

Children's Museum of Memphis, 220
Chocolate Soup (Memphis), 238
Christ Episcopal Church (Nashville), 108
Christmas at Belmont (Nashville), 19–20
Christmas lights, 4
Chucalissa Archaeological Museum (Memphis), 216
Churches, Nashville, 98
Church of the Assumption of the Blessed Virgin Mary (Nashville), 46
Church Park (Memphis), 218–219, 222
Circle Players (Nashville), 136
Circuit Playhouse (Memphis), 253
City Wide Cab Company (Clarksdale), 25
City Wide Cab Company (Memphis), 30
Civil rights movement, Memphis, 149
Civil War
- Memphis, 149
- Nashville, 9–10

Clarksdale, 226–228
Clarksdale/Coahoma County Chamber of Commerce, 226
Club 152 (Memphis), 251–252
CMA (Country Music Association) Music Festival, 18
CMT Music Awards (Nashville), 16
Coal Miner's Daughter **(movie), 13**
The Cocoa Tree (Nashville), 119
Columbia, 140–141
The Commercial Appeal **(Memphis), 15, 244**
Consulates, 255–256
Continental Airlines, 23
Cool Springs Galleria (Nashville), 117, 120
Cooper-Young Festival (Memphis), 21
Cooper-Young neighborhood (Memphis), 155
Cooter's Place (Nashville), 88
Cotten Music Center (Nashville), 121
The Cotton Mill (Nashville), 118
The Cotton Museum at the Memphis Cotton Exchange, 213, 223
Cotton Row (Memphis), 223
Country music, 5–7
- Nashville nightlife, 125–130

Country Music Hall of Fame and Museum (Nashville), 88–89, 121
Court Square (Memphis), 217
Crafts, Nashville, 117
The Crossroads (Clarksdale), 226
Cumberland Art Gallery (Nashville), 113
Curious Heart Emporium (Nashville), 113
Customs regulations, 23

D

Dance clubs
- Memphis, 251–252
- Nashville, 134–135

Dan McGuinness Irish Pub (Nashville), 132
David Lusk Gallery (Memphis), 233
Davis-Kidd Booksellers (Memphis), 236
Davis-Kidd Booksellers (Nashville), 88, 116
Davy Crockett Park Municipal Golf Course (Memphis), 224
Delis
- Memphis, 203
- Nashville, 86

Delphinium (Memphis), 238
Delta Airlines, 23, 24
Delta Blues Museum (Clarksdale), 226
Dentists, 31
Department stores
- Memphis, 236
- Nashville, 117

Dillard's
- Memphis, 236
- Nashville, 117

Dining, 14. ***See also*** **Restaurants Index**
- Memphis, 182–203
  - barbecue, 202
  - best, 145, 182–183
  - by cuisine, 183–185
  - delis, cafes and bakeries, 203
  - downtown, 185–192
  - East Memphis, 196–200
  - family-friendly, 188
  - price categories, 182
  - South Memphis & Graceland area, 201–202
- Nashville, 65–87
  - barbecue and hot chicken, 85–86
  - best, 3, 65–66, 87
  - cafes, delis, bakeries and pastry shops, 86–87
  - chain restaurants, 65
  - by cuisine, 66–68
  - downtown, The Gulch & 12th Avenue South, 68–74
  - family-friendly, 72
  - Germantown & Jefferson Street, 74–75
  - Music Row, The West End & areas southwest, 75–82
  - Music Valley & East Nashville, 82–85
  - price categories, 65
  - Tennessee-based eateries, 87

Dinstuhl's Fine Candies (Memphis), 238–239
Disabilities, travelers with, 32
Disability Information Office, 32
Discount shopping
Memphis, 236
Nashville, 117
The District (Nashville), 37
attractions, 95
nightlife, 125, 128–129
sights and attractions, 102
Dixon Gallery & Gardens (Memphis), 213
Doctors, 31
Dollar Rent-A-Car
Memphis, 29
Nashville, 27
Douglas Corner Cafe (Nashville), 125
Dove Awards (Nashville), 16
Downtown Memphis, 155
accommodations, 168–174
nightlife, 244–248
restaurants, 185–192
Downtown Nashville, 37, 45–46
accommodations, 50–59
restaurants, 68–74
traveling between Music Valley and, 95
walking tour, 105–109
Drinking laws, 255
Driving rules, 255
Memphis, 29
Nashville, 28
Dr. Martin Luther King, Jr., Memorial March (Nashville), 20
DSW Shoe Warehouse (Memphis), 242

Earnestine & Hazel's (Memphis), 245
East Memphis, 155, 162, 164
accommodations, 175–179
nightlife, 251
restaurants, 196–200
East Nashville, 39
attractions, 103
restaurants, 82–85
Eating and drinking. *See* Food and cuisine
Eco Directory, 34
Ecotourism, 33–35
Ecotourism Australia, 34
Edge, John T., 229
Edmonson, William, 11
Edwin Warner Park (Nashville), 102
Eighth Avenue (Nashville), 46
Eighth Avenue South (Nashville), 38
attractions, 103
Elder's Bookstore (Nashville), 116
Elmwood Cemetery (Memphis), 217
Elvis Presley Automobile Museum (Memphis), 208
Elvis Tribute Week (Memphis), 21, 211
Embassies and consulates, 255–256
Emergencies, 256
Enterprise Rent-a-Car
Memphis, 29
Nashville, 27
Environmentally Friendly Hotels, 34
E-Passport, 22
Ernest Tubb *Midnite Jamboree* (Nashville), 129–130
Ernest Tubb Record Shop (Nashville), 88, 108, 121
Escorted tours, 35–36
Exit/In (Nashville), 130

Fall Festival & Tennessee State Pow Wow (Nashville), 19
Families with children
Memphis
accommodations, 176
restaurants, 188
shopping, 238
sights and attractions, 219–220
Nashville
accommodations, 56
sights and attractions, 104–105
Family Wash (Nashville), 133
Farmers' Market
Memphis, 241
Nashville, 72, 119
Fashion (clothing)
Memphis, 236, 238
Nashville, 117–118
Faulkner, William, 228
FedEx Cup St. Jude Classic (Memphis), 20
FedExForum (Memphis), 253
Finer Things Gallery (Nashville), 116
Fire Finch (Nashville), 118
Fire Museum of Memphis, 220
First Baptist Church (Nashville), 108
First Congregational Church (Memphis), 223
Fisk University Galleries (Nashville), 101
Fisk University (Nashville), 33, 38, 101
Flashback (Memphis), 232
Flavour (Nashville), 118
Flea Market, Memphis, 241
Flea markets, Nashville, 119
Flying Saucer Draught Emporium (Memphis), 251
Flying Saucer Draught Emporium (Nashville), 134
Food and cuisine
Memphis, 153–154
restaurants by cuisine, 183–185
Nashville, 14
restaurants by cuisine, 66–68
Southern Foodways Alliance (SFA), 229
Food stores and markets
Memphis, 238–239, 241
Nashville, 119
Food trips, 35
Football
Memphis, 225
Nashville, 112
Fork's Drum Closet (Nashville), 121
Fort Nashborough (Nashville), 9, 97, 106
Four Corners Marina (Nashville), 111
Fox and Hound (Memphis), 251
Fox Meadows Park (Memphis), 224
Franklin, 138–140
Freedom Awards (Memphis), 21
Free or almost free activities, 3
Frist Center for the Visual Arts (Nashville), 99, 108, 136–137
F. Scott's Restaurant & Jazz Bar (Nashville), 132
Full Gospel Tabernacle (Memphis), 219

Gambling on the Mississippi, 254
Gasoline, 256
Gaylord Opryland Resort (Nashville), 93–94
Gaylord Springs Golf Links (Nashville), 111
Gays and lesbians, 32
Memphis nightlife, 252
Nashville nightlife, 134–135
***General Jackson* Showboat (Nashville), 111, 129**
Germantown Charity Horse Show (Memphis), 21, 225
Germantown (Nashville), 37
restaurants, 74–75
Gerst Haus (Nashville), 133
***G.I. Blues* (movie), 209**
Gibson Beale Street Showcase (Memphis), 242
Gibson Showcase (Nashville), 122
Gifts and souvenirs
Memphis, 239–240
Nashville, 118–119
Gigi's Cupcakes (Nashville), 86
GMA (Gospel Music Association) Dove Awards (Nashville), 16
Golf
Memphis, 224
tournaments, 225
Nashville, 111
tournaments, 112
Golf & Games Family Park (Memphis), 220
Goner Records (Memphis), 241
Graceland area (Memphis)
accommodations, 179–181
restaurants, 201
Graceland (Memphis), 208–210
Elvis Presley's Birthday Tribute, 20
sights and attractions, 204–212
Tribute Week, 21
Graham Central Station (Nashville), 131
Grand Ole Opry Museum (Nashville), 89, 93
***Grand Ole Opry* (Nashville), 5–6, 12**
***Grand Ole Opry* (Nashville), 128**
***Grand Ole Opry* (Nashville), 129**
Birthday of, 19
***Grand Ole Opry* (Nashville), Ryman Auditorium, 95**
Gray Line Airport Express (Nashville), 24
Gray Line Nashville, 109
The Great Escape (Nashville), 121
Great Performances at Vanderbilt series (Nashville), 136
Greenbelt Park (Memphis), 217
The Green Directory, 34
Green Hills (Nashville), 39
Greenhotels, 34
Greenlivingonline.com, 34
Green Pages, 34
Greyhound, 26
Greyhound North American Discovery Pass, 26
Greyhound racing, Memphis, 225
Grimey's (Nashville), 121
Ground Zero Blues Club (Memphis), 245
Gruhn Guitars (Nashville), 106, 122
The Gulch (Nashville), 38
attractions, 103
nightlife, 125, 128–129
restaurants, 68–74

Haley, Alex, House Museum (Memphis), 219
Handy, W. C., 151
House (Memphis), 222
Hanks, Tom, 164
Hard Rock Cafe (Memphis), 248
Hatch Show Print (Nashville), 106, 116
Hattiloo Theatre (Memphis), 253
Hayes, Isaac, 210
Health concerns, 31–32
***Hee Haw* (television program), 13**
Heritage Tours (Memphis), 219
Hermitage Hotel (Nashville), 108
The Hermitage (Nashville), 97
Hertz
Memphis, 29
Nashville, 27
Hickory Hollow Mall (Antioch), 117, 120
Highway 61 (U.S. 61), 226
Hillsboro Village (Nashville), 39
Historic RCA Studio B (Nashville), 93
History
of Memphis, 147–152
of Nashville, 8–12
Hi-Tone Cafe (Memphis), 250
Hockey, Nashville, 112
Holiday Inn hotel chain, 178
Holidays, 256
Horseback riding, Nashville, 111–112
Horse shows
Memphis, 225
Nashville, 112
Hospitals, 256, 260
Hotel Association of Canada, 34
Hotels. *See also* Accommodations Index
Clarksdale, 227–228
Memphis, 166–181
airport and Graceland areas, 179–181
best, 2, 167
downtown, 168–174
East Memphis, 175–179
family-friendly, 176
Midtown, 174–175
price categories, 167
Nashville, 49–64
best, 2, 50
downtown area, Music Row & The West End, 50–59
family-friendly, 56
Music Valley and the airport area, 59–64
Oxford (Mississippi), 230
Huey's (Memphis), 250
Hume-Fogg High School (Nashville), 108

International Blues Competition (Memphis), 21
International Market and Restaurant (Nashville), 119
Internet access, 36, 256
Ireland
embassy, 256
passports, 257
visas, 259

Iroquois Steeplechase (Nashville), 18, 112
Isabella (Memphis), 238
Itineraries, suggested
Memphis, 156–161
Nashville, 39–44
Itta Bena (Memphis), 249

Jack Daniel's Distillery (Lynchburg), 141–142
James Davis (Memphis), 236
James K. Polk Home (Columbia), 140
Jamie (Nashville), 118
Java Cabana (Memphis), 249
Jay Etkin Gallery (Memphis), 233
Jazz and blues clubs, Nashville, 131–132
Jefferson Davis Park (Memphis), 217
Jefferson Street (Nashville), 11, 38
restaurants, 74–75
Jimmy Kelly's Steakhouse (Nashville), 133
Johnny Walker Tours (Nashville), 109
Johnston & Murphy Outlet (Nashville), 117
Joseph (Memphis), 238
Joysmith Gallery (Memphis), 233
Jubilee Hall (Nashville), 101
JuRo Stables (Nashville), 112

Katy K's Ranch Dressing (Nashville), 122
Kids
Memphis
accommodations, 176
restaurants, 188
shopping, 238
sights and attractions, 219–220
Nashville
accommodations, 56
sights and attractions, 104–105
King, B. B., 151
King, Martin Luther, Jr., 150
Birthday (Nashville), 20
Memorial March (Nashville), 20
National Civil Rights Museum (Memphis), 214–215
King's Palace Café (Memphis), 248
Kittie Kyle Kollection (Memphis), 238
KLM, 24
Kudzu's (Memphis), 250

Lane Motor Museum (Nashville), 100
Lansky 126 (Memphis), 238
Laundromat, Nashville, 256
Laurelwood (Memphis), 240
Layla's Bluegrass Inn (Nashville), 125
Layout
Memphis, 162, 164
Nashville, 45–46
Lazzaroli Pasta (Nashville), 119
Le Chardonnay Wine Bar (Memphis), 250
Leftwich (Memphis), 224
Legal aid, 256–257
Legends Corner (Nashville), 125
Legislative Plaza (Nashville), 109
Levitt Shell (Memphis), 248
Lewis, John, 11
Liberty Bowl Memorial Stadium (Memphis), 225
Lichterman Nature Center (Memphis), 218
The Links at Galloway (Memphis), 224
The Lipstick Lounge (Nashville), 134
Local Color Gallery (Nashville), 116
Longhorn World Championship Rodeo (near Murfreesboro), 19
Lonnie's Western Room (Nashville), 133
Lorraine Motel (Memphis), 214–215
Lucchesi's (Memphis), 239
LunchLINE shuttles (Nashville), 28

Macy's (Memphis), 236
Macy's (Nashville), 117
Mail, 257
Main arteries and streets
Memphis, 164
Nashville, 46
Main Street Trolley (Memphis), 30
The Mall at Green Hills (Nashville), 117, 120
Malls and shopping centers
Memphis, 240
Nashville, 120–121
Market Street Emporium (Nashville), 106
Mason Temple Church of God in Christ (Memphis), 219
MATA (Memphis Area Transit Authority), 25, 29–30
Medical requirements for entry, 23
Mednikow (Memphis), 240
Memphis Area Transit Authority (MATA), 25, 29–30
Memphis Botanic Garden, 218
Memphis Brooks Museum of Art, 213–214
Memphis Center for Independent Living, 33
Memphis Drum Shop, 242
Memphis Farmers' Market, 241
Memphis Flea Market, 241
***Memphis Flyer*, 15, 244**
Memphis Gay and Lesbian Community Center, 32
Memphis Grizzlies, 225
Memphis in May International Festival, 20
Memphis International Airport, 25
Memphis International Film Festival, 20
Memphis Music, 242
Memphis Music & Heritage Festival, 21
Memphis Redbirds Baseball Club, 225
Memphis Riverboats, 223
Memphis Rock 'N' Soul Museum, 210
Memphis Symphony Orchestra, 253
Memphis Zoo & Aquarium, 216–217
Mercy Lounge/Cannery Ballroom (Nashville), 131
Merry Christmas Memphis Parade, 21
Methodist Healthcare (Memphis), 31
Metro Memphis, 252
Metropolitan Courthouse (Nashville), 106

Metropolitan Transit Authority (MTA), 28
Mid-South Arts and Crafts Show (Memphis), 21
Mid-South Fair (Memphis), 21
Midtown Bike Co. (Memphis), 233
Midtown (Memphis), 155
  accommodations, 174–175
  nightlife, 250–251
  restaurants, 192–196
Minglewood Hall (Memphis), 248–249
Mirimichi Golf Club (Millington), 219
Miss Cordelia's (Memphis), 239
Mississippi River Museum (Memphis), 205, 214
Mollie Fontaine Lounge (Memphis), 250
Money and costs, 30–31
Montana, Patsy, 89
Movies
  Memphis in, 153
  Nashville in, 13–14
Mud Island Amphitheater (Memphis), 214
Mud Island River Park Amphitheatre (Memphis), 253
Mud Island River Park (Memphis), 214
Mulligan's Pub (Nashville), 132
Multicultural travelers, 33
The Muse (Nashville), 131
Musical instruments
  Memphis, 242
  Nashville, 121–122
Music City Jazz, Blues & Heritage Festival (Nashville), 19
Music City July 4th: Let Freedom Sing! (Nashville), 18
Music City Raceway (Nashville), 112
Music City Taxi (Nashville), 28
Musicians Hall of Fame & Museum (Nashville), 93
Music Row (Nashville), 38
  accommodations, 50–59
  restaurants, 75–82
  sights and attractions, 89–95, 102–103
Music stores
  Memphis, 241–242
  Nashville, 121
Music Valley (Nashville), 39
  accommodations, 59–64
  attractions, 103
  nightlife, 124, 129
  restaurants, 82–85
  traveling between downtown and, 95

Nash-Trash Tours (Nashville), 109
Nashville Arcade, 109
Nashville Ballet, 136
Nashville Black Heritage Tours, 110
***Nashville City Vacation Guide*, 32**
Nashville Convention & Visitors Bureau, 15
Nashville Convention & Visitors Bureau Visitors Center, 45
Nashville Cowboy, 123
Nashville Farmers' Market, 72, 119
Nashville International Airport, 24
Nashville International Airport (Nashville), visitor information, 45
***Nashville* (movie), 13**
Nashville Municipal Auditorium, 136
Nashville Opera, 136
Nashville Palace, 129
Nashville Predators, 112
***Nashville Scene*, 15, 124**
Nashville Sounds, 112
Nashville Symphony, 136
Nashville Zoo at Grassmere, 103–104
National Car Rental, Nashville, 27
National Civil Rights Museum (Memphis), 214–215, 222
National Corvette Museum (Columbia), 140
National Ornamental Metal Museum (Memphis), 215
Neighborhoods
  Memphis, 155
  Nashville, 37–39
    sights and attractions, 102–103
Newby's (Memphis), 249
New Daisy Theatre (Memphis), 222, 248
Newspapers and magazines
  Memphis, 260
  Nashville, 257
New Zealand
  customs regulations, 23
  embassy, 256
  passports, 257
  visas, 259
Nightlife
  Memphis, 244–254
    bars, pubs and lounges bars, 249–252
    Beale Street and downtown, 244–248
    performing arts, 252–254
  Nashville, 124–137
    country music, 125–130
    performing arts, 135–137
    rock, blues, jazz and more, 130–132
    tickets, 124
Nixon, Richard, 96
Northwest Airlines, 24
Northwest-KLM, 23

Oak Court Mall (Memphis), 236, 240
Oak Hall (Memphis), 242
Off Square Books (Oxford), 229
Oktoberfest (Nashville), 19
Opera Memphis, 253
Opry Mills (Nashville), 120
Opry Originals: The Shop On Broadway (Nashville), 123
Orpheum Theatre (Memphis), 222, 252
Outdoor activities
  Memphis, 224
  Nashville, 111–112
OutLoud! Book Store, 32
Overton Park (Memphis), 155, 217, 224
Overton Square (Memphis), 155
Oxford (Mississippi), 228–231

P and H Cafe (Memphis), 251
Pangaea (Nashville), 117
Parking
  Memphis, 29
  Nashville, 27–28
Parks and gardens
  Memphis, 217–218
  Nashville, 101–102
The Parthenon (Nashville), 10, 97–98
Passports, 22, 257

The Peabody hotel (Memphis), 222
The Peabody Lobby Bar (Memphis), 250
Peabody Place (Memphis), 241
The Peanut Shop (Nashville), 120
The Peanut Shoppe (Memphis), 239
Percy Priest Lake (Nashville), 112
Percy Warner Park (Nashville), 102
Performing arts
  Memphis, 252–254
  Nashville, 135–137
Petrol, 256
Picnics, Nashville, 105
The Pink Door (Memphis), 238
Pink Palace Museum (Memphis), 215
Planning your trip, specialized travel resources, 32–33
Planning your trip to Nashville and Memphis, 15–36
  calendar of events, 16–22
  entry requirements, 22–23
  escorted tours, 35–36
  getting to Nashville and Memphis, 23–27
  health concerns, 31–32
  money and costs, 30–31
  safety concerns, 32
  staying connected, 36
Playhouse on the Square (Memphis), 253
Police, 257, 260
Posh Boutique (Nashville), 118
Presley, Elvis, 48, 152, 162
  childhood apartment, 180
  Graceland, 208–210
  Memphis
    Birthday Tribute, 20
    Tribute Week, 21
  statue of (Memphis), 222
  trivia, 209
  Ultimate Elvis Tribute Artist Contest (Memphis), 214
Prime Outlets (Lebanon), 117
Printer's Alley (Nashville), 109
Proud Larry's (Oxford), 231
The Pumping Station (Memphis), 252

R

Rack Room Shoes (Memphis), 243
Raiford's (Memphis), 252
RCA Studio B (Nashville), 93
The Regalia (Memphis), 241
Regional Medical Center/ Elvis Presley Trauma Center (Memphis), 31
Regions Morgan Keegan Championships (Memphis), 225
Regions Morgan Keegan Tennis Championship (Memphis), 20
Renaissance Festival, Tennessee (Triune), 16, 18
The Rendezvous (Memphis), 250
Responsible Travel, 34
Restaurants, 14. *See also* Restaurants Index
  Memphis, 182–203
    barbecue, 202
    best, 145, 182–183
    by cuisine, 183–185
    delis, cafes and bakeries, 203
    downtown, 185–192
    East Memphis, 196–200
    family-friendly, 188
    price categories, 182
    South Memphis & Graceland area, 201–202
  Nashville, 65–87
    barbecue and hot chicken, 85–86
    best, 3, 65–66, 87
    cafes, delis, bakeries and pastry shops, 86–87
    chain restaurants, 65
    by cuisine, 66–68
    downtown, The Gulch & 12th Avenue South, 68–74
    family-friendly, 72
    Germantown & Jefferson Street, 74–75
    Music Row, The West End & areas southwest, 75–82
    Music Valley & East Nashville, 82–85
    price categories, 65
    Tennessee-based eateries, 87
  Oxford (Mississippi), 231
Rhodes College (Memphis), 33
Rippy's Smokin' Bar & Grill (Nashville), 133–134
River Arts Festival (Memphis), 21
Riverbluff Walkway (Memphis), 217
Riverboat tours
  Memphis, 223
  Nashville, 111
Riverfront Park, 106 (Nashville)
Riverfront Park (Nashville), 136
RiverGate Mall (Goodlettsville), 117, 121
River Records (Memphis), 242
Riverside Hotel (Clarksdale), 226
River Walk (Memphis), 214
Robert's Western World (Nashville), 125
Rocketown (Nashville), 132
Rowan Oak (Oxford), 228
Rudolph, Wilma, 11
Rum Boogie Cafe (Memphis), 248
Rumours Wine Bar (Nashville), 135
Ru San's (Nashville), 135
Ryman Auditorium (Nashville), 95, 106, 125, 128
The Rymer Gallery (Nashville), 116

S

Safety concerns, 32
St. Jude Classic (Memphis), 225
Sambuca (Nashville), 135
Sam Cooper Boulevard (Memphis), 164
Savannah Tea Company (Nashville), 119
Savarino's Cucina (Nashville), 86
Scarlett Begonia (Nashville), 118
Schermerhorn Hall (Nashville), 136
Second Avenue Historic District (Nashville), 106
Senses (Memphis), 252
SFA (Southern Foodways Alliance), 229
Shangri-La Records (Memphis), 242

Shelby Street Bridge (Nashville), 38
Shoes and boots, Memphis, 242–243
Shopping
  Memphis, 232–243
  Nashville, 113–123
Shopping centers and malls
  Memphis, 240
  Nashville, 120–121
The Shops of Saddle Creek (Memphis), 241
Sights and attractions
  Memphis, 204–225
    Graceland and Beale Street, 204–212
    for kids, 219
    nonmusical attractions, 212–218
  Nashville, 88–112
    for kids, 104–105
    music-related attractions, 88–95
    neighborhoods, 102–103
    organized tours, 109–111
    parks, plazas and botanical gardens, 101–102
Slavehaven Underground Railroad Museum/Burkle Estate (Memphis), 216
Smoking, 257
Social Graces (Nashville), 119
Sole Restaurant & Raw Bar (Memphis), 251
Sommet Center (Nashville), 108, 136
Sommet Entertainment Center (Nashville), 88
Soulsville USA: Stax Museum of American Soul Music (Memphis), 210–211
Southern Festival of Books (Nashville), 19
Southern Foodways Alliance, 35
Southern Foodways Alliance (SFA), 229
Southern Heritage Classic (Memphis), 21
Southland Greyhound Park (Memphis), 225
South Memphis, restaurants, 201
South Nashville, 39
Southside Gallery (Oxford), 229
Southwest, 24
Southwest Airlines, 23
Southwest Airlines Vacations, 24
Spectator sports
  Memphis, 225
  Nashville, 112
Square Books (Oxford), 228–229
The Square (Oxford), 228
Star-Spangled Celebration (Memphis), 21
State Capitol, Tennessee (Nashville), 98, 109
The Station Inn (Nashville), 128
Stax Studio (Memphis), 205
Stoneridge Golf Course (Memphis), 224
Stones River National Battlefield (Murfreesboro), 141
Street maps
  Memphis, 165
  Nashville, 46
Student travel, 33
Sudekum Planetarium (Nashville), 99
Summer, 16
Sunset Symphony (Memphis), 253
Sun Studio (Memphis), 211–212
Super Shuttle International (Nashville), 24
Sustainable tourism/ecotourism, 33–35
Sustainable Travel International, 34
Sustain Lane, 34
Suzy Wong's House of Yum (Nashville), 135
Sweet Dreams (movie), 13
Sweet Magnolia Tours, 36
Sweet 16th-A Bakery (Nashville), 86–87
Swimming, Nashville, 112

TACA Fall Craft Fair (Nashville), 19
Taxes
  Memphis, 260
  Nashville, 257–258
Taxis
  Memphis, 25, 30
  Nashville, 24, 28
Telephones, 258
Television, 13
The Tennessean (Nashville), 15, 124
Tennessee Craft Fair (Nashville), 18
Tennessee Department of Tourism Development (Nashville), 15, 45
Tennessee Jazz & Blues Society (Nashville), 131
Tennessee Jazz & Blues Society's Jazz on the Lawn (Nashville), 18
Tennessee Performing Arts Center (TPAC; Nashville), 135–136
Tennessee Renaissance Festival (Triune), 16, 18
Tennessee Repertory Theatre (Nashville), 136
Tennessee State Capitol (Nashville), 98, 109
Tennessee State Fairgrounds Flea Market (Nashville), 119
Tennessee State Fair (Nashville), 19
Tennessee State Museum (Nashville), 100–101, 109
Tennessee State University (Memphis), 33
Tennessee State Welcome Center (Memphis), 162, 165
Tennessee Titans (Nashville), 112
Tennessee Walking Horse Museum (Lynchburg), 142
Tennessee Walking Horse National Celebration (Shelbyville), 112
Tennessee Walking-Horse National Celebration (Shelbyville), 19
Tennis, Memphis, 224, 225
Ten Thousand Villages (Nashville), 117
TerraPass, 34
Texas Troubadour Theatre/Cowboy Church (Nashville), 129–130
Theater, Memphis, 253
Theatre Memphis, 253
The Thing Called Love (movie), 13–14
Third Man Records (Nashville), 131
3rd & Lindsley Bar and Grill (Nashville), 132
Thrifty Car Rental
  Memphis, 29
  Nashville, 27
Ticketmaster
  Memphis, 244
  Nashville, 124

Timberlake, Justin, 219
Time zones, 258
Timna (Memphis), 240
Tin Pan South (Nashville), 16
Tin Roof (Nashville), 134
Tip-a-Canoe (Nashville), 111
Tipping, 258
Toad Hall Antiques (Memphis), 233
Toilets, 258
Tom Lee Park (Memphis), 217
Tootsie's Orchid Lounge (Nashville), 108, 128
Tourism Concern, 34
Tours
  Memphis, 223–224
  Nashville, 109–111
TPAC (Tennessee Performing Arts Center; Nashville), 135–136
Trail West (Nashville), 123
Train travel, 27
Transportation, 27
Travelers' Aid, 256
Traveling to Nashville and Memphis, 23–27
Travellers Rest Plantation & Museum (Nashville), 98–99
Tread Lightly, 34
Triangle Journal, 32
Tribe (Nashville), 135
Tri-Star Medline (Nashville), 31
Trolleys
  Memphis, 30
  Nashville, 28
12th Avenue South (Nashville), 38
  attractions, 103
  restaurants, 68–74
Twinkle Toes Children's Shoes (Memphis), 238

Ultimate Elvis Tribute Artist Contest (Memphis), 214
Union Avenue (Memphis), 164
Union Station Hotel (Nashville), 108
United Airlines, 23, 24
United Cab (Nashville), 28
United Kingdom
  customs regulations, 23
  embassy, 256
  passports, 257
  visas, 259
University of Memphis, 33
University of Memphis Tigers, 225
Uptown Square (Memphis), 180
Urban Outfitters (Nashville), 118
US Airways, 23, 24
USA Rail Pass, 27
U.S. Customs House (Nashville), 108

Vanderbilt Medical Group Physician Referral Service (Nashville), 31
Vanderbilt University (Memphis), 33
Viking Culinary Arts (Memphis), 240
Virago (Nashville), 135
Visas, 22, 259
Visa Waiver Program (VWP), 22
Visitor information
  Clarksdale, 226
  Memphis, 260
  Nashville, 45, 259
  Oxford (Mississippi), 228
Visit USA, 24
Volunteer International, 34

Walking
  Memphis, 30
  Nashville, 28
Walking tours, self-guided
  Memphis, 220–223
  Nashville, 105–109
Walk the Line (movie), 14
War Memorial Building (Nashville), 109
Wave Country and Skatepark (Nashville), 105
W. C. Handy House (Memphis), 222
W. C. Handy House Museum (Memphis), 212, 218
W. C. Handy Park (Memphis), 218, 222
The West End (Nashville), 38–39, 46
  accommodations, 50–59
  restaurants, 75–82
Western wear, Nashville, 122
Whale and Dolphin Conservation Society, 34
Wheelchair accessibility, 32–33
Wheelchair Getaways of Memphis, Tennessee, 33
Whiskey Kitchen (Nashville), 134
White, Jack, 131
Whole Foods Market (Memphis), 239
Wi-Fi access, 36
Wild Bill's (Memphis), 249
Wildhorse Saloon (Nashville), 106, 128–129
Williamson County Visitor Information Center (Franklin), 138
Williams-Sonoma Clearance Outlet (Memphis), 236
Willie Nelson & Friends Museum & General Store (Nashville), 94–95
Winfrey, Oprah, 11
Withers, Ernest C., 205
Wolfchase Galleria (Memphis), 241
Woodcuts (Nashville), 116
Woodruff-Fontaine House (Memphis), 216
WSM Barn Dance, 5, 12

Xenogeny, 32

Yellow Cab (Nashville), 28
Yellow/Checker Cab (Clarksdale), 25
Young Avenue Deli (Memphis), 251

Zanies Comedy Club (Nashville), 133
Zoos
  Memphis Zoo & Aquarium, 216–217
  Nashville Zoo at Grassmere, 103–104

ACCOMMODATIONS—NASHVILLE AND ENVIRONS

Alexis Inn and Suites, 64
Best Western Airport Inn, 64
Best Western Music Row, 58
Comfort Inn, 64
Comfort Inn Downtown-Music Row, 58

Courtyard Nashville Downtown, 51, 54
Courtyard Vanderbilt, 57
Days Inn, 64
Days Inn Vanderbilt/Music Row, 59
Doubletree Guest Suites Nashville Airport, 60, 62
Doubletree Hotel Nashville, 54
Embassy Suites Nashville, 62
Embassy Suites Nashville at Vanderbilt, 54
Fairfield Inn Opryland, 62
Gaylord Opryland Resort & Convention Center, 59–60
GuestHouse Inn & Suites Music Valley, 62
Hampton Inn and Suites Downtown, 54–55
Hampton Inn Vanderbilt, 57–58
The Hermitage Hotel, 50–51
Hilton Garden Inn Nashville Vanderbilt, 58
Hilton Nashville Downtown, 51
Holiday Inn Express Nashville Downtown, 55
Holiday Inn Select Music Valley, 63
Holiday Inn Select Opryland Airport, 62
Holiday Inn Select Vanderbilt, 58
Homewood Suites Hilton Downtown, 55
Hotel Indigo West End, 55
Hotel Preston, 63
Hutton Hotel, 54
Hyatt Place Opryland, 63
La Quinta Inn Nashville-Briley Parkway, 64
Loews Vanderbilt Hotel, 51
Morton's of Chicago, 65
Nashville Airport Marriott, 60
Nashville Marriott at Vanderbilt, 56
Radisson Hotel at Opryland, 64
Red Roof Inn-Nashville East, 64
Renaissance Nashville Hotel, 56–57
Residence Inn Airport, 63–64
Sheraton Music City, 60
Sleep Inn Nashville, 64
Springhill Suites by Marriott, 64
Union Station: A Wyndham Historic Hotel, 57

Accommodations—Memphis and Environs

Comfort Inn Downtown, 174
Comfort Inn (Oxford), 230
Courtyard Memphis Airport, 179
Crowne Plaza Memphis, 174
Days Inn at Graceland, 181
Days Inn (Oxford), 230
Doubletree Hotel Memphis, 175
Doubletree Memphis, 172
Elvis Presley's Heartbreak Hotel-Graceland, 180
Embassy Suites, 175
Executive Inn (Clarksdale), 227
Gen X Inn, 174
Hampton Inn & Suites-Beale Street, 172
Hampton Inn Suites-Shady Grove, 178
Hilton Memphis, 175–176
Holiday Inn Express Hotel & Suites (Oxford), 230
Holiday Inn Select, 178–179
Holiday Inn Select Downtown, 172
Holiday Inn Select Medical Center/Midtown, 174
Holiday Inn Select Memphis Airport, 180
Homewood Suites, 176
Hyatt Place, 179
The Inn at Hunt-Phelan, 172–173
512 Inn (Oxford), 230
La Quinta Inn & Suites, 179
Madison Hotel, 168
Memphis Marriott Downtown, 168
Motel 6, 175
The Peabody, 168–169
Puddin' Place (Oxford), 230
Radisson Hotel Memphis Airport, 180
Red Roof Inn, 175
Residence Inn by Marriott, 176, 178
Residence Inn by Marriott Memphis Downtown, 173
River Inn of Harbor Town, 169
Shack Up Inn (near Clarksdale), 228
Sleep Inn-Downtown at Court Square, 174
SpringHill Suites by Marriott, 173
Talbot Heirs Guesthouse, 173
The Westin Memphis Beale Street, 169, 172

Restaurants—Nashville and Environs

The Acorn, 75–76
Allium, 84
Aquarium, 82
Arnold's Country Kitchen, 73
Back Yard Burgers, 87
Bailey & Cato Family Restaurant, 85
Bar-B-Cutie, 85
Blackstone Restaurant & Brewery, 77–78
Bobbie's Dairy Dip, 80
Bongo Java, 86
Bound'ry, 76
Cabana, 78
Caney Fork Fish Camp, 84
Cantina Laredo, 69, 72
Capitol Grille, 68
Chappy's on Church, 68
City House, 74–75
Cock of the Walk, 84
Couva Calypso Cafe, 87
Cracker Barrel Old Country Store, 87
DaVinci's Gourmet Pizza, 78
Elliston Place Soda Shop, 80–81
Fido, 86
Fleming's Prime Steakhouse and Wine Bar, 65
Frothy Monkey, 86
F. Scott's Restaurant & Jazz Bar, 76
German Town Café, 75
Gerst Haus, 72
Goten, 78
Grins Vegetarian Café, 86
Harper's, 75
Hot Diggity Dogs, 73
Jack's Bar-B-Que, 85
J. Alexander's, 87
Jimmy Kelly's, 76–77

Kalamatas, 81
Las Paletas, 73
Loveless Cafe, 78–79
The Mad Platter, 74
MAFIAoZA's, 73
Mambu, 77
Marché Artisan Foods, 84
Margot Café & Bar, 82
Mary's Old-Fashioned Bar-B-Q, 85
The Merchants, 68–69, 108
Midtown Cafe, 77
Miro District Food & Drink, 79
Mirror, 72
Miss Mary Bobo's Boarding House Restaurant, 142–143
Monell's, 75
Nashville Farmers' Market, 72
Noshville, 81
Old Hickory Steakhouse, 82
The Old Spaghetti Factory, 73, 106
The Palm Restaurant, 69
Pancake Pantry, 81
Paradise Park Trailer Resort, 73–74
PM, 79
Portland Brew, 86
Prince's Hot Chicken Shack, 85
Provence Breads & Café, 86
Rainforest Cafe, 84
Rotier's Restaurant, 81–82
Ruth's Chris Steak House, 65
Savannah Tea Company, 86
Savarino's Cucina, 86
SoBro Grill, 86
South Street, 79
Stock-Yard Restaurant, 69
Stoney River Legendary Steaks, 65
Sunset Grill, 77
Sweet 16th-A Bakery, 86
Swett's, 74
Taqueria La Hacienda, 79–80
tayst Restaurant & Wine Bar, 80
Tin Angel, 80
Watermark Restaurant, 69
Whitt's Barbecue, 86
The Yellow Porch, 80

Restaurants—Memphis and Environs

A&R Bar-B-Q, 202
Abe's Bar-B-Que (Clarksdale), 228
Alcenia's, 191
Andrew Michael Italian Kitchen, 196
The Arcade Restaurant, 191
Automatic Slim's Tonga Club, 190
Beauty Shop, 193
Beignet Café, 191
Blue Plate Cafe, 199–200
Blues City Café, 202
Bonefish Grill, 182
Bottletree Bakery (Oxford), 231
brontë: A Novel Bistro, 203
Brother Juniper's, 200
Brushmark Restaurant, 203
Cafe 1912, 194
Café Eclectic, 195
Café Society, 194
Café Toscana, 198
Carrabba's, 182
Casa Grill, 194
Chez Philippe, 185
Circa, 185, 188
City Grocery (Oxford), 231
Corky's Ribs & BBQ, 199
Cozy Corner, 202
Currents, 188
D'Bo's Wings n' More, 201
Dyer's Burgers, 191
Erling Jensen, 196, 198
Folk's Folly Prime Steak House, 198
Four Way Restaurant, 201
Frank Grisanti, 198
Grace Restaurant, 193
Grill 83, 188
The Grove Grill, 199
Gus's World Famous Fried Chicken, 191–192
Huey's, 192
The Inn at Hunt Phelan, 188–189
Interstate Bar-B-Que, 201, 202
Java Cabana, 203
Just for Lunch, 203
Krispy Kreme Doughnuts, 201–202
Kwik-Chek Deli, 195
La Baguette, 203
Leonard's Pit Barbecue, 202
The Little Tea Shop, 203
Madidi Fine Dining (Clarksdale), 227
The Majestic Grille, 190
McEwen's on Monroe, 189
Miss Polly's Soul City Cafe, 203
Mosa Asian Bistro, 200
Muddy's Bake Shop, 203
Napa Café, 198
Neely's B-B-Q, 202
Noodle Doodle Do, 195
Otherlands, 203
Owen Brennan's, 199
Patrick's Steaks & Spirits, 200
Paulette's, 194–195
Payne's, 202
Pearl's Oyster House, 192
P.F. Chang's, 182
Pho Saigon, 195
Piccadilly, 202
Proud Larry's (Oxford), 231
The Rendezvous, 192
Restaurant Iris, 193
Ruth's Chris Steak-house, 182
Saigon Le, 195–196
Salsa Cocina Mexicana, 200
Sarah's Kitchen (Clarksdale), 228
Sekisui of Japan, 190
Sekisui Pacific Rim, 190
Sole Restaurant & Raw Bar, 189
Soul Fish Cafe, 196
Spaghetti Warehouse, 192
Spindini, 189–190
Texas de Brazil Churrascaria, 182
Tsunami, 193–194

NOTES

NOTES

NOTES